The
Measurement
and
Evaluation of
Library Services

The Measurement and Evaluation of Library Services

Second Edition

SHARON L. BAKER
F. WILFRID LANCASTER

INFORMATION RESOURCES PRESS I$\frac{R}{P}$

Available from
Information Resources Press
1110 North Glebe Road
Suite 550
Arlington, Virginia 22201

Library of Congress Catalog Card Number 91-072908

ISBN 0-87815-061-7

To Shiao–Feng

CONTENTS

EXHIBITS

PREFACE

Many of those who read this book may have had, at one time or another, the sense that our libraries are not serving their clientele as well as had been planned. Perhaps a patron has been overheard commenting that he or she cannot find anything good to read. Or maybe we have noticed someone becoming increasingly frustrated while using the catalog. Or perhaps we've watched a client turn away from the long line at the reference desk.

Unfortunately, few librarians have been adequately trained to evaluate the effectiveness of library service. This book was designed to help fill that gap and to encourage the growth of library evaluation by familiarizing librarians with various evaluation techniques. There are other works on library evaluation, most notably the first edition of this book (by F. W. Lancaster, Information Resources Press, Arlington, Va., 1977), published 14 years ago as a review of the literature on evaluation, and the recently published work *If You Want to Evaluate Your Library* . . . (by F. W. Lancaster, University of Illinois, Champaign, Ill. 1988), designed as a beginning text to practical evaluation within libraries. This volume seeks to combine the best of these two works. It includes a large number of evaluative studies that have been conducted since the first edition of this work was published, synthesizing major, consistent findings of past evaluation efforts for practicing librarians who have little time to track down and review these evaluative studies. Many of the studies reviewed used enhanced or revised techniques. These techniques are described and evaluated for their rigor and practical application within a library setting. This edition also reviews the substantial body of literature on evaluation for each service area to determine if any consistent patterns of findings appear. Patterns are discussed to help increase librarians' knowledge about a particular phenomenon and to improve the design of individual studies by alerting librarians to potential problem areas.

Further, the book serves as a practical guide to performing evaluations of public service activities in libraries. The emphasis on public services is a departure from the first edition of this work, which included chapters on several technical service areas (for example, the evaluation of automation in libraries). Because of the large volume of research on the subject, however, it is impossible to discuss the evaluation of *all* public services here. Therefore, services that are not widely available in all types of libraries (for instance, bibliographic instruction and outreach programming) are excluded. Instead, this book concentrates on the evaluation of collections and materials availability, certain types of reference services (including database searching), and catalog use, as well as the effects of accessibility and ease of use on public services, the range and scope of library services, the relevance of standards to evaluation activities, and evaluation by means of user studies.

One further point should be made. A very high percentage of studies discussed in the first edition of this work were conducted in academic libraries. Since that edition's publication, evaluation activities have increased in all types of libraries. This book reflects that change, including findings of studies in public, school, and special libraries as well.

A number of people have made important contributions to this book: Jim Rice and Esther Bierbaum read and commented on various chapters; graduate assistants Brian Schuck, Andrea Halverson, Julie Wullner, and Lorraine Haricombe located research articles, selected exhibits, checked citations, and proofread chapters; Jay Semel, Lorna Olson, and faculty working at the University House at the University of Iowa provided a quiet place to write, support services, and stimulating discussions; Carl Orgren, Joyce Hartford, and Ethel Bloesch offered tangible and emotional support; and Pat Kondora typed (and retyped) the manuscript.

SHARON L. BAKER
F. WILFRID LANCASTER

PREFACE TO THE FIRST EDITION

In the past 10 years, librarians, in common with other professionals, have become increasingly interested in techniques that might be used to evaluate the services they provide. One reason for this concern is, of course, financial: growing competition for funds, inflationary pressures, and the need to justify the importance of library services to those responsible for funding them. It seems important, then, that graduate programs in librarianship should include courses relating to the measurement and evaluation of library services, the major objectives being to survey work already done in this area, and, perhaps more importantly, to encourage students to adopt an "evaluative attitude" toward library activities. Such a course has been offered since 1970 at the Graduate School of Library Science, University of Illinois.

The present volume was developed primarily as a textbook for this course and, perhaps, for similar courses in other schools. It should be regarded largely as a survey and synthesis of, as well as a guide to, published literature in the field. It should not, however, be regarded as a substitute for reading the various studies directly. A serious effort has been made to include all important or interesting approaches to evaluation and to put these into meaningful and, where appropriate, critical perspective. The book concentrates primarily on techniques that can be used to evaluate the public service of a library, preferably by means of reasonably objective procedures, although some consideration also is given to the evaluation of technical services. The emphasis is on evaluation methodology; however, in reviewing studies which have been conducted, major findings are frequently presented to show the types of results that have been achieved by various procedures. As pointed out in the first chapter, the book is concerned only with how well the library satisfies the immediate tangible needs of its users. It deliberately excludes any consideration of the evaluation of libraries in terms of their broader, intangible, and largely unmeasurable "benefits" to society.

I would like to express my appreciation to Walter Allen, Michael Buckland, Charles Bunge, George Bonn, and Don Swanson for reading and commenting on various chapters, and to Herbert Goldhor for reviewing the entire volume.

I also would like to thank two of my graduate assistants, Elana Hanson and Gini Gale, for their assistance at various stages of the manuscript. Both made significant and useful contributions. Jane Gothard helped immeasurably with her efficient typing. My greatest debt, however, is to Mary Jane Joncich, who helped me both as a graduate assistant and as a critic, and who was largely responsible for writing Chapters 10 and 11.

F. WILFRID LANCASTER

CHAPTER 1

THE EVALUATION OF LIBRARY SERVICES: AN INTRODUCTION

WHY IS EVALUATION NEEDED?

The 1960s were prosperous years for most libraries. Libraries have always competed for funds with other agencies and departments, but the economy of that decade was so favorable that, even with competition, the funding of libraries increased. When librarians asked their funding bodies for resources to implement or maintain services, they generally received them, even though few data on the success of existing programs had been collected. Library services grew in this relaxed climate.

The picture changed as libraries entered two decades of unprecedented increases in the costs of running facilities capable of coping with more advanced information needs. Since the early 1970s, costs have risen faster than income. With various agencies competing for ever more limited funds, the governmental and business organizations that fund today's libraries are increasingly concerned with providing quality services while keeping costs down. These organizations have developed various techniques to aid in measurement, evaluation, planning, and decision making and expect the departments they fund to use these techniques to identify what is being done, why it is being done, and how much is being done. No longer can librarians simply ask for resources and expect to get them. Instead, they must indicate, in some meaningful and measurable way, the results of their services. In effect, they have to show that their programs are appropriate for the intended users and are achieving their objectives in an effective and efficient manner. The pressing need for data collection of this type was illustrated recently in an Association of Research Libraries (ARL) survey, which showed that 90 percent of the respondents used quantitative data to support their budget requests (Association of Research Libraries, 1987).

Orr (1973) noted more than 17 years ago that the request for ongoing evaluation of library services is reasonable. Evaluation tools have proved success-

1

ful in other fields, and many of the organizations that support libraries have adopted these tools. Moreover, the increasing complexity of the alternatives that librarians face—alternatives created in part by ever more powerful technological advances and increasing formalization of library networks—makes it harder to make critical decisions without a way to monitor what is currently happening. In fact, some authors have argued that failure to evaluate the new alternatives in terms of changing user needs may result in the ultimate demise of the library as we know it (for example, see Rose, 1971). Librarians should not view evaluation as a burden imposed by funding officials but rather as a means of improving services by providing information that can be used to solve problems or make better decisions. If an administrator knows how a library is currently performing and why it is performing as it is, he or she should be able to make better choices about how that performance can be improved. Indeed, the ARL study showed that 74 percent of the responding libraries use such information when deciding how to allocate resources like staff and space (Association of Research Libraries, 1987).

Weiss (1982) argued that most evaluation decisions relate to whether or how a library should

- *Continue a program.* For example, should a junior high school library continue purchasing extensively in the field of mathematics if that material is rarely used?
- *Institute similar programs elsewhere.* For instance, should a public library expand a practice of interfiling adult and juvenile nonfiction to all its branch libraries or just to those with no separate children's room?
- *Improve its practices or procedures.* How can special librarians improve their recall rates for online searching, for instance, without overloading company researchers with irrelevant citations?
- *Add, drop, or change specific program strategies and techniques.* Should an academic library change the locations of its displays after discovering that some less-accessible locations fail to promote use of the displayed titles?
- *Allocate resources among competing programs.* Should a 30 percent serials budget cut be applied across the board, or should the heavily used scientific journals be cut less than the less frequently consulted humanities journals?
- *Accept or reject a program approach or theory.* Should a corporate library reject the notion that its researchers will voluntarily use the library to keep up to date and instead establish a selective dissemination of information (SDI) service?

Evaluation may also help establish a benchmark by showing the level of performance at which a service is currently operating. If librarians subsequently change the service, they can compare the results with the benchmark to see if the service has improved. Routine inspection of benchmark figures can also alert the library to signs of trouble if the quality or quantity of service suddenly declines. Seventy-one percent of the ARL respondents collected evaluation statistics to serve as an early warning signal for trouble spots, and 55 percent used such statistics to establish benchmark figures for staff productivity (Association of Research Libraries, 1987).

Many libraries also use evaluation data to compare their services and resources with other libraries of a similar size, type, or nature, and there is growing pressure at state and national levels for library associations to provide such comparable data. For example, the Public Library Association is working to establish a national database of public library statistics. The movement for comparable statistics is fueled by the fact that librarians seeking increased funding to improve substandard services can use the data to support their pleas.

Expertise gained in conducting an evaluation may be a valuable organizational resource. Consider the case of a newly hired media specialist in a small elementary school who spends the month before school opens evaluating the nonfiction collection. This is done by determining whether the size of the collection meets that recommended in the standards for the state, checking the holdings against titles recommended for purchase in the most recent edition of *The Elementary School Library Collection* (Winkel, 1988), comparing the holdings in various subject areas against the school's curriculum guide to determine if the same areas are emphasized, examining past records of use for the items, and noting dated materials that need to be replaced. It would be expected that, as the result of the evaluation process, the media specialist would become very familiar with old and current nonfiction sources that are used and needed in the collection, thus increasing his/her effectiveness in acquiring future materials and weeding out current ones, as well as in providing better reference service.

At least one article has described the benefits to staff of the evaluation process (Nugent and Carrow, 1977). When the National Criminal Justice Reference Service (NCJRS) conducted an in-house evaluation of its indexing and retrieval capabilities, management and staff both gained additional insight into the nature of NCJRS problems and strengths. Staff gained expertise in conducting evaluations that could be used on future projects, and communication increased among the different functional groups dealing with indexing and abstracting.

Evaluation, therefore, should be thought of as a management tool whose main purposes are to identify current strengths, limitations, and failures, and to suggest ways to improve service.

WHY ISN'T MORE EVALUATION DONE?

Many librarians still seem reluctant to evaluate their services. If evaluation will lead to better service, why has it been resisted? One major reason is that some librarians believe that the effects of library service are so intangible that it is impossible to determine objectively whether or not the library's goals have been met (Orr, 1973). Hamburg et al. (1974) summarized many of these goals. Consider, for example, the following:

- To aid in the creative use of leisure time for the promotion of personal development and social well-being
- To help people become better family and community members by promoting rational, democratic attitudes and values
- To help people discharge political and social obligations, thereby establishing an enlightened citizenship
- To develop creative and spiritual capacities
- To sustain the increasingly complex operations of government
- To assist people in their daily occupations, thereby sustaining economic growth

Social, spiritual, and economic goals of this type sound impressive but are of little use in helping librarians provide effective, efficient service. Such goals may be related to the ultimate benefits of library services, but they do not relate directly to the immediate functions of the library and are too vague and impractical to be used as criteria for evaluating a library or its services.

As Drucker (1973) pointed out, public service institutions may have long-term goals and missions that are relatively intangible, but they also need short-term objectives that are both tangible and measurable to aid them in evaluating their progress and the quality of their service.

"Saving souls," as the definition of the objectives of a church is, indeed, "intangible." At least the bookkeeping is not of this world. But church attendance is measurable. And so is "getting the young people back into the church."

"The development of the whole personality" as the objective of the school is, indeed, "intangible." But "teaching a child to read by the time he has finished third grade" is by no means intangible; it can be measured easily and with considerable precision . . .

Achievement is never possible, except against specific, limited, clearly defined targets, in business as well as in a service institution. Only if targets are defined can resources be allocated to their attainment, priorities and deadlines be set, and somebody be held accountable for results. But the starting point for effective work is a definition of the purpose and mission of the institution—which is almost always "intangible," but nevertheless need not be vacuous. (pp. 48–49)

Most librarians used to operate with nebulous missions and goals in mind. But many of today's librarians have taken Drucker's words to heart. Increasingly, librarians are recognizing the need to have a multitiered, cyclical planning process which takes into account that each library is unique and should be assessed in the context of its own history, constraints, users, and environment. Such a planning process requires that a library decide what its major functions will be, write a mission statement expressing this philosophy, and set long-term goals to guide the direction of the organization. The process, however, also emphasizes creating short-term measurable objectives to guide day-to-day activities, designing strategies to meet the objectives, and evaluating the success of those strategies. (An explanation of the process is offered by Bunge [1984].) Several national library organizations are promoting this very type of planning process. The Public Library Association's *Planning and Role Setting for Public Libraries: A Manual of Options and Procedures* (McClure et al., 1987) is an example of this.

The planning process recognizes that evaluation is not an isolated, sporadic event but rather an integral part of the planning cycle. Indeed, Schlachter and Belli (1976) showed that libraries writing specific objective statements were more likely to use evaluation techniques than libraries with no stated goals or with more nebulous goals. They concluded that agencies explicitly identifying what they are trying to do will usually want to know if they have been successful in doing it. The emphasis on planning cycles should give impetus to evaluation activities in libraries.

There are other potential barriers to evaluation. One of these is a stated lack of staff time. Baker (1987) studied 61 public libraries in North Carolina to determine how many were using the evaluation measures listed in *Output Measures for Public Libraries* (Zweizig and Rodger, 1982). She discovered that although library directors thought evaluation was important in these days of limited funding and use of these output measures had been recommended by both the Public Library Association and the state library, 58 percent of the libraries were not using the measures. In 59 percent of these, library directors stated that staff did not have time to collect the data. Even those libraries that collected this type of evaluative data concentrated their efforts on those measures that were quickly and easily calculated, based on statistics that all North Carolina public libraries are required to report to the state library, namely, circulation per capita, reference transactions per capita, program attendance per capita, library visits per capita, registration as a percentage of population, and turnover rate. Libraries were much less willing to collect statistics requiring the use of a separate survey or other specialized data collection measures and a larger investment of staff time to collect and analyze the data, such as reference fill rate, title fill rate, subject and author fill rate, browser fill rate, document delivery rate, and in-library materials use.

The findings of this study are not surprising given that most libraries have not assigned evaluation duties to a particular person but rather expect regular staff to do evaluation in addition to their other duties. Frequently, however, it is those libraries experiencing the severest shortages that most need evaluation. After all, evaluation has the potential to save staff time in the long run by making library operations more efficient and effective. Hiring an outside consultant to perform initial evaluations may be the best way to resolve the difficulties here.

A third barrier to library evaluation is the prevalence of staff with humanities and fine arts backgrounds (DuMont and DuMont, 1979; Schlachter and Belli, 1976). These staff members may not be experienced in or knowledgeable about the collection and analysis of empirical data. Recently, public library directors confirmed that their staff lacked the skills to conduct even simple evaluations (Baker, 1987). This problem can be overcome by continuing education; however, this can only happen if library educators are themselves comfortable with the techniques used for research and evaluation and if research is consistently emphasized in graduate programs in library and information science. At this point, a growing number of studies suggest that many library school faculty do not have research-oriented degrees; that their research is less in quantity and is more naive and unsophisticated than that produced in comparable disciplines; and that the new librarians these people teach often lack the ability to understand, use, or perform research (Haas and Kraft, 1984; Houser and Lazorick, 1978; Katz, 1975; Peritz, 1980, 1981; Stroud, 1982; Van de Water et al., 1976; Wallace, 1985; Wyllys, 1978). The situation appears to be changing slowly, as research and publication requirements for university faculty become more stringent (Peritz, 1981).

The fact that library managers and staff, who might not fully understand the nature of evaluation, may fear the final results is yet another barrier to evaluation (DuMont and DuMont, 1979; Neenan, 1986). Staff members often are afraid that any service flaws will reflect negatively on their own abilities. But evaluation is not meant to pinpoint individual flaws with the intent of punishing someone. Rather, it should be a developmental activity that is undertaken to improve services, either those provided by an individual or by the library. Evaluation results should yield objective data that identify program strengths and weaknesses. The former should be supported; the latter should be corrected through staff training, the addition of appropriate resources, and the like. The ultimate goal of evaluation—a goal that every professional librarian can support—is the improvement of service to users.

One of the best ways to overcome the fear of evaluation is to foster staff involvement. Indeed, at least two authors (Bonn, 1974; Futas, 1985) suggest that evaluation may in some instances be futile unless staff, who have in-depth knowledge of existing services, patron needs, and limitations of the library, are involved. Training can help improve staff understanding of what evaluation is, how evaluation procedures can be designed to meet local needs, how evaluation data can be interpreted, and how evaluation findings can be used (Alkin, Stecher, and Geiger, 1982). Since training fosters both understanding and involvement, the evaluator may be better able to cope with staff expectations for the evaluation and determine the most appropriate manner of reporting the final results. Direct staff involvement may also foster an increased understanding by the evaluator of the program in general and of the internal and external political environments that are in operation in a particular library. This may lead to more realistic suggestions for improvement and thus to increased utilization of evaluation results (Braskamp and Brown, 1980).

A final barrier to evaluation has not been well researched: that management must be committed to evaluation for it to work. It is not enough merely to collect evaluative data and statistics; for evaluation to be effective, management must be prepared to use the results to make changes where indicated. Schlachter and Belli (1976) found that in 78 percent of the California public libraries in which evaluations were performed, no changes were made. Perhaps some needed changes were not made for valid reasons, such as an immediate lack of resources to solve the problem. The fact that so many libraries failed to make any changes, however, may indicate that the evaluations often were conducted on a pro forma basis rather than as a coordinated effort to improve the quality of service. This pattern has been documented in settings other than libraries (Dickey, 1979) and may be overcome to some extent if the evaluator takes an active role in fostering the use of the information, rather than merely assuming that management will act on the information contained in a final evaluation report (Braskamp and Brown, 1980; Reisner et al., 1982).

In spite of these barriers, there is growing evidence that more libraries are becoming interested in regularly and comprehensively evaluating their programs and that various library associations are promoting this trend. Some libraries, such as the Fairfax County (Virginia) Public Library, have hired full- or part-time specialists in evaluation. This trend is most pronounced in academic libraries; a recent survey showed that 66 percent of the ARL libraries had officers with librarywide responsibility for the collection, manipulation, and dissemination of statistics (Association of Research Libraries, 1987).

LEVELS AND TYPES OF EVALUATION

It is feasible to evaluate any type of library service at three possible levels: effectiveness, cost-effectiveness, and cost-benefit.

Effectiveness must be measured in terms of how well a service satisfies the demands placed on it by its users.[1] An effectiveness study might, for example, ask whether reference questions are answered to the users' satisfaction or whether a library provides wanted materials to its users when needed.

An evaluation of a system's *cost-effectiveness* is concerned with its internal operating efficiency. Such a study measures how efficiently (in terms of costs) the system is satisfying its objectives, that is, meeting the needs of its users.

---

[1] The authors agree with DuMont and DuMont (1979) that the effectiveness of the overall library can be measured in other ways (for instance, the ability of the library to survive in a changing environment and to retain capable staff over time). The focus of this work, however, is to address the effectiveness of specific library services, and the definition of effectiveness reflects this.

Libraries can improve the cost-effectiveness of a service by holding costs constant while raising the level of effectiveness or by maintaining a particular level of effectiveness while reducing costs.

Costs are tangible so long as they are thought of only in monetary terms. But it is easy to be shortsighted in this respect. The fallacy that time spent using information services is free must be avoided. User time is not free, at least not within the broad context of society as a whole. In fact, the costs of operating an information service may be small compared with the cost of using it. For some evaluation purposes, a realistic cost analysis of an information service should consider all costs, including those incurred by users.

A *cost-benefit* evaluation is concerned with whether the value (worth) of the service is more or less than the cost of providing it. In other words, a cost-benefit study attempts to determine whether the expense of providing a service is justified by the benefits derived from it. Such a study might determine, for example, whether the amount and quality of past use of a community information and referral directory justify the cost of continuing to compile and update the resource. Librarians can improve the cost-benefit relationship by increasing benefits without increasing costs or by reducing costs without reducing benefits.

If libraries were profit-making entities, cost-benefit studies would be easy to conduct, because the primary benefit is profit, a tangible and therefore easily measured variable. The reality is that cost-benefit studies are almost impossible to conduct in libraries because many of the presumed benefits of information services are intangible (for example, an informed electorate). It is, however, possible to measure user perceptions of the benefits of library services. Indeed, White (1979) argued quite convincingly that, at least for corporate libraries, the value of the service is worth more than the cost of providing it if corporation managers feel it to be a positive influence on the company's employees. The value of the service is less than the cost of providing it if the managers perceive a negative impact or no impact on the employees. This line of reasoning could be modified and used in public, school, academic, and other special libraries.

The expression *cost-performance-benefit* refers to the interrelationships among costs, performance (level of effectiveness), and benefits. These interrelationships cannot be completely separated (Lancaster, 1971). In practice, it is difficult to differentiate between cost-effectiveness and cost-benefit studies: a particular change in a system may increase its effectiveness, its cost-effectiveness, and its benefits. (This book deals primarily with the effectiveness of library services, although cost-effectiveness also is considered. The ultimate benefit of library services—that is, the value to users of having these services available—is not discussed in detail.)

Another distinction, which King and Bryant (1971) have explained, is the difference between *macroevaluation* and *microevaluation*. The effectiveness of a system or service may be evaluated at either level. Macroevaluation, which is descriptive in nature, measures how well a system operates, that is, its success rate. The results usually can be expressed in quantitative terms, such as percentage of success in satisfying requests for interlibrary loans.

Consider the case of a user entering the library to borrow a particular item for which there is no substitute. The evaluator would like to know whether the user leaves with the item in hand. Although this situation seems simple, the user's success actually depends on the answers to several questions, including: Does the library own the item? Is it cataloged or accessible in some other manner? Is it on the shelf when sought? Can the user find it on the shelf?

Success rate can be considered to be the product of a series of probabilities that some event will occur. Suppose that in the above example the library owns 85 percent of the items sought by users, that 80 percent of the owned items can be located in the catalog, that 75 percent of these are on the shelf when users look for them, and that users succeed in finding items on the shelf (when actually there) 90 percent of the time. The probability that a particular user will leave the library with an item sought is thus $0.85 \times 0.80 \times 0.75 \times 0.90$, or 46 percent. In other words, a user of this library has about a 46 percent chance of finding a particular item. One of the objectives of macroevaluation is to establish probabilities of this kind.

Macroevaluation reveals that a particular system operates at some benchmark level but does not indicate why the system operates at this level or what might be done to improve performance in the future. If changes are subsequently made to the service, the effects can then be compared with the benchmark. The recently updated *Output Measures for Public Libraries* (Van House et al., 1987) is an example of a manual designed to aid libraries in macroevaluation. It suggests that libraries collect 12 sets of data indicative of performance, all designed to show what is happening in a library at a given time.

Microevaluation is diagnostic in nature, investigating how a system operates and why it operates at a particular level. Because microevaluation deals with factors affecting the performance of the system, it is necessary if the results of the investigation are to be used to improve performance. The study should demonstrate under what conditions the service performs well and under what conditions it performs badly, thereby allowing identification of the most efficient ways to improve performance.

The most important element of this diagnosis is the identification of reasons why particular failures occur. For example, a user might not have received a complete and accurate answer to a reference question because the librarian did not take time to verify the user's real (and often ambiguously stated) need, used an inadequate strategy to search the catalog and other bibliographic aids for the answer, or was too busy to help the user locate the item on the shelf. Alternatively, the failure might have been due to collection inadequacy, poor indexing of a book that contains the answer, or poor subject access in the card catalog.

If an evaluation is to be more than an academic exercise, it should be diagnostic, collecting data that indicate how a service performs and why it performs as it does, including reasons why failures occur. It should be of practical use to the librarian, providing guidance on what actions might be taken to improve the effectiveness of the services provided.

It is important to differentiate between *subjective* and *objective* evaluation. Subjective evaluation is based on opinion. For example, a geology expert might be called in to give an opinion on whether the library's collection of materials on plate tectonics is adequate. Subjective opinion certainly has value, because all aspects of service cannot always be measured objectively. Subjective judgments may, however, by their very nature, be biased and should be checked against objective measures whenever possible to verify their validity. For instance, studies have shown that subjective opinions can be "wrong." As an example, users do not always know whether they have been given complete and correct responses to reference questions. (See Chapter 8, "Evaluation of Reference Services: Question Answering," for a more thorough discussion of this phenomenon.) Objective criteria and procedures allow librarians to be more analytical and diagnostic and are often more useful when seeking to determine how a service can be improved.

One last distinction in terms is called for. Evaluation may either be *formative* or *summative*. Formative evaluation produces information that is fed back during the development of a program to help improve the program (Scriven, 1967). Summative evaluation is performed at the end, generally to measure the overall

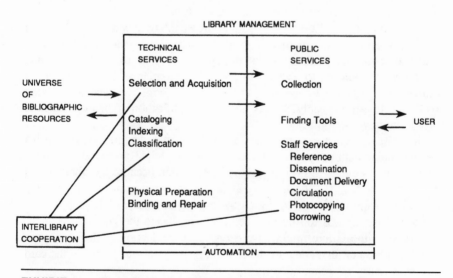

EXHIBIT 1-1   Organization of a library to serve the interface function.

PRINCIPAL FUNCTIONAL COMPONENT   PUBLIC MANIFESTATION

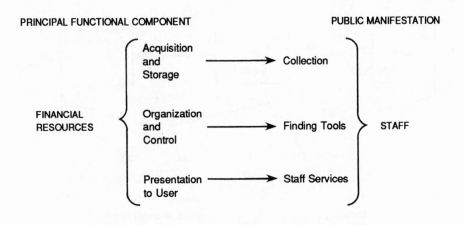

EXHIBIT 1-2 Major library functions and manifestations of these functions.

success or failure of a program. For example, in a literacy program presented by a library, the formative element in the evaluation program may seek to determine whether the methods of instruction used appear to be satisfactory or whether they should be modified or replaced. The summative evaluation, on the other hand, should be conducted to assess the achievement of the program, most obviously in terms of demonstrated improvement in reading ability.

LIBRARY FUNCTIONS AND OBJECTIVES

The functions of all libraries are essentially the same: to acquire bibliographic materials related to the interests of a particular user population, actual or potential; to organize and display these materials; and to make the materials available to users. To satisfy its overall objectives, a library generally is organized into technical services and public services (Exhibit 1-1). Technical, or "behind-the-scenes," services interface directly with the universe of bibliographic resources and provide a bridge between these resources and the user. Public services interface directly with the user community and provide a bridge between the user and the resources. The library staff is involved in both types of activities; "management" directs and coordinates both. The library may cooperate with other institutions in both public and technical services and today may apply automated procedures to many of them.

Libraries are involved primarily in three major activities: (1) acquiring materials and storing them, (2) identifying materials and locating them, and (3) presenting these materials to library users in a variety of forms (Exhibit 1-2). The library staff is involved in all three activities, and library costs are

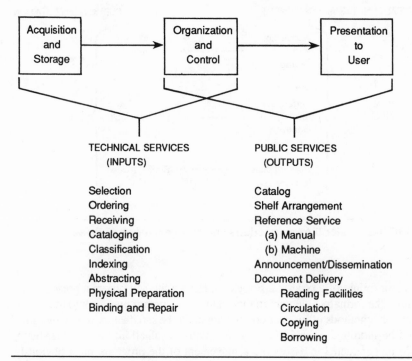

EXHIBIT 1-3   Major library functions and the most important services—public and technical—associated with them.

distributed over all of them. The activities are manifested to the library user in the form of the collection, the tools available to exploit this collection (including shelf arrangement, catalogs, and indexes), and the services provided to the user. All three facets—collection, tools, and services—are closely interrelated, and all must be considered in any overall evaluation of the library. Whereas technical services are concerned mostly with inputs to the library, public services are concerned mostly with outputs. Exhibit 1-3 depicts the three major library activities and the most important services—technical and public—associated with them.

In a broader context, libraries are part of the entire process of transferring information via the published record (Exhibit 1-4). The process comprises the composition, publication, and distribution of a document; acquisition of the document by libraries and others; organization and control of the document (the library processes that are designed to make it accessible to users, including cataloging, classification, indexing, abstracting, shelf arrangement, and related activities); physical presentation to the user; and assimilation of the document's contents by the user. This transfer process can be thought of as a cycle.

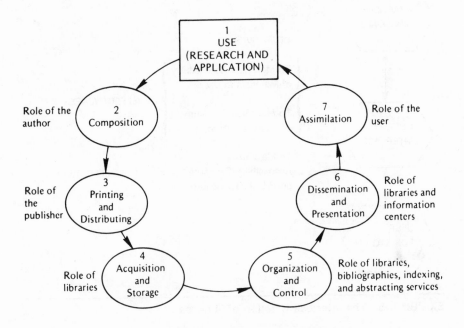

EXHIBIT 1-4   The transfer of information by published documents. Adapted from King and Bryant (1971), courtesy of Information Resources Press.

Assimilation, the stage at which a user is informed by a publication, could lead to some application of this newly acquired knowledge (for example, in research). This may, in turn, result in the composition of a new document.

Although librarians should be interested in all the activities illustrated in this diagram, libraries are directly concerned only with steps 4, 5, and 6 in Exhibit 1-4. The library exists to bring documents and users together. It seeks to ensure that users gain access to publications that are pertinent and comprehensible (in other words, written in a readable language at an understandable level). The assimilation of a document by a user, once it has been supplied, is generally outside the library's sphere of influence. The librarian has no direct control or influence over users and usually does not know whether they used or were informed by the items supplied. This is why the ultimate benefits of library service are difficult to measure.

It has been suggested that the ultimate product of the library is not the use of materials. Armstrong (1968), for example, claims that when a person borrows

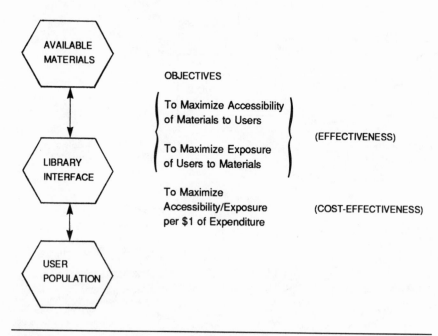

EXHIBIT 1-5   The interface function of libraries.

books on how to construct a house, the house built is the real product. This approach is unacceptable. The library has adequately served its function if it has a supply of good, readable, up-to-date materials on how to construct a house and can make these materials available at the time the user needs them. Whether or not the reader actually builds the house is governed by myriad factors that are beyond the control of the library. Moreover, of all these factors, the availability of suitable reading materials is likely to be one of comparatively minor importance. Assume, for example, that user A and user B come to a library seeking books on house construction. Both borrow materials that they consider suitable for their present purposes. User A subsequently builds a house; B does not. It is doubtful that anyone could say that the library succeeded in the first case and failed in the second. It can, however, legitimately be said that the library failed if user B was unable to find suitable materials in the library at the time they were needed. Therefore, a library can only be evaluated in terms of whether or not it is able to provide the materials sought by users when they are needed.

The overall mission of the library is to make the universe of bibliographic resources (using "bibliographic" in the widest sense), or at least that portion having the most immediate relevance and interest, maximally accessible to its particular user population (restricted geographically or by institutional affiliation)

(Exhibit 1-5). Hamburg, Ramist, and Bommer (1972) and Hamburg et al. (1974) stated the mission differently: to maximize the exposure of library users to the universe of bibliographic materials.

These two facets (accessibility/exposure) of the mission are really opposite sides of the same coin. Maximization of accessibility suggests a somewhat passive information service—one in which the library makes materials available but waits for users to request them. Maximization of exposure, on the other hand, carries a more active connotation—such as bringing materials to the attention of potential users through some dynamic means like a current awareness service, such as SDI. In the past, most academic, public, and school libraries have been passive, providing services "on demand" only. Many industrial libraries and other specialized information centers have been more dynamic, providing services—not directly solicited—designed to keep users current with literature in their areas of specialization.

The major criterion by which to evaluate the effectiveness of a library is the degree to which it maximizes accessibility, exposure, or both; the major criterion by which to evaluate the cost-effectiveness of a library is the degree to which it maximizes accessibility/exposure per dollar expended.

The accessibility/exposure objectives of the library were perhaps enunciated most clearly by Hamburg, Ramist, and Bommer (1972) and Hamburg et al. (1974); however, they have been described by many others as well. The five "laws" of library science written by Ranganathan (1957) present these objectives in a highly concentrated form:

1. Books are for use.
2. Every reader his book.
3. Every book its reader.
4. Save the time of the reader.
5. The library is a growing organism.

The first three laws are closely interrelated. The statement "Books are for use" implies the entire concept of the library as an interface between users and bibliographic resources. It also suggests that collections and services must be evaluated in terms of user needs. The second law relates directly to accessibility. It is not enough that the item sought by a user is owned by the library; it must also be available when the reader needs it. The third law implies exposure in the sense that the library, as a more active information service, makes bibliographic resources known to potential users.

In his fourth law, Ranganathan recognized a secondary, but still important, objective relating to the internal efficiency of the library: to make bibliographic resources accessible in ways that are most convenient to the user. Rzasa and Baker (1972) restated this, noting that the primary goals of a library were to maximize user satisfaction and to minimize time loss to the user. They also recognized a secondary goal: to increase the number of actual library users. These three goals all involve the maximization of exposure and the minimization of cost to the user.

The fifth and final law, "The library is a growing organism," indicates that the library must be willing to adapt to new conditions (changing social and technological conditions as well as changing needs among its clientele) if it is to meet its goal of maximizing accessibility and exposure while minimizing the user's time and effort.

The accessibility/exposure goals of the library can also be seen in the evaluation of information retrieval systems. A group of "user requirements" for automated information retrieval systems have been identified. Summarized, they are

- *Coverage* of the collection (or database)—the scope of the collection in terms of the extent to which it is complete in various subject areas.
- *Recall*—the ability to retrieve the relevant literature when a request is made to the system.
- *Precision*—the ability not to retrieve irrelevant literature in response to a request to the system. Jointly, recall and precision measure *filtering capacity*—the ability to let through only what the user wants.
- The amount of *effort* the user must spend in exploiting the system—if the effort required is excessive, the system will not be used. Some people may even prefer to do without needed information if the task of locating such information is particularly burdensome to them. As "Mooers's Law" states, "An information retrieval system will tend *not* to be used whenever it is more painful and troublesome for a customer to have information than for him not to have it." (Mooers, 1960, p. ii)
- The *response time* of the system—how long the user has to wait to obtain needed literature or references to such literature.
- The *form of output* provided by the system.

Coverage and recall relate directly to the accessibility/exposure missions of information services, and the other criteria relate directly to the additional goal of providing this accessibility/exposure as efficiently as possible to save the time of the user. These criteria are applicable to the evaluation of library service in general. They provide a precise restatement of the overall accessibility/exposure objectives of libraries and are clearly within the spirit of Ranganathan's laws.

MEASURING EXPOSURE THROUGH MACROEVALUATION

The most complete discussion of procedures for measuring exposure was by Hamburg, Ramist, and Bommer (1972) and Hamburg et al. (1974). Users may be exposed to library materials either directly or indirectly. Direct exposure refers to the user's own exploitation of library materials and can be expressed quantitatively by the number of items borrowed or consulted in the library, the number of photocopies made, and so on. Indirect exposure refers to staff exploitation of the library's materials on behalf of the users. It can be measured by the number of telephone inquiries handled or the number of individuals attending a library function such as a book discussion or a storytelling session for children. Exposure is always measured quantitatively.

Hamburg et al. tried to develop an overall index to measure exposure and tentatively came up with three measures of increasing sophistication: exposure counts, item-use days, and exposure time. In the exposure count, each single use of the library's resources counts as a single exposure, either direct or indirect. Although this method provides an easy way to measure exposure, it has a number of disadvantages:

- Dissimilar events, like borrowing a book, consulting an index, and answering a telephone inquiry, may be combined into one overall count. Of course, it is possible to divide these various events into separate counts, but this may complicate subsequent manipulation and analysis of the data collected.
- Volume of use is measured, but amount of use is not. For example, five separate uses of *The Official Airline Guide,* each taking one minute, would count as five separate exposures. On the other hand, a book borrowed and used continuously for five days would count as a single exposure.
- It is possible to increase exposure counts artificially. For example, a reduced loan period would presumably result in more individual loans per year. The exposure count would thus increase, but the actual level of service offered might not.

Item-use days measures exposure in number of days of use. For example, an item used within the library for part of one day counts as one item-use day, whereas a book borrowed for five days is counted as five item-use days. This measure, which appears to have first been suggested by Meier (1961), indicates use more precisely than does the exposure count, but it too has disadvantages:

- A book borrowed for five days is not necessarily used for five days or, indeed, used at all. Actual use can only be determined by interviewing users, or a sample of users, at the time they return materials to the library—a difficult and time-consuming process. Also, the accuracy of the measures thus made depends entirely on how accurately the users remember how much they used a particular publication.

- Events that should be considered approximately equal in value may be weighted differently. For example, a document used for one hour during each of five days counts as five item-use days, whereas the same document used for five hours in one day counts as only one item-use day.

Exposure time measures the actual hours of use. This is a more exact measure of the amount of use and can be determined only by sampling—by observing users, selected at random, in the library and by questioning users, again at random, when they return borrowed materials (a difficult and costly process). The object of the sampling is to determine the average amount of time associated with each type of exposure.

De Prospo, Altman, and Beasley (1973) developed a completely different index to measure exposure: *effective user hours*—the number of hours of actual use recorded during a sampling period divided by the number of hours in that period. Take, for example, a sampling period of 50 consecutive hours during which a library is open; 620 hours of actual use are accumulated (the sum of all hours spent in the library by all users during the sampling period). The final number of effective user hours, therefore, is 620/50, or approximately 12.4 hours of user time for each hour that the library is open.

Exposure, by its very nature, is measured in quantitative terms and thus is subject to all the problems associated with measuring quantity only. The most obvious is that a unit of exposure does not indicate the quality of use. The loan of a novel for recreational reading, for example, may count the same as the scholarly use of a rare manuscript in the library. Although it is theoretically possible to incorporate some qualitative elements into exposure measures by weighting the various exposures according to type of user, type of use, or both, it is unlikely that much consensus would be reached (among librarians or others) as to what weights should be assigned to these different use categories.

A fully acceptable index of exposure has not yet been found, much less an "index of effectiveness," but this does not mean that library services cannot or should not be evaluated (Aversa, 1981). In any case, Spray (1976) found that administrators generally do not require the use of one overall index of effectiveness but rather consider a variety of factors, including qualitative ones, when making program decisions. In other words, macroevaluation may not require the development of a single measure of use but rather the examination of a large number of measures in a particular library setting. For example, when evaluating the overall success of reference services, the following questions are all appropriate: To what extent is the population aware that reference service is provided? How many questions are received? Are the answers given both complete and correct? How often are patrons satisfied with the answers they receive? All these questions are valid, and the answers to each of them may contribute information that is useful in the decision-making process.

Ultimately, all activities in which the library engages are designed to increase accessibility/exposure. As pointed out by Hamburg, Ramist, and Bommer (1972) and Hamburg et al. (1974), one should be able to assess the effects of changes in the collection, tools, and services in terms of exposure. Consider the following examples.

- The more branch locations provided, the greater the exposure.
- The more hours the library is open, the greater the exposure.
- The more titles provided, the greater the exposure.
- The more copies provided, the greater the exposure.
- The more physically accessible the collection, the greater the exposure.
- The more liberal the usage period (up to a point), the greater the exposure.
- The more explicit the shelf arrangement, the greater the exposure.
- The more assistance given to users, the greater the exposure.
- The more accessible the catalog, the greater the exposure.
- The more indexes provided, the greater the exposure.
- The more widely publicized the services, the greater the exposure.

Although all library activities are designed to increase exposure, not all are intended to increase immediate exposure. Some activities, including the purchasing of new materials and publicizing of services, represent an investment in future exposure.

MEASURING EXPOSURE THROUGH MICROEVALUATION

Exposure is a measure of the volume of use. It is an appropriate indicator of a library's effectiveness; presumably, the more effective the library, the more it will be used. The amount of use per dollar expended is an appropriate measure of cost-effectiveness. But volume of use is a relatively gross, quantitative measure, suitable only for macroevaluation. Microevaluation of library services involves the identification of factors affecting the amount of use and degree of user satisfaction (Exhibit 1-6). In general, microevaluation of any service should take into account quality, time, and costs (including costs represented by human effort). There are a variety of relevant criteria by which the various technical and public services of a library can be evaluated (Exhibit 1-7).

Ultimately, the public services of a library should be judged in terms of user satisfaction. The extent to which the library is used (the amount of exposure actually provided) presumably reflects user satisfaction. This satisfaction could also be measured with subjective methods such as questionnaires or interviews. These have some value but are of limited use for purposes of microevaluation. Users are not always able to recognize "failures." For example, a user who cannot locate a particular item in the catalog may be unaware of entries filed under headings that were not consulted. Or a user seeking a particular item may

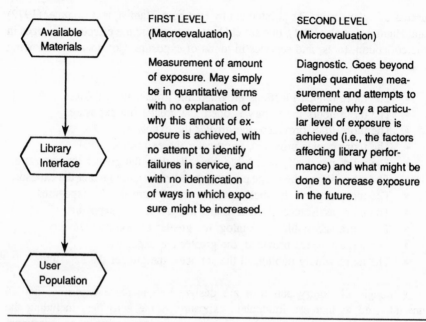

FIRST LEVEL
(Macroevaluation)

Measurement of amount of exposure. May simply be in quantitative terms with no explanation of why this amount of exposure is achieved, with no attempt to identify failures in service, and with no identification of ways in which exposure might be increased.

SECOND LEVEL
(Microevaluation)

Diagnostic. Goes beyond simple quantitative measurement and attempts to determine why a particular level of exposure is achieved (i.e., the factors affecting library performance) and what might be done to increase exposure in the future.

EXHIBIT 1-6   Relationship between macroevaluation and microevaluation.

not know that the item is shelved in another part of the library. To be able to identify various types of failures in library services, and particularly to identify their causes, more objective, quantitative measures of performance often are needed, such as the percentage of time users are successful in finding items on the shelves or the percentage of time staff members are successful in answering telephone inquiries.

Some aspects of library service are more easily evaluated than others. Generally, the more concrete the user requirement, the easier it is to measure user satisfaction in absolute terms. For example, if a user comes to a library seeking a particular book for which no substitute is acceptable, then that individual either finds the book and is presumably completely satisfied or does not and is dissatisfied. The degree to which a "known-item" requirement is met is relatively easy to measure; and it also is relatively easy to identify the factors determining whether or not particular books are available when needed. But consider the user who comes to the library seeking bibliographic material about a particular subject. It is not too difficult to determine whether or not *some* material is found on this subject. It is much more difficult to determine whether the *best* material is found, or whether *all* relevant material is located (assuming that the user wants a comprehensive search). Whereas a known-item search can be scored as

	Technical Services	Public Services

Quality	1. Selection and acquisition
	    Size, appropriateness, and balance
	    of collection
	2. Cataloging and indexing
	    Accuracy, consistency, and completeness
		1. Range of services offered
		2. Helpfulness of shelf order and guidance
		3. Catalog
		    Completeness, accuracy, and ease of use
		4. Reference and retrieval
		    Completeness, accuracy, and percentage success
		5. Document delivery
		    Percentage success

Time	1. Delays in acquisition 2. Delays in cataloging and other processing 3. Productivity of staff	1. Hours of service 2. Response time 3. Loan periods

Cost	1. Unit cost to purchase
	2. Unit cost to process
	    Accession
	    Classify
	    Catalog
		1. Effort to use
		    Location of library
		    Physical accessibility of collection
		    Assistance from staff
		2. Charges levied

EXHIBIT 1-7   Examples of possible performance criteria applied to various services of a library.

0 or 1 (a failure or a success), depending on its outcome, a subject search is not as readily amenable to such an absolute scoring system. Moreover, a user may come to a library, particularly a public library, with no specific requirement in mind beyond finding an entertaining book. The degree to which this user is satisfied is more difficult to evaluate and is certainly not susceptible to any absolute score. It can be easily determined whether the user borrows one or more books, but it is quite difficult to discover if he or she is actually entertained by them. If not, the reason most likely is beyond the control of the library.

The satisfaction of this "browsing" type of requirement, although more difficult to measure and express in quantitative terms, is not completely unmeasurable, but it may be necessary to express the results as subjective statements of user satisfaction. Moreover, factors influencing the satisfaction of various types of users certainly can be identified to ensure that library shelves contain a wide selection of materials that are likely to satisfy most browsers.

The technical services of a library, unlike the public services, cannot be evaluated directly in terms of user satisfaction. Technical processes must be evaluated from two viewpoints: (1) internal efficiency and (2) external, long-term effects such as the effects on public service and, ultimately, user satisfaction. Internal evaluation is concerned largely with time and cost factors—for example, how much it costs to acquire a book and catalog it accurately, and how long it takes to process a new book (the time lag between receipt in the library and appearance on the shelf). From such calculations, various comparisons can be made with published standards, other organizations, or performance at other times. Some qualitative internal evaluation of technical processes may also be possible. For instance, the consistency and quality of cataloging activities can be checked.

The external evaluation of technical processes involves longer term considerations: the effect of the technical processes on the public services of the library. Selection and acquisition, for example, determine adequacy of the collection and thus greatly influence use, whereas the quality of indexing and cataloging influences use of the catalogs and other tools, as well as the degree of success achieved in locating needed documents. Baker's (1988) article on fiction classification is one example of a study showing that changing the method of access can both improve user satisfaction and increase use of certain areas of the collection.

CONCLUSION

Before an individual can use the services of a library, he or she must know of its existence and of the resources it provides. One important factor affecting the extent of library use is physical accessibility. Libraries must be conveniently located. The typical person visits a library because there is some need for its services. Needs generally fall into four major categories:

1. To obtain one or more bibliographic items whose existence is already known
2. To obtain one or more items dealing with a particular subject
3. To obtain the answer to a specific factual question
4. To locate some unspecified item (book, videotape, record, or the like) for purposes of diversion or entertainment.

The extent to which these needs are promptly satisfied depends on the size and quality of the library's collections; the adequacy of collection organization; the usefulness of the tools—especially catalogs, indexes, and shelf arrangement—providing access to the collections; and the ability and willingness of the staff to exploit these resources. Whether or not a user is satisfied with the service of the library depends largely on how long it takes, and how much effort must be expended, to obtain a particular known item, one or more items dealing with a particular subject, or the correct answer to some question. The evaluation of library service should be regarded as a management tool, applied to determine how effectively and efficiently the library is serving the needs of its users, to identify limitations and failures of service, and to suggest ways in which the service might be improved. If implemented, these improvements in immediate service should lead to improvements in the ability of the library to reach its longer term, largely unmeasurable goals.

REFERENCES

Alkin, Marvin C.; Brian M. Stecher; and Frederica L. Geiger. *Title I Evaluation: Utility and Factors Affecting Use.* Northridge, Calif., Educational Evaluation Associates, 1982.

Armstrong, Charles M. "Measurement and Evaluation of the Public Library." In: *Research Methods in Librarianship: Measurement and Evaluation.* Edited by Herbert Goldhor. Urbana, Ill., University of Illinois, Graduate School of Library Science, 1968, pp. 15–24.

Association of Research Libraries, Office of Management Studies. *Planning for Management Statistics in ARL Libraries.* Washington, D.C., ARL, 1987. (Systems and Procedures Exchange Center) SPEC Kit 134

Aversa, Elizabeth. "Organizational Effectiveness in Libraries: A Review and Some Suggestions." *Drexel Library Quarterly, 17*(2):27–45, Spring 1981.

Baker, Sharon L. "Exploring the Use of *Output Measures for Public Libraries* in North Carolina Public Libraries." Iowa City, Ia., University of Iowa, School of Library and Information Science, 1987. ERIC ED288538

_____. "Will Fiction Classification Schemes Increase Use?" *RQ, 27*(3):366–376, Spring 1988.

Bonn, George S. "Evaluation of the Collection." *Library Trends, 22*(3):265–304, January 1974.

Braskamp, Larry A., and Robert D. Brown. *Utilization of Evaluation Information.* San Francisco, Calif., Jossey-Bass, 1980.

Bunge, Charles A. "Planning, Goals and Objectives for the Reference Department." *RQ,* 23(3):306–315, Spring 1984.

De Prospo, Ernest R.; Ellen Altman; and Kenneth E. Beasley. *Performance Measures for Public Libraries.* Chicago, Ill., Public Library Association, 1973.

Dickey, Barbara. "Utilization of Evaluations of Small Scale Innovative Educational Projects." Master's Thesis. Minneapolis, Minn., University of Minnesota, 1979.

Drucker, Peter F. "Managing the Public Service Institution." *The Public Interest,* (33):43–60, Fall 1973.

DuMont, Rosemary R., and Paul F. DuMont. "Measuring Library Effectiveness: A Review and an Assessment." In: *Advances in Librarianship.* Vol. 9. Edited by Michael Harris. New York, Academic Press, 1979, pp. 103–141.

Futas, Elizabeth. "The Role of Public Services in Collection Evaluation." *Library Trends,* 33(3):397–416, Winter 1985.

Haas, David F., and Donald H. Kraft. "Experimental and Quasi-Experimental Designs for Research in Information Science." *Information Processing and Management,* 20 (1–2):229–237, 1984.

Hamburg, Morris; Leonard E. Ramist; and Michael R. W. Bommer. "Library Objectives and Performance Measures and Their Use in Decision Making." *Library Quarterly,* 42(1):107–128, January 1972.

Hamburg, Morris, et al. *Library Planning and Decision-Making Systems.* Cambridge, Mass., MIT Press, 1974.

Houser, Lloyd J., and Gerald J. Lazorick. "Introducing a Significant Statistics Component into a Library Science Research Methods Course." *Journal of Education for Librarianship,* 18(3):175–192, Winter 1978.

Katz, Ruth M. "Library Education and Library Research: An Analysis of Institutional and Organizational Context." Doctoral Dissertation. New Brunswick, N.J., Rutgers University, 1975.

King, Donald W., and Edward C. Bryant. *The Evaluation of Information Services and Products.* Arlington, Va., Information Resources Press, 1971.

Lancaster, F. W. "The Cost-Effectiveness Analysis of Information Retrieval and Dissemination Systems." *Journal of the American Society for Information Science,* 22(1):12–27, January–February 1971.

McClure, Charles R., et al. *Planning and Role Setting for Public Libraries: A Manual of Options and Procedures.* Chicago, Ill., American Library Association, 1987.

Meier, Richard L. "Efficiency Criteria for the Operation of Large Libraries." *Library Quarterly,* 31(3):215–234, July 1961.

Mooers, Calvin N. "Mooers' Law or, Why Some Retrieval Systems Are Used and Others Are Not." *American Documentation,* 11(3):ii, July 1960.

Neenan, Peter A. "Impact Evaluation: Context and Function." *RQ,* 25(3):305–309, Spring 1986.

Nugent, Joan, and Deborah Carrow. "Ins and Outs of an In-House Evaluation: Problems and Solutions from a Working Information System." In: *The Value of Information: Collection of Papers Presented at the Sixth Mid-Year Meeting, American Society for Information Science, May 21, 1977.* Washington, D.C., American Society for Information Science, 1977, pp. 127–135.

Orr, R. H. "Measuring the Goodness of Library Services: A General Framework for Considering Quantitative Measures." *Journal of Documentation, 29*(3):315–332, September 1973.

Peritz, Bluma C. "The Methods of Library Science Research: Some Results from a Bibliometric Survey." *Library Research, 2*(3):251–268, Fall 1980.

————. "Citation Characteristics in Library Science: Some Further Results from a Bibliometric Survey." *Library Research, 3*(1):47–65, Spring 1981.

Ranganathan, Shiyali R. *The Five Laws of Library Science.* 2nd Edition. Bombay, India, Asia Publishing House, 1957.

Reisner, Elizabeth R., et al. *Assessment of the Title I Evaluation and Reporting System.* Washington, D.C., U.S. Department of Education, 1982.

Rose, Priscilla. "Innovation and Evaluation of Libraries and Library Services." *Drexel Library Quarterly, 7*(1):28–41, January 1971.

Rzasa, Philip V., and Norman R. Baker. "Measures of Effectiveness for a University Library." *Journal of the American Society for Information Science, 23*(4):248–253, July–August 1972.

Schlachter, Gail, and Donna Belli. "Program Evaluation—An Alternative to Divine Guidance." *California Librarian, 37*(4):26–31, October 1976.

Scriven, Michael. "The Methodology of Evaluation." In: *Perspectives of Curriculum Evaluation.* Edited by Ralph W. Tyler, Robert M. Gagne, and Michael Scriven. Chicago, Ill., Rand McNally and Company, 1967, pp. 39–83. (Area Monographic Series on Curriculum Evaluation No. 1)

Spray, S. Lee. *Organizational Effectiveness: Theory, Research, Utilization.* Kent, Ohio, Kent State University Press, 1976.

Stroud, Janet G. "Research Methodology Used in School Library Dissertations." *School Library Media Quarterly, 10*(2):124–134, Winter 1982.

Van de Water, Nancy, et al. "Research in Information Science: An Assessment." *Information Processing and Management, 12*(2):117–123, 1976.

Van House, Nancy A., et al. *Output Measures for Public Libraries: A Manual of Standardized Procedures.* 2nd Edition. Chicago, Ill., American Library Association, 1987.

Wallace, Danny P. "The Use of Statistical Methods in Library and Information Science." *Journal of the American Society for Information Science, 36*(6):402–410, November 1985.

Weiss, Carol H. "Purposes of Evaluation." In: *Strategies for Library Administration: Concepts and Approaches.* Edited by Charles R. McClure and Alan R. Samuels. Littleton, Colo., Libraries Unlimited, 1982, pp. 238–251.

White, Herbert S. "Cost-Effectiveness and Cost-Benefit Determinations in Special Libraries." *Special Libraries, 70*(4):163–169, April 1979.

Winkel, Lois, ed. *The Elementary School Library Collection: A Guide to Books and Other Media. Phases 1-2-3.* Williamsport, Pa., Broadcast Co., 1988.

Wyllys, Ronald E. "Teaching Descriptive and Inferential Statistics in Library Schools." *Journal of Education for Librarianship, 19*(1):3–20, Summer 1978.

Zweizig, Douglas L., and Eleanor Jo Rodger. *Output Measures for Public Libraries: A Manual of Standardized Procedures.* 1st Edition. Chicago, Ill., American Library Association, 1982.

CHAPTER 2

THE EFFECTS OF ACCESSIBILITY
AND CONVENIENCE
ON LIBRARY USE

Libraries exist primarily to link a particular user population with a universe of bibliographic resources needed for some purpose. Librarians attempt to maximize the user's accessibility or exposure to those resources. The ideal library is organized so that its patrons expend minimum effort to obtain access to bibliographic materials when they need them. This is because many patrons, consciously or unconsciously, will weigh the cost of a service against the benefits of using it.

Two models of information-seeking behavior exist in the library literature (Hardy, 1982). The *cost-benefit model* suggests that people select information sources primarily on the basis of their benefits, with cost as a secondary criterion. The *least-effort model* suggests that people first select those information sources that require the least effort to use, even if they have to make sacrifices in the quality of information obtained. (The principle of least effort was first described by Zipf, 1949.) A great deal of evidence exists to support the least-effort model, which is perhaps best exemplified by Mooers's famous law:

An information retrieval system will tend *not* to be used whenever it is more painful and troublesome for a customer to have information than for him not to have it. (Mooers, 1960, p. ii)

Poole (1985) reviewed dozens of studies on information-seeking behavior and confirmed Mooers's law, although he stated it in a slightly longer version that he called the avoidance–least-effort theory. The theory is as follows:

1. A first principle of human behavior is to avoid pain.
2. All human behavior has the purpose of problem solving.

3. In solving problems, man will calculate the possible consequences of his acts.

4. In solving problems, man will attempt to reduce all negative consequences of his acts to a minimum.

5. One negative consequence of the expenditure of effort in problem solving is the discomfort of fatigue.

6. So as to minimize the probability of fatigue, man will attempt to minimize his expenditure of effort.

7. By expending least effort, man seeks to avoid pain. (p. 95)

Mooers's law and the various least-effort principles imply that librarians can increase use by reducing the amount of effort patrons need to expend to use the library facilities, services, or resources. Therefore, librarians should concentrate on increasing accessibility-convenience to library services, because this will decrease the "pain" or "cost" of using these services.

Various types of accessibility—including societal, institutional, psychological, intellectual, bibliographic, and physical—have relevance to libraries (Culnan, 1985; Dervin, 1973; Wilson, 1968). *Societal accessibility* is the need for society to provide certain types of information, allocating the resources necessary to satisfy these information needs. *Institutional accessibility* is the need for the existence of organizations that can provide the desired information to a particular individual or group of individuals. The public library movement was born when one community recognized books and other publications as a public good and devoted public funding to maintaining and staffing a collection designed to meet the reading needs of its citizens. *Psychological accessibility* relates to the "friendliness" of the information source. For example, a library user may refuse to consult a librarian who is perceived to be unsympathetic to the user's needs. *Intellectual accessibility* is an individual's capacity for understanding library resources (for example, the catalog) and using the information sources provided. Some librarians, for instance, have initiated literacy programs to increase intellectual accessibility; others have deliberately selected a variety of materials for users who differ in terms of reading ability, general intelligence, or sophistication.

The two types of accessibility with which librarians are most familiar are *bibliographic* and *physical accessibility*. Librarians typically provide bibliographic accessibility through catalogs, various indexing and abstracting tools (in paper, online, or CD-ROM form), or some type of selective dissemination of information (SDI) services. Physical accessibility is the ability of an individual to have easy access to the information service and to the resources it provides.

Over the years, several dozen studies have examined how the accessibility or convenience of facilities, services, or materials affects their use. A review of the literature reveals four recurring findings, noted more than 20 years ago by Allen and Gerstberger (1967):

1. For the typical user, perceived accessibility is the single most important determinant of the overall extent to which an information channel is used.

2. The more experience a user has with a channel, the more accessible he or she will perceive it to be.

3. After the user finds an accessible source of information, he or she will screen it on the basis of other factors (for example, technical quality).

4. High motivation to find specific information may prompt users to seek out less-accessible sources of information.

PERCEIVED ACCESSIBILITY-CONVENIENCE

For the typical person, those information sources perceived to be the most accessible or convenient are used the most. Consider, for example, the many studies that examine the effects of distance on public library use (Elrick and Lavidge, Inc., 1977; Hayes and Palmer, 1983; Monat, 1967; Palmer, 1981; Schlipf, 1973). The studies generally show that most users reside within 5 miles of the library, that use declines rapidly as distance from the nearest branch or bookmobile stop increases, and that few active users live 10 or more miles from library facilities. Moreover, various studies show that adding or changing library locations can greatly increase use. For instance, a new library situated on the pedestrian walkway at the McGill metro station in Montreal attracted 5,000 new library users in its first year of operation (Lavigne, 1984).

Although public libraries have special problems because of the comparatively large geographic areas they serve (for example, Onadiran and Onadiran, 1981), the effect of physical accessibility on library use is not exclusive to this type of library. McCabe et al. (1976) assessed use by nonaffiliated users of all types of libraries within a six-county area in Pennsylvania; 67 percent of these users said convenience of location was the primary factor influencing their choice of library. Other studies have shown that student use of academic libraries is related to the distance students live from the university (for example, Orten and Wiseman, 1977). Even the specific location of a library within a campus or school can influence its use to a considerable degree, and the precise location of a special library within a corporate complex can affect significantly the type and amount of its use (Culnan, 1980; Neal and Smith, 1983; Slater, 1963). The extent to which an individual uses any library depends at least partly on how easily it can be reached from home or office.

Accessibility is a primary criterion influencing the public's selection of materials used for pleasure reading or as information sources (Baker, 1986a; Culnan, 1985; Ennis, 1965; Hernon, 1984; Waples, 1932). In fact, the typical person considers accessibility or convenience before considering other selection factors relating either to one item or to the collection as a whole—factors like currency, quality, comprehensiveness, and relevance (Adedigba, 1985;

Dougherty and Blomquist, 1974; Hardy, 1982; O'Reilly, 1982; Rosenberg, 1966). In the McCabe et al. study (1976) previously mentioned, only 21 percent of the respondents chose to visit a library because of its collection.

Patrons often use information sources that are readily at hand even when they know that better sources are available elsewhere. Many students, for example, use the closest accessible sources of information (for example, friends, teachers, and family) even when they know more authoritative sources can be found at the university library (Dunn, 1986). Herron (1986) observed a similar pattern among journalists working for large metropolitan newspapers, even though they had reasonable access to library facilities. Faculty, in both schools and colleges, tend to use personal library collections more than they do departmental collections; use departmental collections more than the main library; and use the main library more than less-accessible libraries, materials housed in remote storage facilities, or interlibrary loan systems (Holmes, 1987; Neal and Smith, 1983; Soper, 1972, 1976; Woodburn, 1969). Few patrons in any type of library reserve or recall books checked out to other patrons; this is true even when such options are advertised as being available and even when the material desired is considered better in some way than the material in hand (for example, Fullmer, 1981).

The general public's desire for convenience and easy access to information resources also is illustrated by the popularity of four other types of services:

1. *Selective dissemination of information (SDI) services.* Special librarians profile the interests of company scientists, managers, and other employees and provide them, on a regular basis, with abstracts of current materials that match their profiles. Most users of such services feel they are better informed as a result of the service, state that their satisfaction with the library has increased, or are able to quantify significant savings in the time associated with collecting information in general (for example, Estabrook, 1986; Houlson and Jax, 1987; Universiti Sains Malaysia Library, 1983).

2. *Other current awareness services.* Publishers have developed a number of journals that provide rapid and convenient access to the new literature in a given area. Most notable is *Current Contents,* which reproduces the contents pages of journals in various areas. One study found that scientists prefer *Current Contents* because it is comprehensive and provides the authors' addresses. The scientists often found it easier to write the authors directly for reprints of important articles than to use their local libraries, which had "lots of red tape" or access barriers (Lancaster, 1974).

3. *Document delivery services.* University libraries allow faculty and staff to order needed bibliographic materials by telephone. Library staff retrieve each item from the stacks, charge it out, and have it delivered to the office of the requester. Patron satisfaction with the library increases, and patron use of the services increases if patrons perceive the services to be easier to use than

obtaining library materials themselves (D'Elia and Hutkins, 1986; Dougherty, 1973).

4. *Curriculum consulting services.* In some universities and schools, librarians work with faculty and staff to identify bibliographic materials to support particular courses, conduct appropriate literature searches, and acquire all materials needed by faculty and students for use in the course, ordering materials when necessary (for example, Mavor and Vaughan, 1974; Oberg, 1986; Roggenbuck, 1985; Tovell, 1985).

Each of the library-related services listed here (SDI, document delivery, and curriculum consulting) could, if the service was made sufficiently convenient, increase use of or user satisfaction with the library, or both.

Other studies have shown that if particular materials or services are made more accessible within a particular library, they are more likely to be used. Moving materials from closed stacks or the reserve area to open stacks, from the regular stack to a prominent display, or closer to the library's door all increase usage (Baker, 1986a, 1986b; Carnovsky, 1933; Forbes, 1935; Goldhor, 1972, 1981; Osundina, 1975; Pings, 1967). Moving specific services, such as the reference department, closer to incoming traffic significantly increases their use (Harris, 1966; Osundina, 1975).

The principle that access is the single most important determinant of the overall extent to which an information source is used applies to all types of accessibility, not just physical accessibility. For example, Markey (1985) found that patrons avoided using subject heading guides for choosing the correct term under which to conduct a catalog search because they did not understand what the "x," "xx," or "s.a." abbreviations meant. The guides were not "intellectually accessible" to the average user.

Moreover, it is not enough for the librarian to make a particular service, tool, or library accessible. The item will not be used until the user *perceives* it as accessible. Taylor (1982) demonstrated this when she increased bibliographic access to specific materials (for example, through the addition of multiple entries in the card catalog) and found that usage of the materials did not increase. It is probable that most patrons do not perceive subtle differences in bibliographic access. Most patrons find the card catalog hard to use; therefore, minor changes like adding more entries for a very small number of items are likely to go unnoticed. Taylor later increased the physical accessibility of the same group of titles by displaying them in prominent locations; this change was readily apparent to library patrons and use increased significantly.

Perception of accessibility may affect willingness to use an information resource or service more than actual accessibility. Factors that influence this perception may relate to many different facets of accessibility. For example, patron perceptions of the accessibility of facilities are influenced by topographical features such as rivers and major highways, physical barriers such as limited parking and steep stairs, limitations imposed by youth or age such as lack of transportation, and psychological barriers such as cultural perceptions of "community boundaries" (for example, D'Elia, 1980; Hubbard, 1978). They also are influenced by the hours a library is open; for example, patrons in portions of New York City perceive many branches in their general home territory as equidistant and tend to look for those with the most convenient hours (Getz, 1980).

Furthermore, user perceptions of accessibility can vary extremely, even when a service is being rated by one fairly homogeneous client group. For example, D'Elia and Hutkins (1986) discovered that some college faculty found that a document delivery service on a major university campus saved them more time, required less effort, and was less frustrating to use than searching for items in the library themselves. Other faculty on the same campus did not use the service because they found it faster and easier to get the documents from the library themselves.

Potential library users often differ from librarians in their perceptions of how accessible services are, as Geppert (1975) demonstrated in a study of patrons and staff of school library media centers. Consider, for example, patron perceptions of the willingness of reference librarians to answer their questions. Several studies have shown that a number of patrons will not ask a librarian for assistance when they have a question, primarily because they perceive that the librarian is busy and, thus, unavailable to help them (for example, Durrance, 1986; Swope and Katzer, 1972; Westbrook, 1984). Both patrons and librarians perceived the librarian as busy any time another patron was being helped; patrons also perceived librarians as being too busy to help any time the librarians were working on something else at their desks or did not immediately make eye contact when patrons approached.

Collectively, these studies illustrate that improving the quality or performance of a particular information service will not, in and of itself, lead to increased use of the service (Allen and Gerstberger, 1967). Use will not rise unless resources, services, and facilities are made more accessible and more convenient to the library's clientele. This may require either major or minor redesign of facilities and services.

INFLUENCE OF EXPERIENCE ON PERCEPTIONS OF ACCESSIBILITY

Experience with a particular library service or tool, or with the library in general, can change a person's perception of its accessibility and ease of use. Many studies support this principle. For instance, various researchers have documented that people who were exposed to libraries as children tend to use them more than people who were not (for example, Duncan and Goggin, 1982; Powell, Taylor, and McMillen, 1984). Other studies have shown that most users of reference services and online searching services are repeat users, people who have already been exposed to and are satisfied with the service they received (for example, Bayer and Jahoda, 1981; Warden, 1981; Weech and Goldhor, 1984). Researchers have also shown that the more experience people have with information sources in general, the more accessible they perceive them to be (Allen and Gerstberger, 1967; Kremer, 1980). For example, frequent library users are less likely than moderate users to consider distance from the library as an accessibility problem (Zweizig and Dervin, 1977).

The implications are simple: If people use a service, tool, or library and see its benefit, they will perceive it as accessible to them and will be likely to use it again; however, it is not enough for librarians simply to tell people about the benefits. Librarians must somehow make patrons perceive the relevance of a service to their lives and to experience the rewards of using it before the patrons' opinion of its accessibility will change.

SCREENING ACCESSIBLE SOURCES

Several dozen studies show that patrons choose information sources that are most accessible and then screen them to meet any other selection criteria they might have. For example, once engineers in a study had chosen accessible sources to solve some information problem, they then screened the sources for technical quality (Allen and Gerstberger, 1967; Kremer, 1980). Forest Service professionals determined whether the contents of accessible sources were relevant to the problem at hand (Hardy, 1982). Even fiction readers browsed first those portions of the collection that were most accessible, making their selections based on factors such as the book's author, genre, or length (Baker, 1986a).

Another series of studies concentrated on how people screen items they locate through the catalog. Two of the most frequently used screening devices are publication date and content notes or annotations (for example, Palmer, 1972; Simmons and Foster, 1982). This suggests that entries under a single subject heading in a card catalog should be arranged in reverse chronological order rather than alphabetically by author and that entries should include item descriptions or notes. When patrons are unable to screen materials on the basis of the brief descriptive information contained in the catalog entry, they simply record the appropriate call number and browse among the titles in that area until they find items they believe will meet their needs (for example, Miura et al., 1980).

Studies such as these imply that librarians need to consider whether to conduct further research into the specific criteria that patrons use to screen accessible sources. Access tools, like the catalog, can then be redesigned to help patrons make their selections.

SEEKING OUT LESS-ACCESSIBLE SOURCES

A few users—those with a strong motivation to find a particular information source, the answer to a particular question, or a special type of information—will seek out less-accessible sources of information to meet their specific needs. Consider, for example, a woman who is planning to buy an inexpensive item, say a curling iron, within the next few weeks. Even though the various consumer magazines rate curling irons, noting their features, strengths, and weaknesses, this woman would probably not take the time to visit the library to read *Consumer Reports* and determine which curling iron is the best buy. She would feel it was not worth her time to spend an hour or more researching an item that cost less than $20.00.

But what if she were considering buying a new sports car? Since the cost of the vehicle is high, she is more likely to take the time to search for information on various makes and models of sports cars before making her purchase decision, even if she has to seek out sources that are less accessible to her, such as those housed at her local library.

At this point, the research is not sufficiently comprehensive to make broad generalizations about whose motivation will be high enough to overcome the access problem. But several studies shed light on the issue. Hodgart (1978) found that people with highly inelastic demands—that is, with some very specific need—were willing to travel farther to meet that need. This would explain, for example, the finding that professionals, business people, and students are likely to travel farther to meet their information needs (Gallup Organization Inc., 1976; Neale, 1950) and that graduate students, who often are highly motivated to find specific information relevant to their research, are much heavier users of interlibrary loan than most other categories of user (Montgomery, Seinola, and Vance, 1985). Fullmer (1981) discovered that people browsing the shelves do not file recall requests to retrieve books already in circulation. This is understandable given that browsers' demands are more elastic; they are looking not for one specific title, but rather for any "good" book that will meet their need for recreation or information. Lipetz (1970) reported that users who need formal documentation, or have time to wait for a source, are more likely to seek less-accessible sources.

REFERENCES

Adedigba, Yakub A. "Forestry Researchers as Information Users in Nigeria." *Information Development,* 1(4):229–233, October 1985.

Allen, Thomas J., and Peter G. Gerstberger. *Criteria for Selection of an Information Source.* Cambridge, Mass., Massachusetts Institute of Technology, 1967.

Baker, Sharon L. "The Display Phenomenon: An Exploration into Factors Causing the

Increased Circulation of Displayed Books." *Library Quarterly,* 56(3):237–257, July 1986a.

—————. "Overload, Browsers, and Selections." *Library and Information Science Research,* 8(4):315–329, October–December 1986b.

Bayer, Alan E., and Gerald Jahoda. "Effects of Online Bibliographic Searching on Scientists' Information Style." *Online Review,* 5(4):323–333, August 1981.

Carnovsky, Leon. "The Dormitory Library: An Experiment in Stimulating Reading." *Library Quarterly,* 3(1):37–65, January 1933.

Culnan, Mary J. "Organizational Information Flows and the Industrial Library." Doctoral Dissertation. Los Angeles, Calif., University of California, 1980.

—————. "The Dimensions of Perceived Accessibility to Information: Implications for the Delivery of Information Systems and Services." *Journal of the American Society for Information Science,* 36(5):302–308, September 1985.

D'Elia, George. "The Development and Testing of a Conceptual Model of Public Library User Behavior." *Library Quarterly,* 50(4):410–430, October 1980.

D'Elia, George, and Charla Hutkins. "Faculty Use of Document Delivery Services: The Results of a Survey." *Journal of Academic Librarianship,* 12(2):69–74, May 1986.

Dervin, Brenda. *The Information Needs of Urban Residents.* Washington, D.C., U.S. Department of Health, Education, and Welfare, Office of Education, Bureau of Libraries and Learning Resources, 1973.

Dougherty, Richard M. "The Evaluation of Campus Library Document Delivery Service." *College and Research Libraries,* 34(1):29–39, January 1973.

Dougherty, Richard M., and Laura Blomquist. *Improving Access to Library Resources: The Influence of Organization of Library Collections, and of User Attitudes Toward Innovative Services.* Metuchen, N.J., Scarecrow Press, 1974.

Duncan, Patricia W., and William F. Goggin. "A Profile of the Lifetime Reader: Implications for Instruction and Resource Utilization." Paper presented at the 26th College Reading Association Annual Conference, October 28, 1982. Philadelphia, Pa., College Reading Association, 1982. ERIC ED223994

Dunn, Kathleen. "Psychological Needs and Source Linkages in Undergraduate Information-Seeking Behavior." *College and Research Libraries,* 47(5):475–481, September 1986.

Durrance, Joan C. "The Influence of Reference Practices on the Client-Librarian Relationship." *College and Research Libraries,* 47(1):57–67, January 1986.

Elrick and Lavidge, Inc. "Public Library Usage in Illinois." Springfield, Ill., Illinois State Library, 1977.

Ennis, Philip H. *Adult Book Reading in the United States: A Preliminary Report.* Chicago, Ill., National Opinion Research Center, 1965. (Report No. 105)

Estabrook, Leigh Stewart. "Valuing a Document Delivery System." *RQ* 26(1):58–62, Fall 1986.

Forbes, Harriet R. "The Geography of Reading." *ALA Bulletin,* 29(8):470–476, August 1935.

Fullmer, Shaun M. "Improving the Effectiveness of Browsing." Master's Thesis. Chicago, Ill., University of Chicago, 1981.

Gallup Organization, Inc. *The Role of Libraries in America: A Report of the Survey Conducted by the Gallup Organization, Inc. for the Chief Officers of State Library Agencies and the American Library Association.* Frankfort, Ky., Kentucky Department of Library and Archives, 1976.

Geppert, Alida L. "Student Accessibility to School Library Media Center Resources as Viewed by Media Specialists and Compared to Students in Southwestern Michigan Secondary Schools." Doctoral Dissertation. Kalamazoo, Mich., Western Michigan University, 1975.

Getz, Malcolm. *Public Libraries: An Economic View*. Baltimore, Md., The Johns Hopkins University Press, 1980.

Goldhor, Herbert. "The Effect of Prime Display Location on Public Library Circulation of Selected Adult Titles." *Library Quarterly, 42*(4):371–389, October 1972.

—————. "Experimental Effects on the Choice of Books Borrowed by Public Library Adult Patrons." *Library Quarterly, 51*(3):253–268, July 1981.

Hardy, Andrew P. "The Selection of Channels When Seeking Information: Cost-Benefit vs. Least Effort." *Information Processing and Management, 18*(6):289–293, 1982.

Harris, Ira W. "The Influence of Accessibility on Academic Library Use." Doctoral Dissertation. New Brunswick, N.J., Rutgers University, 1966.

Hayes, Robert M., and E. Susan Palmer. "The Effects of Distance Upon Use of Libraries: Case Studies Based on a Survey of Users of the Los Angeles Public Library." *Library and Information Science Research, 5*(1):67–100, Spring 1983.

Hernon, Peter. "Information Needs and Gathering Patterns of Academic Social Scientists, with Special Emphasis Given to Historians and Their Use of U.S. Government Publications." *Government Information Quarterly, 1*(4):401–429, 1984.

Herron, Nancy Lee. "Information-Seeking Behavior and the Perceptions of Information Channels by Journalists of Two Daily Metropolitan Newspapers." Doctoral Dissertation. Pittsburgh, Pa., University of Pittsburgh, 1986.

Hodgart, R. L. "Optimizing Access to Public Services: A Review of Problems, Models and Methods of Locating Central Facilities." *Progress in Human Geography, 2*(1):17–48, March 1978.

Holmes, Gloria Price. "An Analysis of the Information-Seeking Behavior of Science Teachers in Selected Secondary Public Schools in Florida." Doctoral Dissertation. Tallahassee, Fla., Florida State University, 1987.

Houlson, Van C., and John J. Jax. "An Automatic Current Awareness Service: The Stout Experience." Menomonie, Wis., University of Wisconsin–Stout, 1987. ERIC ED283523

Hubbard, R. "A Review of Selected Factors Conditioning Consumer Travel Behavior." *Journal of Consumer Research, 5*(1):1–21, 1978.

Kremer, Jeannette M. "Information Flow Among Engineers in a Design Company." Doctoral Dissertation. Urbana, Ill., University of Illinois, Graduate School of Library Science, 1980.

Lancaster, F. W. "A Study of Current Awareness Publications in the Neurosciences." *Journal of Documentation, 30*(3):255–272, September 1974.

Lavigne, Nicole. "A Library in the Metro Station." *Public Library Quarterly, 5*(2):47–57, Summer 1984.

Lipetz, Ben-Ami. "Information Needs and Uses." In: *Annual Review of Information Science and Technology*. Vol. 5. Edited by Carlos A. Cuadra. Chicago, Ill., Encyclopaedia Brittanica, 1970, pp. 3–32.

Markey, Karen. "Subject-Searching Experiences and Needs of On-Line Catalog Users: Implications for Library Classification." *Library Resources and Technical Services*,

29(1):34–51, January–March 1985.

Mavor, Anne S., and W. S. Vaughan, Jr. *Development and Implementation of a Curriculum-Based Information Support System for Hamline University.* Landover, Md., Whittenburg, Vaughan Associates, Inc., 1974.

McCabe, James P., et al. "Census of Use by the Public of Different Types of Libraries: A Survey Indicating the Needs of Users with Regard to Cooperative Ventures." Allentown, Pa., Greater Lehigh Valley Council, 1976. ERIC ED134210

Miura, Itsuo, et al. "Information-Seeking Behavior of Catalog Users in the Library of International Christian University." *Library and Information Science, 18*:29–57, 1980.

Monat, William R. "The Community Library: Its Search for a Vital Purpose." *ALA Bulletin, 61*(11):1301–1310, December 1967.

Montgomery, K. Leon; Jill Seinola; and Pamela Vance. "The Investigation of Demand for a Rapid Document Delivery Service for the University of Pittsburgh Library System." Pittsburgh, Pa., University of Pittsburgh, 1985. ERIC ED272205

Mooers, Calvin N. "Mooers' Law or, Why Some Retrieval Systems Are Used and Others Are Not." *American Documentation, 11*(3):ii, July 1960.

Neal, James G., and Barbara J. Smith. "Library Support of Faculty Research at the Branch Campuses of a Multi-Campus University." *Journal of Academic Librarianship, 9*(5):276–280, November 1983.

Neale, Doris L. "Study of the Relation Between Distance from the Public Library Branch and Its Use." Master's Thesis. Chicago, Ill., University of Chicago, Graduate Library School, 1950.

Oberg, Antoinette. "The School Librarian and the Classroom Teacher: Partners in Curriculum Planning." *Emergency Librarian, 14*(1):9–14, September–October 1986.

Onadiran, G. T., and R. W. Onadiran. "Public Library Development: An Assessment of Present Trends in Nigeria." *Annals of Library Science and Documentation, 28* (1–4):119–123, March–December 1981.

O'Reilly, Charles A. "Variations in Decision Makers' Use of Information Sources: The Impact of Quality and Accessibility of Information." *Academy of Management Journal, 25*(4):756–771, December 1982.

Orten, Larry, and John Wiseman. "Library Service to Part-Time Students." *Canadian Library Journal, 34*(1):23–27, February 1977.

Osundina, Oyeniyi. "Nigerian Studies: Improved Accessibility and Undergraduate Use of the Academic Library." *International Library Review, 7*(1):77–81, January 1975.

Palmer, E. Susan. "The Effect of Distance on Public Library Use: A Literature Study." *Library Research, 3*(4):315–354, Winter 1981.

Palmer, Richard P. *Computerizing the Card Catalog in the University Library: A Survey of User Requirements.* Littleton, Colo., Libraries Unlimited, 1972.

Pings, Vern. "A Study of the Use of Materials Circulated from an Engineering Library, March to May 1956." *American Documentation, 18*(3):178–184, July 1967.

Poole, Herbert H. *Theories of the Middle Range.* Norwood, N.J., Ablex Publishing, 1985.

Powell, Ronald R.; Margaret A. T. Taylor; and David L. McMillen. "Childhood Socialization: Its Effects on Adult Library Use and Adult Reading." *Library Quarterly, 54*(3):245–264, July 1984.

Roggenbuck, Mary June. "Curriculum Involvement: Choices and Challenges for the School Library Media Specialist." *Catholic Library World, 57*(3):125–132, November–December 1985.

Rosenberg, Victor. "The Application of Psychometric Techniques to Determine the Attitudes of Individuals Toward Information Seeking." Master's Thesis. Bethlehem, Pa., Lehigh University, Center for Information Sciences, 1966.

Schlipf, Frederick A. "The Geographical Distribution of Urban Public Library Use and Its Relationship to the Location of Branch Libraries." Doctoral Dissertation. Chicago, Ill., University of Chicago, Graduate Library School, 1973.

Simmons, Peter, and Jocelyn Foster. "User Survey of a Microfiche Catalog." *Information Technology and Libraries, 1*(1):52–54, March 1982.

Slater, M. "Types of Use and User in Industrial Libraries: Some Impressions." *Journal of Documentation, 19*(1):12–18, March 1963.

Soper, Mary Ellen. "The Relationship Between Personal Collections and the Selection of Cited References." Doctoral Dissertation. Urbana, Ill., University of Illinois, Graduate School of Library Science, 1972.

————. "Characteristics and Use of Personal Collections." *Library Quarterly, 46*(4): 397–415, October 1976.

Swope, Mary Jane, and Jeffrey Katzer. "The Silent Majority: Why Don't They Ask Questions?" *RQ, 12*(2):161–166, Winter 1972.

Taylor, Margaret Ann Thomas. "The Effect of Bibliographic Accessibility Upon Physical Accessibility of Materials in a Public Library Setting." Doctoral Dissertation. Ann Arbor, Mich., University of Michigan, Graduate School of Library and Information Science, 1982.

Tovell, W. A. "Professional Cooperation: An Area for Development." *Education Libraries Bulletin, 28*(2):2–4, Summer 1985.

Universiti Sains Malaysia Library. "The Evaluation of SISMAKOM (Computerized SDI Project)." Paris, United Nations Educational, Scientific and Cultural Organization, 1983. Report #PGI-83/WS/16. ERIC ED241060

Waples, Douglas. "The Relation of Subject Interests to Actual Reading." *Library Quarterly, 2*(1):42–70, January 1932.

Warden, Carolyn L. "User Evaluation of a Corporate Library Online Search Service." *Special Libraries, 72*(2):113–117, April 1981.

Weech, Terry L., and Herbert Goldhor. "Reference Clientele and the Reference Transaction in Five Illinois Public Libraries." *Library and Information Science Research, 6*(1):21–42, January 1984.

Westbrook, Lynn. "Catalog Failure and Reference Service: A Preliminary Study." *RQ, 24*(1):82–90, Fall 1984.

Wilson, Patrick. *Two Kinds of Power: An Essay on Bibliographic Control.* Los Angeles, Calif., University of California Press, 1968.

Woodburn, Ian. "A Mathematical Model of a Hierarchical Library System." In: *Planning Library Services: Proceedings of a Research Seminar Held at University of Lancaster, 9–11 July 1969.* Session 3. Edited by Alexander G. Mackenzie and Ian M. Stuart. Lancaster, Eng., University of Lancaster Library, 1969.

Zipf, George K. *Human Behavior and the Principle of Least Effort.* Cambridge, Mass., Addison-Wesley, 1949.

Zweizig, Douglas, and Brenda Dervin. "Public Library Use, Users, Uses: Advances in Knowledge of the Characteristics and Needs of the Adult Clientele of American Public Libraries." In: *Advances in Librarianship.* Vol. 7. Edited by Melvin J. Voigt and Michael H. Harris. New York, Academic Press, 1977, pp. 231–255.

CHAPTER 3

COLLECTION EVALUATION: MATERIALS-CENTERED APPROACHES

Over the years, more work has been performed on the evaluation of collections of books and other materials than on any other facet of the library. This can be attributed to at least three major factors: (1) good collections are vital to the fulfillment of a library's goals; (2) the collection is tangible and therefore easier to evaluate than various library services, which are intangible; and (3) the declining economy and leaner budgets have forced librarians to buy only the "best" items for their clients. This chapter concentrates on the criteria that are used to evaluate the collection of a library or library system after the collection has been purchased and organized for public use. It also focuses on how to assess the strengths and weaknesses of the collection.

One major point underlies the evaluation techniques discussed in this chapter. Collection evaluation is most effective when it takes into account the goals and objectives of the library or information system and the institution of which it is a part. This means that there is no one best technique to use for collection evaluation in all libraries. Rather, the best ongoing and comprehensive collection evaluations combine techniques that are appropriate for the library's size, type, clientele, and the like. A community college library at an institution that focuses on teaching may choose evaluation methods that differ from those selected by a large library that supports scholarly research, a public library that provides recreational reading and general information, or a corporate library that helps company members keep the business profitable.

Other factors that may influence the evaluation choice include the cost of the evaluation method, the experience and skill of the library staff, and how soon the information is needed. Even more important may be the librarian's opinion of the desirability or effectiveness of the evaluation techniques. In the past, many librarians have relied heavily on qualitative methods of collection evaluation, apparently believing that subjective methods best utilize their professional judgment. Betts and Hargrave (1982), however, argue convincingly that

Traditional skills (of book selection and evaluation) are insufficient without a quantitative *context* in which to exercise them. Indeed, the existence of such a context both increases the degree of skill required in selection and provides an objective means of evaluating past selection. (p. 4)

Finally, the method of evaluation chosen depends on why the study is being conducted. Different techniques are used, depending on whether the library's intent is to revise its written collection development policy, document for the governing authority what has been accomplished with funds provided for collection development, record the changing interests and needs of the user community, determine which areas of the collection can be heavily weeded to provide needed shelf space, attain accreditation of either the library or its parent institution, or merely respond to a survey or request for statistics.

Once the purpose of the evaluation is understood, the librarian needs to consider which of two basic approaches will be used. The first approach focuses on the materials in the collection and addresses such factors as collection size and diversity; it also seeks to answer questions such as "How many and what kinds of books are in the collection?" and "How valuable is each book in the collection?" This chapter focuses on this type of collection evaluation. The second approach focuses on the use the collection receives and the library's clientele—actual or potential. It asks whether the materials in the collection are appropriate to the clientele served regardless of some abstract evaluation of the worth of each book or set of books. Chapter 4 focuses on use-centered approaches to collection evaluation.

Various authors have discussed specific techniques used in both the collection-centered and client-centered approaches. General overviews are provided by Altman (1980), the American Library Association (1979), Bonn (1974), Christiansen, Davis, and Reed-Scott (1983), and Futas and Intner (1985). Collection evaluation has also been discussed in the context of specific types of libraries. Magrill (1985) gives the best overview. Robinson (1981, 1982) reviews techniques suitable for evaluating government document collections, Mancall (1982) for school library collections, and Sandler and Barling (1984) for sociology collections. Several bibliographies listing both overviews and actual evaluation studies have also been compiled (for example, Ifidon, 1976; Nisonger, 1982; *Pacific Northwest Collection Assessment Manual,* 1990).

Six basic evaluation approaches focus on the collection itself:

1. Outside evaluators can conduct a subjective collection review and give their impression of collection adequacy.

2. Holdings can be checked against lists of best books or standard bibliographies in a subject area.

3. Holdings can be checked against lists of sources cited by researchers in a discipline.

4. The absolute size of a collection and its growth rate can be compared against quantitative standards issued by the profession or other formulas that state the optimal size of a collection to meet patron needs.

5. The size of various subject collections in learning institutions can be determined and compared against the emphasis placed on these materials in the curriculum.

6. Collection depth, or comprehensiveness, can be estimated.

Each of these approaches to collection evaluation is discussed separately.

THE IMPRESSIONISTIC METHOD

The impressionistic method, described in detail by Hirsch (1959) and Robinson (1981), occurs when one or more individuals—subject specialists, librarians, or scholars—thoroughly examine and evaluate the collection. Ideally, this is done after the specialist becomes familiar with the library's mission, its collection development policies, and any statistical data that have been gathered (for example, on collection size, the acquisitions budget, or collection use). The specialist then physically examines the collection and the shelf list (since the most frequently used materials may be checked out). This type of evaluation is entirely subjective, but it is valuable if done by individuals with sound knowledge of various subject areas and, more important, of the literature. Academic libraries in particular have relied on the expertise of faculty members when conducting impressionistic studies of this sort. For example, more than 50 years ago, the University of Chicago used 200 faculty members to evaluate its collections (Raney, 1933).

Bonn (1974) reviewed a number of impressionistic evaluations of library collections, including several studies where faculty members from various academic departments were asked to rate the quality of the collection in their own subject area. The product of the evaluation is generally a report identifying collection strengths and weaknesses and making specific recommendations for improvement. Many of these reports actually end up rating each subset of the collection on the comprehensiveness of its coverage (for example, discussing its size, scope, and depth). Indeed, Bonn notes that there is "a striking similarity between these rating scales and the levels or degrees of subject coverage which many libraries now specify in the acquisition policy statements" (p. 281).

Several libraries that have tried the impressionistic approach have specified general criteria that the evaluator can use to determine overall collection quality.

Exhibit 3-1 lists the set of criteria developed for use by academic, public, and special librarians in the Pacific Northwest. Other aspects that may be readily revealed in an impressionistic evaluation are the physical condition of the collection and the types of formats represented.

The greatest advantage of an impressionistic evaluation is its versatility. Any segment of the collection can usually be evaluated quickly with this method. Such an approach is most successful when specialists are available who are willing to undertake the evaluation, who know both their subject and its literature, who extensively use both the library being studied and others so that they have a better idea of what an ideal collection might be, and who have kept themselves well informed about whether the library is meeting user needs (Williams, 1967). Although the impressionistic method has been used most often to evaluate academic library collections, it is also applicable to other types of libraries.

The biggest limitation of this method is finding enough skilled, knowledgeable evaluators (preferably within the institution) who are willing to devote the time necessary to conduct a thorough evaluation. Academic libraries may find that faculty, who face increasingly heavy pressure to spend time doing and publishing research, are reluctant to help out with major collection evaluation efforts. Indeed, Kim (1979) found that fewer than 10 percent of faculty were committed to helping their library on even recommending books for purchase. It is also unlikely that many school teachers, with heavy class loads, will devote extensive amounts of energy to similar collection evaluations in media centers. Although evaluators with the necessary expertise can be hired, the cost of paying them to evaluate a large variety of subject areas may be prohibitive.

Another problem is that the experts hired might be unfamiliar with unique local conditions and their effects on collection development (Robinson, 1981). Also, the judgment of some experts may be impaired by their specialized focus or some other form of bias. These two problems may be lessened to some degree if the expert chosen to complete the review is given a clear understanding of the library's goals and the conditions affecting collection development, along with any general criteria to use when conducting the evaluation.

EVALUATION AGAINST STANDARD LISTS AND BIBLIOGRAPHIES

A common way of evaluating a library collection in toto, or in one or more specified subject areas, is to check the collection against another authority, such as a standardized list representing a core or basic collection, a subject bibliography that is accepted as complete and authoritative, or the catalog of another library that emphasizes the subject being evaluated. If the list is very large, a random sample of titles may be chosen to check against the collection. Presumably, an adequate collection is one that owns a high percentage of titles

Criteria	Description
Number of Volumes	Count of shelf list, or approximation based on 10 volumes per foot of shelf occupancy.
Checking the Collection Against Standard Bibliographies	This reflects:
	Principal Authors: Are the standard, chief, or more important authorities and authors included?
	Principal Works: Are the classic, standard, essential, and important works in the collection?
	Primary Sources: Are critically edited original texts and documents included? How extensively?
	Criticisms/Commentary/Interpretation: How complete is secondary monographic or critical treatment?
Chronological Coverage	Are older and newer materials consistently represented? Should they be?
Complete Sets	Are sets and series well represented in the collection? Are they complete?
Periodical Coverage	How extensive is periodical coverage of the subject? Are the chief titles included?
Access to Periodicals	Are the major indexes or abstracts in the field available either in paper or online?
Other Formats and/or Special Collections	Is the collection significantly strengthened by audiovisual materials, documents, microfilms, or other special collections?
Language	Is the collection primarily in English, or does it include extensive foreign-language materials?
Acquisition Level	How does the number of monographs and new serial titles acquired annually compare to standard annual publishing statistics?
Level of Funding	How does the level of funding correlate with the acquisition rate and the materials price inflation rate for the last 3–5 years?
Collection Goals	Do the collection goals reflect the library's mission?

EXHIBIT 3-1 **Criteria developed for use by academic, public, and special librarians in the Pacific Northwest for assessing a collection by the impressionistic method. Reprinted from *Pacific Northwest Collection Assessment Manual* (1990), courtesy of the Oregon State Library Foundation.**

on the list chosen. What is considered high will vary from library to library and subject to subject, depending on such factors as the library's purpose and the level of resources devoted to collecting in that subject area. This means that some degree of interpretation and judgment is involved in this method of evaluation. If the bibliographies are well chosen, examining the percentages of titles owned will reveal both strengths and weaknesses in the collection and identify particular titles that should be purchased.

Most libraries also will wish to analyze the list of books not held to see if there are consistent weaknesses in the coverage of particular periods, languages, or types of materials. Diagnostic analysis of this kind requires larger samples than would be needed simply to establish a probability of ownership. A sample of 300 is reliable for estimating the coverage of a collection, but 1,000 or more references might be needed to learn anything useful about what items or types of items are missing from the collection.

One of the most critical steps in this list-checking process is choosing the best list or set of lists from which to work, because various factors relating to the lists that are chosen may affect the quality of the evaluation results. These might include the scope, size, dates of inclusion, languages covered, and even the selectors' judgment, taste, and knowledge. Evaluators can ensure a good match by carefully reading the scope notes and introductory material in each list that is chosen to determine whether these are relevant to a particular library's size and goals.

There are literally hundreds of bibliographies and book lists that libraries can use in an evaluation that focuses on popular, general, specialized, or research materials. The American Library Association (1979), Bonn (1974), Comer (1981), and the *Pacific Northwest Collection Assessment Manual* (1990) list the major sources, such as *Public Library Catalog, Fiction Catalog, Elementary School Library Collection, Books for College Libraries, Choice*'s "Opening Day Collection," and the various "best books" lists put out regularly by the American Library Association and its divisions. Other lists are prepared or recommended by agencies of accreditation, are specifically mentioned in various library standards, or are listed in major guides to reference works such as *American Reference Books Annual*.

These standard lists are most useful for evaluating the quality of small- and medium-sized libraries with basic collections. They are generally inadequate for evaluating the special subject collections of larger or more specialized libraries, which prefer to use some of the numerous authoritative and comprehensive subject bibliographies such as those published by technical and professional organizations (Comer, 1981). Many special bibliographies are available. Gallagher (1981) located several that were useful for evaluating books in an ophthalmology collection at Washington University, and Tjarks (1972) proposed 29 bibliographies appropriate for evaluating resources in English and American literature and languages. These special bibliographies can be located by scanning *Biblio-*

graphic Index, the subject descriptor "Bibliography" in *Subject Guide to Books in Print*, and guides to major reference sources. For example, the 10th edition of *Guide to Reference Books* (Sheehy, 1986) lists a number of recently published bibliographies in the field of medicine, including those relating to medical education in the United States, environmental health, health care administration, health statistics, health maintenance through nutrition, consumer health information, and bioethics. Also available are standard lists for formats other than books, such as *Magazines for Libraries.*

It is possible to use, as a checklist, the catalog from another library perceived to have a strong collection in the area being evaluated. The University of Florida did this on a very extensive basis, comparing its holdings in various subject areas against a printed catalog of Library of Congress holdings (Kebabian, 1966). The University of Texas Health Science Center compared its holdings with those of the University of Texas Medical Branch and the National Library of Medicine (Kronick and Bowden, 1978). The latter operation was much less labor intensive than the University of Florida study because it used computer-generated databases to compare the holdings.

University and school librarians should not forget one good source of lists: the syllabi and bibliographies prepared by faculty. These lists are especially relevant because they were prepared to meet immediate student needs. Many librarians have assumed that these bibliographies will include only sources owned by the library, so they have not thought it necessary to check them. Olaosun (1984), however, discovered that his library could provide only a small percentage of the readings recommended for students in his university's French department.

Any library can combine or edit published checklists to meet a special evaluation need. This may be essential if the scope of a given bibliography, as defined by its compilers, does not exactly coincide with the needs of the library. In the Public Library Inquiry study, researchers were interested in obtaining an evaluation of collection adequacy in terms of the "best" and the most popular books. They compiled their fiction checklist from a number of sources: lists of best-sellers in *Publishers Weekly,* the American Library Association's "notable books of the year" bibliographies, best books lists prepared by professional critics in *Nation* and *The New York Times,* and lists of books appearing in *Book Review Digest* that were noted as suitable for public libraries (Leigh, 1951). Some authors have even compiled checklists of banned or controversial works, generally for the purpose of seeing whether librarians have purchased such titles or have themselves been censors by failing to include them in their collections (Serebnick, 1982). The expense of preparing a special-purpose list varies, depending on the purpose and scope of the evaluation.

List checking has a number of advantages. It is a simple, practical approach to providing rough evaluations of collection adequacy or completeness in small libraries or collections in fairly restricted subject areas. The list of books not owned may serve as a basis for future purchase consideration. And, once appropriate lists have been chosen and edited, the evaluation can be completed by a well-trained nonprofessional, making this approach fairly inexpensive.

List checking also is amenable for use by library consortia. For example, the Research Libraries Group (RLG) checked the holdings of member libraries against samples of titles taken from *The New Cambridge Bibliography of English Literature* and *The MLA Bibliography* to verify the depth of coverage in English literature:

In this case, the evaluation [was] designed not to conform to the needs and priorities of any individual library, but rather to the interests of RLG in establishing comparable and reliable indicators of collection strength and collecting levels, in order that national-level planning may be based on firm understandings of the strengths and weaknesses of each member's collections. (Wiemers et al., 1984, p. 70)

A number of consortia studies have checked member holdings in specific areas against the catalogs of other libraries to accomplish the same purpose. Potter (1982) and Shaw (1985) provide overviews of such studies.

The list-checking technique of collection evaluation does have limitations, as noted by Comer (1981), Hirsch (1959), and McInnis (1971). Lists become dated quickly. The use of standard lists may lead to conformity among collections. Bonn (1974) has even mentioned the possibility that the standard lists used to check adequacy of collections may be the very ones that were used earlier to build these collections. When this occurs, their use as evaluative tools is essentially nil.

Other serious criticisms are that the lists are not necessarily tested for user satisfaction and may not reflect local needs. Moreover, lists usually concentrate on what libraries should have, but fail to identify what they should not have, such as any outdated or superseded material that the library already owns. As Goldhor (1973) pointed out, the titles checked against a list in a particular subject area may represent only a small percentage of the library's total holdings in that field, and the checking operation reveals nothing about the other books held by the library, which may actually be better in terms of meeting local needs than those on the list.

To overcome some of these problems, Goldhor (1959, 1967, 1973, 1981) suggested a different approach to list checking, which he referred to as an "inductive method." It involves assessing the quality of a collection by taking a complete list of the library's holdings in a particular subject area and comparing the titles with a number of book-reviewing tools and selected bibliographies, both current and retrospective. He (1973) pointed out that "presumably the titles held by the library which are upon multiple lists are clearly desirable, those which are included on no list are probably not desirable, and those which are on only one list are of borderline quality" (p. 6). This makes sense, because a lower quality book presumably gets few initial reviews and is not included in the selected bibliographies. Goldhor applied his method to several evaluations, including one of books in a public library in Jamaica, and found it to be a viable alternative to checking one standard list. The time needed to check several sources, however, increases substantially the cost of the evaluation.

List checking in general seems most appropriate for smaller, nonspecialized libraries; it is not quite as useful for evaluating major research collections. This is partly because the cost of this methodology grows in proportion to the size and depth of the collection being evaluated. Even a large collection could be checked against innumerable lists covering a broad range of subject fields. In fact, this was done in a University of Chicago evaluation that used more than 400 lists and bibliographies (Raney, 1933) and a later evaluation at Stanford University (Mosher, 1979), but the expense of this kind of extensive, comprehensive analysis may prevent many libraries from undertaking it. Even if cost were not an issue, "uniqueness" is likely to be important in a research collection; that is, the collection should contain items that are not held elsewhere and do not appear on any standard lists.

EVALUATION USING CITATION ANALYSIS

Because of the limitations of checking standard lists, bibliographies, and catalogs, Coale (1965) suggested that large research collections should be evaluated one subject area at a time, using lists of citations (the bibliographic references that accompany a scholarly work) selected by the library staff. Often, the citations are chosen from a randomly selected sample of current journal articles or from a core group of "good" works in a subject collection.

As with other forms of list checking, the source of the citations must be carefully chosen to provide a group of citations that represent what should be present in a given library. This is particularly true because the time lag in publishing means that this method will emphasize retrospective materials. Although this may be appropriate for some disciplines (for example, nineteenth century American literature), others will suffer if the citations selected are not as current as possibe (for example, research on AIDS). If currency is important, the citations should be chosen from recent issues of major journals in a field rather than from classic works.

Regardless of the citation source used, the goal is to evaluate the collection not against some theoretical list of best books, but against lists of works actually consulted by scholars writing in the field, thereby indicating the ability of the library to support this type of research. The major assumption is that library users pay attention to bibliographic citations when seeking materials on a specific subject. A growing number of studies suggest that this assumption is valid. Broadus (1977) presents a good overview of these studies. Few scholars rely on abstracting and indexing tools to identify relevant citations, in part because such tools provide only the title or give a brief (generally nonevaluative) description of a work. Instead, when looking for further material on some subject, researchers rely on references in scholarly papers as the best indicator of which additional papers are worth reading. Broadus also found evidence of "parallels between use of materials as indicated by citation patterns and as shown by studies of requests in libraries, especially in relation to the needs of people engaged in research" (p. 319).

Several evaluators have used this evidence of "use" to shift collection acquisition patterns after completing a citation analysis. After Kriz (1978) had analyzed citations from master's theses in engineering, he shifted money from the serials budget to allow the purchase of the more heavily cited monographs. Griscom (1983) used a citation analysis study to determine the use of music periodicals and subsequently cut music serial subscriptions.

Citation analysis, in addition to identifying references within the core discipline itself, will also yield references to closely allied disciplines and to disciplines far removed from the main discipline. In other words, it recognizes the importance to scholarly research of material that would not normally be included in standard bibliographies of a particular subject area. This can be an advantage because it allows the evaluator to check the strengths of the general library collection as well as the specialized area. This is particularly helpful for those developing departmental collections in university libraries because it provides insight into how much overlap there needs to be between related departmental collections (for instance, chemistry and biology). Once the initial list of citations has been compiled, the library can determine the percentage of titles held to measure collection adequacy or can use the list of titles cited often but not held as a list of possible purchases.

Citation analysis is not as useful as standard list checking in identifying future titles for purchase. The latter identifies individual titles that should be in the collection, either because they appear on best book lists or because they are needed, in the case of a library trying to build a comprehensive collection, to fill in collection gaps. Citation analysis was designed to identify the overall ability of a library to meet the needs of its researchers. It provides an index of adequacy by determining whether the library has a sample of materials cited in a subject area. Because of its concentration on sampling, an individual work of any type, whether a journal article, monograph, or videotape, has a fairly slim chance of being cited in any one citation study.

Librarians also can determine whether selection trends need to be corrected by looking at the types of materials that are and are not often cited. Schad and Tanis (1974) noted that an inexperienced science bibliographer in a small academic library could argue that, because neither faculty nor students typically cite foreign-language materials, the library should not buy several large and costly serials sets in German when these are available at another library in the immediate area. Budd (1986) analyzed a sample of entries on the topic of American literature from the *International Bibliography* of the Modern Language Association. His analysis verified that, for this field, monographs were the primary information sources used, constituting 64 percent of the citations. Serials constituted 27 percent and unpublished items the remainder. Information such as this may be used to redistribute acquisitions budgets, if indicated.

Periodicals most frequently cited in a particular subject field can be identified by examining the relevant subject headings in *Journal Citation Reports,* published by the Institute for Scientific Information. This work, however, is really most useful for academic and special libraries that are interested in collecting in depth. Citation analysis can provide a viable alternative for school librarians who want to provide a few general magazines that are useful to their students. Drott and Mancall (1980) demonstrated this when they examined papers written by high school students and analyzed the number, types, and recency of materials cited. As Exhibit 3-2 shows, 25 percent of the use was supplied by only four general interest magazines; more than half was supplied by only 17 titles. The analysis allowed specific recommendations to be made for magazine collection policies.

Several authors have described how they select citations for the initial list used to evaluate a collection. When evaluating the Newberry Library's collection of works on the colonial history of Latin America, Coale (1965) drew two groups of samples so as to cover both retrospective and current works. The first group of samples consisted of 100–400 titles in classic works written by recognized colonial history scholars. The second group consisted of items drawn from relevant subject areas listed in the most recent edition of the *Handbook of Latin American Bibliography.*

Nisonger (1983) selected citations from journals rather than subject bibliographies. To determine which journals would provide the most reliable data for evaluating the political science research collections in five university libraries, he selected four samples of citations for comparison purposes. For the first two samples, he selected 150 citations each—1 citation at random from each article that appeared in the most prestigious political science journal, *American Political Science Review,* in 1977, 1978, and 1979. For each of the second two samples, he selected one citation from every article in the 1978 volume of five political science journals, each representing a major branch of the field. The second set of samples was comparable in size to the first. He tried to answer three questions:

1. Are consistent results obtained between [each set of] samples?
2. Are the relative rankings of the five universities consistent throughout the four samples?
3. And do the relative rankings of the five universities correspond to what one would expect, based on their academic programs? (p. 167)

Magazine Rank	Number of References to Magazine*	Cumulative References to Magazine	Cumulative Percent of All References
1 Newsweek	135	135	9.1
2 Time	112	247	16.6
3 U.S. News & World Report	76	323	21.7
4 Sports Illustrated	55	378	25.4
5 New Republic	38	416	27.9
6 Saturday Review	35	451	30.2
7 Scientific American	33	484	32.5
8 Science Digest	32	516	34.6
9 Science News	31	547	36.7
10 Nation	30	577	38.7
11 Reader's Digest	29	606	40.6
12 Business Week	29	635	42.6
13 National Geographic	27	662	44.4
14 America	26	688	46.1
15 American Heritage	25	713	47.8
16 Science	23	736	49.4
17 Current History	22	758	50.8
18 Congressional Digest	22	780	52.3
19 Psychology Today	20	800	53.7
20 National Review	16	816	54.7
21 thru 23	14 (14 × 3)	858	57.5
24 thru 26	12 (12 × 3)	894	60.0
27 thru 30	11 (11 × 4)	938	62.9
31 thru 34	9 (9 × 4)	974	65.3
35 thru 37	8 (8 × 3)	998	67.0
38 thru 41	7 (7 × 4)	1,026	68.9
42 thru 46	6 (6 × 5)	1,056	70.9
47 thru 57	5 (5 × 11)	1,111	74.6
58 thru 74	4 (4 × 17)	1,179	79.1
75 thru 99	3 (3 × 25)	1,254	84.2
100 thru 138	2 (2 × 39)	1,332	89.4
139 thru 296	1 (1 × 158)	1,490	100.0

NOTE: Total number of references equals 1,490.

*Numbers in this column indicate first the number of articles contributed by each magazine in the group listed in the Magazine Rank column. The calculation in parentheses shows the number of articles contributed, multiplied by the number of titles in the group. This product is the number which is added to the Cumulative References to Magazine column in each row.

EXHIBIT 3-2   Citation analysis: dispersion of magazine articles cited by high school students. Reprinted from Drott and Mancall (1980), courtesy of the American Library Association.

	Sample 1		Sample 2		
Library	*Number Held*	*Percent Held*	*Number Held*	*Percent Held*	*Percent Difference*
Georgetown University	125	83.3	133.5*	89.0	6.4
The George Washington University	122	81.3	128	85.3	4.7
Howard University	118	78.7	116.5*	77.7	1.3
The Catholic University of America	112	74.7	109.5*	73.0	2.2
George Mason University	102	68.0	99.5*	66.3	2.5

NOTE: Samples were compiled by randomly selecting one citation from every article in the *American Political Science Review*, 1977 through 1979.

*If the edition in the collection varied from the edition cited, it was counted as 0.5.

EXHIBIT 3-3 Comparisons of coverage of five collections based on two samples drawn from the *American Political Science Review (n* = 150). Reprinted from Nisonger (1983), courtesy of the American Library Association.

Results are given in Exhibits 3-3 and 3-4. Because the answers to all three questions were positive, Nisonger concluded that either method of drawing citations would yield reliable results.

Lopez (1969) suggested taking a multitiered sample of citations to test the depth of a subject collection. This method requires selecting, from a critical subject bibliography, a set of references and checking these against the library's holdings. A sample is then taken from the items cited in the works found during this search. This process is repeated until either the library lacks the materials cited or a fourth and final citation is obtained. Each succeeding sample is assumed to represent a level of greater depth of the collection. Thus, the citations found at the first level receive a score of 10, while the point value is doubled for each succeeding level (20 at the second level, 40 at the third, and 80 at the fourth). Although Lopez used citations from a critical subject bibliography, the study could be done using randomly selected citations from a carefully chosen list of current journals that are important in a discipline.

Nisonger (1983) was particularly impressed with the possibilities of the Lopez method because of its capabilities for measuring collection depth. It allows references to be traced back to earlier sources, approximating the steps followed by a scholar doing in-depth research on a specific topic. The tracing process yields citations that increase in average age and diversity of subject from the first level to the fourth. Nisonger (1980) verified that a library can logically expect to find fewer of the older citations when he tested the Lopez method at the University of Manitoba. Eighty-two percent of the searches at the first level

| | Sample 3 | | Sample 4 | | |
Library	Number Held	Percent Held	Number Held	Percent Held	Percent Difference
Georgetown University	116.5*	82.0	112	78.9	3.9
The George Washington University	109	76.8	105	73.9	3.7
Howard University	97.5*	68.7	95	66.9	2.6
The Catholic University of America	92.5*	65.1	95	66.9	2.6
George Mason University	78	54.9	79	55.6	1.3

NOTE: Samples were compiled by randomly selecting one citation from every article in 1978 issues of the *American Journal of Political Science, Comparative Politics, Political Theory, Journal of Politics,* and *World Politics.*

*If the edition in the collection varied from the edition cited, it was counted as 0.5.

EXHIBIT 3-4   Comparisons of coverage of five collections based on citations selected at random from five political science journals (n = 142). Reprinted from Nisonger (1983), courtesy of the American Library Association.

were successful, compared to 72 percent at the second level, 67 percent at the third, and 64 percent at the fourth.

One other finding by Nisonger (1980) is significant. When he compared the scores obtained by using the Lopez method on two samples of 25 references from each of four critical subject bibliographies, he observed large differences in the results. As Exhibit 3-5 shows, this ranged from a low of 3.1 percent for family therapy to a high of 43.6 percent for medieval French literature. The large variations may be partly because Nisonger's samples were not large enough to guarantee representative data. The scoring method used by Lopez, however, is a problem for three other reasons. First, it assigns higher point values to the retrospective materials. This may be appropriate for some disciplines, like history, that emphasize older materials, but as Lopez (1983) pointed out, this scoring system is inappropriate for disciplines like engineering that place more value on current materials.

Second, this scoring system ignores the fact that the intent of citation analysis is to identify the overall ability of a library to meet the needs of its researchers. Any individual work has a fairly slim chance of being cited, since the study seeks to verify the overall ownership of a sample of citations. It makes little sense, therefore, to assign higher point values to any individual work or set of works in a citation study:

Subject Field	Scores		Percent Difference	Adjusted Percent	
	High	Low		High	Low
American novel	1,130*	930†	17.7	44.7	32.4
Family therapy	1,930†	1,870*	3.1	57.5	53.8
Medieval French literature	1,010†	570*	43.6	27.8	17.0
Modern British history	1,140*	700†	38.6	30.4	21.4
Composite	4,710*	4,570†	3.0	36.6	34.2

*Results from sample 2.

†Results from sample 1.

EXHIBIT 3-5 Results from two samples selected by the Lopez method to evaluate the University of Manitoba library collections. Reprinted from Nisonger (1980), courtesy of the American Library Association.

In accordance with this reasoning, the high value assigned to the fourth level [of citations] would skew the overall results. . .The luck of finding or not finding one or two references at the higher levels would cause a large variation in the final score. (Nisonger, 1980, p. 332)

Third, the end result of the Lopez method is merely a numerical score. It would have value only in comparing two different libraries, using the same citations as the starting point for each, or comparing the collections of one library in different subject fields (with the starting point varied by using books selected from different disciplines). For these reasons, it is suggested that libraries ignore Lopez's scoring system, concentrating instead on determining a simple percentage of materials owned at each level and using professional judgment to determine whether current or retrospective materials are more valuable in a particular subject area.

In selecting the initial citations, special care must be taken to avoid biasing the citation study in favor of the library. This happens when the library limits its list of citations to works prepared by scholars conducting research at that institution. This mistake was made by Bolgiano and King (1978), Chambers and Healey (1973), Emerson (1957), and Griscom (1983), among others. All had good intentions: they wanted to document the research interest of their users, who were the scholars working there. A number of studies (for example, Soper, 1972), however, have shown that selection of an information source is based to a large extent on the accessibility of that source, with the most accessible source being chosen first. This means that libraries are more likely to have larger percentages of materials cited by researchers at their own institutions than materials cited by the general population of researchers in a specific subject area.

Several evaluators have been astute enough to avoid such bias by modifying their studies accordingly. When Popovich (1978) measured the adequacy of his university library's research collection in business/management, he supplemented the citations from the dissertations completed in his library with citations from dissertations completed by recently appointed faculty who had received their degrees elsewhere. Sineath (1970) used citations of faculty publications from both the University of Michigan and the University of Illinois to test the adequacy of collections in both libraries.

These types of citation analysis are most suitable for large academic and research libraries because they measure scholarly use. They have little relevance to public libraries because citation is not really applicable to many of the materials with which public libraries deal. For instance, cookbooks tend not to cite other cookbooks, so it would be difficult to compile a bibliography useful in evaluating a library's collection of this type of publication. Bland (1980), however, recommended a variation of citation analysis that could readily be applied to small academic or high school libraries: compiling checklists of citations from texts currently used in the curriculum. He argued that because a textbook is selected to meet specific local teaching and learning needs, the citations it contains can be presumed to be both relevant and pertinent to local interests of the students, as well as the faculty and scholars, using the collection. Gallagher (1981) later used a classic text as a basis of citation analysis in one subject area.

Like all evaluation methodologies, citation analysis has its share of drawbacks. It focuses primarily on the needs of those who do research (unless some variation of Bland's methodology is used). Sources cited by researchers may not be the most important or useful to the practitioners, teachers, or students in a field (for example, medicine). Citation analysis also tends to underrepresent those items read but not often quoted in scholarly research, including abstracts and indexes, news-oriented journals, and some secondary sources. And, because of the time lag inherent in the nature of citation studies, the emergence of new core titles may not be reflected in the results. A further practical difficulty is that many published citations are incorrect or incomplete. Tracking down the correct citations with erroneous information is at best a time-consuming process that requires the costly skill of a professional; at worst, it results in a large number of unusable references.

Another criticism is that the sources cited by an author writing on some topic may not be central to that topic, but may be only peripherally related. In some areas, though, this is actually an advantage: a collection often needs more than just the "core" to support research in a given area.

EVALUATION AGAINST QUANTITATIVE STANDARDS

For many years, the library community has been evaluating its collections against national, regional, or state standards set by library associations or by the accrediting bodies of the institution of which the library is a part. Those standards that relate to collection development may specify how large the book budget should be, what formats the library should have (for example, videotapes and compact disks), what the ratio of fiction to nonfiction should be, and the like. Presumably a collection that meets the standards is better than one that does not. The two standards most often specified, probably because they are tangible and relatively easy to measure, are the size and the rate of growth of the collection.

Size most often is measured by examining holdings records to determine the number of volumes or titles held overall or broken down by some variable such as location, subject, publication date, or format. If the library does not have an accurate record of holdings, an estimate can be used instead. The easiest way to obtain an estimate is to measure the number of linear inches of cards contained in the library's shelf list. The average number of cards per inch is determined through some type of systematic sampling—for instance, by sampling every 100th inch of the shelf list, counting the number of volumes represented in each inch of cards, determining the mean number of volumes per inch, then multiplying this figure by the total number of inches in the shelf list.

The concept of absolute size is important because a library is unlikely to function effectively if its collection falls below a certain level. Presumably, the larger the collection, the greater the probability that it will satisfy the information needs of its users. This assumes that the collection is appropriate in terms of subject matter and level of treatment to meet user needs.

Research has verified that the larger the collection, the greater the library's circulation (McGrath, 1976–1977; Pierce, 1976); however, there appears to be a diminishing return on circulation once a library reaches a particular size. Hodowanec (1978) made this point in a study of 400 academic libraries in the United States when he developed a formula that could accurately predict use in those libraries. He found that increasing the per student acquisition (PSA) yielded a corresponding incremental increase in per student circulation (PSC). At some point, however, the rate at which circulation rose leveled off. A PSA of 2.65 led to a PSC of 23.64. As Exhibit 3-6 shows, increasing the PSA 13 percent, to 3, will increase circulation by 6 percent. Increasing the PSA 126 percent, to 6, will only increase circulation by 34 percent. And increasing the PSA beyond approximately 8 has no significant effect in raising the PSC. Detweiler (1986) discovered a similar pattern for more than 100 public library branches in the Washington, D.C. area. Circulation per volume increased slowly for libraries with fewer than 50,000 volumes, increased drastically for libraries with 50,000–100,000 volumes, then leveled off for libraries with more than 100,000 volumes.

PSC	PSA	Percent Increase in PSC*	Percent Increase in PSA†
23.64	2.65	—	—
25.00	3.00	6	13
27.70	4.00	17	51
29.90	5.00	26	89
31.60	6.00	34	126
32.80	7.00	39	164
33.50	8.00	42	202
33.69	9.10	42	243

NOTE: PSC = per student circulation; PSA = per student acquisition.

*Percent increase calculated from base level PSC of 23.64.

†Percent increase calculated from base level PSA of 2.65.

EXHIBIT 3-6   Incremental range of per student circulation for a corresponding increase in per student acquisition. Adapted from Hodowanec (1978), courtesy of the American Library Association.

Neither Hodowanec nor Detweiler explained this phenomenon, but a study by D'Elia and Walsh (1985) suggested a possible cause. The latter authors found that patrons are not able to perceive differences in collection quality until the quality of the collection falls below some minimally acceptable (to the patron) level of service.

This minimally acceptable level of service may be related to size. Librarians who are designing their collections to meet user needs should be selecting first those basic items that patrons are likely to find of use, such as materials in heavy demand among students or other clientele. Up to a point, larger collections should have more of the most wanted materials, patrons should be satisfied, and circulation should increase significantly. In Detweiler's (1986) study, circulation per item was lowest in the smallest libraries, those with fewer than 50,000 volumes. Potential users who could not find what they needed might have considered these collections below minimally acceptable levels. Circulation per volume increased significantly when collection size was between 50,000 and 100,000 volumes, a size that enabled patrons to find more of the materials they wanted. For collections of more than 100,000 titles, circulation per user or per volume began to fall off. This is because libraries with large collection budgets will at some point have chosen most of their "basic" materials and then added other works to the collection—works that may be used by a more specialized (and smaller) clientele. Taken together, these studies suggest that the absolute size of the collection is related to patron satisfaction only up to a point and should be just one of a number of factors considered when examining collection quality.

There is also evidence, at least for academic libraries, that absolute size is related to the perceived quality of the institution. Quality in this case generally is measured by some ranking of academic excellence. This relationship was noted by Blau and Margulies (1974–1975), Jordan (1963), and Reichard and Orsagh (1966), among others.

The question of whether a library is continuing to grow should also be addressed when measuring collection quality. Current materials are requested and used more frequently by library patrons. A large library that stops acquiring new publications will decline rapidly in value except, perhaps, for purposes of historical research. Collection growth generally is measured by the percentage rate of growth or the actual number of new items added. It can be related to size of the user community (items added per capita) and evaluated separately for different subject areas.

A number of libraries have, in the past, defined a quality collection as one that grows by a certain percent per year. For example, the most recent set of college library standards (Association of College and Research Libraries, 1986) recommended that libraries not meeting the standard for absolute size should attempt to maintain a 5 percent annual growth rate. But percentage growth rate alone can give a distorted picture of collection quality. A library may show a high rate of growth if it fails to discard obsolete items while collecting new ones. Such a library, however, is performing a great disservice to its users. In addition to creating chronic storage problems, this type of policy is likely to reduce overall collection quality. Percentage rate of growth as an indicator of collection utility penalizes the library that actively weeds. Large libraries should also be cautious when using percentage rate of growth to evaluate collection quality, because there is a threshold beyond which one can expect the rate of collection growth to decelerate (Leach, 1976). In other words, as libraries get larger, the number of volumes they must purchase to maintain a consistent percentage rate of growth also rises. An academic library with 50,000 volumes needs to purchase only 2,500 volumes to maintain a 5 percent annual growth rate, one with 500,000 volumes needs to buy 25,000, and a library with 5 million volumes needs to acquire 250,000 volumes. Eventually the library reaches a point where it cannot afford to continue purchasing, processing, or storing so many materials, and percentage growth drops off.

A better indicator of collection vitality may be growth measured by the absolute number of items added. Institutions can easily document whether this number is increasing steadily from year to year (the preferred mode for many libraries), is fairly constant (the preferred mode for libraries that lack expansion space), or is declining. Libraries can use data that show purchasing declines to support requests for more funding, to counteract inflation's effects on the acquisitions budget.

A notable trend has been the attempt to develop formulas that address absolute size, growth rate, or both. Some are rather simple, such as the large number of public and school library formulas that base collection size on the number of community residents or students served. Other, more complex formulas are predicated on the belief that minimum collection size should depend on many different variables, including the size and composition of the population served; the levels of use or, in academic and school libraries, curriculum; methods of instruction; and geographic location of the campus. The formula that Beasley (1968) created for public libraries factors in resources, population, circulation, and research capability. For academic libraries, a number of formulas exist, including that of Washington State University (Interinstitutional Committee of Business Officers, 1970) and those developed by Alexander (1976), Association of College and Research Libraries, (1986), Cartter (1966), Hodowanec (1978), Power and Bell (1978), and Voigt (1975). The strength of these formulas is that they consider the different levels of use by various groups of the library community. But the formulas make two big assumptions, which may or may not be valid: that all materials in the collection are carefully chosen in accordance with institutional goals and that the weeding program is active and realistic.

The most widely cited formula is the one designed by Clapp and Jordan (1965). Its premise is that an academic library collection should begin with 50,750 volumes, a figure the authors arrived at after examining several standard lists of basic collections for undergraduate libraries (the comparable figure in 1991 will probably exceed 80,000 volumes). The library then adds more volumes on the basis of the exact population served, with fewer volumes being added for undergraduate use and proportionately more for use by master's students, faculty, and doctoral students (Exhibit 3-7).

The Clapp/Jordan formula, like others of its type, has been criticized over the years. Some authors take issue with the weighting scheme. Rogers and Weber (1971) pointed out that the formula does not distinguish between demands placed on the library by users in different disciplines but rather assumes that demands will be uniform. McInnis (1972) noted that the weight applied for the number of doctoral fields exerts too strong an influence on the final results. Mitchell (1976) believed the formula needs to take other variables into account, including price factors, level of service desired, rates of obsolescence and rates of publishing in a given discipline, and the need for multiple copies. The most serious criticism is that the Clapp/Jordan formula underestimates the size of the collection needed (McInnis, 1972). This is a particular problem because all too often minimum standards, like those expressed in the Clapp/Jordan formula, are interpreted by the people controlling a library's funding as optimum levels; as a result, some library acquisitions may be curtailed.

This was the problem faced by some of the State University of New York (SUNY) libraries, which were in danger of having their growth restricted to the levels recommended by Clapp and Jordan. The librarians who authored a

	Books		Periodicals		Document	Total
	Titles	*Volumes*	*Titles*	*Volumes*	*Volumes*	*Volumes*
To a basic collection, namely:						
Undergraduate library	35,000	42,000	250	3,750	5,000	50,750
Add for each of the following as indicated:						
Faculty member (full-time equivalent)	50	60	1	15	25	100
Student (graduate or undergraduate in full-time equivalents)	0	10	0	1	1	12
Undergraduate in honors or independent study programs	10	12	0	0	0	12
Field of undergraduate concentration—"major" subject field	200	240	3	45	50	335
Field of graduate concentration—master's work or equivalent	2,000	2,400	10	150	500	3,050
Field of graduate concentration—doctoral work or equivalent	15,000	18,000	100	1,500	5,000	24,500

EXHIBIT 3-7 Formula for estimating the size for liminal adequacy of the collections of senior college and university libraries. Reprinted from Clapp and Jordan (1965), courtesy of the American Library Association.

report on the matter (State University of New York, 1970) clearly indicated that standards established by the formula are applicable only to the threshold period of an institution's growth. They are set at the "bread and water level" and are not appropriate to assess the adequacy of a collection in a well-established institution, a point supported by the McInnis (1972) study. The SUNY report emphasizes that

threshold criteria set forth in *minimal* terms are inadequate as budgeting devices for the State University of New York and . . . that minimal criteria devised in the early 1960's must be appreciably more minimal and less adequate in 1970 . . . Indeed a formula that confines itself to merely liminal levels, with no exponential factor to provide for growth beyond the threshold, should have, in theory, a built-in mechanism to keep it current and relevant. (p. 4)

The compilers of the SUNY report found that none of the Clapp/Jordan factors were superfluous and that "no significant growth factor" was omitted from the formula. They developed a modified formula, based on the same factors but with the values raised above those proposed in the original formula.

Raising the level of resources suggested in the standards is one possible solution to the minimum-levels problem. Indeed, the Association of College and Research Libraries did this when it developed Formula A for determining the adequacy of college library collections (Association of College and Research Libraries, 1986). Formula A, shown in Exhibit 3-8, is similar to that developed by Clapp and Jordan (1965) except that it increases both the base number of volumes recommended for a collection and the number of volumes to be added for some of the enrichment factors. Another solution to the minimum-levels problem is to have the standards specify both minimum and higher levels of adequacy. The standards of the Association of College and Research Libraries recommend four levels of resources for libraries, ranging from grade A (excellent) to grade D (minimum). "A" libraries own 90 percent of the number of volumes recommended by Formula A, "B" libraries own 75–89 percent, "C" libraries own 60–74 percent, and "D" libraries own 50–59 percent.

Another serious problem with quantitative formulas and standards is that they emphasize the number of resources rather than the quality of the service those resources can provide; the central question of how well the resources are managed still is unanswered. Twenty-five years ago, Krikelas (1966) argued that no one had effectively demonstrated a relationship between a library's size and the quality of the titles purchased. A review of the literature shows that the statement still holds true. In fact, at least one study shows that small libraries (with correspondingly small book budgets and collections) do not select materials of lower quality, they just select fewer materials overall (Vitolins, 1963).

FORMULA A

1. Basic collection	85,000 vols.
2. Allowance per FTE faculty member	100 vols.
3. Allowance per FTE student	15 vols.
4. Allowance per undergraduate major or minor field*	350 vols.
5. Allowance per master's field, when no higher degree is offered in the field*	6,000 vols.
6. Allowance per master's field, when a higher degree is offered in the field*	3,000 vols.
7. Allowance per 6th year specialist degree field*	6,000 vols.
8. Allowance per doctoral field*	25,000 vols.

A "volume" is defined as a physical unit of a work which has been printed or otherwise reproduced, typewritten, or handwritten, contained in one binding or portfolio, hardbound or paperbound, which has been catalogued, classified, or otherwise prepared for use. Microform holdings should be converted to volume-equivalents, whether by actual count or by an averaging formula which considers each reel of microfilm, or ten pieces of any other microform, as one volume-equivalent.

*For example of List of Fields, see Malitz (1981).

EXHIBIT 3-8 Formula A for determining the adequacy of college library collections. Reprinted from Association of College and Research Libraries, College Library Standards Committee (1986), courtesy of the American Library Association.

Many authors have argued against determining a collection's quality solely by examining its size. Some representative and reasonable arguments that have been made repeatedly include the following:

- The numbers of books or periodicals owned conveys only the most general impressions of the overall strength or weakness of a library (McInnis, 1971).
- The probability of locating a useful resource depends ultimately on the nature of the request as well as on the collection (Krikelas, 1966).
- Two collections purchased with identical budgets can vary greatly in quality, depending on the wisdom of the purchaser (Hirsch, 1959).
- Collection adequacy should be judged by performance—the percentage of time the patron finds the book he or she wants (Gore, 1976).
- There may be no relationship between the number of items held and a collection's ability to meet its user needs (Robinson, 1981).
- Collection quality depends on diversity as well as on size (Kister, 1971).

For a detailed review of other problems associated with quantitative standards in general, see Chapter 10 in this book.

The general dissatisfaction with quantitative standards and formulas for collection development has led some groups like the Public Library Association to drop prescriptive standards. Rather, they encourage libraries to set their own standards after examining current measures of service, use, or output (Van House et al., 1987). Many of these measures, such as stock turnover rate and fill rate, are discussed in Chapters 4 and 5 of this book. Not all librarians feel comfortable with abandoning quantitative standards entirely; many individuals feel such standards have upgraded libraries by providing substandard institutions with realistic targets toward which they can strive. This is why collection standards written at the state level, particularly for underfunded public and school libraries, are retaining some prescriptive, quantitative elements. The best also include output measures. Two good examples of collection standards that use both types of measures are those developed for public libraries in Illinois and North Carolina (Illinois Library Association, 1989; North Carolina Library Association, and North Carolina Public Library Directors Association, 1988).

EVALUATING THE SIZE OF SUBJECT COLLECTIONS

Libraries often find it more useful to have an indication not just of the absolute number of volumes in a collection or the growth rate but of the number of holdings in a particular subject. This statistic can provide objective evidence for determining whether the collection is adequate to meet user needs, can support impressionistic evaluations, and can be used in cooperative collection development efforts. Goldstein and Sedransk (1977), for example, sampled the shelf lists to compare the size (and the age and distribution of materials in terms of language) of the Jewish history collections in seven libraries. This type of comparative analysis is favored among consortia seeking to determine which library has the largest collection. It also is useful for librarians who want to know how the size of their collection relates to similar libraries.

Many libraries keep statistics about how many titles are held within a particular subject area, especially subject areas defined by whatever classification system is used (for example, the 400s of the Dewey Decimal System schedule or the Zs of the Library of Congress schedule). If a library has input its holdings in an automated system, a program can be written to obtain specific information on how many items are owned in each subject area. Kim (1982) discussed how libraries subscribing to OCLC-MARC tapes can get accurate counts of holdings in certain classification areas. If a library has converted all of its holdings to machine-readable form, the MARC tapes can be used to analyze the entire collection; otherwise, monthly and annual cumulative tapes provide data for the materials added to the collection in a given time frame.

If a library does not have an accurate record of holdings, a considered estimate can be made instead. Many libraries simply measure the number of linear inches of cards contained within each major classification area of the library's shelf list and multiply this by the average number of volumes represented in an average inch of cards (determined by sampling). Black (1981) suggested that estimating size in a particular subject area is more complex because the number of volumes per inch of shelf list may differ from subject to subject. For each separate subject area, he suggested following seven steps, illustrated in Exhibit 3-9, to estimate collection size:

1. Count the number of shelves of books.
2. Count the number of books on every 10th shelf, then average these to get a mean number of volumes per shelf.
3. Multiply the number of shelves by the mean number of volumes per shelf to determine the total number of volumes currently shelved in each area.
4. Count the number of volumes currently in circulation.
5. Count the number of volumes housed in the reference collection.
6. Count (if known through an inventory) the number of missing volumes.
7. Add the results of steps 3 through 6 to obtain the total number of volumes in each subject area.

One advantage of Black's method is that once a total volume count has been determined for each area, the number of linear inches of shelf list can be measured and divided by the total number of volumes obtained in step 7 to yield an average volume-per-inch count. This average varies from subject to subject and can easily be used to calculate the growth of the subject collection. For example, if the collection in medicine grows by 30 linear inches over a 3-year period, one can estimate the new size of the medical collection (Exhibit 3-9) to be 36,519 volumes (32,469 volumes + [135 volumes/inch × 30 linear inches]).

It is questionable whether Black's method of adding the number of missing volumes to the holdings count is valid, because missing volumes are, for whatever reason, no longer held and because ideally the cards for such volumes have been removed from the shelf list. Still, Black's method, even if it is somewhat complicated and labor intensive, may yield accurate data if a count of subject holdings is needed.

Neither the simple method of estimating the number of volumes per linear inch of shelf list nor Black's method is perfect for measuring subject size, because a library classification schedule assigns books to only one subject, whereas many titles fall into more than one subject area or may end up separated from other books on the same or closely related subjects, owing to the vagaries of the classification system used. In other words, a large percentage of titles relevant to a given subject may not appear under the notation assigned to that subject in a particular classification scheme. Saunders, Nelson, and Geahigan (1981) demonstrated that for some disciplines—such as philosophy—the match is relatively good (that is, 70 percent or higher congruence) between books

Dewey Decimal Number	Number of Shelves	Mean Number of Volumes per Shelf	Number of Volumes					Inches of Shelf List	Volumes per Inch
			Total Currently Shelved	Circulating	Reference	Missing	Total Volumes		
600-609 (General Technology)	56	19.5	1,092	30	319	20	1,461	7.875	186
610-619 (Medicine)	1,187	24.1	28,607	1,708	1,236	918	32,469	240.500	135
620-629 (Engineering)	758	22.4	16,979	715	882	411	18,987	134.375	141
630-639 (Agriculture)	712	21.7	15,450	484	509	315	16,758	80.500	208
640-649 (Home Economics)	100	23.0	2,300	184	46	125	2,655	26.500	100
660-669 (Chemical Technology)	162	21.4	3,467	237	346	90	4,140	30.75	135
670-679 (Manufacturing)	59	25.5	1,505	58	72	43	1,678	15.000	112
680-689 (Special Manufacturing)	19	32.5	618	52	12	33	715	7.375	97
690-699 (Construction)	24	27.0	648	86	61	37	832	8.500	98
600-699 (Summary)	3,077	26.8	70,666	3,554	3,483	1,992	79,695	551.375	145

EXHIBIT 3-9   Steps in estimating collection size in a specific subject area. Reprinted from Black (1981), courtesy of the *Journal of Academic Librarianship.*

deemed relevant by professionals in the discipline and their actual classification within the Library of Congress scheme. But for other disciplines—for example, anthropology and sociology—the match was not good (40 percent or lower congruence).

To overcome this problem, Saunders, Nelson, and Geahigan proposed two alternatives to shelf list measurement. The first modifies a standard shelf list count by factoring in the percentage of books within a discipline that are classified outside that area. This is determined by selecting, from a journal that reviews books in all subfields of a discipline, a random sample of books, then determining what percentage of these are classified outside the expected class numbers. The second alternative to the shelf list count is somewhat simpler. An expert in a particular discipline randomly selects 1,000 titles from the card catalog and identifies those titles from the sample that relate to the discipline. The number of titles held within the discipline is the percentage of the total sample identified as belonging to the discipline times the total number of titles in the library.

Regardless of how the size of a subject collection is determined, the evaluator examines the final holdings count to see if it seems too high, too low, or just right. This decision could be made using the librarian's best judgment, based on his or her knowledge of the clientele served. But the classified profile approach can provide quantitative data to help academic and school librarians determine whether the size of each subject area is appropriate.

Classified Profile Approach to Determining the Size of a Subject Collection

The classified profile approach has been used frequently in university libraries since its development in the late 1960s (McGrath, 1968; McGrath and Durand, 1969). During the last few years, a variation of this approach, called collection mapping, has gained growing acceptance in the school library field. Loertscher (1985) described the value of the classified approach as follows:

The sage advice that in order to eat an elephant, cut it into small pieces is a sound strategy for collection building. The idea is to divide a collection into a number of small but manageable segments which match the various parts of the curriculum. Each of these segments can be built, weeded, or maintained as curriculum needs dictate. Each segment has the corresponding piece of the total budget, depending on the priorities assigned to the goals of expansion, replacement only, or deemphasis. . . . Do not build the collection as a whole. Build pieces of the collection. Create a collection that is tailored specifically for the school it serves. (p. 11)

The premise of this type of evaluation is that the key to collection evaluation is knowledge of the curriculum, specifically, knowing how many items support certain subject areas in the curriculum. Generally, librarians use curricular guides to learn about the resource needs of school teachers and catalog course descriptions to learn about the resource needs of university faculty.

Golden (1974) described how a typical profile is created. First, librarians read the published description for each course, supplementing these as necessary with information obtained directly from the faculty or from current class outlines. They then assign numbers to the description from the classification scheme used in their library. No limit is placed on how many classification numbers are assigned to a course; however, numbers are assigned only for the primary topics of each class, rather than for peripheral subjects covered. The shelf list then is counted to determine how many books are held in each classification number supporting a course. The evaluators also examine the course enrollment statistics for the year just ended to provide a more balanced view of collection support for specific classes. A sample of the data collected for courses in religion at the University of Nebraska is shown in Exhibit 3-10. The ultimate result is a profile of the collection that shows which collection areas should be emphasized and which are emphasized. Needed changes can then be made to purchasing policies.

Whaley (1981) varied this approach at two university libraries in the late 1970s. Instead of scrutinizing catalog course descriptions, bibliographers met with individual faculty members to identify, for each course taught, pertinent classification numbers. The shelf list was then checked to determine how many titles were held within each area.

Burr (1979) showed that the classified profile approach can successfully be combined with an evaluation using collection standards. His main goal was to identify which parts of the collection provided support for the course offerings of each of four major schools: arts and sciences, engineering, education, and business administration. The catalog descriptions of all courses offered were reviewed, and relevant Library of Congress classification numbers were assigned on the basis of the subject matter covered. These classification numbers were then matched with the library's holdings to see how many resources supported the curricula of each school. This was done by estimating, through a shelf list sample, the number of volumes in each area.

Burr then compared the number of volumes that supported each curricular area with those recommended in a modified version of the collection development formula specified in the standards of the Association of College and Research Libraries. The standards required that there be an 85,000-volume core collection, with additional holdings added on the basis of institutional characteristics such as the number of faculty, students, and undergraduate majors or minors. Using information about the program characteristics and enrollments in all four areas, Burr determined how much of the core and supplementary collections should support the programs of each school. The final step in the process was to compare recommended holdings in each area with actual holdings. Burr concluded that, although the overall size of the collection was generally adequate, there were significant deficiencies in the support the library was providing

Course Number	Course Title	Library of Congress Classification Numbers	Total Number of UNO* Books	Course Credit Hours	Enrollment 1971–1972			
					Fall		Spring	
					Under-graduate	Graduate	Under-graduate	Graduate
211	African and American Indian Religion	BL2400–2499 E59.R38 E98.R3	38	3	37	0	32	0
215	Old Testament	BS1–1830	676	3	111	0	—	—
216	New Testament	BS1–680, 1901–2970	817	3	—	—	124	0

*University of Nebraska at Omaha.

EXHIBIT 3-10 Example of quantitative data collected for courses in religion at the University of Nebraska. Reprinted from Golden (1974), courtesy of the American Library Association.

for the schools of engineering, education, and business administration. Purchasing policies were changed as a result of the study.

Evans and Beilby (1983) described collection evaluation through a sophisticated management information system used in the SUNY libraries. One machine-readable file stores student enrollment data that are classified according to the U.S. Office of Education's Higher Education General Information Survey (HEGIS) codes. The evaluators use OCLC tapes, together with a conversion tape showing equivalencies between the HEGIS codes and Library of Congress class numbers, to relate the acquisitions data of a library to the enrollment. Thus, for each HEGIS code (for example, 1103, German language) the system generates a printout showing the number of titles acquired by the library and the percentage of the total acquisitions that this represents, and the number of student credit hours and the percentage of the total credit hours that this represents. Subject areas in which strong or weak relationships exist between student credit hours and acquisitions patterns can thus be identified.

Palais (1987) significantly refined the reporting of collection profile data. Librarians at the Arizona State University libraries complete classified profiles and place the results in a computer database, making the numbers subject both to quick revision and to sorting in various fashions. Four sortings are by

1. *Library of Congress (LC) classification record.* All LC class numbers are interfiled in one sequence and displayed to show the selector the total demand on each class by all university courses. It thus becomes easy to tell how much emphasis should be placed on collection in a given area. The practice may reveal some surprising connections. For example, Palais found that the history of civilization class was used (as expected) by the history, religion, philosophy, sociology, and English departments and (unexpectedly) by the engineering department.

2. *Subject.* The report is arranged by LC subject headings, giving the corresponding LC class or range of classes. It can be used as a reference tool to determine LC classes or ranges for a particular subject.

3. *Department.* The departmental profile lists the course number and relevant LC classes and subject headings. It can be particularly useful when determining what subjects ought to be emphasized in departmental library collections.

4. *Course number.* The report lists both the LC classes and the subject headings for each course and is helpful when discussing new or revised course needs with teaching faculty.

Like all evaluation methods, the classified approach has drawbacks. It does not consider such qualitative factors as collection age, condition, variety, and duplication. Moreover, the success of the approach depends on the evaluator's ability to match accurately the course offerings to the classification schemes. This is sometimes difficult, since the Library of Congress and Dewey classification schedules hinder precise assignment when a subject area is relatively undeveloped. A second problem is vague or out-of-date course descriptions. This difficulty can be overcome by contacting faculty directly or by obtaining class outlines to supplement the course descriptions when necessary, but this approach increases the cost of the evaluation. And cost is a concern because the methodology is time-consuming. Libraries can economize, as Golden (1974) did, by having student assistants measure the shelf list to determine holdings in each classified area. But the assignment of subject categories and, when pertinent, the individual meetings with faculty members should be handled by professionals. Of course, the cost will increase with the number of courses in a university's curriculum. Because it concentrates so heavily on the curriculum, the classified profile approach may also ignore the research needs of faculty and graduate students. Again, this can be overcome, at some cost, by holding meetings with these groups to determine their needs.

In spite of these difficulties, the classified profile approach is generally viable and has some important fringe benefits. Librarians often understand more clearly the relationship between the curriculum and the collection; this knowledge should result in better purchasing decisions. Discussion between faculty and librarians about what the collection should include is promoted. Finally, the quantitative data gathered can be used when analyzing budget allocations for specific collection areas; that is, a library can target deficient areas and allocate a higher-than-normal percentage of the book budget to strengthening these.

School media specialists have, during the past decade, adapted the classified profile approach to meet their needs. They, too, calculate the number of materials within specific subject areas and compare these data to the emphasis given a subject in the curricular guide. They then use these data to create a visual map of their holdings that displays collection breadth and depth. The map can be used to draw the attention of teachers, students, administrators, and parents to the strengths of a collection and, by omission, to its weaknesses.

As described by Loertscher (1985), refined by Ho and Loertscher (1985), and demonstrated by Murray et al. (1985), three specific sets of data are mapped visually. These are shown, in simplified form, in Exhibit 3-11 and are explained as follows:

1. The number of items owned per student is mapped at the bottom of the chart and is graphed horizontally, using a scale ranging from mediocre to exemplary. An exemplary collection is one that meets the national standard of 40 items held per student.

2. The left side of the chart shows the major areas of general emphasis—the materials that support major courses of instruction such as biology or American history.

3. The right side of the chart shows specific subjects that are emphasized in the curriculum.

School name:
Number of students: 597
Total collection: 8,289
Number of total collection items per student: 13.88

	Number of Items	Number of Items per Student
General Emphasis Areas		
Folklore and Fairy Tales	305	0.5108
Animals	263	0.4405
Specific Emphasis Areas		
Dinosaurs	53	0.0887
Frontier and Pioneer Life	79	0.1323
Indians of North America	150	0.2512

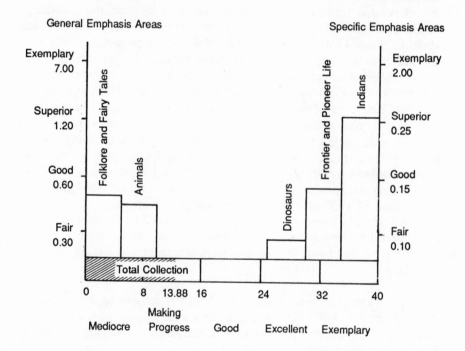

NOTE: All numbers are charted in items per student.

EXHIBIT 3-11   Example of a collection map for a school library. Reprinted from Ho and Loertscher (1985), courtesy of *Drexel Library Quarterly*.

The numerical scales used on the map for the areas of general and specific emphasis were determined during a study of the collections of 68 elementary, junior high, and high schools nationwide. Exemplary collections were defined as those in the top 25 percent for number of volumes per student, superior collections were in the second 25 percent, good collections were in the third 25 percent, and fair collections were in the lowest 25 percent. The number of volumes per student representing the top of each quartile is indicated on each scale.

Loertscher (1985) suggested that each area of curricular emphasis be evaluated every time a major demand is made on it (for example, when a class assignment is made). In other words, the media specialist and the teacher, working with input from students, should rate each segment of the collection on the diversity of formats available to meet student needs, the recency of the materials, the relevance of the collection to the assignment, the level of duplication of materials (were there enough materials for the number of students taught?), and the appropriateness of the reading or viewing levels. This kind of added evaluation emphasizes the quality of the materials in each area and is a welcome modification to the emphasis on quantification of holdings, which is the basis for most classified profile studies. In fact, there is only one real weakness to the collection mapping approach: the implication that only strong areas of the collection should be visually displayed. Rather, weaknesses should also be shown, so that librarians, administrators, and others can see what action should be taken to improve collection development efforts.

Comprehensiveness of the Collection and Its Subsections

Information about a collection's comprehensiveness is also of use in collection evaluation, given the desire of most libraries to have a balanced, complete collection that will meet patron needs. Comprehensiveness, in this sense, refers to the breadth of subject coverage rather than the number of items in the collection. Garland (1982) visualized comprehensiveness

as a continuum ranging from a collection in which documents are acquired in a single subject field to a collection in which documents are acquired in all subject fields. The lower the degree of comprehensiveness, the more related the subject collection; the higher the degree of comprehensiveness, the more diverse the subject collection. (p. 110)

A library's goals would determine, to a large extent, how well it should perform on a comprehensiveness scale. A large public library might strive for a high degree of comprehensiveness by collecting materials in many subject fields; a small special library may collect in only a handful of areas designated by the parent corporation as being vital to its research and development efforts.

Garland (1979, 1982) suggested using the Brillouin information measure to track comprehensiveness. This measure is a single numerical value that expresses the degree of collection diversity. The lower the degree of comprehensiveness, the less diverse the collection; the higher the comprehensiveness, the more diverse the collection. Garland (1982) believed that this type of comprehensiveness scale is more useful than list-checking methods, "which provide only a rough guide as to the degree to which the system's goals are being met. A scale of comprehensiveness would provide collection evaluations with a precise measure" (p. 111). This is questionable. It is difficult to see how a measure that yields only a numerical value and cannot in itself identify types of deficiencies can be judged more valuable than list-checking methods that, if properly applied, can identify areas of deficiency, types of documents, or individual works that need to be added to a collection.

Even though a single index of comprehensiveness is not particularly useful when evaluating collections, there is growing interest in describing various subject "intensity" levels to reveal the depth to which a library would like a particular collection to grow. The American Library Association (ALA), the Library of Congress, and the Research Libraries Group (RLG) have all developed similar measures. These are described in ALA's collection evaluation guidelines (American Library Association, 1979) and SPEC Kit 87 (Association of Research Libraries, 1982). The most used of the three measures is that of RLG, which assigns intensity levels on a scale from 0 to 5 as follows:

0: *Out of scope*—The library does not collect in this area.

1: *Minimal level*—Few selections in the collection are beyond basic works.

2: *Basic information level*—The material is up to date and general and serves to introduce and define a subject and to indicate the varieties of information available elsewhere. A basic information collection is not sufficiently intensive to support any courses or independent study in the subject area involved.

3: *Instructional support level*—The collection is adequate to support undergraduate and most graduate instruction, or sustained independent study.

4: *Research level*—The collection includes the major published source materials required for dissertations and independent research.

5: *Comprehensive level*—The library endeavors, so far as is reasonably possible, to include in the particular collection all significant works of recorded knowledge in all applicable languages for a defined field.

The strength of such descriptions is that they recognize that a library cannot collect comprehensively in all areas. The procedures RLG uses to collect information on collection intensity levels were designed to provide uniformly gathered data to form a framework for future cooperative actions among libraries, such as cooperative collection development and interlibrary loan. For example, the RLG Conspectus has been adopted by the Association of Research

Libraries for use in the North American Collection Inventory Project. Further refinement of the collection intensity levels developed by RLG and other groups are expected in the next decade. Stielow and Tibbo (1987) have already suggested one refinement that should further improve collection description efforts: they want RLG to follow ALA's example by subdividing the instructional support level into initial (undergraduate) and advanced (graduate) levels to reflect more clearly existing university library practices.

The uses and benefits of the RLG Conspectus have been discussed by Ferguson et al. (1988). Although Oberg (1988) referred to the Conspectus method as an evaluation technique, this is misleading. A library that applies the Conspectus criteria does not really evaluate the strength of its collection in various subject areas; rather, it merely identifies its stated collection development policies in these areas. For more detailed information on the Conspectus approach, consult SPEC Kit 151 of the Association of Research Libraries (1989).

REFERENCES

Alexander, Norman D. "Suggested Model, Designed to Serve as a Guide for Evaluating the Adequacy of Academic Library Collections in American Colleges and Universities." Doctoral Dissertation. Los Angeles, Calif., University of Southern California, 1976.

Altman, Ellen. "Collection Evaluation—What It Means; How It's Done." *Unabashed Librarian*, (35):13–14, 1980.

American Library Association, Resources and Technical Services Division, Collection Development Committee. "Guidelines for the Evaluation of the Effectiveness of Library Collections." In: *Guidelines for Collection Development*. Edited by David L. Perkins. Chicago, Ill., ALA, 1979, pp. 9–19.

Association of College and Research Libraries, College Library Standards Committee. "Standards for College Libraries, 1986." *College and Research Libraries News*, 47(3):189–201, March 1986.

Association of Research Libraries, Office of Management Studies. *Collection Description and Assessment in ARL Libraries*. Washington, D.C., ARL, 1982. SPEC Kit 87

———— *Qualitative Collection Analysis: The Conspectus Methodology*. Washington, D.C., ARL, 1989. SPEC Kit 151

Beasley, Kenneth E. "A Theoretical Framework for Public Library Measurement." In: *Research Methods in Librarianship: Measurement and Evaluation*. Edited by Herbert Goldhor. Urbana, Ill., University of Illinois, Graduate School of Library Science, 1968, pp. 2–14.

Betts, Douglas A., and Roger Hargrave. "How Many Books?" *Library Management*, 3(4):1–31, 1982.

Black, George W., Jr. "Estimating Collection Size Using the Shelf List in a Science Library." *Journal of Academic Librarianship*, 6(6):339–341, January 1981.

Bland, Robert N. "The College Textbook as a Tool for Collection Evaluation, Analysis, and Retrospective Collection Development." *Library Acquisitions: Practice and Theory*, 4(3/4):193–197, 1980.

Blau, Peter M., and Rebecca Zames Margulies. "A Research Replication: The Reputations of American Professional Schools." *Change,* 6(10):42–47, December–January 1974–1975.

Bolgiano, Christina E., and Mary Kathryn King. "Profiling a Periodicals Collection." *College and Research Libraries,* 39(2):99–104, March 1978.

Bonn, George S. "Evaluation of the Collection." *Library Trends,* 22(3):265–304, January 1974.

Broadus, Robert N. "Applications of Citation Analyses to Library Collection Building." In: *Advances in Librarianship.* Vol. 7. Edited by Melvin J. Voigt and Michael H. Harris. New York, Academic Press, 1977, pp. 299–335.

Budd, John. "A Citation Study of American Literature: Implications for Collection Management." *Collection Management,* 8(2):49–62, Summer 1986.

Burr, Robert L. "Evaluating Library Collections: A Case Study." *Journal of Academic Librarianship,* 5(5):256–260, November 1979.

Cartter, Allan M. *An Assessment of Quality in Graduate Education.* Washington, D.C., American Council on Education, 1966.

Chambers, George R., and James S. Healey. "Journal Citations in Master's Theses: One Measurement of a Journal Collection." *Journal of the American Society for Information Science,* 24(5):397–401, September–October 1973.

Christiansen, Dorothy E.; C. Roger Davis; and Jutta Reed-Scott. "Guide to Collection Evaluation Through Use and User Studies." *Library Resources and Technical Services,* 27(4):432–440, October–December 1983.

Clapp, Verner W., and Robert T. Jordan. "Quantitative Criteria for Adequacy of Academic Library Collections." *College and Research Libraries,* 26(5):371–380, September 1965.

Coale, Robert Peerling. "Evaluation of a Research Library Collection: Latin–American Colonial History at the Newberry." *Library Quarterly,* 35(3):173–184, July 1965.

Comer, Cynthia. "List-Checking as a Method for Evaluating Library Collections." *Collection Building,* 3(3):26–34, 1981.

D'Elia, George, and Sandra Walsh. "Patrons' Uses and Evaluations of Library Services: A Comparison Across Five Public Libraries." *Library and Information Science Research,* 7(1):3–30, January–March 1985.

Detweiler, Mary Jo. "The 'Best Size' Public Library." *Library Journal,* 111(9):34–35, May 15, 1986.

Drott, M. Carl, and Jacqueline C. Mancall. "Magazines as Information Sources: Patterns of Student Use." *School Media Quarterly,* 8(4):240–244, 249–250, Summer 1980.

Emerson, William L. "Adequacy of Engineering Resources for Doctoral Research in a University Library." *College and Research Libraries,* 18(6):455–460, November 1957.

Evans, Glyn T., and Albert Beilby. "A Library Management Information System in a Multi-Campus Environment." In: *Library Automation as a Source of Management Information.* Edited by F. W. Lancaster. Urbana, Ill., University of Illinois, Graduate School of Library and Information Science, 1983, pp. 164–196.

Ferguson, Anthony W., et al. "The RLG Conspectus: Its Uses and Benefits." *College and Research Libraries,* 49(3):197–206, May 1988.

Futas, Elizabeth, and Sheila Intner, eds. "Collection Evaluation." *Library Trends,* 33(3):237–436, Winter 1985.

Gallagher, Kathy E. "The Application of Selected Evaluative Measures to the Library's Monographic Ophthalmology Collection." *Bulletin of the Medical Library Association, 69*(1):36–39, January 1981.

Garland, Kathleen. "The Brillouin Information Measure Applied to Materials Selection." *Collection Management, 3*(4):371–380, Winter 1979.

_____. "Developing a Scale of Comprehensiveness to Serve as a Collection Evaluation Criterion." In: *Information Interaction: Proceedings of the 45th ASIS Annual Meeting.* Vol. 19. Edited by Anthony E. Petrarca, Celianna I. Taylor, and Robert S. Kohn. White Plains, N.Y., Knowledge Industry Publications, 1982, pp. 110–112.

Golden, Barbara. "A Method for Quantitatively Evaluating a University Library Collection." *Library Resources and Technical Services, 18*(3):268–274, Summer 1974.

Goldhor, Herbert. "Are the Best Books the Most Read?" *Library Quarterly, 29*(4):251–255, October 1959.

_____. *A Plan for the Development of Public Library Service in the Minneapolis-St. Paul Metropolitan Area.* Minneapolis, Minn., Metropolitan Library Service Agency, 1967.

_____. "Analysis of an Inductive Method of Evaluating the Book Collection of a Public Library." *Libri, 23*(1):6–17, 1973.

_____. "A Report on an Application of the Inductive Method of Evaluation of Public Library Books." *Libri, 31*(2):121–129, August 1981.

Goldstein, Marianne, and Joseph Sedransk. "Using a Sample Technique to Describe Characteristics of a Collection." *College and Research Libraries, 38*(3):195–202, May 1977.

Gore, Daniel. "Farewell to Alexandria: The Theory of the No-Growth, High Performance Library." In: *Farewell to Alexandria.* Edited by Daniel Gore. Westport, Conn., Greenwood, 1976, pp. 164–180.

Griscom, Richard. "Periodical Use in a University Music Library: A Citation Study of Theses and Dissertations Submitted to the Indiana University School of Music from 1975–1980." *Serials Librarian, 7*(3):35–52, Spring 1983.

Hirsch, Rudolph. "Evaluation of Book Collections." In: *Library Evaluation.* Edited by Wayne S. Yenawine. Syracuse, N.Y., Syracuse University Press, 1959, pp. 7–20.

Ho, May Lein, and David V. Loertscher. "Collection Mapping: The Research." *Drexel Library Quarterly, 21*(2):22–39, Spring 1985.

Hodowanec, George V. "An Acquisition Rate Model for Academic Libraries." *College and Research Libraries, 39*(6):439–447, November 1978.

Ifidon, Sam E. "Qualitative/Quantitative Evaluation of Academic Library Collections: A Literature Survey." *International Library Review, 8*(3):299–308, June 1976.

Illinois Library Association. *Avenues to Excellence II: Standards for Public Libraries in Illinois.* Springfield, Ill., ILA, 1989.

Interinstitutional Committee of Business Officers. *A Model Budget Analysis System for Program 05 Libraries.* Olympia, Wash., Evergreen State College, 1970.

Jordan, Robert T. "Library Characteristics of Colleges Ranking High in Academic Excellence." *College and Research Libraries, 24*(5):369–376, September 1963.

Kebabian, Paul B. "The Distance to a Star: Subject Measurement of the Library of Congress and the University of Florida Collections." *College and Research Libraries, 27*(4):267–270, July 1966.

Kim, David U. "OCLC-MARC Tapes and Collection Management." *Information Technol-*

ogy and Management, 1(1):22–27, March 1982.

Kim, Ung Chon. "Participation of Teaching Faculty in Library Book Selection." *Collection Management, 3*(4):333–352, Winter 1979.

Kister, Kenneth F. "Let's Add Diversity." *Library Journal, 96*(16):2745, September 15, 1971.

Krikelas, James. "Library Statistics and the Measurement of Library Services." *ALA Bulletin, 60*(5):494–499, May 1966.

Kriz, Harry M. "Subscriptions vs. Books in a Constant Dollar Budget." *College and Research Libraries, 39*(2):105–109, March 1978.

Kronick, David A., and Virginia M. Bowden. "Management Data for Collection Analysis and Development." *Bulletin of the Medical Library Association, 66*(4):407–413, October 1978.

Leach, Steven. "The Growth Rates of Major Academic Libraries: Rider and Purdue Reviewed." *College and Research Libraries, 37*(6):531–542, November 1976.

Leigh, Robert D. "The Public Library Inquiry's Sampling of Library Holdings of Books and Periodicals." *Library Quarterly, 21*(3):157–172, July 1951.

Loertscher, David V. "Collection Mapping: An Evaluation Strategy for Collection Development." *Drexel Library Quarterly, 21*(2):9–21, Spring 1985.

Lopez, Manuel D. "A Guide for Beginning Bibliographers." *Library Resources and Technical Services, 13*(4):462–470, Fall 1969.

——————. "The Lopez or Citation Technique of In-Depth Collection Evaluation Explicated." *College and Research Libraries, 44*(3):251–255, May 1983.

Magrill, Rose Mary. "Evaluation by Type of Library." *Library Trends, 33*(3):267–295, Winter 1985.

Malitz, Gerald S. *A Classification of Instructional Programs.* Washington, D.C., National Center for Education Statistics, 1981.

Mancall, Jacqueline C. "Measurement and Evaluation of the Collection." *School Library Media Quarterly, 10*(2):185–189, Winter 1982.

McGrath, William E. "Measuring Classified Circulation According to Curriculum." *College and Research Libraries, 29*(5):347–350, September 1968.

——————. "Predicting Book Circulation by Subject in a University Library." *Collection Management, 1*(3–4):7–26, Fall–Winter 1976–1977.

McGrath, William E., and Norma Durand. "Classifying Courses in the University Catalog." *College and Research Libraries, 30*(6):533–539, November 1969.

McInnis, R. Marvin. "Research Collections: An Approach to the Assessment of Quality." *Institute of Professional Librarians of Ontario Quarterly, 13*(1):13–22, July 1971.

——————. "The Formula Approach to Library Size: An Empirical Study of Its Efficacy in Evaluating Research Libraries." *College and Research Libraries, 33*(3):190–198, May 1972.

Mitchell, Ruth K. "A Methodology for Assessing Academic Library Collection Development." Doctoral Dissertation. Pittsburgh, Pa., University of Pittsburgh, 1976.

Mosher, Paul H. "Collection Evaluation in Research Libraries: The Search for Quality, Consistency, and System in Collection Development." *Library Resources and Technical Services, 23*(1):16–32, Winter 1979.

Murray, William, et al. "Collection Mapping and Collection Development." *Drexel Library Quarterly, 21*(2):40–51, Spring 1985.

Nisonger, Thomas E. "An In-Depth Collection Evaluation at the University of Manitoba

Library: A Test of the Lopez Method." *Library Resources and Technical Services,* 24(4):329–338, Fall 1980.

—————. "An Annotated Bibliography of Items Relating to Collection Evaluation in Academic Libraries, 1969–1981." *College and Research Libraries,* 43(4):300–311, July 1982.

—————. "A Test of Two Citation Checking Techniques for Evaluating Political Science Collections in University Libraries." *Library Resources and Technical Services,* 27(2):163–176, April–June 1983.

North Carolina Library Association, Public Libraries Section, and North Carolina Public Library Directors Association. *Standards for North Carolina Public Libraries.* Raleigh, N.C., North Carolina Department of Cultural Resources, Division of State Library, 1988.

Oberg, Larry R. "Evaluating the Conspectus Approach for Smaller Library Collections." *College and Research Libraries,* 49(3):187–196, May 1988.

Olaosun, Adebayo. "Materials Provision Survey at the University of Ife Library, Nigeria." *College and Research Libraries,* 45(5):396–400, September 1984.

Pacific Northwest Collection Assessment Manual. 3rd Edition. Salem, Oreg., Oregon State Library Foundation, 1990.

Palais, Elliot. "Use of Course Analysis in Compiling a Collection Development Policy Statement for a University Library." *Journal of Academic Librarianship,* 13(1):8–13, March 1987.

Pierce, Thomas J. "The Economics of Library Acquisitions: A Book Budget Allocation Model for University Libraries." Doctoral Dissertation. Notre Dame, Ind., University of Notre Dame, 1976.

Popovich, Charles J. "The Characteristics of a Collection for Research in Business/ Management." *College and Research Libraries,* 39(2):110–117, March 1978.

Potter, William G. "Studies of Collection Overlap: A Literature Review." *Library Research,* 4(1):3–21, Spring 1982.

Power, Colleen J., and George H. Bell. "Automated Circulation, Patron Satisfaction and Collection Evaluation in Academic Libraries: A Circulation Analysis Formula." *Journal of Library Automation,* 11(4):366–369, December 1978.

Raney, McKendree L. *The University Libraries.* Chicago, Ill., University of Chicago Press, 1933.

Reichard, Edwin W., and Thomas J. Orsagh. "Holdings and Expenditures of U.S. Academic Libraries: An Evaluative Technique." *College and Research Libraries,* 27(6):478–487, November 1966.

Robinson, William C. "Evaluation of the Government Documents Collection: An Introduction and Overview." *Government Publications Review,* 8A(1–2):111–125, 1981.

—————. "Evaluation of the Government Documents Collection: A Step-by-Step Process." *Government Publications Review,* 9(2):131–141, March–April 1982.

Rogers, Rutherford D., and David C. Weber. *University Library Administration.* New York, H. W. Wilson Company, 1971.

Sandler, Mark, and Cathryn H. Barling. "Departmental Evaluation and Maintenance of the Library Sociology Collection." *Teaching Sociology,* 11(3):259–280, April 1984.

Saunders, Stewart; Harriet Nelson; and Priscilla Geahigan. "Alternatives to the Shelflist Measure for Determining the Size of a Subject Collection." *Library Research,*

3(4):383–391, Winter 1981.

Schad, Jasper G., and Norman E. Tanis. *Problems in Developing Academic Library Collections.* New York, R. R. Bowker, 1974.

Serebnick, Judith. "Self-Censorship by Librarians: An Analysis of Checklist-Based Research." *Drexel Library Quarterly, 18*(1):35–56, Winter 1982.

Shaw, Debora. "Overlap of Monographs in Public and Academic Libraries in Indiana." *Library and Information Science Research, 7*(3):275–298, July–September 1985.

Sheehy, Eugene P. *Guide to Reference Books.* 10th Edition. Chicago, Ill., American Library Association, 1986.

Sineath, Timothy W. "The Relationship Between Size of Research Library Collections and the Support of Faculty Research Studies." Doctoral Dissertation. Urbana, Ill., University of Illinois, 1970.

Soper, Mary Ellen. "The Relationship Between Personal Collections and the Selection of Cited References." Doctoral Dissertation. Urbana, Ill., University of Illinois, Graduate School of Library Science, 1972.

State University of New York, Associates for Library Services and Chancellor's Advisory Committee on Libraries. *Proposals for the Growth of Library Collections of the State University of New York: A Formula for Liminal Adequacy, with Recommendations for Growth Beyond.* Albany, N.Y., State University of New York, 1970.

Stielow, Frederick J., and Helen R. Tibbo. "Collection Analysis and the Humanities: A Practicum with the RLG Conspectus." *Journal of Education for Library and Information Science, 27*(3):148–157, Winter 1987.

Tjarks, Larry. "Evaluating Literature Collections." *RQ, 12*(2):183–185, Winter 1972.

Van House, Nancy A., et al. *Output Measures for Public Libraries: A Manual of Standardized Procedures.* 2nd Edition. Chicago, Ill., American Library Association, 1987.

Vitolins, Ilga. "Relationship Between Quality of Books and Their Acquisition by Libraries." Doctoral Dissertation. Chicago, Ill., University of Chicago, 1963.

Voigt, Melvin J. "Acquisition Rates in University Libraries." *College and Research Libraries, 36*(4):263–271, July 1975.

Whaley, John H., Jr. "An Approach to Collection Analysis." *Library Resources and Technical Services, 25*(3):330–338, July–September 1981.

Wiemers, Eugene, et al. "Collection Evaluation: A Practical Guide to the Literature." *Library Acquisitions: Practice and Theory, 8*(1):65–76, 1984.

Williams, Edwin E. "Surveying Library Collections." In: *Library Surveys.* Edited by Maurice F. Tauber and Irlene R. Stephens. New York, Columbia University Press, 1967, pp. 23–45.

CHAPTER 4

COLLECTION EVALUATION: USE-CENTERED APPROACHES

Like all methods of collection evaluation, use studies have been both criticized and praised by librarians. How valuable an analysis of use will be to a library depends on the library's purpose—that is, on the needs of its users. These needs should be reflected in the library's mission statement. Consider the mission of a hypothetical public library:

> The Marion Public Library's primary mission is to provide the most wanted materials in sufficient quantities to meet the needs of its patrons in a cost-effective way. Its secondary mission is to provide access, through interlibrary loan, to other materials needed by patrons.

The ultimate test of the quality of this library's collection will be the extent and mode of its use. Most public, school, and special libraries, as well as some college libraries, will be interested in measuring use, because use reflects a primary purpose for their existence.

Librarians in institutions whose major purpose is to promote research are much more ambivalent about use studies. More than 10 years ago, Kent et al. (1979) showed that many books at the University of Pittsburgh library had never been used. Some librarians believed that the implications were simple: in these times of rising costs, even academic librarians need to pay more attention to providing what users want and less attention to purchasing esoteric materials that few patrons are expected to ever use. Other librarians, however, thought the Pittsburgh study was based on an erroneous assumption: that the quantity of use of a research library is important. For instance, Schad (1979) admitted that instructional use of a research collection is characterized by the intensive use of a small body of current materials, often requiring the purchase of multiple copies to meet student demand. But he argued that research use is characterized by much less intensive use of a vast body of material. . .scholars must sift through extensive numbers of books, journals and other sources. Sometimes hundreds of volumes must be examined to determine whether or not they contain relevant material. A great deal of interlibrary borrowing for this kind of work is not practical, if for no other reason than cost. What this means is that collections that fall below a certain level inhibit research. (p. 62)

In other words, Schad believed that a research library's main goal is to promote high-quality research, rather than to circulate a lot of material. Today, more than a decade after the Pittsburgh study was published, the value of measuring use in research libraries still is debated.

As discussed in Chapter 3, the most valuable collection evaluation efforts use a variety of techniques to measure both the nature of the collection and its use. Combining studies helps overcome the disadvantages of any one method.

For instance, some measures of use, such as circulation, are imperfect. Knowing that a patron checked out a book does not indicate whether he or she actually read or enjoyed it. Use studies tell little about what the patron wanted but could not find. Moreover, they only record the behavior of people who currently use the collection; they give no information about the type of collection that might convert nonusers to users.

Proponents of use studies argue that circulation and other indicators of use are valuable measures. Circulation does not tell whether patrons read or enjoyed their books, but it does indicate that they were interested enough in the subject, author, or title to think they would read or enjoy their selections. Moreover, Baker (1983) found that patrons overwhelmingly report that they find useful and enjoy the materials they check out from the library. Studies of recorded use can be supplemented by studies that focus on nonuser needs or identify materials that the patron wanted but could not find. And use studies are versatile; libraries of all sizes and types can use them to evaluate all kinds of collections or subsets of collections.

The main reason that libraries have relied increasingly on studies of use is that mistakes in collection development are costly. Librarians may spend large sums of money buying, processing, and storing items that will never be used. They might also lose patrons if enough copies of the right items are not available when wanted or if needed titles have been stored, in an attempt to save money, in a building that is not readily accessible to patrons.

Saving funds by improving collection development is of particular concern today because librarians are more aware that recorded use in many libraries is low. Evaluators have documented repeatedly that most library items have not been used during some specified time. This is particularly true in research libraries, which aim for comprehensive, rather than heavily used, collections. For example, Nothiesen (1960) found that 60 percent of the serials held in the John Crerar Library in Chicago did not circulate at all during a one-year period

Number of Circulations	Number of Books	Percent of Total Books
0	702	36.9
1–5	951	49.9
6–10	166	8.7
11 +	85	4.5
Total	1,904	100.0

NOTE: The total number of circulations was 4,556. Therefore, the average circulation per book was 4,556/1,904 = 2.4 times in the 5-year period.

EXHIBIT 4-1 Five-year circulation of a select sample of DePauw University books. Reprinted from Hardesty (1981), courtesy of Ablex Publishing Corporation.

and 25 percent of the total journal titles (not individual issues) were borrowed only 1–5 times each. Fussler and Simon (1969) discovered that, of a sample of monographs purchased by the University of Chicago Library from 1944 to 1953, more than half did not circulate during the following five-year period. In the Pittsburgh study, Kent et al. (1979) found that only 52 percent of newly purchased monographs circulated at all during a seven-year period.[1]

There is growing evidence that the pattern of low overall use of individual titles exists in many nonresearch libraries as well. Hardesty (1981) found this to be true in a small liberal arts college with a goal of collecting material to support instruction. He drew a large sample from the list of books acquired at DePauw University during a six-month period from late 1972 to mid-1973. He then examined circulation records for a five-year period. As Exhibit 4-1 shows, more than a third of the books never circulated and another half circulated between one and five times during that entire period. The average circulation for the entire five-year period was only 2.4 times, or 0.5 circulation annually. These findings parallel those of Ettelt (1978) and Hostrop (1966). Each observed circulation in small college libraries for more than one year and discovered that more than 70 percent of the titles owned did not circulate. At the Washington State Library, 50 percent of the collection did not circulate during a 35-month period (Reed, 1979). Almost 40 percent of current periodicals in a law library were not used during a one-year period (Goldblatt, 1986). This pattern of use—

---

[1] In a few libraries, the data reveal higher levels of use. For example, Chrzatowski (1989) found that only 24 percent of the journals subscribed to by an academic chemistry library were used two or fewer times in a six-month period; only 9 percent received no use. Presumably, these higher use libraries have carefully analyzed patron demands and determined how best to meet them.

a small part of the collection used intensively and other parts used at a low level—may also be true for other types of libraries, but few data have been collected.

One basic assumption underlies evaluations of collection use: that past use is a good predictor of present or future use. Although Line and Sandison (1974) expressed doubt on the validity of this assumption, much evidence supports it, going back at least to the classic study by Fussler and Simon (1969). There is a considerable built-in inertia associated with large communities. In a university, courses change or disappear and new courses, or even entire programs, emerge. Nevertheless, in terms of the entire university environment, these changes are relatively insignificant. Kent et al. (1979) verified this when they showed that a 3-day use study at the University of Pittsburgh yielded results on the subject distribution of items in circulation equivalent to their 86-month study. Metz and Litchfield (1988) also confirmed, in a study at the Virginia Polytechnic Institute and State University, that the stability of use patterns greatly exceeded the change. This principle also is true in public and school library environments. Interests change but very slowly. Changes likely to significantly affect the use of a collection occur over a long time. Only in the case of special libraries in industrial organizations, especially those heavily involved in short-term contract work, do significant changes of direction occur quickly. And even here, radical changes are likely to be the exception rather than the rule.

In a major study of circulation records, Fussler and Simon (1969) tried to determine whether they could accurately predict how often groups of books with defined characteristics were likely to be used in a research library. If it was possible to determine this, the library could store infrequently used books in a less-accessible, less-costly facility. Fussler and Simon based their study on large systematic samples drawn from the shelf list of the University of Chicago library in two diverse subject areas: economics and Teutonic literature and languages. They also drew smaller samples from many other subject areas. They sampled 9,058 monographs, observing the use of all copies of each title. For serials, they examined the use of all copies of each volume. For each item, they reviewed records of past circulation for the period from 1954 to 1958, as well as the item's language, publication date, and accession date.

Fussler and Simon found that present circulation could be readily predicted on the basis of past use. When circulation records were not available, it was possible to predict use, although less accurately, on the basis of characteristics of the books themselves, the most important predictors being age and language. Use diminished as a title aged, rapidly at first then leveling off (books more than 100 years old circulated about as much per title as those 70–100 years old). The main language of used items was English.

Fussler and Simon attempted to predict accurately the use of items under three different scenarios: (1) when no record of past use was available, (2) when a record of use for 5 years back was available, and (3) when a record of use for 20 years back was available. They found that language and publication date could identify the 25 percent of the economics collection likely to be used least in the future. If the library applied these criteria, then the 25 percent of the economics collection retired to storage would account for only 3 percent of the collection's total future use. Each title retired to storage would have an average use probability of once every 35 years.[2]

Predictions of use based on age and language were more successful in the scientific disciplines than in the humanities, where use was less dependent on these factors. For example, if the same rule was used at the University of Chicago to retire 25 percent of the books in Teutonic languages and literature, the retired portion of the collection would account for 12 percent of the collection's total future use.

The accuracy with which use can be predicted increases considerably when records of past use are factored in. For example, if, in addition to the rule for language and publication date, no book that has been used in the preceding five years is sent to storage, then the 25 percent of the economics collection with the lowest predicted use would account for only 2 percent of the total use in this subject field. The corresponding figure for the Teutonic collection would be 5 percent. When 20-year use records were available, prediction of future use was even more accurate and language and age characteristics were of little value. If the 25 percent to be retired in either the economics or the Teutonic collection was determined on the basis of the 25 percent least used in the preceding 20 years, then the retired portion of the collection would account for only 1 percent of the total use, and it could be expected that, on the average, each monograph would be requested only once every 100 years.

For serials, Fussler and Simon found it most effective to retire the oldest volume of a particular journal, proceeding consecutively until a volume is reached that shows a specified level of use within a set period of time, such as the last five years. This use-based retirement rule is more effective than one based solely on language and age.

Fussler and Simon's primary finding, that the average item's past circulation could accurately predict its future use, has been verified in all types of library settings. For example, Eggers (1976) examined all books returned at a small library in Iowa and found that 93 percent had circulated in the previous year. Slote (1970) noted a similar pattern after examining the circulation of adult fiction in five public libraries, as did Ettelt (1985) when examining use records in a college library. Brooks (1984a, 1984b) worked with data from academic and public libraries and showed that past circulation can forecast the future overall

---

[2] Fussler and Simon's storage rule is as follows: based on publication date alone, the oldest 25 percent of the collection would be retired; based on publication date and language, more would be retired from the less-used languages.

circulation for a library—information that can be used by administrators for long-term planning and resource allocation.

The remainder of this chapter focuses on studies that analyze circulation and interlibrary loan records to determine use. It describes how to use the information for a number of very practical purposes, like deciding which subjects to emphasize in future buying, how many duplicate copies to purchase, and which material should be weeded or stored. Other types of studies also are relevant to use of the collection; the methodologies for these are complex enough and the literature sufficiently extensive that they receive separate treatment. Methods of evaluating in-house or nonrecorded use are discussed in Chapter 5, and ways to assess fill rate or shelf availability are covered in Chapter 6.

ANALYZING RECORDS OF USE

The two types of use data that libraries utilize most often in collection evaluation are records of interlibrary loan borrowing and circulation. The first reflects unmet demands, and the second reflects met demands.

In the simplest type of evaluation, the library examines interlibrary loan records to see if the demand falls within the scope of its collection efforts. For example, a small public library may request, on interlibrary loan, a dissertation on Latvian politics for one of its patrons. Because the library's primary mission is to buy popular materials for community residents, however, it will not add the dissertation to its collection. But some materials borrowed on interlibary loan should be in the collection. The same library could notice that its patrons are filing interlibrary loan requests for Erma Bombeck's latest book. The library may have neglected to purchase this title or may not have purchased enough copies to meet patron demand. Because current in-print titles make up a substantial percentage of interlibrary loan requests (Stevens, 1974; Trevvett, 1979), some libraries routinely screen requests to identify particular items for purchase and to identify the types of new materials patrons want.

Interlibrary loan records can be broken down in various ways. In one early and fairly typical study, Graziano (1962) examined interlibrary loans over a three-year period at the science library of Southern Illinois University. He tabulated loan requests by department and degree program, comparing the number of interlibrary loans to the number of students and faculty in each area. This type of analysis allows a library to see if some group of users is making more frequent use of interlibrary loan, which might indicate that the collection in this area of specialization needs strengthening. Graziano also analyzed interlibrary loan requests by format (for example, books, theses, and serials) to determine any deficiencies.

Brown, Miller, and Pinchoff (1975) tabulated interlibrary loan requests by mode of request (for instance, telephone versus letter), time taken to fill the loan, and number and type of unfilled loans. The library also collected information on the language of the request, the status of the borrower (for example, student or faculty), and the age and format of the requested item (for example, journal article versus monograph).

A university library in Scotland analyzed almost 2,500 interlibrary loan requests (Roberts and Cameron, 1984). The evaluators marked each request with 1 of 37 subject codes reflecting the teaching and research interests of the university. They recorded the borrower's status and department, the number of days taken to fill the request, and the age of the requested materials. One purpose of this study was to determine the feasibility of purchasing materials requested on interlibrary loan. The evaluators discovered that the materials requested were actually good candidates for purchase. They were frequently low priced, in print, and recently published; in fact, more than half of the requested materials had been published within the previous six years.

Pritchard (1980) tried to determine whether materials requested on interlibrary loan represented a transient user demand. Of 114 books requested on interlibrary loan in this medical school library, only 9 had been purchased. Pritchard compared the 105 monographs that were not purchased against the teaching and research program of the school. Forty-five percent appeared to be at least as relevant to the program as the nine titles that had been purchased. Further analysis showed that the books originally requested on interlibrary loan and eventually purchased had circulation ratios comparable with titles selected by library staff.

Increasingly, computers are handling interlibrary loan activities. The statistics generated from this automation make data tabulation easier. For example, a health sciences library in New York used to compile interlibrary loan statistics manually—a time-consuming process that resulted in numerous inaccurate data reports. The library developed a COBOL-based computer program to generate a variety of statistical reports that break down interlibrary loan information into various categories to improve collection development and overall user service (O'Connell and Miller, 1977).

Although records of interlibrary loan borrowing are valuable, they constitute a small percentage of total library use. As a result, most libraries focus on circulation records, which are easily collected and readily understood by the library's funding authority. The numbers most often reported are total circulation, circulation per volume owned, or circulation per capita. This information shows whether use is increasing or decreasing from year to year and can form a basis for comparing a library's performance with that of similar institutions.

Circulation can be broken down by various user characteristics, such as departmental affiliation, occupation, or grade level, to discover who is borrowing what. This can easily be done in an automated environment if a machine-readable file is maintained that links user identification numbers to various user characteristics. It can also be done manually by surveying or interviewing users or by analyzing circulation cards that hold the information. The circulation card at the University of Iowa asks users to record the book's call number, author, and title before writing in their name, address, and status (undergraduate, graduate, or faculty). Such information is tallied to "identify use patterns among subpopulations, thus pointing out materials that are underutilized by certain groups. This information allows the librarian to develop and implement plans to enhance awareness of [materials] in different segments of the user population" (Cook, 1985, p. 223).

As Weech (1978) noted, most studies of this type concentrate on a comparatively narrow group of users. For example, Ray (1974, 1978) tried to determine who uses map collections, and several other authors scrutinized patrons of government documents collections (Cook, 1985; Hernon, 1979; McCaghy and Purcell, 1972). Departmental libraries, whether divided by subject (for example, psychology) or format (such as audiovisuals), also could benefit from such an analysis, as could many small libraries. Picture the library at a company that manufactures rolled oats. If the librarian knows the extent to which various departments, such as research and development, purchasing, or distribution, use the collections, he or she can identify areas that need to be augmented for potentially high use or examined for flaws due to low use.

More complicated breakdowns of circulation statistics, generally by the item used, also are valuable. Stieg (1943) conducted one of the earliest such studies at Hamilton College. Basing his analysis on circulation records for three consecutive academic years, he was able to show the effect of subject matter on circulation, the effect of publication date on circulation, the proportion of titles that circulated n times in an academic year, and the proportion of titles that circulated in all three academic years. Librarians since Stieg's time have continued to analyze circulation by subject and publication date, although they have also tried to determine the effects of other variables on use. And, like Stieg, evaluators have tried to identify the most-used and least-used titles in an effort to improve current collection development practices.

In an automated environment, librarians can accumulate circulation records over a period of years in a machine-readable archive. A properly designed system will have a built-in management information component capable of gathering and formatting the necessary data continuously as an inexpensive byproduct. Libraries that lack automated circulation systems will need to manually sample circulation data for subsequent analysis. Jain et al. (1967) originally discussed three methods for sampling (circulation, shelf list, and stack samples); Trochim (1980) and Trochim, Miller, and Trochim (1985) tested these to determine whether they would yield comparable data and whether one in particular was easier for libraries to use. In general, evaluators taking a circulation sample examine all books checked out from the library during a specified time. Two forms of collection samples exist: one taken from the shelf list, the other from the books on the shelves at a given time. In each case, the evaluator gathers information on past use from a representative sample of the total collection. These methods all presuppose that the library maintains some record of how often a particular book has been borrowed, generally by recording on book cards or date labels affixed inside the books the date on which the borrowed books are due back in the library.

When Trochim compared the three methods, she found that

* Information for both the circulation sample and the stack sample needs to be collected on representative days over a fairly long time (six months to one year). The circulation sample collects information on the books absent from the collection and the stack sample on books present in a collection at any one time. The long sampling period counteracts the fact that use and nonuse vary, depending on the time of year in which the study is conducted.
* The shelf list sample is the most difficult to implement, since it requires that staff sample the shelf list, then locate the sampled item in the stacks. If the item is not present, staff must also file a reserve or recall request. The stack sample is the easiest to perform because all the books are present on the shelf when the sample is taken.
* The circulation sample can be collected as part of other circulation desk tasks, such as checking out materials or collecting daily circulation statistics. Although additional staff do not have to be hired, the sampling procedure may slow the circulation process.
* The stack sample will be slightly weighted toward books that are used less, and the circulation sample will be slightly weighted toward books that are used more. Libraries should use the sample that best meets their purposes. For example, the circulation sample will help identify the currently used sections for librarians who want to know which items to mark first for theft-detection systems or which to convert first to machine-readable form when automating the circulation system. The shelf sample will help identify little-used sections to aid with weeding or selection of materials for storage.
* Evaluators may consider a combination of the circulation and stack samples if there is adequate staff to carry out both and if the library wants a great deal of information about collection use.

If complete records of past use are not readily available, as when a card with circulation information is replaced and only the last few circulations are shown, knowing the last circulation date of an item will enable fairly accurate predictions of use (Trueswell, 1964, 1965, 1966). But some libraries, because of the circulation system used, have no records of past use in the book. These libraries may use the spine-marking method described by Slote (1982). The procedure is fairly simple. Beginning at a preset date, the circulation staff applies two self-sticking dot labels to the spine of every volume as it circulates. The first dot shows the book has been used; the second is a check to improve the reliability of the system, by preventing the loss of information in case one of the dots should fall off or be removed. Staff members conduct another reliability check by examining every volume that is checked in or placed on a reshelving cart; if the item is not already marked, two dots are applied to the spine. In the early stage of marking, this procedure will catch volumes that were already in use when the spine-marking method began. Ideally, the dotting procedures are followed for at least one year.

Spine marking can inexpensively identify those items that are used currrently and, therefore, most likely to be used in the future. As such, it can be a very effective weeding tool (Shaw, 1978; Williams, 1986); indeed, it was designed for this purpose. It can also be used in studies of in-house use (see Chapter 5). Nevertheless, it does, have one obvious limitation. Although it identifies items that are used, it tells nothing about the amount of use each item receives. The librarian cannot distinguish between an item that circulated once during the last year and one that circulated 20 times; both are marked by two spine dots. This problem can be overcome, although at some cost in time, if circulation staff places a hash mark inside the front cover of the book each time it is used during the study period. If this practice is followed, the spine-marking method can be used for purposes other than weeding.

Evaluators can use data from interlibrary loan and circulation records in a number of practical ways. For example, evaluators can identify types of items and specific items that are likely to be used or not used. Librarians can then change initial and follow-up selection patterns so that more books that are likely to be used are purchased. For example, librarians can buy more duplicate copies of individual books and authors that are likely to be in great demand or can concentrate purchases on subjects that patrons have used heavily in the past. Evaluators can also obtain data that indicate the most effective ways to arrange and promote collections. This information can help libraries meet their goals and improve user satisfaction with the collection. Finally, evaluators can identify a core collection of items likely to satisfy some specified percentage of all circulation demands within the near future. Middle management can use this information to make various decisions, such as which items to weed or store or which items' records to convert first to machine-readable form when the library automates its circulation system.

IDENTIFYING MATERIALS THAT ARE LIKELY TO BE USED

Several studies verify that materials selected by librarians who have studied their clientele and examined past patterns of use in their libraries are used more than those selected some other way. For example, in academic libraries, librarians select more heavily used titles than do teaching faculty. Both librarians and faculty select items that circulate more than materials given to the library or ordered through a blanket-approval plan (Diodato and Diodato, 1983; Evans, 1969; Evans and Argyres, 1974).

The difference in choice of materials is related to the amount of public service contact the selector has. Turow (1978) asked selectors of children's books in a public library whether "a general impression of what children want" was an important factor in their choice. Ninety-one percent of branch librarians, all of whom had daily contact with their patrons, thought this criterion was "very important." None of the system coordinators, who had no public service duties but were responsible for purchasing books for branches without children's librarians, rated this criterion as more than "somewhat important." In an academic library, Evans (1969) found that public service librarians routinely selected a higher percentage of titles in demand than their nonpublic service counterparts. Both studies imply that public service librarians, through observation of use patterns, have gained knowledge of what patrons are likely and not likely to use.

This knowledge may be related to specific characteristics of the items that have been shown to affect use. These include the age of the item, the language in which it is written, the current or expected popularity of its author or title, its general subject, and its degree of subject specificity.

Age

Researchers have repeatedly shown that the age of an item affects its use, regardless of category, although the rate of aging may vary from area to area. The overall rate of obsolescence in the social sciences is similar to that of the sciences as a whole (Van Styvendaele, 1981) and much higher than in the humanities (Griscom, 1983; Longyear, 1977; Soper, 1972). On the average, however, a book's circulation declines very quickly within three to five years after its addition to the library (Ettelt, 1978; Hardesty, 1981; Middleswort, 1951; Raisig et al., 1966). Brown, Miller, and Pinchoff (1975) found that materials less than five years old accounted for the bulk of interlibrary loan borrowing in a health sciences library. This is not surprising since most patrons want current books, especially in the case of nonfiction. Also, a major factor in book choice is simply knowing that the work exists; new books tend to receive more publicity than old ones. There are obvious implications for libraries interested in maximizing use of items. Works should be purchased when they are fairly new and processed quickly for the collection. Librarians considering replacing a worn and dated book with a newer copy of the same book should determine whether past use records justify the purchase, because an older book is likely to be used less than a new and different book. There are obvious exceptions to the age rule, such as the classics and books that regain popularity after the release of movies that are based on them, but these situations are easily handled on an individual basis.

Age also affects the use of serials. As Griffith et al. (1979) noted, the aging rate varies among journals, based on the subject area, what the journal is used for, and the user community. For example, science journals that support a research front age quickly; journals that receive intense use by a specialized audience age faster than those that receive diffuse use by a diversified audience. Selectors can use information on aging patterns to help make decisions such as those relating to the purchase of back runs of a journal.

Language

Even in academic settings, patrons check out or borrow on interlibrary loan many more items written in their native tongue than they do materials written in other languages. For example, Heussman (1970) found that 95.5 percent of the circulation in two seminary libraries in the United States was of English-language materials. The percentage of such materials borrowed on interlibrary loan in academic libraries in the United States ranges from 67 percent to 99 percent (Stevens, 1974). Ninety-eight percent of the social sciences materials requested from the (British) National Lending Library were written in English (Wood and Bower, 1969). More than 80 percent of the loan requests submitted to the Information Dissemination Service, serving the needs of health professionals in nine New York counties, were for English-language materials (Brown, Miller, and Pinchoff, 1975). Libraries interested in maximizing use will not want to allocate a large part of the budget to the purchase of foreign-language materials.[3]

Current or Expected Popularity of a Title or Author

Librarians have always purchased items appearing on best-seller lists or works by authors with a popular following because patrons have repeatedly requested these materials. During the last two decades, some librarians have begun to purchase more multiple copies of these works to improve the likelihood of meeting patron demands. Exactly how much need is there for duplication in most libraries? Evaluators have not explored this subject extensively; however, a few preliminary studies show that duplication is desirable.

Moreland (1968) found that 25 percent of a particular library's patrons were dissatisfied with the services they received. Of these, 65 percent were unhappy because they could not get the books they wanted when they wanted them. The library decided to increase the rate of duplication for popular titles. Eleven

---

[3]Because of the present dominance of English in scholarly materials, particularly in the sciences, this overwhelming concentration of use on materials in the vernacular may be much less true for non-English-speaking countries.

participating branches identified 122 titles that were thought to be in continuous demand. Most of the titles were modern classics. Staff in each branch regularly checked the shelves to verify that at least one copy of each title was always available for patron checkout. The branch added more copies each time patrons had checked out all copies of the item. Over the 11 months of the study, librarians at the 11 branches purchased a total of 21,821 copies. They bought an average of 16 copies of each title at each branch, a much higher rate of duplication than normal. Today, heeding the lessons of this experiment, many public libraries are purchasing many more multiple copies initially to ensure that patrons have an excellent chance of finding what they want on library shelves. One demand-oriented library, the Baltimore County Public Library in Maryland, has purchased more than 700 copies of a single best seller to be used at 22 branch libraries (Rawlinson, 1986).

Other types of libraries also need to duplicate materials. In academic libraries, Simmons (1970) examined the circulation of books in a single semester at the University of British Columbia. He identified more than 2,000 books for which the level of demand seemed to justify the purchase of additional copies. Metz (1980) found that a substantial number of items owned by university libraries and sought by patrons were checked out to other users, suggesting that some duplication is needed. A five-week study at the University of Tennessee at Knoxville pinpointed reasons why the items patrons wanted were unavailable: 71 percent were checked out to other users (Smith and Granade, 1978).

Evaluators can study duplication needs for items other than books. Goldblatt (1986) measured the use of 770 journals in a law library. She determined that patrons used certain types of journals frequently, such as law school reviews from U.S. schools, and infrequently used others, such as law school reviews from foreign schools. She compared the costs per use of buying each type of journal and revised purchasing patterns as a result; she also identified specific journal titles that patrons used heavily. After reviewing cost figures, Goldblatt determined the level of use that justified a second subscription. She used this information to order duplicates of some titles and to cancel the second subscription of others.

Some evaluators consider information on unmet demands when determining how much duplication is needed. Many librarians automatically order duplicate copies any time the number of reserves reaches an unacceptable level—say, three or more. Evaluators also can use interlibrary loan figures to identify journals from which patrons request more than some given number of articles per year. Data on in-house use can aid in determining how much duplication is necessary, as is discussed in Chapter 5.

Automated circulation systems enable evaluators to quickly collect information about which items should be duplicated. Because each item in the system must carry a unique identifying number, librarians can readily identify the items that are most and least used. This information can form the basis for duplication and future purchase decisions or, for that matter, for decisions to retire materials altogether.

Some libraries with manual circulation systems identify heavily used titles that should be duplicated by taking a sample of the circulating titles. Because the issue of interest is items that are used, it is better to take a circulation sample than a collection sample. Unfortunately, any sample will fail to identify all titles that need duplication. A better solution is to have circulation staff quickly examine each item being returned to the library during some specified time period, say six weeks, and count the number of times it has been checked out during the last year.

All these methods can be used to relate the number of days a book is out on loan to the total number of days the library is open. If the library is open 280 days a year, then circulation for a particular item can be expressed in terms of the number of days the item is absent from the shelves, say, 190/280. This represents the probability that this item will be off the shelves when looked for by any user. Circulation data for two copies of a particular title are combined and related to a potential availability of 560 days. Data for items available in three or more copies are handled similarly.

In cases where the library does not have an automated circulation system, it is necessary to estimate the number of days a particular item is out. Because at least one study (Buckland, 1975) showed that patrons tend to return books when they are due, evaluators can use the length of the circulation period to estimate the length of an item's absence from the shelves. Therefore, if a library is open 360 days a year and a book with a 4-week (28-day) loan period is checked out twice during that year, the book can be expected to be off the shelves for about 56 days (2 × 28).

The library then has to decide subjectively at what level titles will be duplicated. In the last example, the book was unavailable 15 percent of the time (56/360 days). Perhaps this is acceptable. But is 30 percent acceptable? What about 50 percent? Various factors affect a library's decision about when to duplicate and when not to. For example, a cheap book may be duplicated more readily than an expensive one. The cost of processing may also be factored in, as may the ability of a library to take some alternative action, such as reducing the length of the loan period, to increase a particular title's availability.

It is also a good idea, although it appears to rarely be done, to identify authors likely to be heavily or poorly used. Librarians working with automated systems could link the records of each title by the same author and determine an average-use rate for all the author's books. In a manual system, a clerk could average the number of circulations per item for authors thought to be popular or for which the library owned more than some given number of titles. If this average is high, the library could purchase more multiple copies initially, a practice increasingly followed at demand-oriented public libraries. Selectors should also identify, whenever possible, authors whose works have been purchased repeatedly in the past but that have received little use. Predicting future use of individual items is not easy, except for titles that are very esoteric or of blockbuster potential. Libraries that have used these techniques, however, to identify currently owned titles that are heavily used and to base initial purchasing decisions on factors relating to whether a book is likely to be used, have been very successful with their patrons. For example, the Baltimore County Public Library successfully met user demands for 86–97 percent of specific known-title requests (Engel, 1982). This is significantly higher than the 50 percent availability rates obtained by most libraries (Kuraim, 1983). The library's centralized selection staff, assisted by a team of public service librarians, did this by consistently and systematically identifying and purchasing authors and titles likely to be in demand and correcting inadequate purchasing by adding duplicate copies where needed.

Subject

The subject of the item also affects its use. McGrath (1972) used the classified profile approach, described in Chapter 3, to relate books used to the subjects taught at two very different academic libraries, the University of Southwestern Louisiana and the South Dakota School of Mines and Technology. He matched book classification numbers to catalog offerings to create a classified profile of courses taught. Patrons were more likely to check out or use in-house books with classification numbers that matched the course profiles. In a later study, McGrath, Simon, and Bullard (1979) used this approach to determine to what extent graduate and undergraduate students borrow books outside their own disciplines. Jenks (1976) improved the approach by supplementing circulation information for each class with information on the number of students in each department so that he could factor in the effects of large and small enrollments before making collection development decisions. This type of subject analysis is appropriate for community college and school libraries as well as for universities. The reader is referred to Chapter 3 for a complete discussion of the advantages and disadvantages of the classified profile approach to collection evaluation.

Libraries of all types can use simple subject analysis to determine whether the use of or demand for each subject class is rising or declining month by month and year by year. Evaluators can express the rise or decline of a class in terms of a percentage of the total circulation or in terms of the proportion of books existing in the class that are on loan at any time. McClellan (1956) used the latter method in a completely manual environment. On a specified day of each month, he counted more than 150 subject categories to determine how many books were on the shelf and how many were in circulation. Over time, evaluators can observe trends in collection use by this simple method and can identify rising and declining classes. Automated circulation systems allow evaluators to continuously gather data of this type.

Knowing the absolute use of portions of the collection is important, but Jain et al. (1967) correctly noted that relative use is more important—that is, the amount of use actually received compared with the amount of use expected. Suppose that mathematics occupies 12 percent of the total collection of a science library and that geology occupies 9 percent. One would expect that mathematics would receive 12 percent of the use and geology 9 percent of the use. Geology, however, might account for 15 percent of the current circulation and mathematics for only 6 percent. Mathematics would be an underused class and geology an overused class in this library.[4]

An underused class is one whose contents seem to exceed present user needs. A heavily underused class may contain items that are no longer current. Librarians should weed this class to eliminate out-of-date materials and should strengthen it by purchasing newer titles and editions. Underuse also occurs when a library buys the wrong books, especially ones that are too technical or too theoretical for its clientele. Selecting materials more attuned to the user population should correct this. Underuse may also indicate a subject for which interest is declining in the user community. If this is the case, librarians should greatly restrict purchases in this area. When Mills (1982) evaluated the use of the film center at the University of Illinois, he found a fourth type of underused class, containing items "which are categorically different in some way from the bulk of the collection. Seasonal films, films about holidays, and feature films are all examples of films which may appear to be underused when a collection is analyzed in this fashion" (p. 7). As Mills noted, it is inappropriate to compare the use of these kinds of films to the standards of use set by the rest of the films in the collection.

An overused class is one that seems to need strengthening. Because the present use exceeds expectations, the danger exists that the class is not strong enough to support existing and future demands of users. The more overused a class, the lower the probability that any particular book will be on the shelf when sought by a user. When books are absent from the shelves, most of the users looking for specific titles leave dissatisfied (Hitchingham, 1976), although a small number will file interlibrary loan requests for the materials (Aguilar, 1984). Librarians can strengthen overused classes by purchasing new titles or purchasing duplicate copies of titles known or expected to be in great demand.

Evaluators can easily exploit an automated circulation system to obtain data comparing actual use versus expected use. Exhibit 4-2 presents an example of this type of data from the library at the Goddard Space Flight Center. For each Library of Congress class number, the exhibit shows the total number of

---

[4] Interpretation of relative-use data of this kind requires caution. The data simply indicate a deviation from expected behavior; they do not explain why the deviation exists. The librarian must carefully scrutinize heavily overused and heavily underused classes to determine what corrective action to take.

	Total Holdings		Circulation Year			
			1976		1977	
HF1001	1	0.00%	0	0.00%	0	0.00%
HF1002	1	0.00%	0	0.00%	0	0.00%
HF1007	2	0.00%	0	0.00%	0	0.00%
HF1017	1	0.00%	0	0.00%	0	0.00%
HF1042	2	0.00%	0	0.00%	0	0.00%
HF1231	1	0.00%	0	0.00%	0	0.00%
HF1253	4	0.00%	0	0.00%	0	0.00%
HF1455	4	0.00%	0	0.00%	0	0.00%
HF3002	1	0.00%	0	0.00%	0	0.00%
HF3007	1	0.00%	0	0.00%	0	0.00%
HF3010	6	0.01%	4	0.03%	0	0.00%
HF3031	1	0.00%	0	0.00%	0	0.00%
HF5351	2	0.00%	2	0.02%	2	0.02%
HF5353	2	0.00%	0	0.00%	0	0.00%
HF5371	3	0.00%	0	0.00%	5	0.04%
HF5381	3	0.00%	1	0.01%	1	0.01%
HF5381.7	1	0.00%	0	0.00%	0	0.00%
HF5382	4	0.00%	0	0.00%	0	0.00%
HF5382.5	1	0.00%	0	0.00%	0	0.00%
HF5383	3	0.00%	3	0.02%	4	0.04%
HF5386	5	0.00%	4	0.03%	12	0.11%
HF5415	4	0.00%	2	0.02%	0	0.00%
HF5415.1	1	0.00%	0	0.00%	0	0.00%
HF5415.13	2	0.00%	0	0.00%	0	0.00%
HF5437	4	0.00%	0	0.00%	0	0.00%
HF5500	25	0.04%	16	0.13%	7	0.06%
HF5500.2	9	0.01%	7	0.06%	9	0.08%
HF5547	43	0.07%	1	0.01%	8	0.07%
HF5547.5	6	0.01%	1	0.01%	1	0.01%
HF5548	10	0.01%	0	0.00%	1	0.01%
HF5548.2	76	0.13%	35	0.28%	43	0.38%
HF5548.3	5	0.00%	0	0.00%	0	0.00%
HF5548.5	8	0.01%	4	0.03%	2	0.02%
HF5548.6	2	0.00%	0	0.00%	0	0.00%
HF5548.8	13	0.02%	10	0.08%	16	0.14%
HF5549	58	0.10%	31	0.25%	37	0.33%
HF5549.5	53	0.09%	29	0.23%	20	0.18%
HF5550	12	0.02%	5	0.04%	25	0.22%
HF5621	2	0.00%	6	0.05%	0	0.00%
HF5625	2	0.00%	0	0.00%	1	0.01%
HF5629	1	0.00%	0	0.00%	0	0.00%
HF5630	2	0.00%	2	0.02%	2	0.02%
HF5635	8	0.01%	5	0.04%	2	0.02%
HF5657	3	0.00%	0	0.00%	0	0.00%
HF5657.9	1	0.00%	0	0.00%	7	0.06%
HF5667	4	0.00%	0	0.00%	0	0.00%
HF5679	2	0.00%	1	0.01%	1	0.01%
HF5686	2	0.00%	0	0.00%	0	0.00%
HF5688	3	0.00%	1	0.01%	4	0.04%
HF5695	2	0.00%	2	0.02%	0	0.00%
HF5714	1	0.00%	0	0.00%	0	0.00%
HF5726	1	0.00%	0	0.00%	0	0.00%
HF5736	6	0.01%	1	0.00%	2	0.00%

EXHIBIT 4-2 Sample of circulation data from the Goddard Space Flight Center library. Reprinted from Lancaster (1982), courtesy of Haworth Press.

volumes held by the library, the percentage of the total collection occupied by that class, the number of items from that class circulating in 1976 and 1977, and the percentage of the 1976 and 1977 circulation accounted for by that class. Class HF5549, for example, contains 58 items that constitute 0.10 percent of the total collection. But this class accounted for 0.25 percent of total circulation in 1976 and 0.33 percent of total circulation in 1977. It is an overused class.

Exhibit 4-3 presents summary circulation and holdings data from Goddard's library for each main class and discloses both overused and underused classes. The two major classes in the collection, Q (Science) and T (Applied Science and Technology), are overused and underused, respectively. Evaluators find these kinds of data extremely valuable when establishing collection development policies.

Library of Congress Class	Percent of Collection	Percent of 1976–1977 Circulation	1977 Use Compared with 1976 Use*
A	0.38	0	=
B	0.19	0.16	=
C	0.17	0.30	+
D	0.15	0.06	+
E/F	0.13	0.06	−
G	1.78	1.75	+
H	3.26	4.71	−
J	0.72	0.31	−
K	0.13	0.07	+
L	2.22	0.77	−
N	0.04	0.02	=
P	0.91	0.41	−
Q	54.90	65.24	−
R	0.54	0.24	−
S	0.41	0.32	+
T	31.04	24.39	−
U	0.16	0.09	−
V	0.23	0.15	−
Z	2.64	0.33	+

*+ indicates a rising class, − represents a declining class, and = indicates no change. Many of the + and − indicators are not statistically significant.

EXHIBIT 4-3 Macrolevel analysis of circulation/holdings data from the Goddard Space Flight Center library. Reprinted from Lancaster (1982), courtesy of Haworth Press.

Class	Percent of Holdings	Percent of Circulation	Underuse or Overuse*
Q (Science)	2.63	1.68	−
QA	15.13	28.07	+
QB	9.03	9.45	=
QC	20.54	21.15	=
QD	3.50	1.23	−
QE	2.18	2.40	=
QH	1.12	0.81	−
QK	0.24	0.16	−
QL	0.11	0.04	−
QM	0.01	0.01	=
QP	0.32	0.20	−
QR	0.09	0.05	−

*+ indicates overuse, − signifies underuse, and = indicates that the level of use is as expected.

EXHIBIT 4-4 Circulation versus holdings from class Q (Science). Note that the overuse of class Q is due solely to the overuse of subclass QA (Mathematics). Reprinted from Lancaster (1982), courtesy of Haworth Press.

Whenever possible, librarians should break down the data into their smallest components to avoid jumping to the wrong conclusions. For example, Exhibit 4-4 shows that whereas class Q (Science) as a whole is overused, all of this overuse is accounted for by subclass QA (Mathematics). The other subclasses are either underused or used at the level expected.

Several authors discuss how to distinguish among overused, underused, and average-use classes. Trochim (1980) and Trochim, Miller, and Trochim (1980) suggested that the evaluator should simply examine the raw differences between the percentage of holdings and the percentage of circulation of each class. Mills (1982) was very critical of this. A difference of 0.2 percent would apply equally to a subject occupying 0.5 percent of the collection and getting 0.7 percent of the use and to a subject occupying 2.5 percent of the collection and receiving 2.7 percent of the use. But the discrepancy between holdings and use is much greater for the smaller class than for the larger—40 percent as opposed to 8 percent.

Mills suggested a better method for determining underused and overused classes: multiply the relative-use factor (which is expressed as a percentage) by 100 to create a related variable, percentage of expected use (PEU). The PEU concept is easy to understand, suggesting as it does that the expected use of a subject will be 100 percent. Subjects that are above 100 percent are tentatively designated as overused; those below 100 percent are considered underused.

It is necessary, however, to distinguish those categories that vary significantly from the PEU from those that vary only slightly. Mostyn (1974) developed a formula to test, for each subject area, the following null hypothesis: the proportion of circulation observed in a subject area is equal to the proportion of circulation expected in that area. Subject areas for which the null hypothesis is rejected are those that are either overused or underused.

Dowlin and Magrath (1983) ranked the PEUs of various subjects in a continuum from high to low. They labeled those subjects with PEUs one standard deviation below the mean as underused and those with PEUs one standard deviation above the mean as overused.

Librarians can, of course, subjectively define a threshold that represents overused or underused classes. For example, a library could decide that any class whose PEU is less than 80 percent is an underused class, and, similarly, that any class whose PEU exceeds 120 percent is an overused class. This method seems the easiest for most libraries to apply.

Several other points need to be made about relative use. First, librarians may calculate use for only one or two areas of the collection. Say, for example, that a school library has 10,000 titles and a circulation of 30,000 annually. The new librarian does not have time to determine use for all subject areas but does suspect that mathematics is an underused class. Circulation and holdings in this one area are measured. Assume that the 100 mathematics books in the collection circulated 25 times during the last academic year. Logically, mathematics should account for 1 percent of total circulation (100/10,000), but it accounts for only 0.25 percent (25/10,000), making it a grossly underused class. Corrective action can now be taken.

Second, librarians should note the close relationship between the concepts of relative use and stock turnover rate. Relative use compares the proportion of circulation expected in one area to the proportion of holdings in that area. Stock turnover rate is the ratio of total holdings to total circulation within some specified time period (that is, the average circulation per item). Like relative use, turnover rate allows identification of patterns of strengths and weaknesses for any collection or its subsets. For example, a public librarian who knows that the library's average fiction turnover rate is 1.5 can quickly tell that mystery fiction, with a turnover rate of 4.0, is an overused class and that classic fiction, with a turnover rate of 0.5, is an underused class. The National Oceanic and Atmospheric Administration library has regularly used computerized circulation and acquisition data to calculate stock turnover rates (Wenger, Sweet, and Stiles, 1979). The rates are then used to improve collection development efforts.

Third, the concept of relative use does not limit itself to subject analysis; librarians can calculate relative use for materials of a particular format, those located in a particular department or branch, or those of a particular age or language. Again, evaluators compare the expected use of each category, based on size alone, to the actual recorded use and note any patterns of overuse or underuse. Many evaluators find it especially beneficial to analyze the relative use of particular formats. Several studies have shown that the ratio of journal to book use varies considerably from discipline to discipline (for example, Hodowanec, 1980; Stangl and Kilgour, 1967). Knowing this ratio will help a library determine whether books or journals should receive the most emphasis. The public library in Oklahoma City found that the average circulation of its 76,862 uncataloged paperbacks was 4.75, compared with an average circulation among the 465,326 cataloged hardbacks of 2.31 (Little, 1979). If this information is converted to relative-use form, it can be shown that although 14 percent of the book collection is composed of uncataloged paperbacks, these account for 25 percent of the circulation. This entire category of materials is overused. The automated circulation system described by Nimmer (1980) allows relative use to be simultaneously cross-analyzed by subject and departmental library location. This type of breakdown would be particularly helpful in academic and public libraries, because departmental or branch libraries within the system might receive different amounts of use depending on who their primary patrons are. A library could discover, for instance, that microbiology books located in a chemistry library receive substantially less use than the microbiology books in a biology library. The evaluator could then determine how much overlap there needs to be in these collections. Indeed, Bulick (1982) found so much overlap between the social sciences in a university library that he recommended not having separate departmental libraries for social science disciplines.

Fourth, librarians can calculate relative use manually with data from collection or circulation samples. Jain (1965, 1966, 1969) and Jain et al. (1967) suggested combining data from three samples: one drawn from the total collection, one drawn from monographs borrowed for home use, and one drawn from monographs used within the library. He suggested that this combination is more reliable than any one type of data alone.

Finally, evaluators can calculate a type of relative-use data from interlibrary loan records by determining the ratio of borrowings to holdings. Aguilar (1986) arranged the ratios in a continuum from low to high, designating classes one standard deviation above the mean as overused and those one standard deviation below the mean as underused. He then determined the percentage of expected use from circulation records in these areas, again designating overused and underused classes as those more than one standard deviation from the mean. If overuse or underuse was significant in some subject area, Aguilar determined the library's next action from a preset decision table. The table illustrated four separate actions:

1. A specific subject is being used heavily at the local level, and the number of interlibrary loans needed to supplement the local collection is high. This is definitely an overused class; therefore, the library should purchase additional or duplicate titles.

2. A subject is being used heavily at the local level, but patrons do not think it is necessary to go outside for additional materials. This is the ideal situation. The library should continue its current purchasing patterns.

3. Even though local materials are underused, users frequently find it necessary to go outside the institution for materials they want on the subject. Something appears to be wrong with the local collection. This category should be examined closely to determine exactly what is causing the problem (an outdated collection, emphasis on the wrong titles, or the like).

4. Local materials are not being used, nor are users requesting materials from other institutions. This is a "dead" subject; materials in this subject area should be deemphasized.

Byrd, Thomas, and Hughes (1982) also calculated relative-use data from interlibrary loan records. They constructed a graph with the x-axis representing different subjects and then plotted two lines: the percentage of total acquisitions for each new field and the percentage of borrowing each field represents. Exhibit 4-5 illustrates this for the National Library of Medicine (NLM) classification areas in clinical medicine at the University of Missouri–Kansas City Health Sciences Library. Such a graph readily shows the relationship between the subject distribution of new books added to these collections and the same distribution of books borrowed on interlibrary loan. Evaluators can identify areas where the percentages are not close. These classes are broken down into even narrower classes and regraphed to see exactly where the problem lies. When Byrd and his coauthors did this for NLM's WM class (psychiatry), they found that users were requesting more titles on psychotherapy, schizophrenia, neuroses, organic psychoses, and social behavior disorders than the library was processing.

Generally, the theory expressed here is that the classes needing the most attention are those in which the volume of materials borrowed most exceeds the volume of materials purchased. This discrepancy is expressed as a collection balance indicator (CBI)—a relative percentage—as follows:

$$100 \quad \times \quad \frac{\text{new acquisitions in this class}}{\text{total acquisitons}} \quad - \quad \frac{\text{titles borrowed in this class}}{\text{total titles borrowed}}$$

A positive CBI indicates a relatively strong subject area in terms of current acquisitons, whereas a negative CBI indicates a relatively weak area. This can be illustrated through two simple examples:

$$100 \quad \times \quad \frac{100}{400} \quad - \quad \frac{12}{120} \quad = \quad +15$$

$$100 \quad \times \quad \frac{40}{400} \quad - \quad \frac{30}{120} \quad = \quad -15$$

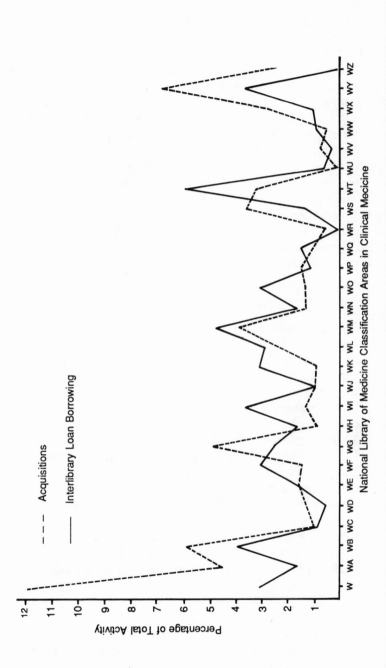

EXHIBIT 4-5 Subject distribution of new acquisitions and books borrowed on interlibrary loan for fiscal year 1980 at the University of Missouri–Kansas City Health Sciences Library. Reprinted from Byrd, Thomas, and Hughes (1982), courtesy of the Medical Library Association.

In the first case, 25 percent of the acquisitions are made in a subject field, but only 10 percent of the titles borrowed fall in this area. The CBI is a high +15. The second case puts the proportions exactly in reverse—10 percent of acquisitions and 25 percent of titles borrowed—and the value is a low −15. The librarian will need to examine the second subject area to determine why the local collection is not being used even though the interlibrary loan borrowing indicates patron interest in this subject.

The more useful data that the librarian has available, the more likely it is that collection development decisions will be made wisely. Krueger (1983) described a coordinated collection evaluation program in which Illinois librarians collected the following data for each subject area: percentage of collection occupied, percentage of use accounted for, percentage of interlibrary loan requests accounted for, percentage of current acquisitions, percentage of American publishing output (from *Publishers Weekly* and the *Bowker Annual of Library and Book Trade Information*), median age of materials used, median age of materials owned, and percentage of books available on the shelf during a specific time. These data were used to improve cooperative collection development efforts.

Specialized Nature of the Item

The degree of subject specificity of a title affects its use. Sargent (1979) analyzed 129 books that had not circulated at the University of Wisconsin–Oshkosh since their purchase more than seven years before and discovered that half were specialized and generally of a technical or scholarly nature. Schmitt and Saunders (1983) found that 77 percent of the titles recommended in *Choice* as being suitable for a "broad audience" and 74 percent of those "generally recommended for most undergraduate levels" had been used since their acquisition, in comparison with only 59 percent of the more specialized titles. Lee (1986) read the preface and introductory materials for all items contained in the anthropology collection at a small college library. He discovered that books labeled by their authors as "introductory" or "for a general audience" circulated significantly more than those written for a specialized or advanced audience. In fact, titles of a general nature on any subject are likely to appeal to a larger audience than titles on specific aspects of the same subject. Some demand-oriented libraries, such as the Baltimore County Public Library, have used this information to emphasize items of a more generalized nature.

Quality

Many librarians think that the quality of a book should influence its use, although no evidence exists that this is true. Indeed, studies conducted 20 years apart in locales as diverse as Indiana and Jamaica suggest it is not true. Using the inductive method of evaluation described in Chapter 3 of this book, Goldhor

(1959, 1981b, 1981c) found no correlation between book quality and use in public libraries. Rather, he suggested that "if libraries buy good books and poor books in equal quantities, they will be read in approximately equal numbers" (1959, p. 255). Goldhor believed that public library patrons do not differentiate better books from the poorer books or read better books more often. Further research is needed on this issue.

IDENTIFYING PATTERNS OF ARRANGEMENT AND PROMOTION OF MATERIALS

Use studies enable librarians to see which patterns of arrangement and promotion work best. More than 50 years ago, Shaw (1938) studied circulation patterns of books on each shelf of a regular stacks section. Books on shelves at eye level circulated more than books on the bottom shelves. When Shaw tilted the bottom four shelves so that patrons could more easily read the titles on the books' spines, circulation of these books increased.

Promoting titles by increasing their visibility and accessibility affects their use. For example, books located near the library's door circulate more than those housed further away (Carnovsky, 1935). University faculty use books housed in their offices more than those located in departmental libraries. In turn, they use books in nearby departmental libraries more than books in main libraries and books in main libraries more than those in libraries farther away (Soper, 1972, 1976).

In a series of studies, Aguilar (1982), Goldhor (1972, 1981a), Mueller (1965), and Taylor (1982) showed that displayed books circulate more than nondisplayed books. Building on this research, Baker (1986a, 1986b) found that displays can increase the use of any type of book they contain, but only if they are located in easily accessible, highly visible areas. Books displayed face front so that their covers are more visible circulate more than books displayed spine out (Long, 1986).

Book lists also can increase usage, but only when librarians distribute the lists widely and in a way that requires little patron effort to obtain them (Baker, 1986b). Taylor (1982) failed to increase the use of book list titles when, following the test library's usual practice, she left them out for voluntary patron pickup. Many patrons did not visit those sections of the library where the book lists were placed. Those who did still had to notice the book list, among all the other stimuli competing for their attention, had to comprehend what the list was, and had to consciously pick up the list before they could consider using it as a selection aid. Any breakdown in this process resulted in the book list not being used. Golden (1983), Goldhor (1972, 1981a), and Parrish (1986) were more effective in distributing book lists. Parrish set up a large poster and display at the library's entrance to promote use of the lists. Each of these three researchers also placed one book list in each set of books borrowed by an adult patron. Circulation of book list titles increased significantly in each of these studies.

Another series of studies focused on the use of books arranged in genre fiction categories. Ninth graders found a classified fiction scheme easier to use than an alphabetically arranged fiction section (Briggs, 1973). Most patrons browsing for fiction generally said they wanted a book in a particular genre (Spiller, 1980). And fiction categorized into genre areas was used more than fiction categorized other ways (Baker, 1988). Patrons in Baker's study felt the genre markings saved time, were easy to use, and allowed them to identify authors, previously unknown to them, who wrote the type of book they liked.

The research reviewed in this section consists primarily of experimental studies. The researchers developed a hypothesis and tested it, measuring changes in use before and after a new promotion or arrangement feature was tried. Librarians can use results of studies like these in many practical ways. For example, in a library with a goal of promoting "quality" works, Hermenze (1981) increased the use of classics by displaying them prominently near the circulation desk. After receiving patron complaints about the difficulty of browsing for fiction classified under the Library of Congress scheme, Wood (1985) distributed genre fiction book lists. Circulation of these titles subsequently increased.

IDENTIFYING CORE COLLECTIONS OF MATERIALS

Evaluators have successfully identified core collections in libraries. Generally, some optimal number of volumes constitutes a core collection that is capable of satisfying a specified percentage of all demands (Trueswell, 1966). Librarians generally determine the core by examining the circulation records for each item borrowed during a specified time, although they also could factor in recall or reserve requests for an item, records of interlibrary loan borrowing of owned items, or measures of in-house use. They can then make a graph similar to the one in Exhibit 4-6. The graph shows the percentage of books borrowed now (that is, during some current circulation period) that were last borrowed within some specified period. For example, approximately 25 percent of the items borrowed currently had not been borrowed within the preceding 6 months, approximately 10 percent within the preceding 18 months, and approximately 3 percent in the preceding 36 months. In other words, approximately 97 percent of the items being borrowed now were borrowed at least once in the preceding 36 months. The core collection could be defined as all books circulating at least once in the past 36 months. This collection, which is expected to account for approximately 97 percent of the total circulation, could be a small subset of the entire collection.

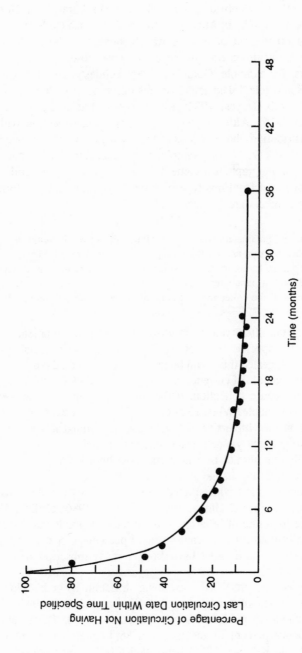

EXHIBIT 4-6 Distribution of book use on the basis of last circulation date. Reprinted from Trueswell (1966), courtesy of *Libri.*

Trueswell (1966) identified core collections in libraries at Northwestern University, the University of Massachusetts, and Holyoke College. In each case, he found that 80 percent of the use was accounted for by approximately 20 percent of the collection; enough evaluators have observed this same pattern over the years (for example, Goldblatt, 1986; Hardesty, 1981) that it has been termed "the 80/20 rule." The actual figures observed in such a study, however, may not be 80/20 (Hayes, 1981; Kaske, 1979; Lancaster, 1982; Urquhart and Urquhart, 1976). Although the use of any book collection will follow a hyperbolic distribution, the steepness of the curve may vary from one institution to the next. Reed (1979), for example, found that during a 35-month period, 90 percent of monograph use came from 50 percent of the collection. The information obtained from this type of study is useful in guiding further action when the two numbers are far apart:

If, for example, the parameters were 50/50, 60/60, and so on, it would indicate that all the parts of the collection are, on the average, equally in demand. In such a case, there would be no point in trying to decide which parts are not heavily in demand . . . On the other hand, with a parameter set such as (90/10) one would be encouraged to look for the 90 percent of the collection that is in very low demand. (Kantor, 1980, p. 514)

In applying the 80/20 rule to improve collection development efforts, it is assumed that the specific rule derived for a given library is stable over time. Kantor (1980) suggested this could be tested. A library could compare the results obtained from a sample of current circulating titles with the results obtained from a sample of the entire collection. If the rule is the same for the two samples, the distribution is stable. When Kent et al. (1979) tested the subject distribution of circulation at the University of Pittsburgh, they found it was very stable: a 3-day circulation study yielded results equivalent to those of a 36-month study. Subject distribution should be stable for most libraries because user interests and circulation patterns change slowly.

Many evaluators have concentrated on identifying core collections of serials (for example, Advani and Gupta, 1984; Goldblatt, 1986; Sridhar, 1986). This is because the high rate of inflation in the price of journals has forced libraries to drop the least-used titles. Because a small percentage of titles accounts for a high percentage of use, libraries have dropped many subscriptions to expensive, low-use periodicals.

Two early studies are worth describing in detail. Kilgour (1962) analyzed three months' worth of canceled charge slips at Yale's medical library. The slips were for journals published between 1956 and 1960. Thirty-seven journals accounted for 49 percent of the use, and 86 journals for 73 percent of the use. Fleming and Kilgour (1964) conducted a follow-up study at the medical libraries of Yale and Columbia to identify a core of biomedical journals capable of satisfying 75 percent of current demand. They examined canceled charge slips for journal issues published during a designated 42-month period. These were collected for one year at Yale and six months at Columbia. Although Columbia subscribed to more than 2,000 journals and Yale to more than 1,500, a core of 262 journals supplied 80 percent of the total journal use. As few as 69 journals satisfied more than half the demand in both libraries.

It seemed odd that the number of journals supplying half the use at Yale was 37 in 1962 and 69 in 1964. Fleming and Kilgour attributed this difference to the saturation effect of heavily used titles. The rate of use of the most popular titles, virtually to maximum capacity, remains relatively constant over a given period (unless duplicate copies are added to satisfy higher demand). The less-used materials, however, accumulate additional loans over time. This means that the shorter the period for which circulation records are analyzed, the fewer the number of different titles that will contribute to a fixed percentage of the total usage. Conversely, the longer the circulation period studied, the greater the number of journals that will contribute to a fixed usage percentage:

Sixty-nine Yale titles supplied 50 percent of use in one year as opposed to thirty-seven in three months, not so much because the heavily used titles were more heavily used during a year, but rather because the little-used titles accumulated more loans over a year and thereby depressed the 50 percent level. (p. 240)

Academic and research-oriented libraries interested primarily in the extent of scholarly use (as opposed to the absolute quantities of use) should study serials use for a longer, rather than a shorter, time. A study of journal use at the Air Force Cambridge Research Laboratories (Groos, 1966) showed that many patrons felt low-use journals were an important part of the collection. Thirty-eight percent of the patrons requested a low-use title (one with only one use during a six-month period); these titles accounted for 51 percent of total use.

Librarians can use core collection information in a number of ways. Miller (1981) described three small midwestern college libraries that worked together to identify their core distributions. In each case, approximately 40 percent of the collection met 80 percent of the demand. Lake Forest used the results to determine which items in the collection should be the first to receive security tape when a new theft-detection system was installed. Knox determined which parts of the collection to convert first from Dewey to Library of Congress classification. And St. Olaf's decided which means of storage was best for items in its collection.

This last use—resolving the ongoing problem of inadequate space to house collections—is the primary reason many libraries identify core collections. Librarians consider various options when they run out of space, such as purchasing microforms initially, whenever available, converting bound volumes to a less-bulky format, using compact shelving, or building a new, larger facility to house materials. Researchers have dismissed some of these options as unrealistic. The amount of material available on microform is small when compared to that available in paper form (Lawrence, 1981); it may cost more to microfilm bound volumes than to provide more space to house the paper copies (University of California, 1977); and the initial capital outlay for new full-service buildings is difficult to raise in tight budget times (Stayner, 1983). Researchers are still exploring other options. For example, the Library of Congress is assessing the costs, benefits, and problems of storing the content of materials on optical disks (Price, 1985). Kountz (1987) has described automated storage and retrieval approaches, and Creaghe and Davis (1986) have discussed such a system adopted by one university that can house 950,000 volumes.

The two most common solutions to space problems are those that librarians have used for decades: weeding the collection and storing some materials remotely. Weeding not only saves space, it saves the time of patrons and staff, makes the library more appealing, enhances the collection's reputation for reliability and currency, provides a check for needed mending and binding, identifies lost or stolen books, and provides feedback on the collection's strengths and weaknesses (Segal, 1980). Remote storage has these same benefits but allows a library to keep titles that a researcher or scholar may someday use.

Librarians weigh space options after considering constraints set by the parent institution and the library's purpose. School libraries, for example, are unlikely to store materials remotely because their primary mission is to house items that will meet current curricular needs and because they often have limited space and no storage options. On the other hand, corporate libraries can be expected to maintain a company archive, and academic libraries a collection that will support faculty research; in these cases remote storage is an option.

Librarians should take three kinds of costs into account when deciding whether to weed or store: (1) the cost of circulations "lost" because discarded or stored books were unavailable to the user at the time requested, (2) the costs of various retirement methods, and (3) the costs of various types of storage. The cost of lost circulation is an interesting concept, first explored by Raffel and Shishko (1969). They assumed there would be some loss of circulation if items were weeded or stored in less-expensive, but less-convenient, locations. Some librarians have argued that this assumption is simplistic and does not take into account the fact that a book badly needed will be requested from storage or that a substitute may be found for a book not available in the library. Overall, however, the assumption is valid, because physical accessibility is a primary factor influencing most patrons' use. For example, one library found that moving items to a storage facility reduced loans by 30 percent, even though patrons could have requested the stored materials and obtained them that same day (Douglas, 1986). Few patrons use interlibrary loans or recall services, which take several days or weeks to deliver requested items, even when they believe the items in question are relevant to their needs (Hitchingham, 1976). Readers are referred to Chapter 2 in this book for a full discussion of accessibility.

Evaluators can estimate the maximum number of books that would be lost using certain weeding or storage criteria. Suppose that an evaluator selects a sample of all books in some subject area that are at least 10 years old and then establishes different sets of weeding guidelines. Let us assume that two sets of guidelines, each with two weeding criteria, are established. The first set says that a book should be weeded if its physical condition is poor and if it has not circulated during the past five years. The second set says that a book should be weeded if its physical condition is poor and if it has not circulated during the past three years. For each of these two sets of criteria, the evaluator plots the number of circulations that would have been lost during the past several years (using actual circulation data from the sample works) if these criteria had been used to weed or store each item in the collection. This practice will slightly overestimate lost circulations, because it assumes that no patron will seek an item not currently on the shelf. It can, however, determine which set of weeding or storage criteria will result in the fewest lost circulations for a particular library.

Existing evidence (for example, Ash, 1974; Basart, 1980) shows that retirement decisions based on usage are more sound, in terms of identifying books likely to be requested in the future, than those of any other *single* criterion. Evaluators, however, may supplement use information by a number of other factors when making weeding and storage decisions, as librarians at a California public library did. These librarians began their weeding program by obtaining a computer-generated list of all materials that had not circulated in three years. They examined individual titles on the list, factoring in a number of other weeding criteria, before making their discard decisions (Hayden, 1987). The most-used weeding criteria are listed in "Guidelines for the Review of Library Collections" (American Library Association, 1979). These criteria include, among others, the age, subject, language, physical condition, obsolescence of content, or "quality" of the title (this last generally is determined through the list-checking approach described in Chapter 3). Librarians do not have to apply any set of retirement rules on a librarywide basis, but rather may modify them depending on the format or subject area involved. Thus, the Massachusetts Institute of Technology and an IBM library developed different sets of critera for weeding monographs, periodicals, internal company reports, and materials of other formats (Hulser, 1986; Lucker, Herzog, and Owens, 1986).

Making storage decisions based on use requires examining each title and modifying each catalog card to show which items are stored off-site. This is expensive when a large number of books are involved. If saving money is very important, evaluators may substitute the publication date for the use criterion when making storage decisions (Ford, 1980; Moss, Brophy, and Hargreaves, 1982). Publication-date storage decisions are

easy for junior staff to carry out and could be implemented with the minimum of documentation, if users could be successfully instructed (perhaps with a notice prominently posted in the catalog areas) that any book published before a certain date is on closed access. However, it would mean that catalogue entries would be inaccurate and might lead to user frustration at the shelves. (Best, 1980, p. 232)

The publication-date approach to storage often is more cost-effective for materials that age rapidly, such as medical research reports, or for large libraries. Gradmann and Pinkwart (1987) illustrated this graphically. Staff at the university library in Bonn, West Germany wanted to weed the collection by checking each individual title and examining its use, age, and various other aspects. The library rejected this method after determining that it would take existing professional staff members 39 years to weed the 550,000-item collection using a volume-by-volume approach, because there was no money for additional help and the staff was already overburdened with work.

Even those libraries that retire complete groups of material to storage on the basis of publication date (or for that matter, some other criterion) often make exceptions when necessary; that is, a particular book will not be discarded or retired to storage if it has been used above some threshold level, even though it falls within a general category of materials identified as prime candidates for storage.

Librarians must consider still another cost in the storage of less-used materials. In stacks that are open to the public, library staff must arrange the volumes systematically, using the library's classification scheme, to allow for browsing and to permit the user to find a particular item easily once its call number is known. But materials in book stacks that are accessible only to members of the library staff, particularly items in remote storage areas, do not have to be stored by a classified subject arrangement. These materials can be stored compactly and economically in other ways. More than 25 years ago, Metcalf (1965) suggested compactly shelving stored materials by size or date of acquisition. He also described ways of implementing compact storage. More recently, the Brookhaven National Laboratory Research Library doubled the linear footage of its remote storage facility by shelving items one behind the other on two-foot-deep shelves (Ryan and Galli, 1983).

Boll (1982) and Gilder et al. (1980) gave good overviews of the types of compact shelving units that a number of large libraries are using for storage. If these are properly designed to be mobile and easy to use, they will not even interfere with patron access to materials. Although space is conserved by all compact-storage techniques, there may be an added cost if mechanical and mobile shelving units are used. These costs may offset much, if not all, of the gain derived from saving space.

Some libraries use several space-saving options concurrently. When the American Jewish Archives became full, librarians devised a three-part plan to handle the problem: they weeded extraneous materials, microfilmed others, and placed a third group of little-used items in off-site storage (Proffitt, 1986).

Evaluators can decide which of these options are more cost-effective, substituting local cost figures into various formulas that researchers have proposed. Most of these formulas originally were written for large university libraries that have severe storage needs (for example, Ford, 1979; Lawrence and Oja, 1979), but the models apply to other library settings as well. Lister (1967) demonstrated that the storage cost per volume decreases for books stored in a compact form in less-accessible storage areas, but that the cost per circulation increases, especially if evaluators factor in some form of cost penalty for the delay and inconvenience caused to users. Stayner and Richardson (1983) compared costs associated with four storage solutions: (1) a conventional, low-density storage building or extension, (2) a remote, high-density storage facility, (3) a shared storage facility, and (4) no new building of any type. They figured in the costs for building the necessary storage facility, as well as the recurring costs of weeding and altering catalog records. Brown (1980) and Thompson (1980) also compared weeding and storage costs.

Using a fairly sophisticated relegation model, Lawrence (1981) compared the costs of (1) retaining materials on the shelves in a new larger library, (2) relegating material to compact shelving at a remote storage facility, and (3) weeding the material from the collection. For the first option, Lawrence determined the annual capital cost of constructing and equipping a new full-service library expected to last 40 years, the annual recurring cost of building maintenance, and the average circulation cost. For the storage option, he figured in the annual capital cost of constructing and equipping a storage facility (approximately 23 percent of the cost of a new full-service library), the annual building maintenance cost, the cost of selecting storage candidates from the collection, the cost of changing the location on the catalog record, and the unit cost of circulation. The selection cost included a small fee that users would be willing to pay to avoid a two-day delay in the delivery of materials housed in the storage facility and the cost of round-trip transportation for each item a user requested. For the weeding option, Lawrence added the cost of selecting books to be discarded and the cost of borrowing these items on interlibrary loan. The latter cost included a fee that users would be willing to pay to avoid a two-week delay in obtaining materials.

Lawrence then used a formula to determine which space-saving option was best, given the average number of years expected between circulations of each item. Exhibits 4-7 and 4-8 show the results of his analysis. These data— and, incidentally, data in studies by Brown (1980) and Stayner and Richardson (1983)—showed that no one treatment is cost-effective for every item. Rather, librarians should choose different space-saving treatments, depending on the number of times an item has circulated. In the Lawrence study, if a storage facility was already built, the most cost-effective solution would be for the librarian to retain, in the campus library, items that had circulated at least once in the past 10 years, to discard items that had circulated less than once in 35

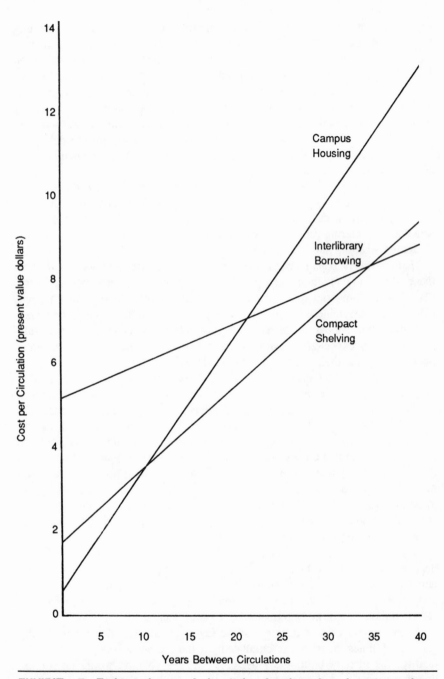

EXHIBIT 4-7   Estimated cost of circulation for three housing alternatives. Reprinted from Lawrence (1981), courtesy of the American Library Association.

Disposition		Years Between
From	*To*	*Uses*
Campus	Disposal	20.93
Campus	Storage	10.17
Storage	Disposal	34.22

EXHIBIT 4-8 Crossover points for storage and disposal. Reprinted from Lawrence (1981), courtesy of the American Library Association.

years, and to store the rest. If no storage facility was available, the librarian would retain on campus those items that had circulated once in the past 21 years and would discard the remainder.

Two final points must be made about these least-cost decision rules. First, they do not generally consider in-house use. This is less important than one might think, however, because materials that circulate tend to be those that are used in-house and vice versa (this is explained in detail in Chapter 5). Second, the rules affecting relegation decisions are very sensitive to changes in unit costs; even small differences in costs can result in a major shift in the decision rules.

CONCLUSION

There are a variety of approaches to evaluating the use of library collections. At this point, it must be reemphasized that a library should choose the evaluation method or methods best suited to its purpose. Often this involves conducting a multitiered evaluation using a combination of collection-oriented and use-oriented methods. Many authors report using evaluations of this type. For example, when Bolgiano and King (1978) evaluated a periodicals collection, they compared their holdings to those on recommended lists, analyzed current titles in relation to the academic programs they might be expected to support, reviewed interlibrary loan requests for periodicals, and conducted a citation analysis of graduate theses finished at the university during the previous five years. Researchers in a Virginia health sciences library evaluated periodical holdings by measuring the availability of titles in other area libraries, recording in-house use, surveying users, and examining lists of titles held by other selected libraries (Alligood, Russo-Martin, and Peterson, 1983). Although using a variety of methods will increase the cost of the evaluation, the results often provide a more balanced and comprehensive review than those obtained by using just one method.

Ultimately evaluators will scrutinize most collections in terms of the proportion of the demands they are able to satisfy. If a collection is sufficiently large, is well chosen in relation to the needs of the community served, is accessible, and is updated and weeded, it should satisfy the bulk of demands—both known-item and subject-related requests—placed on it.

REFERENCES

Advani, N., and M. G. Gupta. "Reader Utilization of Journals in Maulana Azad Medical College Library (University of Delhi)." *Library Herald,* 22(4):201–206, January 1984.

Aguilar, William. "The Influence of a Book Display on Circulation in a Two-Year College Library." Urbana, Ill., University of Illinois, Graduate School of Library and Information Science, 1982. (Unpublished paper)

―――――. "Relationship Between Classes of Books Circulated and Classes of Books Requested on Interlibrary Loan." Doctoral Dissertation. Urbana, Ill., University of Illinois, 1984.

―――――. "The Application of Relative Use and Interlibrary Demand in Collection Development." *Collection Management,* 8(1):15–24, Spring 1986.

Alligood, Elaine C.; Elaine Russo-Martin; and Richard A. Peterson. "Use Study of *Excerpta Medica* Abstract Journals: To Drop or Not to Drop." *Bulletin of the Medical Library Association,* 71(3):251–258, July 1983.

American Library Association, Collection Development Committee. "Guidelines for the Review of Library Collections." In: *Guidelines for Collection Development.* Edited by David L. Perkins. Chicago, Ill., ALA, 1979, pp. 20–30.

Ash, Joan. "Library Use of Public Health Materials: Description and Analysis." *Bulletin of the Medical Library Association,* 62(2):95–104, April 1974.

Baker, Sharon L. "An Adult User Survey." *Illinois Library Statistical Report,* 7:1–33, May 1983.

―――――. "The Display Phenomenon: An Exploration into Factors Causing the Increased Circulation of Displayed Books." *Library Quarterly,* 56(3):237–257, July 1986a.

―――――. "Overload, Browsers, and Selections." *Library and Information Science Research,* 8(4):315–329, October–December 1986b.

―――――. "Will Fiction Classification Schemes Increase Use?" *RQ,* 27(3):366–376, Spring 1988.

Basart, Ann. "Criteria for Weeding Books in a University Music Library." *Notes: the Quarterly Journal of the Music Library Association,* 36(4):819–836, June 1980.

Best, Sheila. "A Book Relegation Project in the Biological and Medical Sciences Division, Glasgow University Library." *Journal of Librarianship,* 12(4):229–237, October 1980.

Bolgiano, Christina E., and Mary Kathryn King. "Profiling a Periodicals Collection." *College and Research Libraries,* 39(2):99–104, March 1978.

Boll, John J. *To Grow or Not to Grow: A Review of Alternatives to New Academic Library Buildings. Library Journal* Special Report No. 15. New York, Bowker, 1982.

Briggs, Betty S. "A Case for Classified Fiction." *Library Journal,* 98(22):3694, December 15, 1973.

Brooks, Terrence A. "Naive vs. Sophisticated Methods of Forecasting Public Library

Circulations." *Library and Information Science Research,* 6(2):205–214, April–June 1984a.

_____. "Using Time-Series Regression to Predict Academic Library Circulations." *College and Research Libraries,* 45(6):501–505, November 1984b.

Brown, A. J. "Some Library Costs and Options." *Journal of Librarianship,* 12(4):211–216, October 1980.

Brown, Helen J.; Jean K. Miller; and Diane M. Pinchoff. "Study of the Information Dissemination Service—Health Sciences Library, State University of New York at Buffalo." *Bulletin of the Medical Library Association,* 63(3):259–271, July 1975.

Buckland, Michael K. *Book Availability and the Library User.* New York, Pergamon Press, 1975.

Bulick, Stephen. *Structure and Subject Interaction: Toward a Sociology of Knowledge in the Social Sciences.* New York, Marcel Dekker, 1982.

Byrd, Gary D.; D. A. Thomas; and Katherine E. Hughes. "Collection Development Using Interlibrary Loan Borrowing and Acquisitions Statistics." *Bulletin of the Medical Library Association,* 70(1):1–9, January 1982.

Carnovsky, Leon. Personal correspondence cited by Harriet Forbes in "The Geography of Reading." *ALA Bulletin,* 29(8):470–476, August 1935.

Chrzatowski, Tina E. "Where Does the Money Go? Measuring Cost-Effectiveness Using a Microcomputer to Analyze Journal-Use Data." In: *Building on the First Century: Proceedings of the Fifth National Conference of the Association of College and Research Libraries, Cincinnati, Ohio, April 5–8, 1989.* Edited by Janice C. Fennell. Chicago, Ill., Association of College and Research Libraries, 1989, pp. 201–204.

Cook, Kevin L. "Gathering Useful Circulation Data in the Documents Department." *RQ,* 25(2):223–228, Winter 1985.

Creaghe, Norma S., and Douglas A. Davis. "Hard Copy in Transition: An Automated Storage and Retrieval Facility for Low-Use Library Materials." *College and Research Libraries,* 47(5):495–499, September 1986.

Diodato, Louise W., and Virgil P. Diodato. "The Use of Gifts in a Medium-Sized Academic Library." *Collection Management,* 5(1/2):53–71, Spring–Summer 1983.

Douglas, Ian. "Effects of a Relegation Programme on Borrowing of Books." *Journal of Documentation,* 42(4):252–271, December 1986.

Dowlin, Ken, and Lynn Magrath. "Beyond the Numbers: A Decision Support System." In: *Proceedings of the 1982 Clinic on Library Applications of Data Processing.* Edited by F. W. Lancaster. Urbana, Ill., University of Illinois, Graduate School of Library and Information Science, 1983, pp. 27–58.

Eggers, Lolly. "More Effective Management of the Public Library's Book Collection." *Minnesota Libraries,* 25(2):56–58, Summer 1976.

Engel, Debra. "Putting the Public First: The Baltimore County Approach to Collection Development." *Catholic Library World,* 54(3):122–126, October 1982.

Ettelt, Harold J. "Book Use at a Small (Very) Community College Library." *Library Journal,* 103(20):2314–2315, November 15, 1978.

_____. "What Price Weeding?" *Community and Junior College Libraries,* 3(3):69–77, Spring 1985.

Evans, G. Edward. "The Influence of Book Selection Agents Upon Book Collection Usage in Academic Libraries." Doctoral Dissertation. Urbana, Ill., University of Illinois, 1969.

Evans, G. Edward, and Claudia White Argyres. "Approval Plans and Collection Development in Academic Libraries." *Library Resources and Technical Services, 18*(1):35–50, Winter 1974.

Fleming, Thomas P., and Frederick G. Kilgour. "Moderately and Heavily Used Biomedical Journals." *Bulletin of the Medical Library Association, 52*(1):234–241, January 1964.

Ford, Geoffrey. "The Costs of Relegation." In: *Financing Serials from the Producer to the User.* Edited by David P. Woodwarth. Oxford, Eng., U.K. Serials Group, 1979.

_____. "Stock Relegation in Some British University Libraries." *Journal of Librarianship, 12*(1):42–55, January 1980.

Fussler, Herman H., and Julian L. Simon. *Patterns in the Use of Books in Large Research Libraries.* Chicago, Ill., University of Chicago Press, 1969.

Gilder, L., et al. *The Relegation and Storage of Materials in Academic Libraries: A Literature Review.* Loughborough, Eng., Centre for Library and Information Management, Department of Library and Information Studies, Loughborough University, 1980. Claim Report No. 3

Goldblatt, Margaret A. "Current Legal Periodicals: A Use Study." *Law Library Journal, 78*(1):55–72, Winter 1986.

Golden, Gary A. "Motivation to Select Books: A Study of Annotated and Unannotated Booklists in Public Libraries." Doctoral Dissertation. Urbana, Ill., University of Illinois, 1983.

Goldhor, Herbert. "Are the Best Books the Most Read?" *Library Quarterly, 29*(4):251–255, October 1959.

_____. "The Effect of Prime Display Location on Public Library Circulation of Selected Adult Titles." *Library Quarterly, 42*(4):371–389, October 1972.

_____. "Experimental Effects on the Choice of Books Borrowed by Public Library Adult Patrons." *Library Quarterly, 51*(3):253–268, July 1981a.

_____. "Evaluation of a Sample of Adult Books in the Kingston and St. Andrew Parish Library of Jamaica." Urbana, Ill., University of Illinois, Graduate School of Library Science, 1981b. ERIC ED201334

_____. "A Report on an Application of the Inductive Method of Evaluation of Public Library Books." *Libri, 31*(2):121–129, August 1981c.

Gradmann, Stefan, and Doris Pinkwart. "Über die Bunutzung 'alterer' Literaturi Recherchen und Überlegungen zum Problem 'veralteter' Monographienbestande am Biespeil der Universitätsbibliothek Bonn." (The Use of Older Literature: Research into and Consideration of the Problem of Obsolete Monograph Stocks as Exemplified by Bonn University Library.) *Mitteilungsblatt (Verband der Bibliotheken des Landes Nordrhein-Westfalen), 37*(2):172–185, June 1987.

Graziano, Eugene E. "Interlibrary Loan Analysis: Diagnostic for Scientific Serials Backfile Acquisitions." *Special Libraries, 53*(5):251–257, May–June 1962.

Griffith, Belver C., et al. "The Aging of Scientific Literature: A Citation Analysis." *Journal of Documentation, 35*(3):179–196, September 1979.

Griscom, Richard. "Periodical Use in a University Music Library: A Citation Study of Theses and Dissertations Submitted to the Indiana University School of Music from 1975–1980." *Serials Librarian, 7*(3):35–52, Spring 1983.

Groos, Ole V. "Less-Used Titles and Volumes of Science Journals: Two Preliminary Notes." *Library Resources and Technical Services, 10*(3):289–290, Summer 1966.

Hardesty, Larry. "Use of Library Materials at a Small Liberal Arts College." *Library Research,* 3(3):261–282, Fall 1981.

Hayden, Ron. "If It Circulates, Keep It." *Library Journal, 112*(10):80–82, June 1, 1987.

Hayes, Robert M. "The Distribution of Use of Library Materials: Analysis of Data from the University of Pittsburgh." *Library Research,* 3(3):215–260, Fall 1981.

Hermenze, Jennie. "The 'Classics' Will Circulate!" *Library Journal, 106*(20):2191–2195, November 15, 1981.

Hernon, Peter. *Use of Government Publications by Social Scientists.* Norwood, N.J., Ablex Publishing, 1979.

Heussman, John W. "The Literature Cited in Theological Journals and Its Relation to Seminary Library Circulation." Doctoral Dissertation. Urbana, Ill., University of Illinois, 1970.

Hitchingham, Eileen E. "MEDLINE Use in a University Without a School of Medicine." *Special Libraries,* 67(4):188–194, April 1976.

Hodowanec, George V. "Analysis of Variables Which Help to Predict Book and Periodical Use." *Library Acquisitions: Practice and Theory,* 4(1):75–85, 1980.

Hostrop, Richard W. "The Relationship of Academic Success and Selected Other Factors to Student Use of Library Materials at College of the Desert." Doctoral Dissertation. Los Angeles, Calif., University of California, 1966.

Hulser, Richard P. "Weeding in a Corporate Library as Part of a Collection Maintenance Program." *Science and Technology Libraries,* 6(3):1–9, Spring 1986.

Jain, Aridaman K. *A Sampled Data Study of Book Usage in the Purdue University Libraries.* Lafayette, Ind., Purdue University, 1965.

————. "Sampling and Short-Period Usage in the Purdue Library." *College and Research Libraries,* 27(3):211–218, May 1966.

————. "Sampling and Data Collection Methods for a Book-Use Study." *Library Quarterly,* 39(3):245–252, July 1969.

Jain, Aridaman K., et al. *Report on a Statistical Study of Book Use.* Lafayette, Ind., Purdue University, School of Industrial Engineering, 1967.

Jenks, George M. "Circulation and Its Relationship to the Book Collection and Academic Departments." *College and Research Libraries,* 37(2):145–152, March 1976.

Kantor, Paul B. "On the Stability of Distributions of the Type Described by Trueswell." *College and Research Libraries,* 41(6):514–516, November 1980.

Kaske, Neal K. "An Evaluation of Current Collection Utilization Methodologies and Findings." *Collection Management,* 3(2–3):187–199, Summer–Fall 1979.

Kent, Allen, et al. *Use of Library Materials: The University of Pittsburgh Study.* New York, Marcel Dekker, 1979.

Kilgour, Frederick G. "Use of Medical and Biological Journals in the Yale Medical Library." *Bulletin of the Medical Library Association,* 50(3):429–449, July 1962.

Kountz, John. "Robots in the Library: Automated Storage and Retrieval Systems." *Library Journal, 112*(20):67–70, December 1987.

Krueger, Karen. *Coordinated Cooperative Collection Development for Illinois Libraries.* Springfield, Ill., Illinois State Library, 1983.

Kuraim, Faraj Mohamed. "The Principal Factors Causing Reader Frustration in a Public Library." Doctoral Dissertation. Cleveland, Ohio, Case Western Reserve University, 1983.

Lancaster, F. W. "Evaluating Collections by Their Use." *Collection Management, 4* (1–2):15–43, Spring/Summer 1982.

Lawrence, Gary S. "A Cost Model for Storage and Weeding Programs." *College and Research Libraries, 42*(2):139–147, March 1981.

Lawrence, Gary S., and Anne R. Oja. *An Economic Criterion for Housing and Disposing of Library Materials Based on Frequency of Circulation.* Berkeley, Calif., University of California Systemwide Administration, 1979. Research Report RR-79-2

Lee, Paul. "Evaluation of the Anthropology Collection at the University of North Carolina at Greensboro." Greensboro, N.C., University of North Carolina, Department of Library Science and Educational Technology, 1986. (Unpublished Student Paper)

Line, Maurice B., and A. Sandison. "'Obsolescence' and Changes in the Use of Literature with Time." *Journal of Documentation, 30*(3):283–350, September 1974.

Lister, Winston Charles. "Least Cost Decision Rules for the Selection of Library Materials for Compact Storage." Doctoral Dissertation. Lafayette, Ind., Purdue University, School of Industrial Engineering, 1967.

Little, Paul. "The Effectiveness of Paperbacks." *Library Journal, 104*(20):2411–2416, November 15, 1979.

Long, Sarah P. "The Effect of Face-Front Display on the Circulation of Books in a Public Library." Greensboro, N.C., University of North Carolina, 1986. ERIC ED278415

Longyear, R. M. "Article Citations and 'Obsolescence' in Musicological Journals." *Notes: the Quarterly Journal of the Music Library Association, 33*(3):563–571, March 1977.

Lucker, Jay K.; Kate S. Herzog; and Sydney J. Owens. "Weeding Collections in an Academic Library System: Massachusetts Institute of Technology." *Science and Technology Libraries, 6*(3):11–23, Spring 1986.

McCaghy, Dawn, and Gary R. Purcell. "Faculty Use of Government Publications." *College and Research Libraries, 33*(1):7–12, January 1972.

McClellan, A. W. "New Concepts of Service." *Library Association Record, 58*(8):299–305, August 1956.

McGrath, William E. "The Significance of Books Used According to a Classified Profile of Academic Departments." *College and Research Libraries, 33*(3):212–219, May 1972.

McGrath, William E.; Donald J. Simon; and Evelyn Bullard. "Ethnocentricity and Cross-Disciplinary Circulation." *College and Research Libraries, 40*(6):511–518, November 1979.

Metcalf, Keyes D. *Planning Academic and Research Library Buildings.* New York, McGraw-Hill, 1965, pp. 157–165.

Metz, Paul. "Duplication in Library Collections: What We Know and What We Need to Know." *Collection Building, 2*(3):27–33, 1980.

Metz, Paul, and Charles A. Litchfield. "Measuring Collections Use at Virginia Tech." *College and Research Libraries, 49*(6):501–513, November 1988.

Middleswort, L. E. "A Study of Book Use in the University of Chicago Library." Master's Thesis. Chicago, Ill., University of Chicago, 1951.

Miller, Arthur H., Jr. "A Model for Collection Use Study at Small Academic Libraries." Paper presented at the American Library Association Conference, San Francisco, Calif., 1981.

Mills, Terry R. "The University of Illinois Film Center Collection Use Study." Urbana,

Ill., University of Illinois, Graduate School of Library and Information Science, 1982. ERIC ED227821

Moreland, George B. "Operation Saturation: Using Paperbacks, Branch Libraries in Maryland Conduct an Experiment to Equate Book Supply with Patron Demand." *Library Journal, 93*(10):1975–1979, May 15, 1968.

Moss, R.; P. Brophy; and P. Hargreaves. *Time Factor Classification and Relegation: Final Report for the Period August 1978–December 1981.* Middlesbrough, Eng., Teesside Polytechnic, 1982. British Library Research and Development Department Report 5744

Mostyn, Gregory R. "The Use of Supply-Demand Equality in Evaluating Collection Adequacy." *California Librarian, 35*(2):16–23, April 1974.

Mueller, Elizabeth. "Are New Books Read More Than Old Ones?" *Library Quarterly, 35*(3):166–172, July 1965.

Nimmer, Ronald J. "Circulation and Collection Patterns at the Ohio State University Libraries, 1973–1977." *Library Acquisitions: Practice and Theory, 4*(1):61–70, 1980.

Nothiesen, Margaret A. "A Study of the Use of Serials at the John Crerar Library." Master's Thesis. Chicago, Ill., University of Chicago, 1960.

O'Connell, Michelle D., and A. Patricia Miller. "COCTAILS: Automated Interlibrary Loan Statistics at Health Sciences Library, SUNYAB." *Bulletin of the Medical Library Association, 65*(2):250–254, April 1977.

Parrish, Nancy. "The Effect of a Booklist on the Circulation of Fiction Books Which Have Not Been Borrowed from a Public Library in Four Years or Longer." Greensboro, N.C., University of North Carolina, 1986. (Unpublished Student Paper)

Price, Joseph W. "Optical Disks and Demand Printing Research at the Library of Congress." *Information Services and Use, 5*(1):3–20, February 1985.

Pritchard, S. J. "Purchase and Use of Monographs Originally Requested on Interlibrary Loan in a Medical School Library." *Library Acquisitions: Practice and Theory, 4*(2):135–139, 1980.

Proffitt, Kevin. "Collection Management at the American Jewish Archives." *American Archivist, 49*(2):177–179, Spring 1986.

Raffel, Jeffrey A., and Robert Shishko. *Systematic Analysis of University Libraries.* Cambridge, Mass., MIT Press, 1969.

Raisig, L. Miles, et al. "How Biomedical Investigators Use Library Books." *Bulletin of the Medical Library Association, 54*(2):104–107, April 1966.

Rawlinson, Nora. "The Approach to Collection Management at Baltimore County Public Library." In: *Collection Management in Public Libraries: Proceedings of a Preconference to the 1984 ALA Annual Conference, June 21–22, 1984, Dallas, Texas.* Edited by Judith Serebnick. Chicago, Ill., American Library Association, 1986, pp. 76–80.

Ray, Jean M. "Who Borrows Maps from a University Library Map Collection—And Why?" *Special Libraries, 65*(3):104–109, March 1974.

_____. "Who Borrows Maps from a University Library Map Collection—And Why? Report II." *Special Libraries, 69*(1):13–20, January 1978.

Reed, Mary Jane Pobst. "Identification of Storage Candidates Among Monographs." *Collection Management, 3*(2/3):203–214, Summer–Fall 1979.

Roberts, Michael, and Kenneth J. Cameron. "A Barometer of 'Unmet Demand.' " *Library Acquisitions: Practice and Theory, 8*(1):31–42, 1984.

Ryan, Ken, and Marilyn Galli. "Adapting Non-Library Facilities for Periodical Collections at Brookhaven National Laboratory." *Science and Technology Libraries,* 3(4):31–41, Summer 1983.

Sargent, Seymour H. "The Uses and Limitations of Trueswell." *College and Research Libraries,* 40(5):416–423, September 1979.

Schad, Jasper G. "Missing the Brass Ring in the Iron City." *Journal of Academic Librarianship,* 5(2):60–63, May 1979.

Schmitt, John P., and Stewart Saunders. "An Assessment of *Choice* as a Tool for Selection." *College and Research Libraries,* 44(5):375–380, September 1983.

Segal, Joseph P. *Evaluating and Weeding Collections in Small and Medium-Sized Public Libraries: The CREW Method.* Chicago, Ill., American Library Association, 1980.

Shaw, Ralph R. "The Influence of Sloping Shelves on Book Circulation." *Library Quarterly,* 8(4):480–490, October 1938.

Shaw, W. M., Jr. "A Practical Journal Usage Technique." *College and Research Libraries,* 39(6):479–484, November 1978.

Simmons, Peter. "Improving Collections Through Computer Analysis of Circulation Records in a University Library." In: *Proceedings of the American Society for Information Science, 33rd Annual Meeting, Philadelphia, Pa., October 11–15, 1970.* Vol. 7. Edited by Jeanne B. North. Washington, D.C., American Society for Information Science, 1970, pp. 59–63.

Slote, Stanley J. "The Predictive Value of Past-Use Patterns of Adult Fiction in Public Libraries for Identifying Core Collections." Doctoral Dissertation. New Brunswick, N.J., Rutgers University, 1970.

––––––––. *Weeding Library Collections.* 2nd Edition. Littleton, Colo., Libraries Unlimited, 1982.

Smith, Rita Hoyt, and Warner Granade. "User and Library Failures in an Undergraduate Library." *College and Research Libraries,* 39(6):467–473, November 1978.

Soper, Mary Ellen. "The Relationship Between Personal Collections and the Selection of Cited References." Doctoral Dissertation. Urbana, Ill., University of Illinois, Graduate School of Library Science, 1972.

––––––––. "Characteristics and Use of Personal Collections." *Library Quarterly,* 46(4):397–415, October 1976.

Spiller, David. "The Provision of Fiction for Public Libraries." *Journal of Librarianship,* 12(4):238–266, October 1980.

Sridhar, M. S. "Use of Current Journals by Indian Space Technologists." *Serials Librarian,* 10(3):77–93, Spring 1986.

Stangl, Peter, and Frederick G. Kilgour. "Analysis of Recorded Biomedical Book and Journal Use in the Yale Medical Library." *Bulletin of the Medical Library Association,* 55(3):290–315, July 1967.

Stayner, Richard A. "Economic Characteristics of the Library Storage Problem." *Library Quarterly,* 53(3):313–327, July 1983.

Stayner, Richard A., and Valerie E. Richardson. *The Cost-Effectiveness of Alternative Library Storage Programs.* Clayton, Victoria, Australia, Monash University, Graduate School of Librarianship, 1983.

Stevens, Rolland E. "A Study of Interlibrary Loan." *College and Research Libraries,* 35(5):336–343, September 1974.

Stieg, Lewis. "A Technique for Evaluating the College Library Book Collection." *Library Quarterly, 13*(1):34–44, January 1943.

Taylor, Margaret Ann Thomas. "The Effect of Bibliographic Accessibility Upon Physical Accessibility of Materials in a Public Library Setting." Doctoral Dissertation. Ann Arbor, Mich., University of Michigan, Graduate School of Library and Information Science, 1982.

Thompson, Donald D. "Comparing Costs: An Examination of the Real and Hidden Costs of Different Methods of Storage." *Bulletin of the American Society for Information Science, 7*(1):14–15, October 1980.

Trevvett, Melissa D. "Characteristics of Interlibrary Loan Requests at the Library of Congress." *College and Research Libraries, 40*(1):36–43, January 1979.

Trochim, Mary Kane. "The Associated Colleges of the Midwest Library Collection Use Study: Final Report." Chicago, Ill., Associated Colleges of the Midwest, 1980. (Unpublished Report)

Trochim, Mary Kane, with Arthur H. Miller, Jr., and William M. K. Trochim. *Measuring the Book Circulation Use of a Small Academic Library Collection: A Manual.* Washington, D.C., Association of Research Libraries, 1985.

Trueswell, Richard W. "Two Characteristics of Circulation and Their Effect on the Implementation of Mechanized Circulation Control Systems." *College and Research Libraries, 25*(4):285–291, July 1964.

————. "A Quantitative Measure of User Circulation Requirements and Its Possible Effect on Stack Thinning and Multiple Copy Determination." *American Documentation, 16*(1):20–25, January 1965.

————. "Determining the Optimal Number of Volumes for a Library's Core Collection." *Libri, 16*(1):49–60, 1966.

Turow, Joseph. "The Impact of Differing Orientations of Librarians on the Process of Children's Book Selection: A Case Study of Library Tensions." *Library Quarterly, 48*(3):276–292, July 1978.

University of California, Office of the Executive Director of Universitywide Library Planning. *The University of California Libraries: A Plan for Development, 1978–1988.* Berkeley, Calif., University of California, 1977, pp. 161–166.

Urquhart, John A., and N. C. Urquhart. *Relegation and Stock Control in Libraries.* Stocksfield, Eng., Oriel Press, 1976.

Van Styvendaele, B. J. H. "University Scientists as Seekers of Information: Sources of References to Books and Their First Use Versus Date of Publication." *Journal of Librarianship, 13*(2):83–92, April 1981.

Weech, Terry L. "The Use of Government Publications: A Selected Review of the Literature." *Government Publications Review, 5*(2):177–184, February 1978.

Wenger, Charles B.; Christine B. Sweet; and Helen J. Stiles. "Monograph Evaluation for Acquisitions in a Large Research Library." *Journal of the American Society for Information Science, 30*(2):88–92, March 1979.

Williams, Roy. "Weeding an Academic Lending Library Using the Slote Method." *British Journal of Academic Librarianship, 1*(2):147–159, Summer 1986.

Wood, D. N., and C. A. Bower. "The Use of Social Science Periodical Literature." *Journal of Documentation, 25*(2):108–122, June 1969.

Wood, Richard J. "The Experimental Effects of Fiction Book Lists on Circulation in an Academic Library." *RQ, 24*(4):427–432, Summer 1985.

CHAPTER 5

EVALUATION OF IN-HOUSE USE

WHY MEASURE IN-HOUSE USE?

Librarians have traditionally used circulation data as the primary indicator of library activity; however, circulation data do not give a complete picture of collection use because they fail to take into account materials used within the library. Such use may come from books and periodicals in the general collection that are consulted but not borrowed, as well as from noncirculating special collections, for example reference, archival, or microfiche collections.

There are several reasons why librarians should consider recording in-house use. First, these data are needed to demonstrate the full extent of collection use. This is important because the ratio of in-house use to circulation is high in some libraries. Moreover, the library may be able to attract more financial support if it can show the full range and extent of use.

Second, data on in-house use allow a librarian to more accurately predict total use relating to specific subject areas and specific items, thus aiding decisions on which areas of the collection to augment and which to weed, which journals to discontinue, and so on.

Third, data on in-house use can help librarians make decisions about accessibility of portions of the collection. In libraries where space is at a premium, the librarian can choose to store rarely used materials in less-accessible locations or to convert them to other formats (microcopy or electronic). Having data on in-house use for various portions of the collection enables the librarian to make more informed decisions on other practical matters. For example, more frequent reshelving may be needed to improve the availability of materials in the heavily used sections of the library. These areas may also require greater seating capacity or more photocopying facilities.

DEFINING IN-HOUSE USE

Perhaps the greatest problem with measuring in-house use is deciding how to define it. Circulation is an objective measure; when a book is checked out, a use is recorded, whether the patron actually reads the book or not. But what constitutes an in-library use? Lancaster (1988) described this problem as follows:

If a book is removed from the shelves, casually glanced at and immediately returned, has it been used? If it is removed, some portion of it read at the shelves, and it is then put back, has it been used? If it is carried to a table, along with others, glanced at and pushed to one side, has it been used? (p. 54)

All of these situations have been considered "uses" in one study or another. The main factor that seems to affect the definition chosen by researchers is objectivity. This is not surprising, since distinguishing a rejection from a use can be difficult at best. Most studies have selected a measure that can be defined unequivocally. Many define a used item as one that needs to be returned to its proper location. For example, in a study by McGrath (1971), a book that a user reshelved was not counted as an in-house use, but one left on a table for reshelving was:

We assumed that if [the patron] reshelved a book immediately after a moment's examination, then he demonstrated neither interest nor use and that no count need or could be taken. We also assumed that if he took a book . . . to a table until he had gleaned what he needed, then he had demonstrated measurable interest and the book should be counted. (p. 281)

Clearly, this definition will underestimate use, because patrons often reshelve books they have actually consulted.

Other researchers have considered a book to be used when a slip of paper carefully inserted into it is shown to have been disturbed (for example, Harris, 1977). When using questionnaires or interviews, some investigators have allowed patrons to decide whether books were used or not, generally after providing an appropriate definition of use. For example, a questionnaire used in a study for the Coalition for Public Library Research (Rubin, 1986a) gave users the following definition:

When people visit the library they use books, magazines, or newspapers in different ways: some people use them for "just a minute" by reading or skimming only a few pages; some people use them for a "longer period of time," perhaps by reading one or more books, articles or chapters. Please tell us how many books, magazines or newspapers you used in the library today for "just a minute" or for "a longer period of time." Include adult and juvenile materials but do not count the materials you are taking out today. (p. 204)

A secondary factor in choosing a definition of in-house use appears to be ease of data collection. For example, several evaluators mention having chosen the "left-on-the-table" definition because nonprofessional staff were able to record this type of use quickly and easily, thus providing a cost-effective means of data collection.

THE TABLE COUNT METHOD

The table count is the most frequently used method of measuring in-house use. For a length of time that is long enough to provide a representative picture of use, shelvers collect at predetermined intervals all items left on tables or in specially designated reshelving areas. Shelvers record details of the books they pick up before returning them to the shelves.

Table counts allow the materials used within a library to be categorized by subject, type of document, age of material, or other characteristics of interest. Thus, the counts can give a very specific picture of which books, subjects, and sections of the library are highly used. Other major advantages of the table count method are the relative ease of data collection, since little skill is needed to record the desired figures, and the fact that no direct patron contact is required.

The biggest limitation of the table count method is its tendency to underestimate total use (Elston, 1966; Goldhor, 1979; Rubin, 1986a, 1986b). Taylor (1976–1977) discovered that only 20 to 25 percent of all periodical volumes used within a large academic library were left on tables for reshelving. And a study comparing different methods of collecting data on in-house use found that table counts underestimated use by an average of 50 percent (Rubin, 1986a, 1986b).

The evaluator can increase the percentage of persons who cooperate, and thereby increase the accuracy of the table count, by implementing a publicity campaign. Signs prominently placed in the library can urge users not to reshelve materials they consult. These can be supplemented by notices in library bulletins, cards handed to users entering the library on the days selected for the survey, or any other procedure that seems likely to work in a particular institution. When Taylor (1976–1977) asked patrons to leave used items on tables, he was able to raise the level of cooperation from 25 percent to 40 percent. Nevertheless, 40 percent cooperation is still far from perfect.

If a more precise figure for in-house use is needed, a correction to the results obtained from the table count may be made by determining what proportion of library users reshelve materials. The best way to determine the correction factor is to observe a sample of users during selected brief time periods to see who reshelves books and who does not (for example, see Wenger and Childress, 1977). For instance, if 200 volumes are observed to be used and 40 of these are reshelved by patrons, the table count will underestimate use by 20 percent.

Underestimation of use is not as serious a problem as it initially may appear. So long as sampling shows the underestimate to be constant, the reliability of the table count method is not affected (Morse, 1968). Librarians who are collecting data on total in-house use to document the level of service provided can apply a correction factor to obtain better estimates. Other libraries perform in-house studies to discover which items are being used, not how much the library is being used. But because in-house use is heavily skewed toward the same highly used items, even if the table count underestimates an item's total use it will still show that it is heavily used, compared with other items.

Lancaster (1988) suggests a more serious limitation of the table count. There may be certain factors within a particular library that could cause table counts to seriously distort overall patterns of use. For example, the shelves devoted to subject A could be immediately adjacent to tables, whereas those devoted to subject B could be far away. One could argue, then, that A users would be more likely than B users to carry items to the tables. On the other hand, if B users went to the trouble of taking items to the tables, they might be more likely than A users to leave them there, so one factor might offset the other. To date, no studies have been done on environmental factors such as these that may distort use.

A third limitation of the table count method is the cost of labor associated with recording in-house use over a long time. Although training of nonprofessional workers to collect data will not take long, the continued, consistent recording of the data may. For this reason, libraries usually do table counts either for a few days that are chosen to be representative of the calendar year or as part of a short-term, one-time study. The former is preferable, since both circulation and in-house use may vary, depending on the time of year during which the study is conducted.

The table count method also fails to tell who is using the materials. The data collected provide no information on whether in-house use varies by a patron's age, sex, occupation, status (for example, faculty versus undergraduate), or education. Moreover, table counts do not tell whether the user found anything of value or how long an item was used. Answers to these questions may be important in certain situations.

Variations on the table count method, designed to be more cost-effective in the long run, have been tried. One is the dotting or spine-marking method used by Shaw (1978, 1979), which is virtually identical to the method used by Slote (1982), described in Chapter 4. An adhesive dot is placed on the spine of each volume used so it is clearly visible when the volume is on the library shelf. If dots of different colors are used, one can distinguish items borrowed from items used in the library. Moreover, with different colors, one can identify items borrowed but not used in the library, items used in-house but not borrowed, items borrowed and used in-house, and items not used at all. This method requires extra work during the first few weeks, but soon most items needing to be reshelved will have already been dotted. After several months, the items needing a dot will be the exception rather than the rule, so the procedure can go on indefinitely. One limitation of the dotting variation, however, is that it does not record either frequency of use or time of last use.

Harris (1977) described another variation of the table count method that uses alternate color stamping. Circulating books are stamped with a black due-date stamp, and books that are used in-house and left on tables are stamped with a red date stamp before being reshelved. This allows data on in-house use to be quickly recorded in the book itself. This is extremely useful when weeding individual sections of the stacks or when deciding which books should be moved to less-accessible storage areas.

THE SLIP METHOD

The "slip" method is similar to the table count in its identification of specific materials used in-house, allowing categorization by subject, type, age, and the like. Moreover, it has similar advantages—the ease of data collection—and it requires no direct patron contact. It shares disadvantages as well: failing to tell who used the material, how long it was used, or whether it was useful to the patron. This method is described by Harris (1977):

A slip is placed in the selected book in such a way that it cannot be seen unless the book is removed from the shelf and consulted, in which case it cannot fail to be seen. The user is asked, on the slip, to throw the slip away. The book cannot be used without the slip being obviously disturbed, so even if the user does not do as he is asked, the use of the book is detectable. (p. 124)

Generally, the slips are placed as illustrated in Exhibit 5-1, with both edges of the slip inserted on predetermined page numbers. The person who opens the book for any reason would disturb the slip.

Unfortunately, this method is subject to inaccuracies. Despite Harris's claims to the contrary, someone who opens the book to glance at the title page or the table of contents may not disturb a slip placed further back in the book. It may also be possible that a patron or shelver may inadvertently move the book without examining it, causing the slip to shift or fall out. Depending on how one wants to define "use," the slip method may give an overestimate of use as serious as the underestimate of the table count. Harris found that the slip method yielded an in-house use to circulation ratio more than 10 times that yielded at the same library when using a table count.

PATRON QUESTIONNAIRES

In the most extensive study conducted to date, use of a questionnaire was considered the best way to measure in-house use (Rubin, 1986a). Like the

EXHIBIT 5-1   Placement of the questionnaire when using the slip method. Reprinted from Taylor (1976–1977), courtesy of Haworth Press.

table count and slip methods, questionnaires allow categorization by a variety of factors relating to the specific items used. Moreover, they are not affected by patron reshelving and can record repeated uses of the same item. The questionnaire method requires minimal training of staff, takes little of the patron's time to complete, and is relatively easy to administer (Rubin, 1986b). Perhaps its greatest strength is that it can be used to obtain relevant information about the patrons themselves. Data can be collected to show various demographic characteristics of those who use materials in-house, to provide correlations between patrons and uses (for example, who uses bound periodicals, who uses physics periodicals, how much use is made of physics materials by faculty and students in other departments), and to indicate the extent to which the library's facilities are being used without concomitant use of library materials (Lancaster, 1988). Questionnaires have also been used to determine whether or not readers find anything of value in the works they consult (Taylor, 1976–1977).

Questionnaires can either be placed in a random set of books under study or distributed by staff to patrons entering the library. Fussler and Simon (1969) followed the former practice, arranging each questionnaire in a manner similar to that of the slips described above. The questionnaire asks the user of the book to complete the questionnaire and place it in a designated location.

Ensuring the cooperation of patrons in completing the questionnaires is vital. Fussler and Simon attempted to do this by taping half of the questionnaires, in alternate books, to ball-point pens that provided both a writing instrument and a token reward. Use of the pens was found to have a significant positive effect on the return of questionnaires.

The other method of distributing questionnaires uses library staff (or volunteers) to urge patron cooperation. The staff give patrons entering the library short questionnaires (Exhibit 5-2) and ask them to record information on all items used in-house but not checked out. If no items are used in-house, the patron simply checks the box stating this. The staff then collect the questionnaires as patrons leave. This form of questionnaire distribution allows researchers to determine how many people cooperate. Nevertheless, it does not necessarily allow one to estimate total in-house use because it is not known whether those who use materials in-house are more likely to cooperate by completing the form than those who do not.

As with any method of evaluation, questionnaires have their drawbacks. The results will be good only if the questions are clearly and unambiguously worded and if patrons answer truthfully and accurately. Moreover, some questionnaires ask the library patron to interpret the word "use," thus allowing for ambiguity of interpretation. Ambiguity may be somewhat counteracted by giving a precise definition of use within the questionnaire itself. The cost of continually distributing, collecting, and analyzing questionnaires may also be prohibitive. The library can reduce this cost by conducting the study only for a representative number of days that the library is open.

PATRON INTERVIEWS

The patron interview has all the advantages of the questionnaire: it allows categorization of materials used in-house, collection of information on patrons, and detection of uses that might otherwise be uncounted. Interviews can be conducted with patrons who are leaving the library, simply by asking them to list items they used in-house. Alternately, evaluators can conduct interviews based on a random sampling of the library's seating pattern (Daiute and Gorman, 1974). First, the evaluator gives every chair in a library where a user could be seated an identifying number (Exhibit 5-3). Time slots are established for interviewing users (selected times on selected days in selected weeks), then a sequence of seat numbers is randomly assigned to each time slot. During each time slot, an interviewer approaches the first seat thus identified. If a user is present, he or she is interviewed. If not, the interviewer proceeds to the next seat indicated, and so on, until a user is located (Exhibit 5-4). This procedure has an advantage in that it can readily identify users who bring their own materials for study in the library. On the other hand, it is somewhat more difficult to extrapolate from the complex sample to the total number of in-library uses of materials in a specified period. Moreover, this method gives no indication of materials used by a patron who is not seated.

Interviews tend to be more expensive than the other methods of determining in-house use. Interviewers must be carefully trained and, unless volunteers are available, they must be paid for the extensive amount of time involved in interviewing. Interviews also can produce biased data because some subjects may try to give the responses that they think the interviewer wants.

Illinois Public Library Cooperative Research Group User Survey

Please answer the following questions to help us improve service. Do not sign your name.

1. HOW MANY BOOKS OR OTHER MATERIALS ARE YOU BORROWING
   FROM THE LIBRARY TODAY?.. _____

2. DID YOU USE ANY LIBRARY MATERIALS IN THE LIBRARY TODAY?   Yes _____
   (If "No," go to Question 4.)   No _____

3. When people use books, magazines and other materials in the library, they may look at them for just a few minutes or they may use them for a longer period of time. Below is a chart which we would like you to fill out. Please tell us HOW MANY fiction, nonfiction, reference books and non-book materials you used today and tell us how long you used them by putting your answers under the columns with time limits at the top.

	NUMBER used under 2 min.	NUMBER used 2 to 10 min.	NUMBER used 10 or more min.
Fiction books/novels	_____	_____	_____
Circulating nonfiction books	_____	_____	_____
Reference books	_____	_____	_____
Non-book materials (magazines, newspapers, phonorecords, microfilm, etc.)	_____	_____	_____

4. ARE YOU MALE OR FEMALE? .... Male 1
                                                     Female 2

5. WHAT IS YOUR PRINCIPAL OCCUPATION? (Circle one number)
   a. Professional (teacher, engineer, accountant, etc.) 1
   b. Manager or proprietor (farm owner, store manager, etc.) 2
   c. Clerical or sales 3
   d. Unskilled, semi-skilled or skilled worker (farm laborer,
      carpenter, factory operative, etc.) 4
   e. Student, at any level 5
   f. Housewife 6
   g. Retired or unemployed 7
   h. Other (what? _____) 8

6. HOW FAR HAVE YOU GONE IN SCHOOL? (Circle one number)
   a. No more than completion of elementary school 1
   b. Some or all of high school 2
   c. Some or all of college 3
   d. Study beyond 4 years of college 4

7. IN WHAT AGE GROUP ARE YOU? .... Less than 20 1
                                                    20 – 39 2
                                                    40 – 59 3
                                                    60 or over 4

Thank you for answering these questions. Please put this form in the box provided for that purpose.

EXHIBIT 5-2 Self-administered patron survey of in-house use. Reprinted from Rubin (1986a), courtesy of the University of Illinois, Graduate School of Library and Information Science.

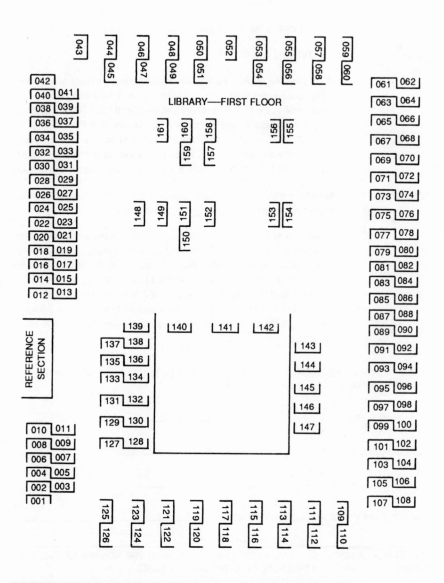

EXHIBIT 5-3 **Assignment of identifying numbers to all seats in the library.**
Reprinted from Daiute and Gorman (1974), courtesy of Oceana Publications.

INSTRUCTIONS: At the time designated below, report to the first library carrel listed. Before proceeding with the interview, the interviewee must meet the following requirements:

1. Seated at the designated carrel.

2. Reading any <u>BOOK</u>.

Then, proceed to obtain the desired information. If reader is a student, obtain student's name, campus address, and full bibliographical description of book, including library call number if book is a library book. Other information on the student can be obtained at the Office of the Dean of Students at a later time. If reader of book is not a student, obtain name and address of the reader, as well as purpose for reading the book. Also, of course, obtain full bibliographical description of book.

REMEMBER: At no time is the normal function of the library to be interrupted. Conduct interviews as <u>QUIETLY</u> and <u>QUICKLY</u> as possible.

SPECIAL NOTE: There is a high probability that you will find a reader at one of the five carrels. If you are unable to find a qualified interviewee at the first carrel listed, proceed to the second listed carrel. If still unable to find a qualified person, proceed to the third listed number, and so forth. If unable to find a suitable interviewee at any of the designated carrels, indicate this fact and the reason at the bottom of this page in the space provided. It should be understood that your interview activities will be monitored.

IT IS OF EXTREME IMPORTANCE THAT THE INTERVIEW BE HELD AT THE DESIGNATED TIME. PLEASE BE PROMPT.

DESIGNATED TIME: _____

DESIGNATED CARRELS: 1. _____   2. _____   3. _____

4. _____   5. _____

UNABLE TO FIND A QUALIFIED INTERVIEWEE: _____

THE UPPER NUMBER ON THE GUMMED LABEL REFERS TO THE NUMBER OF THE INNER CARREL. THE LOWER NUMBER REFERS TO THE OUTER CARREL.

EXHIBIT 5-4   Instructions and interview schedule used when selecting and interviewing patrons, based on a random sampling of the library's seating pattern. Reprinted from Daiute and Gorman (1974), courtesy of Oceana Publications.

EXHIBIT 5-4 *(Continued)*

Name of Interviewer: _____

Time of Interview: _____

Number of Carrel: _____

Name of Reader: _____

Sex of Reader: _____

_____

Complete Bibliographical Description of Book Being Read: _____

_____

_____

_____

_____

_____

_____

_____

_____

_____

Name of Author: _____

Title of Book: _____

Place of Publication: _____ Name of Publisher: _____

Date of Publication: _____

Library Call Number on Book: _____

Place of Residence: Dormitory ☐ Sorority ☐ Fraternity ☐ or Off-Campus ☐

Academic Average of Reader: _____ Major Field of Study: _____

Freshman ☐ Sophmore ☐ Junior ☐ Senior ☐ Evening School Student ☐

Graduate School Student ☐

UNOBTRUSIVE OBSERVATION

One interesting attempt at a different method of evaluating in-house use was made in the Coalition for Public Library Research study (Rubin, 1986a, 1986b). Observers were assigned to record the use behavior of patrons who entered designated sections of the library. Observers were limited to 30 minutes per patron and were asked to record the sex, approximate age, number of items, and types of materials used (Exhibit 5-5). The unobtrusive evaluations were conducted for one day in each of six consecutive months.

Unfortunately, this method failed to provide as much useful information as was originally thought. For example, observers could not always determine exactly which item was being used; rather, they could tell its broad type. Thus, although unobtrusive observation can provide information on the total use of audiovisual as well as print information, it does not give the detailed information on the exact materials used that the other methods do. Moreover, some estimates made by the observer, such as patron age, are necessarily less accurate. Finally, Rubin (1986b) noted that unobtrusive observation failed to produce accurate data on in-house use because observers, who were asked to remain in their assigned sections throughout the study, could not determine how many items were checked out by the subjects. Many observers also found the method "uncomfortable."

MAJOR FINDINGS OF STUDIES ON IN-HOUSE USE

Since 1960, more than 20 in-house use studies have been covered in the library literature. Several consistent sets of findings have been reported and are discussed in this section.

The Level of In-House Use Varies Among Libraries

One major finding is that in-house use varies from library to library, just as circulation does. In fact, in the studies reviewed for this chapter, ratios of in-house use to circulation ranged from 0.1:1 to 11.2:1. Several reasons can be offered for the variation. Some of these relate not to the nature of in-house use itself, but to how the researchers collected their data. For example, Goldhor (1979) noted that the use of table counts results in lower ratios of in-house use than other methods. This was confirmed in the Coalition for Public Library Research study (Rubin, 1986a, 1986b). The study was designed to compare different methods of collecting in-house data and was conducted at six public libraries in the United States. Results showed that table counts produce lower ratios of in-house use to external circulation than either the interview or the questionnaire method (see Exhibit 5-6). The average ratio for table counts was 0.5:1; for interviews, 1:1; and for questionnaires, 1.2:1 (Rubin, 1986a, 1986b).

SECTION UNDER OBSERVATION ———————————————————————

INDIVIDUAL UNDER OBSERVATION ———————————————————————

1. Sex   M   F

2. Age ———————

For EACH item used specify:

TYPE OF MATERIAL	TIME USED	NATURE OF USE
(fiction, nonfiction, magazine, newspaper, record, tape, etc.)		
———————————	————	———————————
———————————	————	———————————
———————————	————	———————————
———————————	————	———————————
———————————	————	———————————
———————————	————	———————————
———————————	————	———————————
———————————	————	———————————
———————————	————	———————————
———————————	————	———————————

DURATION OF OBSERVATION ————————————————————

DATE OF OBSERVATION ————————————————————

NAME OF OBSERVER ————————————————————

EXHIBIT 5-5 Form used in unobtrusive observation of in-house use. Reprinted from Rubin (1986a), courtesy of the University of Illinois, Graduate School of Library and Information Science.

Library	Table Count	Questionnaires	Interviews
All libraries	0.7	1.2	1.0
Arlington Heights (Illinois)	0.3	0.9	0.8
Dauphin County (Pennsylvania)	0.1	0.8	0.7
Iowa City	0.6	1.7	1.2
Minneapolis	0.9	1.2	1.2
Rockingham County (North Carolina)	0.5	0.8	0.4
Dallas	0.7*	1.0	1.5

*Table counts based on data collected prior to the study and annualized over a 5-year period.

EXHIBIT 5-6   Comparison of the rates of in-house use obtained with three methods of data collection. Reprinted from Rubin (1986b), courtesy of the American Library Association.

The differences are attributable largely to the varying definitions of in-house use associated with each method.

Rates of in-house use also vary by the format of the material included in the studies. Studies that measure in-house use of noncirculating periodicals and microforms as well as circulating books will produce higher use ratios than those that only measure books. Other differences pertaining to the nature of the library itself may influence the level of in-house use recorded. For example, Stockard, Griffin, and Coblyn (1978) suggested that the subject content of the library's collection may influence the degree of in-house use. These researchers used similar measurement techniques to determine in-house use in a mathematics and science-oriented academic library and in two general university libraries with extensive humanities and social sciences collections. Noting the much larger use ratios obtained at the former, they suggested that the overall degree of in-library use would be lower in academic libraries with broader subject scope than in libraries that are primarily mathematics or science oriented. This makes sense, considering how people use each of these types of materials. Some items, for example, classic works of literature, tend to be used in their entirety and thus lend themselves to being checked out rather than perused within the library. Other items often are used by patrons to obtain just one piece of information (for example, a statistics text used only to obtain the formula for the chi-square statistic).

This higher level of in-house use may apply by type of material as well as by subject. Indeed,

the shorter the reading time for a given work or the more diverse its contents, the less likely it is to be withdrawn. For example, if a reader is interested in scanning one short article in a large serial volume, he might not bother to withdraw the book. Dictionaries are a good example of books unlikely to be withdrawn; the information they contain is diverse, and use is normally brief. (Fussler and Simon, 1969, p. 107)

A related finding in two separate studies is that in-house use is substantially higher in urban public libraries, where patrons are seeking specific subjects, than in suburban public libraries (Gers, 1982; Goldhor, 1979). This was true even though the suburban libraries studied had considerably higher external rates of circulation per capita.

Other library practices also appear to be capable of affecting the extent of in-library use. For example, a library that places large numbers of its books in reference or on closed reserve, rather than releasing them for circulation, could expect to experience more in-house use. The degree of accessibility to the stacks, the level of seating provided, and the ready availability of photocopying machines within the library have also been mentioned as possible factors that can affect the degree of in-house use. No researchers, however, have determined the exact effect of these variables on in-house use.

Rubin (1986a) hypothesized that four other factors might be good predictors of in-house use in public libraries: (1) the number of reference questions asked, (2) the visitor count, (3) the number of full-time public service staff employed, and (4) the size of the acquisitions budget. Strong positive correlations were obtained for each of these variables. As Rubin noted, this is not surprising because

it is reasonable to assume that the greater number of individuals coming into the library, or the greater the number of reference questions asked, the more likely that materials would be used in the library . . . [And] larger budgets should allow the library to purchase more titles for use and employ more public service staff thus increasing the likelihood of in-house use. (p. 63)

Rubin, however, cautioned that the manner in which ratios between in-house use and some of these variables were calculated imposes limitations on the conclusions drawn; he suggested that in-library use be measured directly rather than using other variables to predict it.

Stockard, Griffin, and Coblyn (1978) noted that

the wide range of in-library to circulation ratios . . . reinforces [the idea] that any library administrator, desiring a figure to be used in conjunction with circulation counts as an indicator of use, will benefit little from the numbers reported in published studies of other libraries. (p. 141)

A review of the studies conducted during the last 20 years confirms this; a librarian who wants to know the ratio of in-house use to circulation should not rely on average figures reported in the literature; rather a separate study should be performed to obtain these data for a particular library.

Ratios of in-house use to circulation remain fairly constant over time, unless the characteristics of the library or the community it serves change drastically (Lancaster, 1982). In other words, if a survey reveals that three items are used in the library for each item borrowed, it is likely that this ratio will hold for some time.

Books Used In-House Are Those that Circulate, and Vice Versa

If one excludes items that are not allowed to leave the library, then the items used within a library probably will not differ much from items that are borrowed. Indeed, a substantial body of evidence suggests that both the general subjects and the individual books used within a library are more or less the same as those borrowed for use outside the library (Lancaster, 1988).

Very strong correlations have been found between the subject matter of books borrowed from the library and that of books used within the library. McGrath (1971) counted the subject matter of books in two ways: (1) within finely delineated Library of Congress (LC) and Dewey class spans relating to academic departments and (2) within the framework most libraries use for their daily circulation counts—the first and second letters of LC and the 10s of Dewey. In the first case, he discovered a correlation of + .86 between circulation and in-house use of the subjects; in the second, he found a correlation of + .84. In related studies in Pennsylvania and Texas, Bommer (1972) and Domas (1978) both found average correlations of + .92. Other authors who have noted the similarities between circulation and in-house use of items by subject include Brooks (1981), Jain et al. (1967), and Kent et al. (1979).

For use of individual titles, Fussler and Simon (1969) were among the first to discover that circulation may be a reasonably good predictor of in-library use. They found, for example, that books that averaged two recorded uses every five years could be expected to average twice as many nonrecorded uses as a group of books that averaged one recorded use every five years. Kent et al. also concluded that borrowing and in-house use were similar when they discovered that three-quarters of the books used in an academic library during a 30-day period had also been borrowed.

Furthermore, no circulation tends to mean no in-house use, as documented by Hardesty (1981), Harris (1977), and Hindle and Buckland (1978). In a small academic library in England, Harris found that approximately 18 percent of the collection accounted for all in-library use, approximately 45 percent accounted for all circulation, and some 51 percent accounted for all use. In other words, only an additional 6 percent of the collection was needed beyond the circulating portion to account for all use.

Some authors (for example, Hayes, 1981a, 1981b; Lawrence and Oja, 1980) suggested that because in-house use and circulation do not exactly agree, in-house use is not as good a predictor of circulation as one would want. These authors, however, failed to consider that demand for a popular title may actually cause this slight discrepancy. In other words,

insofar as in-library use is conditioned by what happens to be available on the shelves, whether because it is browsing not directed at known titles or because the user falls back on what is at hand rather than fill out reservations for absent items, the pattern of in-library use will be influenced by what is available. . . In effect, a library with low standards of availability will cause a higher proportion of in-library use to fall on the unpopular (i.e., least circulated) materials. (Hindle and Buckland, 1978, p. 273)

Age of Materials Used	Frequency (number)	Frequency (percent)	Cumulative Frequency (percent)
1983*	66	5.9	5.9
1982	334	29.7	35.6
1981	172	15.3	50.9
1980	103	9.2	60.0
1979	46	4.1	64.1
1978	44	3.9	68.1
1977	39	3.5	71.5
1976	43	3.8	75.4
1975	31	2.8	78.1
1974	17	1.5	79.6
1973	23	2.0	81.7
1972	14	1.2	82.9
1971	16	1.4	84.3
1970	7	0.6	85.0
1960–1969	66	5.9	90.8
1950–1959	21	1.9	92.7
1940–1949	14	1.2	94.0
1930–1939	37	3.3	97.2
1920–1929	3	0.3	97.5
1910–1919	5	0.4	98.0
1900–1909	8	0.7	98.7
Pre-1900	15	1.3	100.0
Total	1,124		

*Because this retrospective study began early in 1983, frequencies for this year are based on only a few months of use.

EXHIBIT 5-7   Age and frequency of in-house use for government publications. Adapted from Cook (1985), courtesy of the *Journal of Academic Librarianship*.

Occupation	Number of People Surveyed with this Occupation	Percentage of People with this Occupation Using Materials In-house	Percentage of People with this Occupation Not Using Materials In-house
Unemployed	334	71	29
Manager	296	67	33
Student	1,334	65	35
Laborer	654	64	36
Professional	1,934	63	37
Retiree	581	62	38
Clerical worker	613	61	39
Homemaker	615	50	50

EXHIBIT 5-8   Occupation of respondents using materials in the library ($n =$ 6,377). Reprinted from Rubin (1986a), courtesy of the University of Illinois, Graduate School of Library and Information Science.

The work of Fussler and Simon (1969) supported Hindle and Buckland's claim.

In-house Use Decreases with the Age of the Item

It is a well-established fact that an individual item's circulation tends to decrease with age. Several studies have shown a similar pattern for in-house use. Cook (1985) found that use of government publications within the library declines rapidly with an item's age (see Exhibit 5-7), and a comparable pattern has been observed for use of journals (for example, Perk and Van Pulis, 1977; Sullivan et al., 1980–1981; Tibbetts, 1974).

Patrons Who Use Materials In-house

The Coalition for Public Library Research study of in-house use in six public libraries produced data on the people who use materials within libraries (Rubin, 1986a). Between 47 percent and 63 percent of the adult patrons visiting these libraries used materials in-house, as did 67 percent of the children. This substantiates the belief of some library administrators that the full extent of in-house use should be reported to those responsible for the funding of libraries.

The coalition's study documented that patrons in different occupational groups tend to use materials differently. As Exhibit 5-8 shows, unemployed people used more materials in-house than any other group, appearing to depend more on the reference and informational materials of the library than other occupational groups (Rubin, 1986a). In fact, 39 percent of the unemployed people who were using the library said they had come to the library specifically to use materials there. Homemakers (who read a very high percentage of fiction) show a disproportionately low use of materials in-house, and men in general (who use nonfiction materials more heavily) are significantly more likely than women to use materials in the library. No other factors have been shown to influence levels of in-house use, although at least two authors suggest that, in academic libraries, doctoral students and faculty are much more likely than undergraduates to use materials in-house (Hindle and Buckland, 1978).

REFERENCES

Bommer, Michael R. W. "The Development of a Management System for Effective Decision Making and Planning in a University Library." Doctoral Dissertation. Philadelphia, Pa., University of Pennsylvania, Wharton School of Finance and Commerce, 1972. ERIC ED071727

Brooks, Terrence A. "An Analysis of Library-Output Statistics." Doctoral Dissertation. Austin, Tex., University of Texas, 1981.

Cook, Kevin L. "Circulation and In-Library Use of Government Publications." *Journal of Academic Librarianship, 11*(3):146–150, July 1985.

Daiute, Robert J., and Kenneth A. Gorman. *Library Operations Research.* Dobbs Ferry, N.Y., Oceana Publications, 1974.

Domas, Ralph E. "Correlating the Classes of Books Taken Out of and Books Used Within an Open-Stack Library." San Antonio, Tex., San Antonio College Library, 1978. ERIC ED171282

Elston, C. "Survey of In-Library Use in MIT Science Library." Cambridge, Mass., Massachusetts Institute of Technology, 1966. (Unpublished Term Report, Operations Research Course 8.75)

Fussler, Herman H., and Julian L. Simon. *Patterns in the Use of Books in Large Research Libraries.* Chicago, Ill., University of Chicago Press, 1969.

Gers, Ralph. "Output Measurement in Maryland: Book Availability and User Satisfaction." *Public Libraries, 21*(3):77–80, Fall 1982.

Goldhor, Herbert. "The Relationship of Books Borrowed to In-Library Use of Books." Urbana, Ill., University of Illinois, Graduate School of Library Science, 1979. (Unpublished Manuscript)

Hardesty, Larry. "Use of Library Materials at a Small Liberal Arts College." *Library Research, 3*(3):261–282, Fall 1981.

Harris, C. "A Comparison of Issues and In-Library Use of Books." *Aslib Proceedings, 29*(3):118–126, March 1977.

Hayes, Robert M. "Application of a Mixture of Poisson Distributions to Data on the Use of Library Materials." In: *The Information Community—An Alliance for Progress: Proceedings of the 44th American Society for Information Science Annual Meeting, Washington, D.C., October 25–30, 1981.* Vol. 18. Edited by Lois F. Lunin, Madeline Henderson, and Harold Wooster. White Plains, N.Y., Knowledge Industry Publications, 1981a, pp. 295–297.

142   THE MEASUREMENT AND EVALUATION OF LIBRARY SERVICES

_____. "The Distribution of Use of Library Materials: Analysis of Data from the University of Pittsburgh." *Library Research*, 3(3):215–260, Fall 1981b.

Hindle, Anthony, and Michael K. Buckland. "In-Library Book Usage in Relation to Circulation." *Collection Management*, 2(4):265–277, Winter 1978.

Jain, Aridaman K., et al. *Report on a Statistical Study of Book Use.* Lafayette, Ind., Purdue University, School of Industrial Engineering, 1967.

Kent, Allen, et al. *Use of Library Materials: the University of Pittsburgh Study.* New York, Marcel Dekker, 1979.

Lancaster, F. W. "Evaluating Collections by Their Use." *Collection Management*, 4(1/2):15–43, Spring/Summer 1982.

_____. *If You Want to Evaluate Your Library.* . . Champaign, Ill., University of Illinois, Graduate School of Library and Information Science, 1988.

Lawrence, Gary S., and Anne R. Oja. "The Use of the General Collections at the University of California." Berkeley, Calif., University of California, 1980.

McGrath, William E. "Correlating the Subjects of Books Taken Out of and Books Used Within an Open-Stack Library." *College and Research Libraries*, 32(4):280–285, July 1971.

Morse, Philip M. *Library Effectiveness: A Systems Approach.* Cambridge, Mass., MIT Press, 1968.

Perk, Lawrence J., and Noelle Van Pulis. "Periodical Usage in an Education-Psychology Library." *College and Research Libraries*, 38(4):304–308, July 1977.

Rubin, Richard. *In-House Use of Materials in Public Libraries.* Urbana, Ill., University of Illinois, Graduate School of Library and Information Science, 1986a.

_____. "Measuring the In-House Use of Materials in Public Libraries." *Public Libraries*, 25(4):137–138, Winter 1986b.

Shaw, W. M., Jr. "A Practical Journal Usage Technique." *College and Research Libraries*, 39(6):479–484, November 1978.

_____. "A Journal Resource Sharing Strategy." *Library Research*, 1(1):19–29, Spring 1979.

Slote, Stanley J. *Weeding Library Collections.* 2nd Edition. Littleton, Colo., Libraries Unlimited, 1982.

Stockard, Joan; Mary Ann Griffin; and Clementine Coblyn. "Document Exposure Counts in Three Academic Libraries: Circulation and In-Library Use." In: *Quantitative Measurement and Dynamic Library Service.* Edited by Ching-Chih Chen. Phoenix, Ariz., Oryx Press, 1978, pp. 136–147.

Sullivan, Michael V., et al. "Obsolescence in Biomedical Journals: Not an Artifact of Literature Growth." *Library Research*, 2(1):29–45, Spring 1980–1981.

Taylor, Colin R. "A Practical Solution to Weeding University Library Periodicals Collections." *Collection Management*, 1(3/4):27–45, Fall/Winter 1976–1977.

Tibbetts, Pamela. "A Method for Estimating the In-House Use of the Periodical Collection in the University of Minnesota Bio-Medical Library." *Bulletin of the Medical Library Association*, 62(1):37–48, January 1974.

Wenger, Charles B., and Judith Childress. "Journal Evaluation in a Large Research Library." *Journal of the American Society for Information Science*, 28(5):293–299, September 1977.

CHAPTER 6

EVALUATION OF
MATERIALS AVAILABILITY

Availability studies assess a library's ability to provide patrons with the documents they need at the time they need them. Specifically, availability rates, or fill rates, measure the probability that an item sought by a patron will be in the collection, be found in the catalog, be on the shelves, and be found on the shelves. Four major barriers may decrease the chance that an item is available: (1) the library may not own the needed item, (2) another patron may be using the item, (3) a library error (for example, misshelving) may prevent the item from being located, and (4) a patron error (for example, misreading the call number) may prevent the item from being located (Kantor, 1976). In other words, each availability study combines evaluations of the collection and of catalog use (discussed in detail in Chapters 3, 4, 5, and 7) with an evaluation of patron knowledge about how to use the library and an evaluation of library practices that may inhibit access.

The probability that a patron can actually find an item on a library's shelves is the cumulative probability that the patron successfully made it past the four barriers noted above. Kantor (1976) and Saracevic, Shaw, and Kantor (1977) were the first to illustrate this through the use of a branching diagram of the type shown in Exhibit 6-1. The number of requests received by the library is indicated at the top of the diagram. Listed at the far left side of each branch is the number of items that passed a particular barrier; the number that did not pass is listed at the far right side of each branch. Listed immediately below each branch is the probability that the barrier would *not* inhibit patron access in a particular library. The probabilities are calculated by dividing the number of items that made it past the barrier by the number of items that approached the barrier. The product of these probabilities is the overall fill rates—the probability that a patron approaching a particular library with a request for a particular item will leave satisfied.

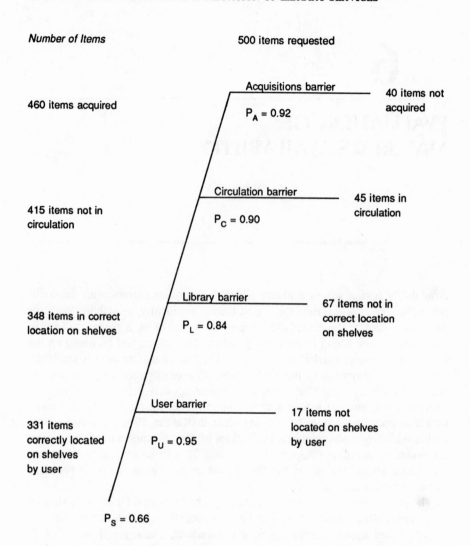

Number of Items   500 items requested

                                                     Acquisitions barrier   40 items not
460 items acquired   acquired
                                                     $P_A = 0.92$

                                                     Circulation barrier   45 items in
415 items not in   circulation
circulation $P_C = 0.90$

                                                     Library barrier   67 items not in
348 items in correct   correct location
location on shelves $P_L = 0.84$ on shelves

                                                     User barrier   17 items not
331 items   located on shelves
correctly located $P_U = 0.95$ by user
on shelves
by user

                             $P_S = 0.66$

where:

P_A = probability of acquisition; P_C = probability that an owned book is not circulating; P_L = probability that an owned book is not circulating and is correctly shelved; P_U = probability that a user has correctly located an owned book on the shelf; and P_S = overall probability that a user finds a sought item.

EXHIBIT 6-1   Branching diagram showing the probability of a user finding a particular item sought. Adapted from Kantor (1976), courtesy of John Wiley and Sons.

In Exhibit 6-1, 92 percent of the books requested at a specific time have been acquired, 90 percent of those are not in circulation, 84 percent of the books not in circulation are actually on the shelves, and 95 percent of the shelved items are located—in the catalog and on the shelves—by patrons. The overall probability rate is $0.92 \times 0.90 \times 0.84 \times 0.95$, which equals 0.66. In other words, in 66 cases out of 100, the patrons of this library are likely to find, on the shelves, the specific items for which they are searching.

Mansbridge (1986) studied findings from more than 40 availability studies conducted in all types of libraries and published during the last 50 years. The fill rates in these libraries ranged from 8 percent to 89 percent and averaged 61 percent. Kuraim (1983) focused on availability studies performed in public libraries. On the average, he found that 50 percent of patron requests were unfilled, even though the public libraries in which the studies were conducted owned 90 percent of the requested titles. The fact that the average fill rates in both studies were relatively low implies that libraries are doing an inadequate job of making owned titles readily available to patrons at the time they are needed. The remainder of this chapter covers how availability studies are conducted and how librarians can use study findings to make improvements.

CONDUCTING AVAILABILITY STUDIES

The first step in an availability study is to select a sample of documents to be used as the basis for the study. Several evaluators have tried to determine how large the sample must be so as to be highly confident that the library's availability score will not vary more than ± 5 points on repeated tests with different samples, unless the availability rate of the library has actually changed between tests. The consensus is that the evaluator should use a sample that contains 300–500 documents (for example, Kantor, 1984; Orr et al., 1968).

The evaluator could compile a list of citations to documents that are presumed to represent the needs of library patrons (a citation-based availability study). Alternatively, the evaluator could ask library patrons to record documents sought during a specified period of time (a patron-based availability study). In either instance, the evaluator notes how often the item was successfully located and, if it was not located, determines why not. Each type of study is discussed in the sections that follow.

The Citation-based Availability Study

The citation-based availability test is an evaluation of both the library's holdings and the availability of items owned; in effect, it is a collection evaluation of the list-checking type (discussed in detail in Chapter 3) carried one step further. To perform such studies, the evaluator creates citation pools—sets of bibliographic items cited in titles that are considered representative of all publications in the subject fields being examined. Most evaluators choose citations from titles that are selected by experts in a field (for example, see Wilson, 1974) or that appear in journals, indexes, abstracts, or general bibliographies in that field (for example, see Murfin, 1980). The evaluator could also choose citations from a standard group of selection tools, as Greenberg (1981) did when evaluating the availability of materials in secondary school libraries.

Compiling a representative set of citations to check against a collection is difficult, particularly when one is trying to measure the availability of items spread over a wide range of subjects in a particular library. Assume that one is checking the availability of journal articles and wants a sample of 300 citations drawn at random from a larger pool of 2,000 citations. A group of recently published articles in a particular subject field could be used to generate the citation pool. If each article contained an average of five citations, a sample of 400 recent articles would form the pool.

It is possible, of course, to select the 400 articles at random from current issues of journals on the shelves of the library to be evaluated. But since many journals have a strong tendency to cite themselves, the citation pool may be biased. It may include a greater proportion of citations to journals held by the library than would be true of a sample drawn some other way. This problem could be avoided by drawing the sample of 400 articles from recent issues of journals on the shelves of a second library, one that is not being evaluated. This second library should be larger than, or at least of comparable size to, the one being evaluated.

Let us assume that this second approach is adopted and that the library chosen to be the source of recent articles subscribes to 60 journals in the field being examined—agriculture. The current issues of all 60 journals are displayed on the open shelves. If the last 7 articles published in each journal are taken, there will be 420 articles. If each article contains an average of 5 citations, a sample of 2,100 citations will be obtained from which to draw the final set of 300 by systematic random sampling.

What can be said about the sample that has been drawn? First, it is a random sample of sources cited by authors contributing to a selected group of agricultural journals. Because it is a random sample, it will represent these sources in proportions (for example, by type of publication, by language of publication, by date of publication) close to which they are cited in the current literature. The extent to which this sample can be accepted as a reasonable approximation of the document needs of a particular library depends on the degree to which the supposition can be accepted that the sources cited in the current literature are those most likely to be brought to the attention of patrons and, thus, to be sought by them. This sample has two weaknesses. First, it will include few, if any, sources of the type that are unlikely to be cited (for example, news-type journals) but that may be needed and asked for by library patrons. Second, it will exclude references to very recently published literature, since the sources cited in current writings are likely to be at least a year old.

The lack of very recent sources may not be too detrimental when assessing the coverage of a library's collection. But it is a problem when assessing document availability because recent materials are those most likely to be in use and, thus, absent from the shelves. One way to compensate for this would be to deliberately include, as representatives of the more current literature, a sample of the current articles from which the citation pool was drawn.

To return to the example previously mentioned, after the 420 current articles have been used to generate the 2,100 citations and, subsequently, the subset of 300, 50 (for instance) of the 420 could be selected at random and used as a supplementary set to assess the availability of the recently published journal literature. In effect, two citation pools would be created, one of 300 items and one of 50, and the results achieved by each group could be compared. The smaller group is really introducing a "correction factor" to account for the more recent literature. To the extent that this group includes journals of the type that are unlikely to be cited, the sample will allow the library's performance on these journals to be compared with its performance on the other items. If there are no significant differences, this factor need not be considered a defect in the total sample.

It is more difficult to draw a citation sample that is meaningful when evaluating the coverage of some broad collection (for example, that of a public library) than it is to evaluate the coverage of a collection with a narrow subject focus. In one of the first availability studies conducted in public libraries, De Prospo, Altman, and Beasley (1973) used a random sample of 500 recently published books from the *American Book Publishing Record* as the major citation pool. This sample is of doubtful utility. Because it is drawn completely at random from everything published in the United States, it measures nothing more than a library's ability to select at random. It is likely to include, for instance, many rather obscure or esoteric items that would be unlikely to appear in any public library, even very large ones. In fact, high scores on this test are correlated with the size of the collection rather than with its quality or the appropriateness of the collection for the community served. When this sample is applied to a small public library, or even one of medium size, the few items found to be held will be completely inadequate for a subsequent analysis of shelf availability.[1] A better practice would be to use one or more selective bibliographies designed specifically for public libraries, such as *Fiction Catalog* and *Public Library Catalog;* this can be done only if the library has not used these as major book selection tools. Nor are the citations contained in these

---

[1] Tamraz (1984) made a similar error when he used a sample selected from *American Book Publishing Record* as the chief basis for an availability study conducted in three Saudi Arabian university libraries.

bibliographies necessarily representative of demands that public library patrons make, because the compilers of these two bibliographies consider a number of factors in addition to patron demand when selecting titles for inclusion.

A few evaluators have used, as the basis of their citation pools, lists of documents that were generated by the selective dissemination of information (SDI) services that a library offers or during online searches that are conducted for library patrons. This type of study has some validity. As patron access to online searching and SDI services increases, so does patron demand for specific items. If this demand cannot be met, patrons will justifiably be dissatisfied with the library. Evaluators, however, should be cautioned. Studies of this nature that are based on the needs of a small number of users of SDI or online services may not yield data that are representative of the library's overall availability rates or even of the availability rates to be expected by users of SDI or online search services. Several evaluators have made this error. For instance, Bourne and Robinson (1973) used, as the basis for their citation pool, 680 citations contained in 23 SDI printouts generated by the Center for Information Services at the University of California, Los Angeles. These printouts represented the requests of only 13 users of the service—hardly a representative sample.

Other evaluators create their citation pools by drawing a systematic random sample from the library's own shelf list. This type of test measures only the availability of items owned. A shelf list sample is relatively cheap to compile and is useful when a library wishes to compare availability at different times during the year. Kaske (1973) and Schwarz (1983) showed that availability could vary greatly. This seems logical in view of changing patron demand patterns in some types of libraries. For example, demand in university libraries varies, depending on whether availability is measured during the first week of class, the middle of the semester, or the end of the semester; demand in public libraries is usually greatest in October and March. Shelf list samples also are helpful in determining potential sources of library error (for example, misshelving problems) that prevent materials from being found. Moreover, reconducting a shelf list study can enable an investigator to determine whether the problem has been corrected. For example, a library that replaces a three-day turnaround time for reshelving materials with a one-day turnaround could draw a second shelf list sample to see if material availability has increased significantly. Availability tests using shelf list samples are simple to apply, take only a few hours to carry out (after the sample is drawn), cause a minimum of disruption to the library being studied, and require no cooperation from the library's patrons.

Shelf list samples, however, have their problems. Because they are based on owned items, they reveal nothing about nonavailability due to acquisition gaps. And an availability study based on a shelf list sample actually biases the results in favor of the library. If the cumulative percentage of the use of a collection is plotted against the cumulative percentage of the collection accounting for this use, a small percentage of the total collection will be shown to account for a

Group*	Number in Circulation	Number on Shelf	Other	Total
Young	24	132	12	168
Middle-aged	1	154	13	168
Elderly	0	151	17	168
Total	25	437	42	504

Circulation availability	95.03968%
Circulation dysfunction	4.960317%
Other availability	91.23173%
Other dysfunction	8.768267%
Stack availability	86.70635%
Stack dysfunction	13.29365%

*Young items are those that had circulated within the last 18 months; middle-aged items had last circulation dates between 19 and 72 months; elderly items had not circulated in 72 months.

EXHIBIT 6-2   Naive results of a shelf list study of item availability with data sorted by last circulation date. Adapted from Schwarz (1983), courtesy of the American Library Association.

large percentage of all use—the 80/20 rule. But the shelf list sample will draw four books from the 80 percent of the collection that is little used for every one book it draws from the 20 percent that is heavily used. Because books in the little-used 80 percent are always likely to be on the shelves, the randomly drawn shelf list sample is likely to give an inflated availability figure, compared with actual availability as reflected by the real demands of library patrons.

Kantor (1981) suggested that this bias toward little-used items could be reduced if the "naive" results from the shelf list sample are weighted to reflect demand for titles that receive heavier use. Schwarz (1983) tested this assumption in a medium-sized academic library. Exhibit 6-2 shows the results of the availability study that was conducted using a sample of 504 titles. Items were grouped into three categories: (1) young items, which had circulated within the last 18 months; (2) middle-aged items, with a last circulation date of between 19 and 72 months; and (3) elderly items, which had not circulated in 72 months. The exhibit indicates the number of items in circulation for each group, the number in their correct locations on the shelves, and the number that were elsewhere (for example, missing, at the bindery, or in the reshelving area). The overall availability rate for the library, calculated from the branching analysis described earlier in this chapter, was 86.7 percent.

Exhibit 6-3 shows the data after they were adjusted to account for current demand. In this exhibit, a weighting factor was added to correct for the fact

| | Raw (Naive) Data | | | Weighting Factor | Adjusted Data | | |
Group*	Number in Circulation	Number on Shelf	Other		Number in Circulation	Number on Shelf	Other
Young	24	132	12	0.1666667	4.000000	22.00000	2.000000
Middle-aged	1	154	13	0.0059880	0.0059880	0.9221557	0.0778443
Elderly	0	151	17	0	0	0	0
Total	25	437	42		4.005988	22.92216	2.077844

Circulation availability	86.18910%
Circulation dysfunction	13.81090%
Other availability	92.83650%
Other dysfunction	7.163501%
Stack availability	79.02560%
Stack dysfunction	20.97440%

*Young items are those that had circulated within the last 18 months; middle-aged items had last circulation dates between 19 and 72 months; elderly items had not circulated in 72 months.

EXHIBIT 6-3   Weighted results of a shelf list study of item availability with data sorted by last circulation date. Adapted from Schwarz (1983), courtesy of the American Library Association.

that an item's demand actually exceeds its circulation, because patrons look for it even though it is not available. The weighting factor was calculated by dividing the number of items in circulation for the row by the number of items on the shelf and in the "other" category. The raw data in each category were then multiplied by the weighting factor to yield the adjusted data. The adjusted availability rate in this library was 79.0 percent.

Whatever the method of drawing the citation pool, an availability test based on citations and applied in a single day in a particular library essentially simulates patrons walking into the library that day, each patron looking for a particular bibliographic item. Again, the object is to determine whether each item is in the collection and, if so, where it is physically located at the time the test is administered.

The investigator enters the library with a set of forms, one form for each citation in the sample. Each citation is checked against the catalogs, lists of serials, and other tools to see if it is owned. If so, the investigator determines where the bibliographic item is located when the availability test is administered. The outcome of each search—that is, the location of each item sought—is recorded on the form.

All types of citation-based availability studies have some major weaknesses. They are valid only if the sample of citations chosen actually represents typical document needs of patrons. They fail to reflect that the lack of availability is often due to very large demands on a small number of items; failures due to the clumping of demand around such popular items will not be clearly identified in this type of study. Finally, they provide the evaluator with no information about patron skills at using the catalog or actually locating desired items. For many purposes, therefore, patron-based availability studies may be preferred.

Nevertheless, when a standard set of citations is used, a citation-based availability study is more valuable than a patron-based study in comparing two or more libraries, because results of patron-based studies may vary greatly in situations where patrons and demands at the libraries are different. Tamraz (1984) and Ajlan (1985) used standard sets of citations to compare availability rates at different academic libraries in Saudi Arabia.

The Patron-based Availability Study

Patron-based availability studies focus on the document needs that actual library patrons have during some specified period of observation. Evaluators can either study the document needs of all library patrons or focus on the needs of a random sample of patrons. Ideally, the study is designed to collect data on representative days of the year, since availability rates may vary at different times of the year (for example, see Kaske, 1973).

Data on availability often are collected through the use of a simple patron questionnaire such as the ones used by Whitlatch and Kieffer (1978) and Rinkel and McCandless (1983). The evaluator asks each patron entering the library to indicate, on a simple form, all items sought that day and all items found. The form should be short, to encourage a high response rate, and should contain brief printed instructions on exactly what the patron is to record; usually, patrons are asked to fill in the author and title and, for owned items, the call number. The form should be designed so that the patron who is not looking for specific materials but is using the library for some other reason can indicate this. Staff collect the forms, either personally or via a drop box, as patrons leave the library.

The quality of the evaluation study that uses patron questionnaires depends largely on the voluntary cooperation of as many patrons as possible. If few questionnaires are completed, the data collected will not reliably represent the demands of all patrons. This means that the evaluator needs to do everything possible to secure patron cooperation. For example, many evaluators post signs throughout the library, informing patrons that a study is in progress and that librarians request their cooperation. Most evaluators attempt to determine the total response rate, so they can determine how reliable the obtained data are. To do this, the evaluator simply divides the number of completed forms received by the total number of forms handed out during a particular period. The higher the response rate, the more reliable the data.

Most patron questionnaires emphasize only known-item requests; that is, most availability studies concentrate on determining success rates for particular items that patrons are seeking when they enter the library. It is easy to study whether or not the library filled a known-item request. Because the answer is objective, patrons simply record whether or not the item was found. It is more difficult to study how well a library meets demands related to a search for materials of a particular subject, class, or form. Wiemers (1981) attempted to do this by asking patrons to indicate whether they were searching for works about a particular subject (and if so, what) or for works of a particular form. A similar questionnaire, shown in Exhibit 6-4, has been promoted by the Public Library Association to determine subject fill rates (Van House et al., 1987). The association also uses the form to measure the fill rate for patrons browsing for "good" books to read. Although the promotion of these types of availability studies is laudable, such a simple questionnaire does not measure whether the patron's request for subject information or for a "good book" was filled satisfactorily. When patrons search for a document on a particular subject or of a particular type, they may find something that partially meets their need. To effectively determine subject or browsing fill rate, an evaluator would need to determine *how well* patron needs were met; this might involve interviewing patrons.

Clearly, subject fill rate is very important in libraries having many subject and browsing requests, compared with known-item requests. Numerous studies suggest that public libraries in particular have large numbers of patrons searching for materials on particular subjects or browsing for good books to read and

Form number _____

LIBRARY SURVEY

Library _____   Date _____

PLEASE FILL OUT THIS SURVEY AND RETURN IT AS YOU LEAVE

We want to know if you find what you look for in our libraries. Please list below what you looked for today. Mark "YES" if you found it, and "NO" if you did not find it.

TITLE

If you are looking for a specific book, record, cassette, newspaper, or issue of a magazine, please write the title below. Include any reserve material picked up.

NAME OF WORK (Example) • Gone with the Wind	FOUND? YES NO
1.	
2.	
3.	
4.	
5.	

SUBJECT OR AUTHOR

If you are looking for materials or information on a particular subject or a special author today, please note each subject or person below.

SUBJECT OR AUTHOR (Examples) • how to repair a toaster • any book by John D. MacDonald	DID YOU FIND SOMETHING? YES NO
1.	
2.	
3.	
4.	
5.	

BROWSING If you were browsing and not looking for anything specific, did you find something of interest?

YES _____   NO _____

OTHER _____ Check here if your visit today did *not* include any of the above activities.

(Example) using the photocopy machine

COMMENTS We would appreciate any comments on our service and collections on the back of this sheet.

THANK YOU!

EXHIBIT 6-4   Materials availability survey form. Reprinted from Van House et al. (1987), courtesy of the American Library Association.

fewer known-item requests, whereas school, academic, and special libraries receive significantly more of the latter. Measuring subject and browsing fill rates separately also is important when such rates are substantially different from known-item fill rates in a particular library, but few evaluators have tried to determine to what extent such differences exist. Logically, the chances of finding a specific item will be lower than the chances of finding at least one of a number of similar items, and thus subject and browsing fill rates should exceed title fill rates. Ciliberti (1985), however, found that availability rates in a particular library were similar for known-item and subject searches. It is unclear why similar rates were obtained; perhaps patrons who wanted subject information were discriminating in choosing titles to meet their specific needs. Further studies need to be conducted to see to what extent Ciliberti's finding can be generalized to all types and sizes of libraries. If item fill rates generally are similar to subject fill rates (which seems unlikely), an evaluator could simply use the former rate to predict the latter.

It also is possible to use patron interviews to obtain all data on which availability rates may be calculated, as Mansbridge (1984), Radford (1983), and Specht (1980) did, or to follow the example of Tagliacozzo and Kochen (1970) and combine direct observation of a patron's search for materials with a follow-up interview. These methods of data collection are more costly and time-consuming than questionnaires, but they may yield higher response rates and allow the evaluator to ask in-depth questions about how the patron went about finding, or not finding, particular items. This will give insight into the types of patron errors that affect availability in a particular library.

Studies suggest that 300–500 requests are needed to yield representative data (for example, Kantor, 1984). The evaluator may examine records of past use to select sample days and times likely to be fully representative of use. If he or she ends up determining that a sample of 40 days would give representative data, then 10 interviews would have to be conducted each day to obtain a sample size of 400. If an average of 500 patrons comes into the library daily, every fiftieth patron would be interviewed.

The investigator sits at a table immediately inside the library's door and interviews each designated patron using a standard set of questions. The first question determines the patron's main purpose for visiting the library that day. If the purpose falls into a category that is outside the scope of the study (for example, the patron is simply meeting a colleague in the library), the investigator records the reason for the visit, then terminates the interview. If the purpose of the visit is to locate specific documents of a particular type, the interviewer records whatever bibliographic data the patron has on each item sought. When the patron leaves the library, the evaluator asks questions designed to determine how each item was looked for and with what degree of success. The evaluator may also ask about the patron's attitudes toward the library, its tools, and its staff and about personal characteristics that may affect library use, such as age or occupation. An exit interview of this kind may take 10–15 minutes to complete. Only patrons who are interviewed at both the entry and exit points are included in the data analysis stage.

Separate availability studies should be conducted for each library facility, because availability rates may differ significantly between branch or departmental libraries within the same system. For example, Detweiler (1980) documented a fill rate of 72 percent in a central public library and 49 percent in a branch. Availability at nine sites in one academic library ranged from 58 percent to 87 percent (Revill, 1987). Meek (1978) even contrasted the availability of general materials to those located in a reserve room and found that although availability rates were comparable at the end of the semester, they were 15 percent lower for reserve materials at mid-semester, because of intense student competition for materials at that time.

An evaluator could conclude an analysis of fill rate by tallying questionnaire and interview results, then recording the proportion of items actually available. If the evaluator stops here, he or she will know what is happening—that is, how many document needs are met—but will not have the diagnostic information necessary to increase the availability rate. It is only when the evaluator determines why the success rate was at a particular level that he or she can intelligently consider where improvements should be made.

The microevaluation analysis is easy to perform. At frequent intervals throughout each day of the study, the evaluator determines the precise cause of each failure: the item was not in the collection, it was in the collection but was not found in the catalog by the patron, it was not on the shelf at the time the patron looked for it, or it was on the shelf but was not found by the patron. If an item is not on the shelf, staff note exactly where it is (for example, in circulation, in use in the library, waiting to be shelved, at the bindery, or recorded as missing) so that the evaluator can identify the precise cause of the "interference." The evaluator then examines the results of the surveys and recommends corrective action.

One major limitation of the patron-based availability study is that it only measures a library's ability to meet the expressed document delivery needs of present patrons. It reveals nothing about the library's possible performance in relation to needs that, for one reason or another, are not converted into demands on the library. For example, if a patron's past experience has been that a library is unlikely to have certain kinds of materials on the shelf, he or she may not even look for these items when visiting the library. In addition, patron-based availability studies reveal nothing about the needs of people who do not currently use the library.

Line (1973) undertook the difficult task of examining latent needs of the population that a particular library is to serve. He tried to identify a sample of bibliographic materials needed by members of the staff at Bath University in England and to determine what proportion actually was available in the university library. On two separate occasions, Line asked faculty members to record bibliographic details of items they would like to see at the time they encountered the reference to each item. On the first occasion, faculty members were asked to record those references they encountered on a given day; the second time they were asked to record the first 12 references (to materials they would like to see) that they encountered in a given month. In addition to recording the citation, each faculty member indicated what steps were taken to obtain the document (including use of the library if this source was selected) and whether or not the search was successful. The process ended when a faculty member completed the set of cards allocated. The data gathering form used on the second occasion is shown in Exhibit 6-5.

In a study such as this, the sum of all cards completed by all cooperating patrons represents a sample of document needs that can be regarded as latent needs so far as the library is concerned; that is, the sample of document needs can be considered legitimate demands on the library. The evaluator can then check the documents to see which are held and which are immediately available.

FINDINGS OF AVAILABILITY STUDIES

Exhibit 6-6 shows a sample of fill rates obtained in nine studies that record data using the "barrier" categories mentioned earlier: acquisition barriers, circulation interference, library error, or patron error (in using the catalog or in finding materials on the shelves). It is likely that many future studies will use these four basic categories to describe the availability situation in many libraries, since these are the ones espoused by the Association of Research Libraries (Kantor, 1984). In order for them to be useful, however, some further breakdowns of the categories for nonavailability are necessary. The finer the breakdown, the more likely the evaluator will determine the cause of the error and correct it. The evaluator determines specifically what type of error is occurring; then, whenever possible, he or she seeks to change library practice to prevent or at least decrease the chances of that error recurring. The best way to proceed is to improve first the factor or factors that show the lowest probability for success or that are expected to give the greatest improvement for the least cost. Possible solutions to the access problems created by each barrier are discussed in turn.

Acquisition Barriers

Metz (1980) suggests that there is little of an acquisitions barrier in large research libraries, because the failure to own a particular title frustrates only about 10 percent of patron searches for specific items; this low failure rate is probably due to the large and diverse collections of these academic libraries. Logically, though, it is expected that the acquisitions barrier will be greater in other types of libraries as well as in smaller academic libraries. Several studies confirm this, including those conducted by Greenberg (1981) in a school setting and Detweiler (1980) in a public library setting.

Evaluators in most availability studies, when looking for a particular title that the patron has been unable to find, have simply noted whether or not that title is in the library's catalog. They should go one step further: checking the acquisitions records to see if any titles are on order, are received but are awaiting cataloging, or are cataloged and shelved but are still "unavailable" because records do not yet appear in the catalog. Especially in large libraries, the excessive length of time for processing new books may be a hidden barrier, one that is related less to the library's selection practices than to the priority placed on the quick processing of new materials. This problem can be corrected, although it usually requires hiring extra staff to handle the processing backlog.

Occasionally, the specific reason for the acquisitions barrier may be easy to identify. For example, Shaw (1980) mapped availability rates over an eight-year period in two libraries in the Case Western Reserve University system. When a significant portion of the library's book fund was reallocated to serials acquisitions, the acquisitions barrier immediately increased and the fill rate for monographs decreased 16 percent. At other times, it may be necessary to break down the availability figures by subject or type of material. Exhibit 6-7 shows a typical subject breakdown at three university libraries. Note that this particular breakdown is reported using the failure rate (the percent of titles unavailable) in a particular subject. Library C could decide that failure rates of 19 percent and 24 percent in the chemistry and physics collections, respectively, were acceptable but that immediate efforts should be made to improve the engineering collection. If such a subject breakdown is contemplated, the evaluator needs to avoid the temptation of breaking down the sample into too many small subject areas, each containing only a handful of items. This is because availability rates calculated on a handful of items may not be representative of any subject field as a whole. To yield data on which accurate availability figures may be calculated, each of these smaller classes should contain enough items to give statistically significant results.

Sometimes the acquisitions barrier may be high, but there may be no obvious pattern to the types of failure patrons are experiencing. When this happens, the evaluator needs to conduct a full-scale collection evaluation to determine what the specific problems are and how to correct them. Such evaluations are discussed in Chapters 3, 4, and 5.

Circulation Interference

Some titles that patrons are seeking will be checked out to other patrons. Although occasional "circulation interference" is normal, most libraries own a number of titles that are so popular that all owned copies are regularly checked

<table>
</table>

AVAILABILITY SURVEY, 1968-69.

For library use only

All references to printed material that you come across which you would like to see personally, *and* all actual printed items of interest to you that you come across for the first time (i.e. without having a prior reference to them), should be recorded, *each on a separate form.*

1-5 Name: —————— School: —————— Date: ———
7-8

1	2	3	4	5

6.   1 2 3
      4 5 6
      7 8 9
      . . X

9,10 Item (brief details): ————————————

11.   Wanted in connection with: (tick boxes as appropriate)
      Research on contact   □
      Personal research   □
      Teaching   □
      Other purposes   □
          please name: ————————————

7-8 [|]

9.   1 2 3
      4 5 6
      7 8 9
      . . X

12.   Estimated importance of reference (please ring appropriate number on the rating scale below)
          (least important) 1 2 3 4 5 (very important)

10.   1 2 .
      . . X

11.   1 2 3
      4 5 .
      . . X

13.   Source of reference: (tick relevant box)
      Reference in another book or periodical
          your own or a colleague's   □
          belonging to Bath University Library   □
          belonging to another library   □
      Abstracting or indexing journal   □
      Bibliography   □
      Library catalogue   □
      Personal (orally or by correspondence)
      Item actually seen while browsing or
          searching in Bath University library   □
          elsewhere   □
              state where: ———————— □
14.   Other source   □
          please specify: ————————————

12.   1 2 3
      4 5 .
      . . X

13.   1 2 3
      4 5 6
      7 8 9
      . . X

14.   1 2 3
      4 5 6
      . . X

PLEASE TURN OVER

EXHIBIT 6-5   Form used in survey of availability of library materials at Bath University, England. Reprinted from Line (1973), courtesy of the Library Association.

EXHIBIT 6-5 *(Continued)*

Action taken

Please tick *all* cells applicable: e.g. if you check Bath
University Library and fail to find it, and then apply on interlibrary loan, three cells should be ticked.

		Action	
	Taken	If taken: Successful	Unsuccessful
Bath University Library			
15. Check branch library			
Check main catalogue			
Consult item			
16. Borrow item			
17. Other Library please name: _____ visit in person			
borrow personally by post			
18. Inter-library loan application	(to be completed by Library)		
Order copy for University Library			
Order personal copy from bookshop			
19. Other action please specify: _____			
No action			

15. 1 2 3
  4 5 6
  7 8 9 X

16. 1 2 3

17.
  1 2 3
  4 5 6
  7 8 9

18. 1 2 3
  4 5 6
  7 8 9 X

19. 1 2 3
  7   X

20. Date of completion: _____

Please retain this form until you have taken all the action you
propose to take on this particular item. When it is completed, please
return to the University Librarian, Northgate House.

20. Y X O
  1 2 3
  4 5 6
  7 8 9

	Not Acquired	Catalog Error	In Circulation	Library Error	User Error	Available Rate
Kantor (1976)	90	*	91	84	94	65
Buckland (1975)	90 (est.)	*	84	85	87	56
Saracevic, Shaw, and Kantor (1977)	97	*	78	89	79	53
	88		77	89	80	48
	91		87	86	82	56
Whitlatch and Kieffer (1978)	87.9†	88.2	88	94	92	58.9
Wulff (1978)	93.8	*	89.6	85.9	87.5	63.1
Shaw (1980)	85	*	86	84	86	53
	74		94	91	92	58
Frohmberg, Kantor, and Moffett (1980)	82.3	96.9	85.7	75.7	92.3	47.7
	90.5	97.9	83.0	79.5	96.1	56.1
	96.8	97.1	85.5	84.4	94.7	64.3
	96.0	97.6	93.9	86.5	94.0	71.6
	93.2	95.6	83.7	86.1	94.0	60.4
Rinkel and McCandless (1983)	97.93	91.00	91.28	92.99	94.52	71.5
	98.10	90.00	94.98	94.72	90.84	72.2
Mansbridge (1984)	89.00‡	88.00	79.4	90.5	98.3	55.3
Average	90.6	93.6	86.6	87.0	90.3	59.4

*Included in user error.
†Includes citation error.
‡Includes citation and bibliographic error.

EXHIBIT 6-6   Comparison of percent fill rates by "barrier" category. Adapted from Mansbridge (1984), courtesy of Ablex Publishing Company.

Library A		Library B		Library C	
Subject	*Percent Failure*	*Subject*	*Percent Failure*	*Subject*	*Percent Failure*
History	36.7	Geography and		Chemistry	19.0
Sociology	54.0	chemistry	38.0	Engineering	40.0
Physics	57.2	Social science	56.0	Physics	24.0
		Language and		Other science	
		literature	36.0	subjects	39.0
		Biological			
		science,			
		medicine, and			
		agriculture	33.0		

EXHIBIT 6-7   Failure rates in three libraries for individual books by subject. Reprinted from Urquhart and Schofield (1972), courtesy of Aslib.

out. In a public library, these titles tend to be recently published best-sellers or titles of long-term, continuing popularity. In a university or school library, they may be titles designated for use in some course. The library's document delivery capability is governed, then, not only by the number of titles in its collection, but also by the number of copies that are available. Libraries have tried to increase the availability of these items in two ways: they duplicate titles that are (or are predicted to be) heavily used, and they shorten the length of the loan period for these popular works.

Buckland (1972, 1975) measured circulation interference when he compared the effects that duplication and shorter loan periods had on availability of titles at the University of Lancaster in England. He noted four relationships between the loan period, the number of copies available, the popularity of particular items, and patron satisfaction:

1. For any given loan period, the chances of a reader finding on the shelves a copy of the book sought varies inversely with the item's popularity. The greater the popularity, the lower the satisfaction level; the lower the popularity, the higher the satisfaction level (see Exhibit 6-8).

2. For any given popularity, the length of the loan period and the user satisfaction level are inversely related. The longer the loan period, the lower the satisfaction level; the shorter the loan period, the higher the satisfaction level (see Exhibit 6-9).

3. For any given satisfaction level, the popularity and length of the loan period are necessarily inversely related. The greater the popularity, the shorter the loan period has to be; the lower the popularity, the longer the loan period (see Exhibit 6-10).

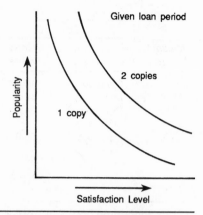

EXHIBIT 6-8   Satisfaction level as influenced by duplication rate and popularity. Reprinted from Buckland (1972), courtesy of the University of Chicago, Graduate Library School.

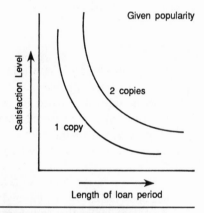

EXHIBIT 6-9   Loan period related to satisfaction level and duplication rate. Reprinted from Buckland (1972), courtesy of the University of Chicago, Graduate Library School.

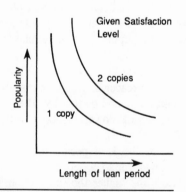

EXHIBIT 6-10   Loan period related to popularity and duplication rate. Reprinted from Buckland (1972), courtesy of the University of Chicago, Graduate Library School.

4. Increasing the number of copies available, like shortening the length of loan periods, increases satisfaction level. To this extent, it is an alternative strategy. The relationship can be seen in Exhibits 6-8, 6-9, and 6-10 by comparing the curve for one copy with the curve for two copies (Buckland, 1972, pp. 99–100).

In other words, the loan period, the duplication policy, or both should be related to the level of demand for the title. In the past, librarians resisted shortening loan periods because they thought this action would result in more overdue books and more renewals. Buckland (1975) and Newhouse and Alexander (1972), however, found that this assumption was invalid. Most borrowers return books before or on the due date. Nor is the frequency with which items are renewed by borrowers significantly influenced by the length of the loan period.[2]

The options of shortening loan periods and changing duplication policies each have strengths and weaknesses and should be considered in the context of the library's goals and objectives, especially those related to patron service. For people borrowing available books, long loan periods are convenient; they are inconvenient, however, for patrons who wish to borrow books already on loan. Moreover, any decision relating to loan periods is complicated by the fact that a few of the books will be in great demand while most will be needed infrequently. Although there is no reason to establish a short loan policy for less-used items, such a policy is beneficial for materials in great demand. Unfortunately, some effort is required to identify those items likely to be in demand. The provision of duplicate copies is convenient for the patron who wants a specific popular title, but it is expensive and uses up funds that could be spent in other ways, including the addition of new titles. Selectors must try to identify, before purchase, titles that need duplication or to systematically analyze use, after purchase, so that heavily used titles can be duplicated.

In the University of Lancaster study, Buckland (1972) used a computer simulation to calculate satisfaction level for various parts of the collection. He used past circulation data to estimate the effect on availability (satisfaction level) of changes made to loan and duplication policies. Exhibit 6-11 shows the estimated satisfaction level for books at five levels of demand (popularity) when the loan period and number of copies are varied.

Buckland (1972) also calculated the probable effect of these changes on "shelf bias" (the fact that the most popular books, which may be the most useful, are likely to be absent from the shelves, whereas the books in least demand will

---

[2] See, for example, Goehlert (1979). Elsewhere, Brophy et al. (1972) have pointed out that "no matter how long the loan period may be, a book will not actually be used for more than about ten hours on average."

Official Loan Period	Number of Copies	Estimated Satisfaction Level for Books at Each of Five Levels of Popularity				
		A	B	C	D	E
5 weeks	1	52	62	72	82	97
5 weeks	2	84	91	97	99	100
1 week	1	90	94	98	99	100

EXHIBIT 6-11 Estimated satisfaction level (in percent) for varying levels of popularity, loan period, and duplication rate. Reprinted from Buckland (1972), courtesy of the University of Chicago, Graduate Library School.

be present; also called "collection bias").[3] Approximately 45 percent of the most-used and most-recommended titles at the University of Lancaster were not available on the open shelves at any one time (a shelf bias of 45 percent). As shown in Exhibit 6-12, shelf bias increases with the length of the loan period.

Buckland (1972) identified three possible actions that could raise the satisfaction level from 60 percent to 80 percent on the average and, at the same time, reduce shelf bias to 20 percent or less:

1. The library could systematically duplicate copies to achieve the higher satisfaction levels. The cost would be significant.

2. The library could change its borrowing policy to one based on the patron's academic status. Undergraduates would be permitted to keep books for two weeks; staff and graduate students would have four return dates per year. This policy would increase the fill rate from 60 percent to 73 percent and reduce shelf bias from 45 percent to 32 percent.

3. The library could establish a variable-length loan policy, giving the most popular books a shorter loan period regardless of the borrower's status. For example, if 10 percent of the items had a one-week loan period and the remaining items had four return dates per year, the fill rate would increase to 86 percent and shelf bias would drop to 8 percent.

The University of Lancaster Library eventually adopted the third strategy. Clerical staff examined the due-date labels in 70,000 volumes in 2.5 days to determine the most-used items in the collection. The change to a variable-length

---

[3] Shelf bias relates to the demand for particular books, but not necessarily to the quality of these books. It is obvious that the books most in demand in a particular subject field are those least likely to be present on the shelves. It is not clear, however, that the books most in demand are necessarily "the best." Goldhor (1959), for example, showed that the best books (in this case, those reviewed most favorably) were not borrowed significantly more than their "less good" counterparts.

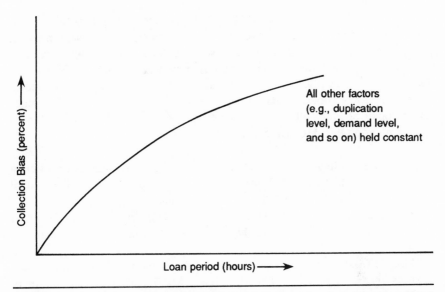

The graph shows a curve. The vertical axis is labeled "Collection Bias (percent)" with an upward arrow. The horizontal axis is labeled "Loan period (hours)" with a rightward arrow. A text annotation near the curve reads: "All other factors (e.g., duplication level, demand level, and so on) held constant"

EXHIBIT 6-12   Relationship between shelf bias and loan period. Reprinted from Brophy et al. (1972), courtesy of the University of Lancaster Library.

loan policy led to a dramatic increase in circulation. Borrowing from open shelves increased by 200 percent in two years, although the user population increased by only 40 percent during that period. In other words, demand for library materials increased when patrons found they could locate needed items on the shelves.

Other studies have also demonstrated how shortening the loan period increases the fill rate. Newhouse and Alexander (1972) estimated that a circulation period of two weeks would satisfy approximately two-thirds of all requests for specific titles at the Beverly Hills (California) Public Library. If the circulation period was increased to three weeks, the fill rate would drop to approximately 60 percent; for a four-week loan period, the fill rate would fall to 55 percent. Shaw (1980) reported that availability increased drastically when an academic library reduced its loan period from one semester to four weeks.

The purchase of additional copies of certain titles is common in public libraries, where large numbers of patrons are competing for the same titles. Moreland (1968) conducted an early, comprehensive study on duplication in the Montgomery County (Maryland) Public Library, after he discovered that 65 percent of the patrons indicating dissatisfaction with library services were unhappy because they could not get the books they wanted when they wanted them. Moreland got staff at 11 branch libraries to participate in an experiment. Selectors at each branch agreed to purchase paperback copies of popular titles at such a rate that there was always at least one copy available on the shelves.

The branch librarians identified 122 titles that were thought to be in popular, continuous demand: most of these were modern classics. At frequent intervals, clerical staff at each branch checked to see that there was at least one copy of each title available. If not, an extra copy was immediately bought, processed, and placed in the collection. To meet demand, selectors at the 11 branches bought a total of 21,821 copies of these titles over an 11-month period, or an average of 15 copies of every title at each branch library. Moon (1968), in an editorial commenting on this research, concluded that

- Librarians too often concentrate on acquiring large numbers of different titles, emphasizing satisfaction of esoteric demands at the expense of satisfaction on the part of regular library patrons.
- Librarians need to spend more time scrutinizing the shelves to determine whether an item, once bought, is ever readily available for the patron.

Moon's words were prophetic in terms of the direction in which libraries are now moving. In particular, public librarians, who regularly receive dozens of requests for the same popular items, are increasingly adopting mass duplication policies. One well-known, demand-oriented library is the Baltimore County Public Library in Towson, Maryland.

The selectors at the Baltimore County Public Library do a large amount of duplicate buying initially; they buy far fewer titles than do selection staff at other public libraries of the same size. In fiscal year 1988–1989, the library's adult fiction budget was $870,000. With this money, the library planned to buy only 1,100 new fiction titles. The library predicts the amount of demand each title will have, and thus the number of copies to be purchased for the system, by examining various use-oriented factors, including the use that past titles by the same author have received, the use of other titles in the same genre or subject area, the amount of money the publisher is spending on advertising a particular book, and whether the book is going to be featured on major radio and television talk shows. Each branch library gets a percentage of the copies purchased equivalent to the percentage of its circulation in the entire system. For example, if the annual circulation for the Towson branch of the library represents 13 percent of the total systemwide circulation, Towson will get 13 percent of the copies for that title. Most fiction best-sellers are initially purchased in the range of 190–450 copies, to be divided among the 23 branch libraries. Fewer than 20 fiction titles are purchased at a rate of more than 450 copies for the system. Two blockbuster authors, Danielle Steel and Sidney Sheldon, are duplicated much more heavily than other authors. The largest branch will receive 125 copies of each new title written by these authors; the smallest full-service branch will get 30 copies of each title. At the other extreme is the formula the Baltimore County Public Library's selectors use for "literary" (high-quality) fiction. The largest branch may get as few as two copies of these works and the smallest none, for a total systemwide purchase of up to eight copies.

Nonfiction is chosen in the same manner, although the total number of individual titles purchased is greater. With a fiscal year 1988–1989 adult nonfiction budget of $770,000, the Baltimore County Public Library planned to purchase approximately 5,100 new titles. An average of 38 copies of each nonfiction title is purchased for the entire library system; this formula gives the highest circulating branch 4 copies of each new title. For any specific title, the number of copies may range from 1 to 20 per branch.

Initial duplication of new titles is not the only technique the Baltimore County Public Library uses to ensure that wanted items are on the shelf. Once a title has been purchased, the central selection staff monitors use so that more duplicate copies can be ordered when the need arises. For example, branch staff who notice that some titles exist for which the library cannot meet demand submit a "beef-up" request to the central selection staff. Beef-up orders are rushed to the jobber for immediate filling. Most beef-up requests are for new titles that were underbought initially, but some are for replacement copies of an older title in which there is resurging interest. When the fiction buyer noted an advertisement for an upcoming television miniseries that was based on the book *The Women of Brewster Place*, she submitted a beef-up request. Within days after the series aired, 95 percent of the 117 copies owned by the library were checked out.

The selection staff developed another technique to respond to what selectors called the "bottomless pit syndrome" in two branches. Patrons at these branches are heavy reservers of adult fiction, seeming to want to read everything new. At any one time, it is common for the branches to have 10–15 titles, not on the best-seller list, with more than 50 reserves each. The collection budgets for adult fiction at these branches are not large enough to meet this type of demand. To avoid having patrons wait for three months to a year before those 10–15 titles actually appear on the shelves, the selection staff developed a computer program that matches reserves with the number of copies ordered:

When one of these two branches has one and one half times more holds than copies ordered, the program subtracts 25% of the available copies due to each branch, and earmarks these copies for one circulation only, to the branch with outstanding reserves. (Wisotzki, 1989, p. 17)

The effect of these programs of duplication and use scrutiny at Baltimore County Public Library has been better patron access to specific items requested. The average fill rate at this system is more than 15 percent higher than the national average. In addition, in fiscal year 1988–1989, Baltimore County Public Library's circulation per capita rate was 14.5, twice the national average for public libraries (personal communication with Lila Wisotzki, April 29, 1989). Because research has shown that there are no significant differences between the average number of items checked out by individual patrons at various public libraries, circulation per capita may actually be an indirect measure of the proportion of the service population that uses a library (D'Elia and Rodger, 1987). In other words, librarians like those in the Baltimore County Public Library, who make the titles their patrons want readily and easily available, may be attracting a broader use base—something that public librarians have been trying to do for years.

Of course, public librarians are not the only ones considering duplication as a way of improving availability. A growing number of academic, school, and special libraries are realizing that circulation interference accounts for a substantial number of patron failures in locating materials. For example, at San Diego State University, circulation interference accounted for 36 percent of patron failures to locate specific items; at San Jose State University, this figure was 42 percent (Whitlatch and Kieffer, 1978). Some academic librarians have tried to develop mathematical models to predict circulation demand for titles in a particular subject area. Bommer (1972) related the rate of circulation to various measures of teaching and research activity within a university. He considered the number of faculty and students working in a particular subject area, the rate of obsolescence of materials, and a factor of diminishing returns, based on the fact that although use of the collection in a particular subject area increases when extra copies are added, the incremental use of each additional copy is successively smaller. His model attempted to predict the number of new titles that would be required in a particular subject area, the number of duplicate copies that would be needed, and the number of copies that would be placed on reserve, the objective being to maximize the use of library materials for each dollar expended. As awareness of the large number of patrons who cannot get needed items because of circulation interference increases, academic, special, and school librarians may consider modifying the demand-oriented techniques used by public librarians to meet their own needs.

Some authors have suggested establishing efficient procedures for easy reservation of materials and for recall of items from circulation when requested by another patron as alternatives to duplicating copies and reducing loan periods. These are not necessarily good substitutes. Neither helps the patron who needs a particular item immediately or the patron who is browsing the shelves in a particular subject area. For the browser, it is important that the shelves display a wide selection of available materials, including books that are current or are, in some sense, regarded as best.

Library Error

A library barrier arises when the library catalog indicates ownership but the title is not in circulation and is not on its regular shelf. The book may be missing, or it may be located in some area not identified in the catalog. This problem of missing items can reach chronic proportions, especially in libraries with very large collections. For example, some researchers studying fill rates in large university libraries have found that 20 percent or more of the collection is "missing" (for example, Urquhart and Schofield, 1972).

In some libraries, a number of items are missing because of theft. This problem is usually solved by installing an electronic security system or some other type of exit control. Such installation has been shown to significantly improve the fill rate (for example, Shaw, 1980).

Other books labeled "missing" may just be misshelved. The solution here is simple, but not inexpensive. The library needs to maintain full strength in the reshelving unit so that items can be reshelved quickly and accurately and so that shelves can be read periodically to correct shelving errors.

Library errors can also be reduced by performing collection inventories, or at least by dealing, on a case-by-case basis, with titles thought to be missing. If a book is missing, a member of the library's selection staff should determine whether or not the item is to be replaced. If so, the order should be placed immediately and the replacement copy processed as soon as it arrives. If not, the catalog should be corrected. The Frieberger Library at Case Western Reserve University significantly increased its availability rate by making a consistent effort to replace missing items (Shaw, 1980).

A more difficult problem is that of books that are temporarily located somewhere other than their regular places on the shelves. A number of studies reported that patrons cannot locate materials because they are at the bindery, are on sorting shelves, or are on reserve (for example, Radford, 1983; Smith and Granade, 1981; Wainright and Dean, 1976.). Although most patrons search the stacks, and a few experienced patrons search the sorting shelves, few check the reserve book room holdings or ask the reference librarian or the circulation staff for assistance (for example, Whitlatch and Kieffer, 1978). The problem has been solved, at least partly, in those libraries with automated catalogs that list temporary locations. Nonautomated libraries can reduce this type of error by installing signs that direct patrons to check with library staff when they cannot find specific items. Such signs should be located at various entrances to, and at strategic locations within, the stacks. Frohmberg, Kantor, and Moffett (1980) showed that installation of an automated circulation system in a college library improved availability in another way. The new system checked in borrowed items more quickly than a former manual system; as a result it allowed faster reshelving of items so that patrons could find them.

Occasionally, a different problem arises: the actual location of some item is changed, but the catalog is not. This may happen, for example, when major shifting of collections occurs between public library branches but the main catalog for the system is not changed. Again, the solution is simple, but not inexpensive. The catalog record for any item that permanently changes its location should be updated to reflect the change.

Patron Error

The term "patron error" is quite misleading; it implies that it is entirely the user's fault that an error has occurred and, therefore, the librarian cannot help correct the error. This is not always the case. Consider, for example, the study by Murfin (1980) which found that nonuse or misuse of the serials directory was a major cause of nonavailability of serials. The patrons erred in their use of the directory, but library staff should also take part of the blame; after all, they did not anticipate errors of this type and plan for ways to avoid them. For example, staff could have displayed the serials directory more prominently, incorporated instruction in use of the directory into bibliographic instruction sessions, and redesigned the directory to be easier to use (for example, adding cross-references from abbreviated versions of journal titles to the main directory entries). Rinkel and McCandless (1983) confirmed that user error was not entirely the patron's fault. They found that these types of errors lessen as a patron's familiarity with the idiosyncracies of a particular library increases.

Patron error in using the card catalog is a serious obstacle to finding a specific title or information on a certain subject. For example, Whitlatch and Kieffer (1978) found that 42 percent of the items that patrons could not find in the card catalog actually were in the catalog and could have been found if the patron had possessed basic catalog-use skills. Librarians can adopt various strategies that will decrease catalog-use error. For example, online catalogs can be designed so that the patron who looks up a subject term that is not used in the catalog will automatically be referred to the correct term. The catalog-use problem is dealt with in detail in Chapter 7.

Another patron error, documented in numerous studies, occurs when the patron correctly locates the item in the catalog but then either relies on short-term memory of the call number when trying to retrieve the book or incorrectly records the call number. Librarians can reduce these errors by providing pencils and paper at the catalog, or by installing printers at catalog terminals so that patrons can carry copies of the actual catalog records to the shelves.

Even when users have the correct call number, they sometimes look in the wrong location for an item (Radford, 1983; Radford, Rossendell, and Sexton, 1983). The simplest solution to this problem is to encourage patrons to ask for help, since all types of libraries report increased fill rates when the librarian helps the patron search for materials (Abduljalil, 1985; Kuraim, 1983; Nwagha, 1983; Rashid, 1985). Few patrons currently ask for help (Whitlatch and Kieffer, 1978). As noted in Chapter 8, this is often because of barriers that libraries and librarians inadvertently create. For example, at San Jose State University, where patrons could not find a full third of the items that were properly shelved, Whitlach and Kieffer correctly found fault with the library's search policy. The policy required that the patron check the stacks twice before the circulation department would agree to conduct a search.

It is doubtful whether those who missed the book the first time in the bookstacks will be any better able to find it the second time and whether searching the first request will educate the user. The best solution is to assist the user physically in finding the book, and if it is not located, to offer to make a complete search immediately. (p. 198)

OTHER VARIATIONS ON AVAILABILITY STUDIES

Whenever possible, evaluators should consider conducting separate availability studies to determine whether fill rates vary, depending on the popularity of a particular format. It is likely, for example, that fill rates in a public library differ for books, videotapes, and compact disks. To date, most libraries have concentrated on measuring book availability, although academic and special libraries that make heavy use of serials are increasingly studying the fill rate for journal articles (for example, Goehlert, 1978b; Murfin, 1980; Rivero Rojas, 1986; and Watson, 1984). The studies conducted to date have shown that overall journal availability rates are similar to those for monographs. Common library errors include the failure to (1) add cross-references to directories of serials to indicate title changes and abbreviated titles, (2) use "dummies" or shelf tags to inform patrons that some journals are not in alphabetic order on the shelves but rather are on microform and housed elsewhere, (3) explain to patrons the difference between current and back issues (since location is often dependent on this distinction), (4) refer patrons who are confused to staff members for help, and (5) reshelve journals quickly after each use.

Evaluators also can determine whether availability rates in a particular library differ, based on patron status, academic department, reason for request, age of material, or other variables (see, for example, Exhibit 6-13). Such studies have been conducted by a number of researchers, including Bush, Galliher, and Morse (1956); Detweiler (1980); Goehlert (1978a); Radford, Rossendell, and Sexton (1983); Rinkel and McCandless (1983); Specht (1980); and Urquhart and Schofield (1972). One consistent finding is that the availability of materials increases as the title gets older. This reflects the fact that use of a title decreases as it ages, a finding discussed in Chapter 4.

Type of User	Percent Failure
Academic staff	30.1
Nonacademic staff	26.3
Postgraduate	45.8
Undergraduate	50.3
Other (for example, students from outside bodies)	56.2
Average	48.7

EXHIBIT 6-13   Failure rates by type of user. Reprinted from Urquhart and Schofield (1972), courtesy of Aslib.

Finally, those libraries that deliver materials that were requested by telephone or mail can study availability in a slightly different way. Consider, for example, university libraries that have established delivery services for faculty. In some such services, faculty members telephone the library with the citation for some desired item. Staff members retrieve the document, then either deliver it by hand or send it to the requesting faculty member by campus mail. Most libraries with such services record the number of requests received, the number of different types of documents requested, and the number of documents filled in each category (for example, D'Elia et al., 1984). Although this type of availability study is fairly easy to conduct, it has one major weakness. It will only identify availability problems related to acquisition failures, circulation interference, and library practices; it will not determine the types of errors that patrons might make in using the catalog and in locating the items on the shelves.

Studies of the types discussed thus far only address how a library can measure and improve fill rates. Various types of follow-up studies also are possible. One of the most logical is the study designed to identify and count the cases in which a library patron needs a particular item, cannot find it in the library, and fails to request it. The reasons for the failure to request the item also need to be recorded. Urquhart and Schofield (1972) performed a study of this type in three university libraries. The actions that patrons said they would take after failing to find the items they were looking for are shown in Exhibit 6-14. These actions are not mutually exclusive; the percentages do not add to 100.0, because a patron might have indicated more than one intended action. Line (1973) collected similar data in his studies of latent needs.

Reilly (1968) believed that a patron's intended action depends heavily on his or her perception that a book will be available. After many experiences, patrons begin to estimate the level of success they will have when looking for a specific title. If they feel their chances for success in finding a title are high, they will be more likely to look for it. If they feel their chances of finding the title are low, they will be less likely to do so. Certainly the findings in the Urquhart and Schofield study back this up. Because Library A has duplicate copies of popular titles, as well as a policy of short loan periods, the probability of finding an unavailable item on a return visit is high, and a large number of patrons (69.2 percent) indicated that they would try later (see Exhibit 6-14).

Librarians cannot simply tell patrons that availability has increased and expect them to believe this. Patrons must be convinced. They must gain, over a period of time, the impression that their chances of obtaining a given item have improved. This was illustrated in a study by Frohmberg, Kantor, and Moffett (1980). Six surveys were mailed to students at one college over a two-year period asking respondents to estimate their chances of successfully finding a book in the main library. At the beginning of the study period, actual availability was low; the library instituted corrective action, and availability slowly increased over the

Intended Action	Library A (n = 692) %	Library B (n = 274) %	Library C (n = 51) %
No action	15.3	10.2	13.7
Come back later	69.2	37.2	29.4
Reservation	11.1	13.9	9.8
Try another library	16.3	39.8	17.6
Try reading room or reserve collection	16.2	25.2	*
Find substitute	25.3	22.6	7.8
Borrow from friend	23.7	13.1	7.8
Buy	14.5	8.0	0
Consult member of staff (either teaching or library)	19.5	16.4	33.3

NOTE: Percentages do not add to 100.0 because patrons might have indicated more than one intended action.

*No reading room or reserve collection.

EXHIBIT 6-14 Follow-up action after failure to locate an item. Reprinted from Urquhart and Schofield (1972), courtesy of Aslib.

two-year period. As actual availability increased, so did patron perceptions of availability, but the former rose much faster than the latter.

Other factors may determine the type of follow-up action that patrons will take. The local environment might influence action; for example, the "try another library" approach depends on the local availability of other resources. Another influence might be the patron's purpose in seeking the item. A scientist seeking an item that he or she believes will help with some vital piece of research might make a strong effort to obtain the item; a public library patron seeking a book that an acquaintance said was enjoyable might not. One major reason that the patron may give up when an item is not immediately available is that he or she is not aware of other options: asking the librarian to purchase the book, to file an interlibrary loan request, or to place a hold or recall on the book. Further research is needed to identify the differences in motivation between patrons who make the effort to continue seeking titles that are not immediately available and those who do not.

Most shelf availability studies measure the immediate availability of library materials. Others measure the availability of materials over time—that is, how long it takes to satisfy some percentage of user needs for particular items. Van House et al. (1987) defined document delivery time as the number of calendar days required to obtain all materials not immediately available to patrons, whether materials are obtained through purchase, interlibrary loan, or a reserve system.

Some libraries conduct an all-purpose study to measure the availability of any items that patrons did not obtain when they were seeking them, regardless of the strategies used to meet the requests. This type of study has been widely promoted by the Public Library Association, which recommends use of the form shown in Exhibit 6-15. This particular form collects data that are useful in a macroevaluation study. For each item that a patron indicates was not found, the staff record the date on which the request was made, the date on which the library made the requested material available to the patron, the total response time (in days), and the strategy that was used to fill the request. A large sample of requests (300–500 items) should be analyzed to obtain reliable data on what the average delivery time is.

Many libraries prefer to conduct separate studies to determine the amount of time that is needed to deliver materials ordered on interlibrary loan, materials recalled from circulation, or materials specially purchased at patron request. Separate studies may allow more information to be collected on possible barriers caused by each type of document delivery.

Evaluating interlibrary loan activities is relatively easy because the evaluation criteria are both simple and unequivocal: a request either is satisfied within a particular time period or it is not. Moreover, it is not difficult to produce an aggregate performance score—the proportion of interlibrary loan requests satisfied within some time period. In fact, the evaluation of document delivery via interlibrary loan is far less difficult than the evaluation of general shelf availability within a particular library. In the former, a written record exists of all demands; in the latter, no such record is available unless a special survey is undertaken.

Kantor (1984) suggests an easy means of evaluating the document delivery capabilities of an interlibrary loan system. The evaluator simply calculates the average time taken for each of five steps in the process: (1) receiving the interlibrary loan forms from patrons and searching to see from which libraries items should be requested, (2) typing and mailing the formal requests (or, if an online system is being used, inputting and sending the formal requests), (3) waiting for responses to these requests, (4) notifying patrons when the requests are filled, and (5) waiting for the patrons to pick up the requested items. Note, however, that the use of online public access catalogs within library networks makes it likely that more and more interlibrary loan requests will be generated at terminals by patrons themselves. For example, the University of Illinois discovered that interlibrary loan borrowing increased from 4,600 items in 1978 to 157,000 items in 1988 ("Stats: AL Asides," 1989). The increase was due to the installation of a computer system that allows patrons to search easily the catalogs of 28 other Illinois libraries and to indicate, with the press of a button, their wish to borrow desired titles directly from any of the other libraries. Evaluation of such activities is readily possible if the automated catalog that is used to generate such requests is programmed to record how many requests are

Library _____

Date Begun _____

Date Ended _____

Request No.	ID for Item	Date Requested Month/Day	Date Available Month/Day	Response Time (days)	Code

Code for source of material: fill in after material arrives
R = Reserve (on your library's copy)
B = Borrowed from another branch (intrasystem loans)
I = Interlibrary loan
O = Purchase
X = Other (e.g., cancelled, does not exist)

EXHIBIT 6-15 Document delivery log. Reprinted from Van House et al. (1987), courtesy of the American Library Association.

made by patrons and how long it takes the lending library to send the requested materials.

Microevaluation of interlibrary loan activities would require more than merely counting the successes and failures and measuring the average times taken to meet patron requests. It would involve analyzing and categorizing the failures (both absolute failures and failures due to unacceptable response time) and determining why they occurred. Factors that affect the success rate might be related to the characteristics of materials requested (such as the date and the form of publication), membership in OCLC or other library networks, the size or training of the interlibrary loan staff, or factors relating to other libraries (for example, material is requested in a timely fashion but the requesting library is slow in filling the order). Library staff can then work to reduce these problems; for instance, if several libraries within an interlibrary loan network are found to be particularly slow in filling material requests, staff should be advised to seek materials from other libraries first.

The evaluation of the effectiveness of recall systems in libraries is another aspect of document delivery that needs to be considered. Goehlert (1979) suggested that the patron who has recalled a circulating item will be satisfied with the library if he or she is reasonably sure that the item will be returned soon (or at least at the end of the current loan period) by the person using it; however, with each additional day of delay in obtaining an item beyond that time, the patron's dissatisfaction with the library tends to increase.

Goehlert (1979) studied all items that were recalled and returned to the main library at Indiana University during a four-month period. He gathered data on the status of the person recalling the book, the status of the person to whom the book was charged, the number of days between sending a recall notice and the book's return, and the number of days between a book's due date and its return. He found that most undergraduate and graduate students returned items when they were due; when books were recalled for another patron, students returned them within an average of six days after the recall notice was sent.

Faculty members also returned books when they were due; however, they took an average of 17 days to return a recalled item, a problem of some importance because 41 percent of all books were recalled from faculty. This delay was undoubtedly because the faculty loan period was one year, as opposed to the two-week loan period for students. The university library corrected the problem by giving faculty an incentive to return materials: they began levying fines on those who failed to return recalled materials quickly. During the next semester, only three faculty members had fines imposed for not returning recalled items within an acceptable amount of time.

Little research has been done to identify the average time for delivery of items that are specially purchased for the patrons who request them, although the type of data collected would be very similar to that collected when measuring the delivery time of interlibrary loan items. It is also valuable for the evaluator to determine what proportion of all items arrive in time to be useful to the individuals requesting them. This could be derived in various ways. The idea of using interlibrary loan, recall, or purchase requests that are canceled by their initiators as an indication of unacceptable delays is unrealistic because few patrons who request such services actually cancel them, even if the item is no longer needed. Nor should the evaluator simply examine those cases where items eventually are made available but are not picked up by the requesters, since there might be other reasons for noncollection (for example, the patron was out of town when the library mailed a notification that the request was filled). To get better data on the impact of document delivery delays, evaluators should survey patrons. A simple way of doing this was demonstrated by Manthey and Brown (1985), who mailed a follow-up questionnaire to all patrons whose requested items were delivered after a certain amount of time. Ideally, the questionnaire should be sent to all patrons whose requests are not met within 10 days. The questionnaire should ask whether the patron is still able to use the material and the effect, if any, of the delivery delay.

REFERENCES

Abduljalil, Mahomed Fituri. "Book Availability and User Satisfaction in School Libraries: A Case Study of Shaker Heights Senior High School and Cleveland Heights High School." Doctoral Dissertation. Cleveland, Ohio, Case Western Reserve University, 1985.

Ajlan, Ajlan Mohammad. "The Effectiveness of Two Academic Libraries in Saudi Arabia: An Enquiry into the Main Factors Affecting Their Services." Doctoral Dissertation. Cleveland, Ohio, Case Western Reserve University, 1985.

Bommer, Michael R. W. "The Development of a Management System for Effective Decision Making and Planning in a University Library." Doctoral Dissertation. Philadelphia, Pa., University of Pennsylvania, Wharton School of Finance and Commerce, 1972. ERIC ED071727

Bourne, Charles P., and Jo Robinson. "SDI Citation Checking as a Measure of the Performance of Library Document Delivery Systems." Berkeley, Calif., University of California, Institute of Library Research, 1973. ERIC ED082774

Brophy, Peter, et al. *A Library Management Game: A Report on a Research Project.* Lancaster, Eng., University of Lancaster Library, 1972.

Buckland, Michael K. "An Operations Research Study of a Variable Loan and Duplication Policy at the University of Lancaster." *Library Quarterly,* 42(1):97–106, January 1972.

————. *Book Availability and the Library User.* New York, Pergamon Press, 1975.

Bush, G. C.; H. P. Galliher; and Philip M. Morse. "Attendance and Use of the Science Library at M.I.T." *American Documentation,* 7(2):87–109, April 1956.

Ciliberti, Anne C. "The Development and Methodological Study of an Instrument for Measuring Material Availability in Libraries." Doctoral Dissertation. New Brunswick, N.J., Rutgers University, 1985.

D'Elia, George, and Eleanor Jo Rodger. "Comparative Assessment of Patrons' Uses and Evaluations Across Public Libraries Within a System: A Replication." *Library and Information Science Research*, 9(1):5–20, January–March 1987.

D'Elia, George, et al. "Evaluation of the Document Delivery Service Provided by University Libraries, Twin Cities Campus, University of Minnesota." Minneapolis, Minn., University of Minnesota, 1984. ERIC ED252241

De Prospo, Ernest R.; Ellen Altman; and Kenneth E. Beasley. *Performance Measures for Public Libraries*. Chicago, Ill., American Library Association, 1973.

Detweiler, Mary Jo. "Availability of Materials in Public Libraries." In: *Library Effectiveness: A State of the Art*. Edited by Neal K. Kaske and William G. Jones. New York, Library Administration and Management Association/American Library Association, 1980, pp. 76–83.

Frohmberg, Katherine A.; Paul B. Kantor; and William A. Moffett. "Increases in Book Availability in a Large College Library." In: *Proceedings of the 43rd ASIS Annual Meeting, Anaheim, California, October 5–10 1980*. Vol. 17. New York, Knowledge Industry Publications, 1980, pp. 292–294.

Goehlert, Robert. "Book Availability and Delivery Service." *Journal of Academic Librarianship*, 4(5):368–371, November 1978a.

————. "Periodical Use in an Academic Library: A Study of Economists and Political Scientists." *Special Libraries*, 69(2):51–60, February 1978b.

————. "The Effect of Loan Policies on Circulation Recalls." *Journal of Academic Librarianship*, 5(2):79–82, May 1979.

Goldhor, Herbert. "Are the Best Books the Most Read?" *Library Quarterly*, 29(4):251–255, October 1959.

Greenberg, Marilyn Werstein. "Availability of Library Materials in Thirteen Secondary Schools." Doctoral Dissertation. Chicago, Ill., University of Chicago, 1981.

Kantor, Paul B. "Availability Analysis." *Journal of the American Society for Information Science*, 27(5–6):311–319, September–October 1976.

————. "Demand-Adjusted Shelf Availability Parameters." *Journal of Academic Librarianship*, 7(2):78–82, May 1981.

————. *Objective Performance Measures for Academic and Research Libraries*. Washington, D.C., Association of Research Libraries, 1984.

Kaske, Neal K. "Effectiveness of Library Operations: A Management Information Systems Approach and Application." Doctoral Dissertation. Norman, Okla., University of Oklahoma, 1973.

Kuraim, Faraj Mohamed. "The Principal Factors Causing Reader Frustration in a Public Library." Doctoral Dissertation. Cleveland, Ohio, Case Western Reserve University, 1983.

Line, Maurice B. "The Ability of a University Library to Provide Books Wanted by Researchers." *Journal of Librarianship*, 5(1):37–51, January 1973.

Mansbridge, John. "Evaluating Resource Sharing Library Networks." Doctoral Dissertation. Cleveland, Ohio, Case Western Reserve University, 1984.

————. "Availability Studies in Libraries." *Library and Information Science Research*, 8(4):299–314, October–December 1986.

Manthey, Teresa, and Jeanne Owen Brown. "Evaluating a Special Library Using Public Library Output Measures." *Special Libraries*, 76(4):282–289, Fall 1985.

Meek, L. "Student Success Rates at Macquarie University Library." *Australian Academic and Research Libraries,* 9(1):33–36, March 1978.

Metz, Paul. "Duplication in Library Collections: What We Know and What We Need to Know." *Collection Building,* 2(3):27–33, 1980.

Moon, Eric. "Editorial: Satisfaction Point." *Library Journal,* 93(10):1947, May 15, 1968.

Moreland, George B. "Operation Saturation: Using Paperbacks, Branch Libraries in Maryland Conduct an Experiment to Equate Book Supply with Patron Demand." *Library Journal,* 93(10):1975–1979, May 15, 1968.

Murfin, Marjorie E. "The Myth of Accessibility: Frustration and Failure in Retrieving Periodicals." *Journal of Academic Librarianship,* 6(1):16–19, March 1980.

Newhouse, Joseph P., and Arthur J. Alexander. *An Economic Analysis of Public Library Services.* Lexington, Mass., Lexington Books, 1972.

Nwagha, Georgiana Kiente Ngeri. "Bibliographical Control in the Field of Agriculture in Nigeria: A Study of Demand and Availability." Doctoral Dissertation. London, Ontario, Can., University of Western Ontario, 1983.

Orr, Richard H., et al. "Development of Methodologic Tools for Planning and Managing Library Services: II. Measuring a Library's Capability for Providing Documents." *Bulletin of the Medical Library Association,* 56(3):241–267, July 1968.

Radford, Neil A. "Failure in the Library—A Case Study." *Library Quarterly,* 53(3):328–339, July 1983.

Radford, Neil A.; Irene Rossendell; and Catherine Sexton. "Why Can't I Ever Find Anything in the Library?" *Vestes,* 26(2):40–44, 1983.

Rashid, Haseeb Fadhel. "Factors Affecting User Satisfaction in a Medical Library and a Comparison with Other Types of Libraries." Doctoral Dissertation. Cleveland, Ohio, Case Western Reserve University, 1985.

Reilly, Kevin D. "User Determination of Library Request Presentation: A Simulation." Los Angeles, Calif., University of California, Institute of Library Research, 1968. ERIC ED030453

Revill, D. H. "'Availability' as a Performance Measure for Academic Libraries." *Journal of Librarianship,* 19(1):14–30, January 1987.

Rinkel, Gene K., and Patricia McCandless. "Application of a Methodology Analyzing User Frustration." *College and Research Libraries,* 44(1):29–37, January 1983.

Rivero Rojas, Jose Guillermo. "Availability of Scientific and Technical Journal Articles and User Dissatisfaction Study in Four Mexican Academic Libraries." Doctoral Dissertation. Austin, Tex., University of Texas, 1986.

Saracevic, Tefko; William M. Shaw, Jr.; and Paul B. Kantor. "Causes and Dynamics of User Frustration in an Academic Library." *College and Research Libraries,* 38(1):7–18, January 1977.

Schwarz, Philip. "Demand-Adjusted Shelf Availability Parameters: A Second Look." *College and Research Libraries,* 44(4):210–219, July 1983.

Shaw, William M., Jr. "Longitudinal Studies of Book Availability." In: *Library Effectiveness: A State of the Art.* Edited by Neal K. Kaske and William G. Jones. New York, Library Administration and Management Association/American Library Association, 1980, pp. 338–349.

Smith, Rita, and Warner Granade. "AL Report: Undergraduate Library Availability Study, 1975–1977, University of Tennessee." In: *User Surveys and Evaluation of Library Services.* Washington, D.C., Association of Research Libraries, Office of

Management Studies, February 1981, pp. 83–90. SPEC Kit 71

Specht, Jerry. "Patron Use of an Online Circulation System in Known-Item Searching." *Journal of the American Society for Information Science, 31*(5):335–346, September 1980.

"Stats: AL Asides." *American Libraries, 20*(5):389, May 1989.

Tagliacozzo, Renata, and Manfred Kochen. "Information-Seeking Behavior of Catalog Users." *Information Storage and Retrieval, 6*(5):363–381, December 1970.

Tamraz, Ahmad Ali. "A Study of Availability and Actual Usage of Arabic and English Monographs in Science and Technology in Three Academic Libraries in Saudi Arabia." Doctoral Dissertation. New Brunswick, N.J., Rutgers University, 1984.

Urquhart, John A., and J. L. Schofield. "Measuring Readers' Failure at the Shelf in Three University Libraries." *Journal of Documentation, 28*(3):233–241, September 1972.

Van House, Nancy A., et al. *Output Measures for Public Libraries: A Manual of Standardized Procedures.* 2nd Edition. Chicago, Ill., American Library Association, 1987.

Wainright, Eric John, and John E. Dean. *Measures of Adequacy for Library Collections in Australian Colleges of Advanced Education: Report of a Research Project Conducted on Behalf of the Commission in Advanced Education.* Perth, Australia, Western Australian Institute of Technology, 1976.

Watson, William. "A Periodical Access Survey in a University Library." *College and Research Libraries, 45*(6):496–500, November 1984.

Whitlatch, Jo Bell, and Karen Kieffer. "Service at San Jose State University: Survey of Document Availability." *Journal of Academic Librarianship, 4*(4):196–199, September 1978.

Wiemers, Eugene, Jr. *Materials Availability in Small Libraries: A Survey Handbook.* Urbana, Ill., University of Illinois, Graduate School of Library and Information Science, 1981. (Occasional Paper No. 149)

Wilson, Thomas D. "Document Delivery Tests for the Evaluation of Basic Reader Service." In: *EURIM: A European Conference on Research into the Management of Information Services and Libraries."* London, Eng., ASLIB, 1974, pp. 134–140.

Wisotzki, Lila. "Duplicate, Circulate: Demand Buying." Unpublished paper presented at the Collection Development Conference, Public Library Association, March 19, 1989, Chicago, Illinois.

Wulff, Yvonne. "Book Availability in the University of Minnesota Bio-Medical Library." *Bulletin of the Medical Library Association, 66*(3):349–350, July 1978.

CHAPTER 7

EVALUATION OF CATALOG USE

The catalog is the single most important key to a library's collections. Its major functions are to show whether the library owns items on a specific subject and items whose identity is known (for example, by author or title) and to indicate where items can be found within the library.

Library catalogs have existed in some form for centuries, but only recently have serious attempts been made to evaluate their effectiveness as finding tools. There are two main reasons that catalog use studies have gained increasing attention. First, librarians are becoming more concerned with the evaluation of library services in general; they want to know how well the catalog performs, what its deficiencies are, and how its effectiveness can be increased. Second, many libraries now are replacing traditional forms of the catalog with online public access catalogs (OPACs). To design effective online catalogs, more information is needed on how existing catalogs are being used, how successfully they are being used, and their major problems and limitations.

Over the years, many studies of catalog use have been conducted. A number of these were on a large scale (for example, American Library Association, 1958; Lipetz, 1970, 1972; Matthews, Lawrence, and Ferguson, 1983; Tagliacozzo and Kochen, 1970; University of Chicago, 1968). These and smaller studies are reviewed by Hafter (1979), Kinsella and Bryant (1987), Lewis (1987), Markey (1980), and Palmer (1972), among others. This chapter deals with both macroevaluation and microevaluation of the catalog. Related topics are dealt with in Chapter 6, which discusses how several factors, including a patron's use of the catalog, affect the probability that a patron will find a particular item in the library at a given time, and Chapter 9, which covers database searching.

MEASURING THE VOLUME OF CATALOG USE

The first step in a catalog use study is to look at how many people use the catalog, for how long, and at what times. These types of data have immediate value in planning schedules of reference assistance in the catalog area and also aid in making decisions on such matters as how many terminals are needed to meet peak-demand, simultaneous-access capacity in an online catalog, how many microfiche readers or copies of a printed catalog are needed, or how a card catalog should be designed to allow multiple users easy access to the drawers. Data on volume of use, if broken down by patron group, may also suggest ways in which librarians can promote the catalog to particular groups.

Some typical studies of this type were conducted by Sage et al. (1981), Taylor (1987, 1988), and Tolle et al. (1983). Sage and his associates observed catalog use in a university library for six weeks. The card catalog area was roped off to allow patrons easy access through a single entrance and exit point and to simplify the counting of arrivals. Observers recorded the number of arrivals and departures during each of 234 randomly selected 10-minute observation periods and the length of each patron's use of the catalog. At the end of each observation period, the evaluators used a schematic drawing to mark the location of each patron using the catalog. From these data, they determined peak periods of use and the average length of use. Peak periods then were monitored for an additional six weeks to determine the maximum number of terminals or microfiche readers that would be needed for a planned replacement of the card catalog. Tolle et al. and Taylor used queuing models to predict the number of terminals that would be needed to achieve various levels of service for online catalogs. Taylor's model (1987) enables evaluators to compare the number of terminals required for 16 different levels of service, based on the number of minutes a patron will have to wait for a machine.

In cases where the number of physical access points to the catalog are limited (that is, there are limited numbers of copies of a book catalog, readers for a microform catalog, or terminals for an online catalog), evaluators should consider recording the number of people who must wait to use the catalog and how long they have to wait. When Pawley (1982) did this she found that 89 percent of the patrons at the University of Guelph had to wait for an available catalog terminal. Thirty-five percent waited one to two minutes; 38 percent, three to five minutes; and 16 percent, six minutes or more. Klugkist, Jacobs, and Bossers (1985) found that all available terminals in two Dutch libraries were in almost constant use. Because inconvenience inhibits use (see Chapter 2), this kind of wait might discourage catalog use. When Wayland (1982) asked students at a junior college what they would do if all the catalog terminals were in use, 55 percent responded that they would use the microfiche catalog—an option not available in many other libraries that have catalogs in only one form. Twenty-four percent said they would ask the librarian for help, an acceptable alternative; 9 percent would browse the shelves for information, an action that could negatively influence retrieval results; and 12 percent would leave the library. In a number of studies of online catalogs, patrons themselves suggested the purchase of more terminals to meet demand (for example, Bosman, 1987; Matthews, Lawrence, and Ferguson, 1983).

A few evaluators have tried measuring the volume and average length of use by photographing the catalog area at 5- or 10-second intervals during representative time periods. Kawakami and Kobayashi (1979) used this technique in an academic library, correctly noting its major flaw: someone must screen the photographs, identifying each user and determining how long each use lasted. This can be more time-consuming than having an observer directly record catalog use data.

One of the strengths of automated catalogs is that they can collect some types of data automatically, including information on volume and length of use, saving the evaluator considerable effort. Unfortunately, online systems do not necessarily differentiate a search conducted by one patron from a search conducted by another; the evaluator ends up with figures on the total number of uses of the catalog but not the total number of users. This has prompted some evaluators to collect data on volume of use by manual surveys of individual patrons (for example, Borgman, 1983). The problem could be solved if the software was reprogrammed to require that each patron log on and off, as in the MELVYL system at the University of California (Larson and Graham, 1983). Note, however, that this is a good example of a possible conflict between the need to collect useful management data and the need to make libraries convenient to use; from the user's viewpoint, it is better not to have to log on and off.

When evaluators measure volume of use frequently and at representative times during the day, week, and year, very clear pictures of use may emerge. For example, Lipetz (1972) found that hourly use in a university library rose steadily until the lunch hour, when it dropped significantly. Use rebounded and peaked between 1:30 P.M. and 4:30 P.M., dropped again over the supper hour, rebounded slightly between 7:00 P.M. and 9:00 P.M., and fell thereafter. Daily use was highest on Monday, Tuesday, and Wednesday. Although use dropped below normal at the beginning of a short holiday or recess, it rose above normal at the end of that interval. As expected, the volume of use fell during summer vacations and during breaks between semesters. More recently, Kaske (1988) reported that the proportion of subject searches made in the catalog may vary widely by time of day, day of week, and week of semester.

A few evaluators have tried to determine whether catalog use can be predicted from some other aspect of library use, such as circulation. The success of these efforts has been mixed. For example, although Krikelas (1972) and Lipetz (1970) found a constant ratio of catalog use to circulation, Sage et al. (1981) found no significant correlation between catalog use and circulation or between catalog use and door count. Further research is needed before any conclusions can be drawn about the ability of other measures to predict accurately the volume of catalog use.

Evaluators have also tried to determine whether volume of use varies by patron group. To date, most studies have divided the use groups by demographic characteristics, for example, gender, age, occupation, or year in school. When conducting these types of analyses, the evaluator needs to consider both the intensity and the total volume of use by a particular group to avoid drawing incorrect conclusions. For example, Palmer (1972) found that faculty members constituted only 4.2 percent of the patrons using the card catalog during an eight-week period at the University of Michigan; however, the 2,150 faculty uses seem quite impressive in terms of the faculty's size—3,800 members.

Information on the volume of use by particular patron groups can help evaluators determine whether catalog services are being promoted effectively. This is of particular concern when the format of the catalog is being changed. For example, Armstrong and Costa (1983) studied the response of second- and fifth-grade students and teachers to the introduction of an online catalog. They collected information on frequency of use and determined patron preference toward and satisfaction with the online catalog and card catalog. These data, shown in Exhibits 7-1 and 7-2, revealed that students and teachers felt more comfortable with the online catalog and used it more often, a sign that the library had done an effective job in designing the new system and in helping patrons adapt to it. Of course, special efforts may be needed to promote catalog use by some patron groups, such as older adults, who have received little instruction in catalog use and may fear new technology.

	Second Grade Students		Fifth Grade Students	
	Online Catalog %	Traditional Catalog %	Online Catalog %	Traditional Catalog %
Student preference for catalog	73	23	83	36
Student comfort in using catalog	58	23	80	51
Frequency of use by individual students	34	19	63	29
Student use of catalog to locate nonfiction	47	31	65	33
Catalog as favorite component of library	31	14	63	19

NOTE: Higher percentages indicate a favorable response.

EXHIBIT 7-1   Student use of an online versus a traditional catalog. Reprinted in modified form from Armstrong and Costa (1983), courtesy of Pierian Press.

	Online Catalog %	Traditional Catalog %
Teacher use of catalog to locate materials in the library	40	11
Teacher feels that catalog allows efficient selection of new materials	45	29
Teacher feels that students have positive reaction to catalog	60	39

NOTE: Higher percentages indicate a favorable response.

EXHIBIT 7-2 Faculty use of an online versus a traditional catalog. Reprinted from Armstrong and Costa (1983), courtesy of Pierian Press.

Evaluators also can examine the reason for patron use of the catalog, as this may influence the volume of use. For example, catalog use might be lower in libraries where patrons often browse to meet recreational reading needs. Bishop's (1983) analysis of data from a major study of catalog use, sponsored by the Council on Library Resources, shows that reasons for patron use vary, as might be expected, among types of libraries. Exhibit 7-3 shows these variations for public and large research libraries.

Although a number of evaluators have concentrated on determining the total number of users, others have examined the percentage of patrons who use the catalog on any particular visit, since this indicates to what extent patrons judge a catalog essential to solving their information needs. Past research has shown that only between 25 percent and 45 percent of patrons use the catalog during a particular library visit (Krikelas, 1972). A more recent study showed that 22 percent of patrons at a college library had never used the catalog (Holgate and Lenton, 1986).

Unfortunately, investigators do not always determine whether patrons who fail to consult the catalog have valid reasons for this nonuse. It is not surprising, for example, if patrons who enter the library to attend meetings or to use the copying facilities do not use the catalog. Other patrons may legitimately bypass the catalog because they prefer to seek help directly from the library staff, a practice that may save their time and give them greater satisfaction. Some patrons may bypass the catalog because they believe they can manage without it. This might indeed be the case when they have very simple requirements, such as seeking a fiction title in a library where novels are shelved alphabetically by author. Even here, however, the patron could often benefit from the catalog, which would show, for example, that a certain author wrote under more than one name. Patrons having to work with more complicated arrangements or

Type of Library	Recreation %	Fixing %	Work %	Personal %	Hobby %	Class %	Report %	Thesis %	Publications %	Teaching %	Keeping-up %
Association of Research Libraries	12.6	1.8	14.8	23.2	6.0	33.0	45.1	11.7	7.5	4.6	13.4
Public	31.1	7.2	17.0	50.6	13.6	17.4	21.1	3.9	3.3	3.7	15.1

EXHIBIT 7-3   Patrons' reasons for seeking information in academic and public libraries. Reprinted from Bishop (1983), courtesy of the American Library Association.

classification schemes are likely to make more serious errors if they fail to consult the catalog. For example, Seymour and Schofield (1973) discovered that undergraduates who bypassed the catalog when looking for specific items in university libraries sometimes failed to find books that were housed correctly on the shelves. Still other patrons may avoid the catalog because they find it too difficult to use (for example, Drone, 1984). This condition suggests that librarians need to either design catalogs that patrons can readily understand and use (the ideal situation) or provide more and better instruction in catalog use, which has been shown to increase both the volume and the effectiveness of use (Bryant and Needham, 1973).

MEASURING THE EFFECTIVENESS OF CATALOG USE

A comprehensive review by Palmer (1972) suggested that, on the average, patrons are able to find entries for 70–80 percent of the items or subjects sought in the catalog; however, the range extends from 15 percent to 94 percent, implying that some libraries are doing a much better job than others in developing and maintaining effective catalogs. Of course, such a wide range in performance might indicate that different performance standards have been used. To make intelligent improvements, librarians must differentiate between search success and search failure, identify specific instances of failure, and determine the precise causes of failure.

Researchers have tried various methods of collecting data for these purposes. In some early studies, investigators analyzed reference questions to determine which could best be answered from standard reference works and which from subject catalogs; they analyzed call slips presented to staff in a closed stack area to determine the types of entries that patrons used to locate desired items; they even "measured" the extent and type of catalog use through observation of the soiled condition of catalog cards (Frarey, 1953; Spalding, 1950). Generally, the methods used in these early studies lacked rigor or failed to distinguish the underlying problems that prevented patrons from locating needed items in the catalog.

Perrine's (1967, 1968) approach was somewhat more successful. Reference staff were stationed in the catalog area to answer patron questions about catalog use. As part of the process, patrons were queried about any search strategy they used that failed. This information was recorded, along with information about any search strategy that the reference staff used that was successful. It was then determined what might be done to make catalogs more effective.

Today, most evaluators use one of four techniques to evaluate the effectiveness of catalog use. They survey library patrons, conduct controlled experiments, analyze transactions that are automatically recorded by online catalogs, or use focus group interviews to identify the problems that patrons have with catalogs. A discussion of each of these techniques follows.

Surveys

Surveying library patrons by questionnaire or interview is the most common method of obtaining information on the effectiveness of catalog use and can be done inexpensively. Investigators who recently conducted such surveys include Markey (1986), Pawley (1982), and Pease and Gouke (1982). Although most surveys concentrate on evaluating the effectiveness of use in a particular library, studies have also been conducted involving a number of different libraries (often libraries of several types). For example, the Council on Library Resources (CLR) collected information on patron use of online catalogs in 29 different public and academic libraries (Ferguson et al., 1982).

Most evaluators design survey instruments to focus on present catalog use because surveys eliciting opinions on past catalog use depend heavily on what respondents remember about past experiences, and human memory is highly unreliable (for instance, see Swanson, 1972). Moreover, surveys on past use gauge only general reactions. Because they do not focus on specific instances of use, they cannot quantify successes and failures or precisely identify instances of failure so that underlying causes can be pinpointed. The best questionnaire or interview schedule, therefore, is designed to determine what each patron is seeking currently and how successful the search is. One typical questionnaire, used in the CLR study of online catalogs, is shown in Exhibit 7-4. It was given to patrons in paper form in most libraries, but staff at one library reprogrammed their catalog to administer the questionnaire online as the patron finished a search (Larson and Graham, 1983). Online questionnaires have been used in other studies as well (for example, Berger and Klemperer, 1981).

Even when designed to focus on a specific instance of catalog use, the questionnaire method of collecting data on catalog use has its flaws. Many people dislike questionnaires and either fail to complete them or do so in such a hurried and careless way that the results are of little value. For example, Seymour

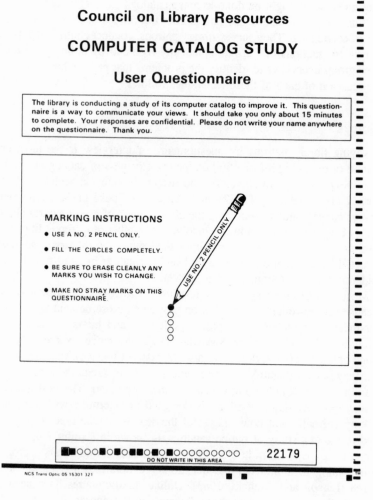

EXHIBIT 7-4 User questionnaire from the Council on Library Resources Computer Catalog Study. Reprinted from Matthews and Lawrence (1984), courtesy of the American Library Association.

EXHIBIT 7-4 *(Continued)*

PART 1: ABOUT YOUR MOST RECENT SEARCH

INSTRUCTIONS: Please answer these questions about the computer catalog search you just completed.

1. I came to this computer search with:
(Mark **ALL** that apply)

a. A complete author's name .... O
b. Part of an author's name .... O
c. A complete title .... O
d. Part of a title .... O
e. A topic word or words .... O
f. A subject heading or headings .... O
g. A complete call number .... O
h. Part of a call number .... O

2. By searching this computer catalog I was trying to find:
(Mark **ALL** that apply)

a. A specific book, journal or magazine .... O

b. Books, journals or magazines on a topic or subject ..... O
c. Books by a specific author .... O

d. Information such as publisher, date, spelling
   of a name, etc. .... O

e. If a book that I know the library has is available
   for my use .... O

f. Another library that has a book, journal or
   magazine that I want .... O

3. I searched for what I wanted by:
(Mark **ALL** that apply)

a. A complete author's name .... O
b. Part of an author's name .... O
c. A complete title .... O
d. Part of a title .... O
e. A topic word or words .... O
f. A subject heading or headings .... O
g. A complete call number .... O
h. Part of a call number .... O

4. I need this information for:
(Mark **ALL** that apply)

a. Recreational uses .... O
b. Making or fixing something .... O
c. My work or job .... O
d. Personal interest .... O
e. A hobby .... O
f. Class or course reading .... O
g. A course paper or report .... O
h. A thesis or dissertation .... O
i. Writing for publication .... O
j. Teaching or planning a course .... O
k. Keeping up on a topic or subject .... O

5. In this computer search I found:
(Mark **ONE** only)

a. More than I was looking for .... O
b. All that I was looking for .... O
c. Some of what I was looking for .... O
d. Nothing I was looking for .... O

6. In relation to what I was looking for, this computer search was:
(Mark **ONE** only)

a. Very satisfactory .... O
b. Somewhat satisfactory .... O
c. Somewhat unsatisfactory .... O
d. Very unsatisfactory .... O

7. I came across things of interest other than what I was looking for:

a. YES .... O
b. NO .... O

8. I got help in doing this computer catalog search from:
(Mark **ALL** that apply)

a. Printed material or signs .... O
b. Instructions on the terminal screen .... O
c. Library staff member .... O
d. Person nearby .... O
e. I did not get help .... O

EXHIBIT 7-4 *(Continued)*

9. My overall or general attitude toward the computer catalog is:
(Mark ONE only)

a. Very favorable .... O
b. Somewhat favorable .... O
c. Somewhat unfavorable .... O
d. Very unfavorable .... O

10. Compared to the card, book, or microfiche catalog in this library, the computer catalog is:
(Mark ONE only)

a. Better .... O
b. About the same .... O
c. Worse .... O
d. Can't decide .... O

PART 2: YOUR EXPERIENCE WITH COMPUTER CATALOG FEATURES

INSTRUCTIONS: Mark the single column for each question that corresponds most closely to how you feel. If the statement does not apply to your experience at the computer catalog, mark the column, "Does Not Apply".

	STRONGLY AGREE	AGREE	NEITHER AGREE NOR DISAGREE	DISAGREE	STRONGLY DISAGREE	DOES NOT APPLY
11. A computer search by title is difficult	O	O	O	O	O	O
12. A computer search by author is easy	O	O	O	O	O	O
13. A computer search by subject is difficult	O	O	O	O	O	O
14. A computer search by call number is easy	O	O	O	O	O	O
15. A computer search by combined author/title is difficult	O	O	O	O	O	O
16. Remembering commands in the middle of the search is easy	O	O	O	O	O	O
17. Finding the correct subject term is difficult	O	O	O	O	O	O
18. Scanning through a long display (forward or backward) is easy	O	O	O	O	O	O
19. Increasing the result when too little is retrieved is difficult	O	O	O	O	O	O
20. Reducing the result when too much is retrieved is easy	O	O	O	O	O	O
21. Understanding explanations on the screen is difficult	O	O	O	O	O	O
22. Using codes or abbreviations for searching is easy	O	O	O	O	O	O
23. Abbreviations on the screen are easy to understand	O	O	O	O	O	O
24. Locating call numbers on the screen is difficult	O	O	O	O	O	O
25. Searching with a short form of a name or a word (truncation) is easy	O	O	O	O	O	O

	STRONGLY AGREE	AGREE	NEITHER AGREE NOR DISAGREE	DISAGREE	STRONGLY DISAGREE	DOES NOT APPLY
26. Using logical terms like AND, OR, NOT is difficult	O	O	O	O	O	O
27. Remembering the exact sequence or order of commands is easy	O	O	O	O	O	O
28. Understanding the initial instructions on the screen is difficult	O	O	O	O	O	O
29. Understanding the display for a single book, journal or magazine is easy	O	O	O	O	O	O
30. Understanding the display that shows more than a single book, journal or magazine is difficult	O	O	O	O	O	O
31. Interrupting or stopping the display of information is easy	O	O	O	O	O	O
32. Typing in exact spelling, initials, spaces and hyphens is difficult to do	O	O	O	O	O	O
33. Knowing what is included in the computer catalog is easy to remember	O	O	O	O	O	O
34. The order in which items are displayed is easy to understand	O	O	O	O	O	O
35. Displayed messages are too long	O	O	O	O	O	O

EXHIBIT 7-4 *(Continued)*

	STRONGLY AGREE	AGREE	NEITHER AGREE NOR DISAGREE	DISAGREE	STRONGLY DISAGREE	DOES NOT APPLY
36. Selecting from a list of choices takes too much time	○	○	○	○	○	○
37. Entering commands when I want to during the search process is difficult	○	○	○	○	○	○
38. The rate at which the computer responds is too slow	○	○	○	○	○	○
39. The availability of signs and brochures is adequate	○	○	○	○	○	○
40. Signs and brochures are not very useful	○	○	○	○	○	○
41. The staff advice is often not helpful	○	○	○	○	○	○
42. It is hard to find a free terminal	○	○	○	○	○	○

YOU ARE MORE THAN HALF - WAY DONE

PART 3: IMPROVING THE COMPUTER CATALOG

INSTRUCTIONS: Select the response or responses that best reflect your views about changes that should be made in the computer catalog.

43. When I use the computer catalog terminal: (Mark YES or NO)

	YES	NO
a. The keyboard is confusing to use	○	○
b. There is too much glare on the screen	○	○
c. The letters and numbers are easy to read	○	○
d. The lighting around the terminal is too bright	○	○
e. There is enough writing space at the terminal	○	○
f. Nearby noise is distracting	○	○
g. The terminal table is too high or too low	○	○
h. The printer is easy to use	○	○

44. Select up to FOUR additional features you would like this computer catalog to have:

a. Providing step by step instructions ○
b. Searching by any word or words in a title ○
c. Searching by any word or words in a subject heading ○
d. Limiting search results by date of publication ○
e. Limiting search results by language ○
f. Ability to search by journal title abbreviations ○
g. Ability to change the order in which items are displayed ○
h. Ability to view a list of words related to my search words ○
i. Ability to search for illustrations and bibliographies ○
j. Ability to search by call number ○
k. Ability to print search results ○
l. Ability to search a book's table of contents, summary or index ○
m. Ability to know if a book is checked out ○
n. Ability to tell where a book is located in the library ○
o. None ○

45. Select up to FOUR computer catalog service improvements you would like the library to make:

a. More terminals ○
b. Terminals at locations other than near the card catalog ○
c. Terminals at places other than library buildings ○
d. A chart of commands posted at the terminal ○
e. A manual or brochure at the terminal ○
f. An instruction manual for purchase ○
g. Training sessions ○
h. Slide/tape cassette training program ○
i. None ○

46. Select up to FOUR kinds of material you would like to see added to the computer catalog:

a. Dissertations ○
b. Motion picture films ○
c. Government publications ○
d. Journal or magazine titles ○
e. Maps ○
f. Manuscripts ○
g. Music scores ○
h. Newspapers ○
i. Phonograph records or tapes ○
j. Technical reports ○
k. More of the library's older books ○
l. None ○
m. Other ○

47. BRIEFLY DESCRIBE ANY OTHER PROBLEMS WITH THIS COMPUTER CATALOG OR CHANGES YOU WOULD LIKE MADE TO IT: ○

EXHIBIT 7-4 *(Continued)*

PART 4: ABOUT YOURSELF

INSTRUCTIONS: Your responses are confidential. Please do not write your name anywhere on this questionnaire.

---

48. I come to this library:

a. Daily .... O
b. Weekly .... O
c. Monthly .... O
d. About four times a year .... O
e. About once a year .... O
f. Not before today .... O

49. I use this computer catalog:

a. Every library visit .... O
b. Almost every visit .... O
c. Occasionally .... O
d. Rarely .... O
e. Not before today .... O

50. I use this library's book, card or microfilm catalog:

a. Every visit .... O
b. Almost every visit .... O
c. Occasionally .... O
d. Rarely .... O
e. Never .... O

51. I use a computer system other than the library's computer catalog:

a. Daily .... O
b. Weekly .... O
c. Monthly .... O
d. About four times a year .... O
e. About once a year .... O
f. Never .... O

52. I first heard about this computer catalog from:
(Mark ONE only)

a. Noticing a terminal in the library .... O
b. Library tour, orientation or demonstration .... O
c. An article or written announcement .... O
d. A course instructor .... O
e. A friend or family member .... O
f. Library staff .... O

53. I learned how to use this computer catalog:
(Mark ALL that apply)

a. From a friend or someone at a nearby terminal .... O
b. Using printed instructions .... O
c. Using instructions on the terminal screen .... O
d. From the library staff .... O
e. From a library course or orientation .... O
f. From a slide/tape/cassette program .... O
g. By myself without any help .... O

54. My age group is:

a. 14 and under .... O
b. 15 - 19 years .... O
c. 20 - 24 years .... O
d. 25 - 34 years .... O
e. 35 - 44 years .... O
f. 45 - 54 years .... O
g. 55 - 64 years .... O
h. 65 and over .... O

55. I am:

a. Female .... O
b. Male .... O

56. Mark your current or highest educational level:
(Mark ONE only)

a. Grade School or Elementary School .... O
b. High School or Secondary School .... O
c. Some College or University .... O
d. College or University Graduate .... O

If you are not completing this questionnaire at a college or university, please stop here. Thank you.

If you are completing this questionnaire at a college or university, please continue.

57. The category that best describes my academic area is:
(Mark ONE only)

a. Arts and Humanities .... O
b. Physical/Biological Sciences .... O
c. Social Sciences .... O
d. Business/Management .... O
e. Education .... O
f. Engineering .... O
g. Medical/Health Sciences .... O
h. Law .... O
i. Major not declared .... O
j. Interdisciplinary .... O

EXHIBIT 7-4 *(Continued)*

58. The main focus of my academic work at the present time is:
(Mark **ALL** that apply)

a. Course Work .... ○
b. Teaching .... ○
c. Research .... ○

59. My present affiliation with this college or university is:

a. Freshman/Sophomore .... ○
b. Junior/Senior .... ○
c. Graduate - masters level .... ○
d. Graduate - doctoral level .... ○
e. Graduate - professional school .... ○
f. Faculty .... ○
g. Staff .... ○
h. Other .... ○

Thank you for participating in this study of the computer catalog. This completes the questionnaire. Please return it.

SUPPLEMENTARY QUESTIONNAIRE ITEMS

60. ○○○○○○○○○○○○○○○○○
61. ○○○○○○○○○○○○○○○○○
62. ○○○○○○○○○○○○○○○○○
63. ○○○○○○○○○○○○○○○○○
64. ○○○○○○○○○○○○○○○○○

Please circle the number in front of the phrase which best describes why you need the information you are looking for in the library.

1. Supplementary reading for a class
2. Writing a term paper for a class
3. Writing a master's thesis
4. Writing a doctoral dissertation
5. Independent research
6. Contract research or grant
7. Interested in the subject, and wish to know more about it
8. Other (Please specify) _____

Please circle the number in front of the phrase which best describes the amount of information you need on the subject you are looking for.

1. A brief explanation of the subject, such as a magazine article or a chapter in a book
2. A book on the subject
3. One *particular* book on the subject whose author and/or title I can't remember
4. Two or three of the best books on the subject
5. All the books listed in the catalog on the subject
6. All the material in the library on the subject whether in books, magazine articles, documents, etc.
7. Everything written on the subject, even if the library doesn't have it
8. Other (Please specify) _____

EXHIBIT 7-5   Two questions about subject searches conducted in the catalog. Reprinted from Broadbent (1984), courtesy of Haworth Press.

and Schofield (1973) asked catalog users at Cambridge University to complete catalog query slips, available in the catalog area, when they were unable to find a known item in the catalog. Follow-up interviews enabled evaluators to estimate the proportion of patrons completing the slips. Of the 446 patrons interviewed, 110 (25 percent) reported at least partial failure; of these, 31 completed query slips, a cooperation rate of only 28 percent. This type of low response rate may bias study results. Evaluators may also find it difficult to design questionnaires that are both user friendly and able to collect the detailed information needed to identify and analyze failures. And most questionnaires are completed at the end of a catalog search; in the case of a subject search, the patron may not recall exactly what he or she was looking for when the search began, since the original concept of the information needed may have changed during the search.

Because of the difficulties inherent in using questionnaires, many evaluators prefer to interview a random sample of patrons while they search the catalog. Although this technique requires more staff time than does questionnaire administration, the results are likely to be more precise and reliable. To obtain the data needed for analysis, the interviewer usually approaches the patron at the moment a search is begun, gathering information on the type of search to be conducted, the motivation for the search, any "clues" that the patron either has in mind or on paper (the evaluator should photocopy these, if possible), the intended search approach, and relevant personal details about the patron. Many variations of these questions are possible. Exhibit 7-5 shows just two of the questions that Broadbent (1984) used to elicit information on subject searches.

In the second stage of the survey, the patron is asked to proceed with the search, and the interviewer may remain nearby to record the precise sequence of entries consulted and the length of time spent on the search. One form used by researchers to record data at this stage is shown in Exhibit 7-6. There is some disagreement about whether the interviewer should try to record data unobtrusively, without letting patrons know they are being watched. Lipetz (1972) and Specht (1980) argued that an unobtrusive approach will result in more accurate data, because the patron will behave more naturally. Many other evaluators have chosen the obtrusive approach, however, because it allows more accurate recording of the steps the patrons take. Markey (1983b) actually asked patrons to think aloud while using the catalog. Their comments were recorded on tape for later transcription and analysis.

In the third stage of the interview process, the evaluator asks patrons whether the desired items were found. It may be necessary to accompany patrons to the stacks to determine the success of their searches, since as many as one-third of those who use the catalog make their final selection at the shelves rather than directly from catalog entries (Miura et al., 1980).

Other information may also be recorded. For example, Lipetz and Stangl (1968) noted the call numbers of the final selections. Later they scrutinized the catalog card for each selection to determine if it actually matched the data that patrons initially brought to the catalog. File arrangement and file headings were compared with the search approaches taken by the patrons. Finally, books identified during the catalog search as being pertinent to the patrons' needs were examined to determine whether a change in cataloging practice might have provided a better match with the data brought to the search.

Controlled Experiments in Catalog Use

Some evaluators have used experiments to measure the effectiveness of catalog use. For example, Siegel et al. (1983, 1984) set up a pair of controlled experiments to study the use of two proposed automated catalogs at the National Library of Medicine. In one experiment, staff were given 14 paired search

INTERVIEW REPORT.   Agency: _____ 1. ___

Date _____ Interview began _____ M   Ended _____ M

Day _____ Patron's occupation _____ 2. ___

(Be as specific as possible, e.g., Undergrad.; Grade-school teacher, Plumber)

SEEKING A KNOWN ITEM (Please record patron's data on verso)

3. Found author or title-main-entry card for desired item . . . . 3. ☐
4. Found title card for desired item . . . . 4. ☐
5. Found item by looking for author or title-main-entry under a SUBJECT . . . . . . 5. ☐
6. Did not find item . . . . 6. ☐
7. Patron's information about author or title was incorrect or incomplete . . . . . . 7. ☐
8. "Author" was not main entry but added entry (like translator) . . . . 8. ☐
9. No entry for "author", altho there *was* a main entry card . . . . 9. ☐
10. No title card, altho there *was* an author card (permanent or temporary) . . . . . 10. ☐
11. Filing arrangements under this author, or before and after him, were unclear to patron . 11. ☐
12. Item was not in this catalog . . . . 12. ☐
13. Other reason_____ 13. ☐
14. Source of patron's information: _____ 14. ___

LOOKING UP A SUBJECT

15. Wanted material on (HIS WORDS)_____ 15. ___
16. That "subject"-field was already familiar to the patron . . . . 16. ☐
    Found catalog cards on that "subject" by locating
17. This subject heading or SEE reference:_____ 17. ☐
18. Title(s) with the meaning he wanted, altho his "subject" was not a Library subject . . 18. ☐
19. Partial or inverted title(s) with the meaning wanted (again, not a Library subject) . . . 19. ☐
20. Relevant title(s) under an AUTHOR known to write on patron's "subject" . . . . . 20. ☐
21. Additional subject headings pertinent to search . . . . 21. ☐
22. Did not find any catalog cards on his "subject" . . . . 22. ☐
23. Patron's "subject" was not a subject heading and there was no SEE reference to
    the subject heading that was used . . . . 23. ☐
24. There was a SEE or SEE ALSO, but it was not understood or not found . . . . . 24. ☐
25. Following up SEE's or SEE ALSO's became burdensome or threatened to; was abandoned 25. ☐
26. Time was lost at heading_____which proved little or no help . . . . . 26. ☐
27. There were no cards on the subject in this catalog . . . . 27. ☐
28. Other reason_____ 28. ☐
29. Took down call numbers for all entries under subject(s) used . . . . 29. ☐
    Took down call numbers for only *some* (or *none*); selection was based in good part on:
30. Alphabetical position of entries . . . . 30. ☐
31. Desire for works in English . . . . 31. ☐
32. Desire for works in other language(s) . . . . 32. ☐
33. Connotation of wording of title(s), subtitle(s) . . . . 33. ☐
34. Date of publication . . . . 34. ☐
35. Prominence of particular classifications (i.e., Where are most books on the subject?) . . 35. ☐
36. Author's reputation . . . . 36. ☐
37. "Illus." statement . . . . 37. ☐
38. Bibliography note . . . . 38. ☐
39. Tracing . . . . 39. ☐
40. (Other)_____ 40. ☐

41. Patron had used this catalog before . . . . 41. ☐
42. Sought help at some point(s) from staff member . . . . 42. ☐
43. Differences among author, title and subject cards were not clear to patron . . . . . 43. ☐
44. Lack of guide-card(s) contributed to confusion, loss of time, or failure . . . . . . 44. ☐
45. Interviewer believes catalog entries were sufficient to meet patron's need . . . . . 45. ☐

INTERVIEWER'S (and Patron's) COMMENT: OVER

EXHIBIT 7-6   Interview schedule designed to record patron actions during a catalog search. Reprinted from American Library Association (1958), courtesy of ALA.

queries (representative of six common search problems) and were asked to search for the materials in both catalogs. In the second experiment, randomly selected patrons conducted self-initiated searches of their own choosing in both catalogs. Immediately after the searches were conducted, staff and patrons completed a survey designed to determine user success and satisfaction with each system. Library staff used results of the evaluation to choose the system that yielded more successful search results (incidentally, the one preferred by both patrons and staff).

In another experiment, Pejtersen and Austin (1983) tested a catalog designed to help patrons select fiction. The entries indexed novels by subject matter and genre, setting, author's intention (for example, humor), and accessibility (for example, readability or size of print). The catalog was shown to be effective.

Experimental studies, if properly controlled, can indicate the types of errors patrons can make when using catalogs. Moreover, they lend themselves to the comparison of catalogs, as in the study by Aanonson (1987), which compared results of keyword searches in six different online catalogs. For some purposes, however, experimental studies may be flawed. One assumption made in such studies is that patrons behave the same when actually using library catalogs as when participating in controlled tests. This is not always true. For example, the fact that most patrons choose fiction either by browsing the shelves or by browsing works by their favorite authors (Spiller, 1980) suggests that few patrons would actually use a catalog such as that described by Pejtersen and Austin to help them select fiction. In addition, experiments often require special expertise and substantial levels of resources, since setting up proper experimental controls is an exacting task.

Analysis of Transaction Logs

Online catalogs have made it possible to monitor many aspects of catalog use through the study of transaction logs. The online catalog is programmed to record each transaction onto a computer disk or tape. The evaluator then screens these transactions to determine various facts about each search. Penniman and Dominick (1980) comprehensively reviewed the types of data that should be collected in a transaction log. At a minimum, these elements should include the date and time of the transaction, the length of the transaction, the types of searches performed, the total number of operations performed by each patron, the number of matches or retrievals obtained after each input access point, the full text of each patron's search, and the type and number of errors made. The most useful systems are programmed to provide summaries of these activities as well as records of individual searches. Studies using transaction logs have been reported by Borgman (1983), Dickson (1984), Freiburger and Simon (1984), and Tolle (1983), among others. Exhibit 7-7, from Cochrane and Markey (1983), is an example of the information that appeared in one transaction log.

LENGTH	TERMINAL ID	DATE	TIME	CHARACTER FORMAT	USER INPUT AND SYSTEM RESPONSE
81	12	308204	13180044302		THE PATH OF THE BUDDHA; NEW YORK, RONALD PRESS CO, 1956
41	12	308204	13180044882	BL1420.M6 C.4;
24	12	308204	13180045252	
52	12	308204	13180045322	9. MORGAN, KENNETH WILLIAM
81	12	308204	13180045692	THE PATH OF THE BUDDHA; NEW YORK, RONALD PRESS CO, 1956
41	12	308204	13180046712	BL1420.M6 C.3;
93	12	308204	13180047322	37 ITEMS. PRESS RETURN FOR DISPLAY, OR S AND RETURN FOR NEW SEARCH:
24	12	308204	13180050341	S
24	12	308204	13180050852	
37	12	308204	13180051022	ENTER SEARCH:
47	12	308204	13180131141	D;PATHOLAGICAL HISTOLOGY
47	12	308204	13180131292	D;PATHOLAGICAL HISTOLOGY
53	12	308204	13180313612	* — MISSING OR BAD SEARCH CODE
24	12	308204	13180131992	
37	12	308204	13180132202	ENTER SEARCH:
41	12	308204	13180204731	WD;PATHO+HISTOLOGY
40	12	308204	13180204782	SEARCHING "PATHO"
45	12	308204	13180205352	SEARCHING "HISTOLOGY"
93	12	308204	13180205952	3 ITEMS. PRESS RETURN FOR DISPLAY, OR S AND RETURN FOR NEW SEARCH:
23	12	308204	13180207671	
24	12	308204	13180207892	
60	12	308204	13180207912	1. BLOOM, WILLIAM, 1899-
89	12	308204	13180208212	HISTOPATHOLOGY OF IRRADIATION FROM EXTERNAL AND INTERNAL SOURCES
66	12	308204	131802088321	ST ED, NEW YORK, MCGRAW-HILL BOOK CO, 1948
50	12	308204	13180209272	RB27.B57 ; ENGR & LIFE SCI
24	12	308204	13180209792	
43	12	308204	13180209832	2. FERLIIO, ALFIJ
94	12	308204	13180210072	HISTOLOGICAL CLASSIFICATION OF LARYNX AND HYPOHARYNX CANCERS AND THEIR
93	12	308204	13180210732	CLINICAL IMPLICATIONS : PATHOLOGIC ASPECTS OF 2052 MALIGNANT NEOPLASMS

Key:
Length (Bytes 1-4): Record Length
Terminal ID (Bytes 5-6): Identifies terminal and location
Date (Bytes 7-12): Date in Gregorian format, YYMMDD
Time (Bytes 13-20): Time this particular record ordinated to 100th of a second, HHMMSShh
Character Format (Byte 21): "1" if record was read from a terminal; "2" if record written to a terminal
User Input and System Response (Bytes 22): Actual text sent to a terminal or entered at a terminal

EXHIBIT 7-7   Transaction log record from Syracuse University. Reprinted from Cochrane and Markey (1983), courtesy of Ablex Publishing Company.

The review of the full text of a sample of searches may provide data useful for microevaluation purposes because it can show what search errors occur frequently and thus can lead to suggestions for system improvements. Some evaluators have reviewed logs from other libraries to see what types of problems appear in more than one system. For example, Kern-Simirenko (1983) suggested the following five changes after she reviewed the transaction logs of three different online systems:

1. Add mnemonic search commands (without punctuation or symbols) to reduce patron errors in entering data.
2. Use various kinds of Boolean operators and other commands that allow patrons to limit results (for example, by publication date or language) to reduce false hits and refine search results.
3. Use automatic truncation to permit simultaneous retrieval of singular and plural forms of search terms.
4. Add a browsable subject heading index so patrons can refine or expand searches.
5. Inform patrons about their various options at each stage of the search.

Although transaction logs most often are used to collect data for improving catalog design, Nielsen (1986) suggested that librarians involved in bibliographic instruction review the logs to gain a better understanding of the types of errors that patrons normally make. Librarians can then design their instructions accordingly, even using actual examples from the logs during instructional sessions to illustrate successful and unsuccessful search strategies that other patrons have used.

Focus Group Interviews

Marketing specialists originally designed focus group interviews to determine how manufacturers could improve product design. In focus group sessions, a moderator leads 5–15 persons in a guided discussion of some product or service. For example, Ferguson et al. (1982) reported on focus group interviews that questioned library staff about online catalogs. Staff members made pointed observations about patron fear and nonuse of the catalogs, difficulties patrons had in using the catalogs, and the perceived impact of the catalogs on the library, staff, and patrons; they also offered specific suggestions for improvement. Although most moderators use interview schedules containing open-ended questions to elicit and focus responses, they are free to pursue any comments the participants make about the issue at hand.

Because of the small number of patrons interviewed, the findings of focus group sessions are not necessarily generalizable. This technique, however, is well suited to determining whether patrons understand the capabilities of current catalogs and to ascertaining what they would like to see changed. Moreover, the technique often unearths points that are not brought out in questionnaires or interviews, which may explain why its popularity with librarians continues to increase (Markey, 1983a).

Choosing the Appropriate Evaluation Method

Cochrane and Markey (1983) pointed out that one evaluation method may be better suited than others for collecting data on some aspect of catalog use. The evaluator who wishes to compare user performance on different types of catalogs (for example, microform versus card) or on different online catalogs might rely on controlled experimental tests. The researcher wishing to obtain patron feedback could use surveys or focus group interviews. Questions about user behavior online might best be examined through transaction logs. Often, a study combining a number of these methods is necessary to collect all the information needed on catalog use in a particular setting. The remainder of this chapter concentrates on common issues that various studies of catalog use have considered.

WHAT TYPE OF SEARCH DID THE PATRON CONDUCT?

Most evaluators try to determine the type of search the patron conducted in the catalog, since this can affect catalog design. Most searches are of two types: a search for some item for which either the author or title is known (called a known-item search) or a search for some item on a particular subject (American Library Association, 1958; Hafter, 1979).

Evaluators who are interested in discriminating between search types need to take extra care to distinguish between known-item searches and "disguised" subject searches. For example, 73 percent of the patrons at the Yale University library originally said they were looking for a known item. But interviews determined that only 56 percent of the searches fell into this category. The other 17 percent were subject searches in disguise: the patron wanted a book on a particular subject and knew of some work on that subject so looked for it rather than others (that may have been of equal or greater value) under the appropriate subject heading in the catalog (Lipetz, 1972). If many patrons are using known-item searches to look for materials on particular subjects, a problem may exist with the subject-searching capability of a particular catalog.

Subject searching is further complicated because some patrons find relevant subject headings in the catalog, jot down the classification numbers, and proceed to these numbers on the shelves, where they browse for the titles that best meet their needs. Miura et al. (1980) found that one-third of the patrons using a university library's catalog followed this practice. This pattern of searching suggests that many patrons have difficulty in determining, from the catalog entry, whether they are interested in perusing a book on a particular subject. As is discussed later in this chapter, this is often because explicit content information is lacking or annotations are not descriptive enough for patrons to discriminate among titles.

Other types of searches may also be conducted (although these constitute such a small percentage of use that they are not discussed in detail here). Lipetz (1972) found that some patrons conduct bibliographic searches. These are initiated to obtain the bibliographic citations for particular items rather than to locate the works themselves. A few evaluators have tried to determine whether patrons will search by access points other than author, title, or subject, if these are provided. Studies so far suggest that alternative search modes will be used. For example, some patrons want the ability to search by call number (Markey, 1986, 1987) or by keyword (Matthews, Lawrence, and Ferguson, 1983). Students in a music library both want and use performer and performing company as access points (Drone, 1984). Further explorations are needed to determine what other access points (for example, SUDOC or ERIC numbers) patrons desire and will use.

Generally, the choice of search strategy is most affected by the access points provided in the catalog and by the amount and kind of information that a patron brings to the catalog. Krikelas (1980), however, verified that search mode also is affected by the actual or perceived ease of searching in a particular mode. He found that, as the information known about an author or title became less distinctive, the extent of subject searching increased. Ultimately, the patron selected the search alternative that he or she thought would be unique; clues that presumably would lead to large sets of catalog entries—difficult and time-consuming to search—were rejected.

The theory that ease of use affects choice of search mode also is supported by studies comparing the ways people search card catalogs to the ways they search other types of catalogs. For example, the vast majority of patrons search by known item when using a card catalog (Corya and Lelvis, 1975; Hafter, 1979; Tagliacozzo, 1972). But, in libraries with book, microform, and online catalogs, the subject approach is used more often (Frost, 1987a, 1987b; Maclaren, 1984; Matthews, Lawrence, and Ferguson, 1983; Sacco, 1973; Siegel et al., 1984).[1] Lipetz and Paulson (1987) recorded that the proportion of subject searches rose from 27 percent to 49 percent when an online catalog was introduced at the New York State Library. The increased use of subject searches generally is attributed to the greater ease in scanning subject entries, because the online, book, and microform catalogs "display a large number of entries on one frame [page or screen], whereas a card file only allows one entry to be seen at a time" (Aveney and Ghikas, 1979, p. 82).

---

[1] Hancock (1987), however, suggested that subject searching in manual catalogs in general may have been underestimated.

In addition to enabling patrons to see alphabetically related subject terms (for example, Protestantism and Protestants), the ease of scanning may help patrons overcome their failure to understand the order in which items are filed in the card, microform, or book catalog. Some evaluators have confirmed this difficulty. For example, Sacco (1973) found that all patrons searching the catalog for periodical titles at the Chester County (Missouri) Library failed in their searches because they did not understand the rules for filing title entries. In a university library, only 17 percent of the patrons knew how subjects and authors were currently filed in the catalog (Simmons and Foster, 1982). Subject filing rules seem particularly difficult for patrons to understand, as Mischo (1981) noted, because subject headings have a variety of phrase constructions. Some are straightforward, but others, such as subdivided headings using hyphens or inverted headings with commas, are difficult for the average person to locate, especially if the catalog contains few cross-references.

Some evaluators have also been interested in determining to what extent the mode of searching varies by patron group. Variations certainly exist. For instance, in academic libraries, the number of known-item searches varies directly with rank: faculty conduct proportionally more of these searches than graduate students, who conduct proportionally more than undergraduates (American Library Association, 1958; Frost, 1987a; Tagliacozzo et al., 1970).

The extent to which search modes vary from one type of library to another has been considered. Most investigators have found that patrons in academic, special, and large public libraries conduct known-item searches more than do patrons in school and small public libraries (American Library Association, 1958; Corya and Lelvis, 1975; Hafter, 1979; Tagliacozzo et al., 1970). This difference presumably reflects the various needs of the client groups of each of these libraries; the patron in a small public library may want something good to read on a particular subject, whereas the faculty member in an academic library is more likely to be seeking a specific item to help with a research project.

Traditionally, library catalogs have provided somewhat limited capabilities for searching by subject. The replacement of the card catalog by online public access catalogs (OPACs) has brought about a great resurgence of interest throughout the library profession in all aspects of subject access. For one thing, it has been found that the proportion of catalog searches that are subject searches has tended to increase considerably as OPACs fall into place. Lipetz and Paulson (1987) confirm this trend in a "before and after" study at the New York State Library. Frost (1985, 1987b) studied catalog users at the University of Houston and concluded that students search more often by subject than do faculty. On the basis of a study at the City University (London) prior to the automation of their catalog, however, Hancock (1987) suggested that subject searching of manual catalogs may have been more prevalent than previously thought. Kaske (1988) found great variability in the proportion of OPAC searches that are subject searches—by hour of day, day of week, and week of semester.

THE SUCCESS OF KNOWN-ITEM SEARCHES

Most studies have shown that patrons searching for known items by author or title experience success rates between 70 percent and 80 percent (for example, American Library Association, 1958; Moore, 1981; Palmer, 1972). Two distinct types of failures exist. The first is failure to find an entry for an item not held by the library. This is a collection failure; methods of identifying and correcting such failures are discussed in Chapters 3 and 4. The second, catalog failure, is failure to find an entry for an item that the library owns. Two types of catalog failure may occur. The more common is that the patron fails to find an entry for an item represented in the catalog. The patron might also fail to find an item that is not represented in the catalog (for example, an uncataloged paperback). The evaluator should determine, for a particular library, why the patron's search failed and what can be done to reduce such failures in the future.

One major factor that determines the success or failure of a known-item search is the completeness and accuracy of information that the patron has brought to the catalog. Various studies, in all types of libraries, have shown that the patron's citation is incorrect or incomplete in 10–45 percent of all cases (for example, American Library Association, 1958; Golden et al., 1982; Seymour and Schofield, 1973). Up to 20 percent of the citations brought to the catalog in written form are incorrect; this percentage rises substantially for memorized citations.

A study described by Swanson (1972) illustrates how unreliable memory can be. The study was designed to explore what people remember about books they once saw. Some 104 persons, mostly students, were exposed to a collection of 180 psychology books. Each participant chose five books, examined them closely, and wrote a brief comment on some aspect of each book that was particularly interesting. Several weeks later the students were tested to determine which of 38 different characteristics they remembered about the books they examined. They were given their own comments on the books, but no other means of identification. Of 440 usable responses, only 10 complete and correct bibliographic citations were provided. In 110 cases (25 percent), students provided sufficient author or title information to allow ready location of the items in the library's catalog. In 312 cases (71 percent), students provided enough information on author, title, or subject to allow the book to be located, but, in most cases, only after a lengthy catalog search.

Some studies have looked at the difference between title and author approaches to known-item searches. The former tend to be more successful; title information is more likely to be complete and accurate than author information, since it often has a mnemonic advantage that author information lacks. In the study by Swanson (1972), for example, only 16 percent of the responses allowed any form of author approach to be made in the catalog. Even when title information is faulty, the searcher generally is better able to compensate for incomplete or partially inaccurate title data than for incomplete author data (Lipetz, 1972). One researcher discovered, for example, that one-fourth of the inexact titles supplied could be found in the catalog because the first word or two, or at least the first five letters, were correct (Hinkley, 1968).

Title searches tend to take less time to perform than author searches because fewer catalog entries have to be examined to find the desired work. For example, Grathwol (1971) used a set of citations gathered from bibliographies, reading lists, and course syllabi to compare the average number of catalog cards that would need to be searched for author and title information. Search length for personal authors varied considerably with the amount of information given in each citation. If the citations gave all personal names in the same form (surname and forename) used in the catalog, the average search length would be 7.8 cards; however, 168 of the citations had the author's first initials only, rather than the complete forename (under which the entry was filed in the catalog). In these cases, the average search length was 26 cards.[2] When the citation provided only the author's surname (without forename or initials), the search length averaged 139 cards. In contrast, the average length of a title search was 1.3 cards.

Despite the greater overall accuracy of title data, the greater probability of success in title searching, and the speed of title searching, more users of card catalogs approach known-item searches by author than by title. Brooks and Kilgour (1964), working in the Yale Medical Library, found the author approach was used in 91 percent of the known-item searches conducted by the staff and 54 percent of those conducted by the public. Tagliacozzo and Kochen (1970) discovered that almost two-thirds of the patrons who conducted known-item searches chose the author as the first access point. When patrons knew both author and title, 85.2 percent began with author searches. Lipetz (1972) found that in 62 percent of the cases, the patron approached a known-item search by author, and in 28.5 percent, by title.

Recent studies have shown that patrons searching in online catalogs conduct more title searches than patrons searching in card catalogs (for example, Alzofon and Van Pulis, 1984; Donkersloot, 1985; Norden and Lawrence, 1981; Steinberg and Metz, 1984). This variation is attributed to the difficulty of conducting title searches in the card catalog, a difficulty caused, at least in part, by patron confusion over where title entries are filed in relation to subject and author entries.

The types of patron errors mentioned so far (incomplete citations and mis-understanding of filing rules) may be compounded by errors made when using online catalog systems. For example, errors related specifically to using the on-line system were made by 16 percent of patrons searching an online catalog at

---

[2] For example, an author is cited as R. A. Brown. If the catalog includes full forenames, the searcher may have to look at every entry from Brown, Ralph to Brown, Ryland. For "expected search length" as a measure of efficiency in subject searching in general, see Cooper (1968).

the University of Illinois (Specht, 1980). Studies by Dickson (1984) and Taylor (1984) illustrated the most common errors that patrons make when searching for known items in an OPAC. Patrons searching by title erroneously typed in the initial article of a title (for example, "the" or "an"); patrons searching by author typed the name in reverse order ("Cyrus Johnson" instead of "Johnson, Cyrus") or entered partial names that did not match the catalog's name authority file (Johnson, C.). Misspellings, typographical errors, difficulties in knowing the proper way to type in punctuation marks or call numbers, and searches made in the wrong mode (for example, searching in the author mode for a title entry) were fairly common. Although some of these errors occur in the use of card, book, and microform catalogs, others, such as asking the computer to search under the word "the" for the title "The Black Stallion," seem to be much more common in the online catalog. In fact, most of the errors

demonstrate clearly a different expectation, an expectation that the computer is "intelligent" or at least has some powers of interpretation. For example, it is probably very rare for a library patron to search for works by William Shakespeare under "W" for "William." And yet this is what many users attempt to do with the computer-held catalog. (Dickson, 1984, p. 35)

The types of errors mentioned thus far would not have such severe effects on the success of a patron's search if the typical patron who met with an initial search failure realized what type of error had been made and corrected it. But more than half of the library patrons do not continue their catalog search when their first attempts fail (Tagliacozzo et al., 1970). The reasons for lack of perseverance have not been well explored. It may be that searchers do not realize they have made an error. Or, as suggested in Chapter 2, searchers might be unwilling to continue in what they may now perceive as a more difficult or futile search. Whatever the reason, the service-oriented librarian should not expect perseverance or condemn the patron who gives up. Rather, to the fullest extent possible, catalogs should be designed to automatically compensate for the most common types of errors.

Various possible solutions exist to the problem of incorrect citation information. Searching could be allowed under various permutations of the title, keyword searching capabilities could be added, or a keyword in the title could be combined with some other aspect of the work that the patron remembers (for example, format). Such modifications can increase substantially the number of inaccurately cited works that can be found (Weintraub, 1979). Other useful solutions include the programming of online catalogs to automatically eliminate initial English-language articles ("the," "an," and "a") when a title search is being conducted, to search under all variations of an author's name, and to automatically correct spelling errors.

Bibliographic instruction, too, may decrease the failure rates of catalog searches. Baker (1986), for example, found that users who attended a 50-

minute workshop covering search basics made fewer errors in searching an online catalog than those who did not attend. Other forms of bibliographic instruction that can be tested are printed guidelines for searching the catalog, online instruction provided through introductory and help screens, informative error messages, and one-on-one instructions provided by librarians located at or near the catalog. Patrons want instruction to be convenient and to have immediate application to the task at hand. They are not generally interested in instruction through audiovisual materials or in a classroom setting, because they perceive such instruction to have less relevance to their information needs (Pritchard, 1981). They will use printed instructional materials only if they perceive their immediate relevance. For example, many patrons have learned to search online catalogs by reading sets of printed instructions located next to the terminals (Steinberg and Metz, 1984). The most preferred form of bibliographic instruction for online catalogs may be computer-assisted instruction at the time of a search; such instruction should include informative error messages (Markey, 1984; Pritchard, 1981). For instance, instead of using the vague message "no match," an OPAC could provide the following: "There is no entry for the title you have typed in. Are you sure you have entered the correct form of the title? If not, please retype the title in proper form OR consider searching by author or by keyword. If you need help in searching by author or keyword, press 'H.' "

THE SUCCESS OF SUBJECT SEARCHES

Success rates for subject searches vary, depending on how the evaluator defines success. Exhibit 7-8, for example, illustrates the success rates found in one major study of catalog use conducted by the American Library Association (1958). Researchers found that the patron was successful in 80 percent of the searches. This study painted a very rosy picture, because a search was judged successful if the user selected one or more items from the catalog. No attempt was made to determine whether the patron found all relevant entries or whether the items that were found were the best (most directly related to the subject sought). Had more stringent evaluation criteria been used, success rates would have been substantially lower; one review of previous research suggested that fewer than 30 percent of all subject searches are successful (Wellisch, 1972). This lower success rate is not surprising because subject searches are more difficult for users to perform than any other type of search (Matthews, Lawrence, and Ferguson, 1983).

For some evaluation purposes, an evaluator will want to know all the reasons that subject searches fail. Perhaps the catalog contains nothing on the subject matter sought—a collection failure rather than a catalog failure. Some catalog failures occur frequently with subject searches because users find it difficult to choose appropriate headings under which to search. A few evaluators, therefore,

Library Category	Subject Searches	Failures No.	Failures Percent	Not in Catalog	Total Adjusted	Failures, Adjusted No.	Failures, Adjusted Percent
College and university, type A	345	80	23	24	321	56	17
College and university, type B	317	51	16	18	299	33	11
College and university, type C	287	40	14	13	274	27	10
College and university, type D	207	16	8	9	198	7	4
Large research	168	23	14	3	165	20	12
High school	353	60	17	26	327	34	10
Special purpose	275	68	25	18	257	50	19
Metropolitan— central	274	56	20	19	255	37	15
Small city	184	19	10	10	174	9	5
Metropolitan— branches	381	138	36	55	326	83	25
Not Coded	1				1		
TOTAL	2,792	551	20	195	2,597	356	13

EXHIBIT 7-8 Incidence of failure in subject searches. Reprinted from American Library Association (1958), courtesy of ALA.

have begun their investigations by exploring how patrons choose their search terms. For example, Tagliacozzo (1972) had each patron record the original query (the topic of the search) in his or her own words. She then noted, in order, the list of terms under which the patron searched. In more than 80 percent of the searches, the search terms were words (or word roots) occurring in the query itself. Only when these terms were unsuccessful did the patron try other approaches. In a more recent study, Diodato (1986) considered search choice from a slightly different point of view. He studied readers' descriptions of books to determine if they matched terms from the tables of contents and indexes of those books; he concluded that both sources are likely to reflect terms that the reader would actually use in searching for the works.

The next question that might be addressed, therefore, is whether the patron's query term successfully matched a subject heading used in the catalog. Those evaluators who used a narrow definition of success—one in which the patron's query term exactly matched the catalog entry—reported success rates in the range of 15–50 percent (for example, Malcolm, 1950; Miura et al., 1980; Swanson, 1972). Other evaluators used a broader definition of success, one in which the patron's query term matches exactly, leads (through a *see* reference) to the correct term, or is sufficiently close (alphabetically) to the correct term to permit the searcher to locate the necessary heading. This definition increases the success rate substantially. For example, in a study reported by Swanson (1972), 18 percent of the query terms used by university students exactly matched the catalog subject headings; a 71 percent match was achieved when the definition of success was broadened. Of course, a partial match between the user's terms and those occurring in the catalog indicates potential success only. Because most studies of this type simulate catalog searches rather than observe real catalog use, it is not known whether a partial match would actually lead a user to a relevant heading in the catalog.

The majority of searches are unsuccessful because the term under which the patron searches is not the one listed in the catalog's controlled vocabulary. Many patrons search under very precise subject terms rather than the more general ones that tend to appear in catalogs (Kaske and Sanders, 1980; Marshall, 1975). For subject fields with precise vocabularies, such as chemistry, failure rates may be lower because the subject headings tend to be more precise; however, patrons searching under specialized subject terms in subject fields that use less-precise, more abstract language, such as education or psychology, may experience far higher rates of failure. Other failures occur because patrons look under currently used terminology, but the subject headings in the catalog include older (or even archaic) terms (Dickinson, 1976).

It is possible for local libraries to provide numerous and extensive cross-references to help patrons access the materials they need. But in these times of tight funding, it is clear that many libraries do not have the resources to do so. In today's environment of standardized cataloging practices and MARC formats, it is a given that libraries will continue to use standardized subject heading lists, even if some of the headings are more general and less current than the terms patrons use in their searches. Therefore, evaluators need to ask whether patrons are aware of the lists of standard subject headings (that is, the controlled vocabulary) used in their libraries, and, if so, how often they consult such lists before beginning their searches.

Many libraries keep the latest editions of the list they use—for instance, *Sears List of Subject Headings* (Sears, 1986) or *Library of Congress Subject Headings* (Library of Congress, 1988)—near the card catalog so that staff and patrons can easily refer to it. But evaluators have found that these lists are little used. For example, not one of the 189 searchers interviewed by Matthews, Lawrence, and Ferguson (1983) consulted such a guide while formulating a subject search strategy. Other researchers have found similar, although less extreme, examples of nonuse of subject heading guides (for example, Kaske and Sanders, 1980; Markey, 1983a). Van Pulis and Ludy (1988) discovered that subject authority files are little used even when they are made available online, and Lester (1988) produced results which suggest that authority files have little effect on subject retrieval in OPACs.

Patrons have given three major reasons for nonuse of subject heading guides. Many said they were unaware that subject searching requires the entry of a subject heading from a controlled vocabulary (Steinberg and Metz, 1984). Others did not understand how to use the subject heading guides; for example, they commented that they did not understand what the "x," "xx," or "s.a." abbreviations in these guides meant (Markey, 1985). Still others reported that the guides were not located next to the online terminal they were using and that leaving the terminal meant they would have to give up their place to another patron (Markey, 1985). Although the last problem is the most easily corrected, solutions to the others may not be too difficult. For example, if the searcher entered an inappropriate subject heading, an online catalog could refer him or her to the appropriate subject guide, while simple instructions on the use of the guide could be taped to the front cover of each volume.

The initial failure experienced by a patron when trying to match a query term to a catalog subject heading would not be so important if the patron would then try other subject headings. A few highly motivated patrons will actually do so. For example, researchers in special libraries and graduate students and faculty in academic libraries may persevere far longer than the general public. The typical patron, however, consults only one subject heading. If that term has no matches, he or she either assumes the library has no materials on the subject or simply gives up (American Library Association, 1958; Bates, 1977; Markey, 1983a; Matthews, Lawrence, and Ferguson, 1983; Tagliacozzo et al., 1970).

The perseverance problem might be overcome if the catalog incorporated some easy-to-use features that would guide the user from an incorrect term to the accepted term. For example, some catalogs generate, from the controlled vocabulary, a list of subject headings that are alphabetically close to the query term a patron uses. Others incorporate more *see* references, a feature that patrons have specifically requested (Markey, 1983b). Evaluators can determine the adequacy of the reference structure of a particular catalog by using tools like the *Library of Congress Subject Headings* to determine whether local catalogers have added relevant synonyms and made references from popular names to the more technical names used in the catalog, from inverted to noninverted forms of entry (or vice versa), and from specific to appropriate generic terms. If not, the cross-reference structure can be augmented.

Jamieson, Dolan, and Declerck (1986) tried to determine whether the ability to search an online catalog with keywords is a reasonable alternative to a built-in cross-reference structure for variant search forms. They found that keyword searching should enable location of at least 15 percent more of the correct subject terms, because 15 percent of the cross-references in the Library of Congress's authority file are from preferred subject terms that are simply arranged in a different order. Keyword subject searching alone, however, is not powerful enough to compensate for the lack of a good cross-reference structure in the catalog; for example, it would not necessarily help the patron who entered a synonym of a correct subject heading.

Other subject enhancements have also been tested. For instance, researchers working on the Subject Access Project (Settel and Cochrane, 1982) augmented the subject headings contained in MARC records with words or phrases from the indexes and tables of contents of selected books. They then conducted a controlled experiment to compare the effectiveness of searching in this set of augmented records with searching in a regular online catalog. They discovered that searches conducted using the augmented MARC records yielded significantly more relevant documents than searches conducted with nonaugmented records. In a related study, Byrne and Micco (1988) added an average of 21 multiword terms, drawn from indexes or tables of contents, to the MARC records for 6,000 books. Results indicated that searches of these augmented records achieved significantly higher recall than searches using titles or subject headings alone. Diodato (1986) considered the same issue from a slightly different point of view when he studied readers' descriptions of books to determine if the descriptions matched terms from the tables of contents and indexes. He concluded that tables of contents and indexes are two sources of terms which are likely to reflect terms that the user would use in searching for the books.

Walker (1987, 1988) and Walker and Jones (1987) evaluated the effectiveness of subject searching in an experimental catalog that incorporates four special features: (1) automatic stemming, a technique in which words are routinely truncated by the computer before searching so as to correct minor problems like patrons searching under the plural, rather than the singular, version of a subject heading; (2) automatic spelling corrections; (3) an augmented cross-reference structure; and (4) a form of relevance feedback. This type of research is important because it shows which techniques will increase the likelihood of the patron matching the search term to the terms used in the catalog so that relevant items can be retrieved. Walker and Jones concluded that weak stemming is beneficial but that strong stemming is of doubtful utility (the former merely conflates singular and plural and removes the "ing" ending, while the latter removes all suffixes), that semiautomatic spelling correction should be used in online catalogs, and that cross-reference lists to allow automatic cross-referencing should be compiled with input from cooperating libraries. The cross-reference lists investigated were extremely simple, incorporating abbreviations (TV), noun-adjective pairs (Wales, Welsh), alternative terminology (Russia, Russian, USSR, Soviet Union), alternative spellings (csar, czar, tsar, tzar), irregular plurals (wife, wives), related terms (third world, underdeveloped countries, developing countries), numbers (6, six, sixth, vi), and phrases. The phrases category is different from the others; it consists of word combinations that should not be split because the meaning of the individual words is quite different from that of the compound (for example, soap opera).

Lester (1988) also studied the ability of various forms of subject enhancement to improve retrieval rates. She randomly selected, from the transaction logs of the NOTIS/LUIS online catalog at Northwestern University, a sample of the actual subject terms typed in by users, then compared these with approved Library of Congress subject headings. When she located user terms that failed to match the headings, she investigated 22 different strategies for achieving a match. Strategies that did not significantly improve matches were use of a spelling checker, singular/plural conflation, phonetic spelling, exact matches in either subject or personal name authority files, and any process involving geographic name authority files. The strategies of right truncation, string searching with adjacency, and searching of keywords with Boolean operators significantly improved the matches whether or not the database was augmented by the inclusion of subject and name authority files or by the ability to search all fields of a bibliographic record.

Other investigators have assessed the value of bibliographic classification schemes for subject searching in OPACs or have explored the limitations of conventional subject headings in providing effective subject access in the online environment. For example, Markey (1987) and Markey and Demeyer (1986) tested the potential of the Dewey Decimal Classification for retrieval in OPACs, and Chan (1986), Huestis (1988), and Williamson (1986) have addressed the problem of applying the Library of Congress Classification in the online environment. Massicotte (1988) described how displays of subject headings in OPACs can be made more browsable, and Markey (1988) investigated the integration of LC subject headings, as a search tool, in online catalogs.

These and other studies have provided many valuable insights that may help librarians design catalogs in which users can more easily locate appropriate subject terms under which to search. For example, an analysis of online subject searches led one group of librarians and information specialists to conclude that an online catalog must compensate for a user's inability to match search terms with subject headings, must provide more than one searching option (such as keywords, subject heading, and class number searches), and should permit users to refine large retrieval sets (Mandel, 1986).

Evaluators need to carry their assessments of subject searches one step further, however, since it is possible that searchers will locate one or more appropriate subject headings but still fail to find items that they consider relevant to their information needs. To some extent, success at this stage of the search "has to do with the user's acceptance of the retrieved material and therefore concerns the user's expectations and attitudes, his satisfaction with the retrieved information, his knowledge of the topic and his ability to discriminate between what is relevant and what is not" (Tagliacozzo and Kochen, 1970, p. 374).

Although many of these factors are beyond library control, librarians can help patrons in various practical ways. First, they can introduce techniques to increase search results when too few subject matches are obtained. Although it is possible for patrons to do this themselves (for example, by using *see also* references listed in the subject headings guide or by examining the tracings field in bibliographic records), few take advantage of such options, possibly because they are unfamiliar with both the mechanics and the benefits of using these techniques (American Library Association, 1958; Matthews, Lawrence, and Ferguson, 1983). The problem of too few subject matches can be overcome in a number of ways. For example, an online catalog could be programmed either to inform patrons of related subject headings or to automatically augment searches by retrieving items under subject headings related to those introduced by the searcher (Doszkocs, 1983).

Second, librarians can introduce procedures to help patrons usefully limit the output of a search when too many items are retrieved. The capability to perform Boolean searches makes this relatively easy in an online catalog. All catalogs, however, would benefit if their entries consistently contained those data elements that patrons found most useful in helping them make (or at least narrow) their selection choices. A number of evaluators have investigated the elements currently contained in each catalog entry with this in mind; studies consistently show that the data elements most used in making selections are the work's language, its title, its date of publication, and, in the few cases where they are available, contents notes or descriptive annotations (for example, American Library Association, 1958; Chwe, 1979; Lipetz, 1972; Simmons and Foster, 1982). Research is now underway at OCLC to determine which of these standard elements are most useful in limiting the results of a keyword search.

Although patrons screen entries first by language, they rely heavily on the title of the book to indicate the book's contents. Most works are selected this way. Titles, however, are not always descriptive, and patrons frequently have trouble selecting the books that are most likely to be relevant to their precise interests, especially when many works are listed under one broad subject heading (Lipetz, 1972; Seal, 1983).

Patrons also seem to use the publication date more frequently than the author as a criterion for selection in subject searches, suggesting that entries under a single subject heading should be arranged in reverse chronological order rather than alphabetically by author. Nitecki (1977) tried this in a large university, then surveyed patrons to obtain their reaction. Because most patrons were searching for current material within a particular subject area, they liked this arrangement. The rearrangement of entries in card, book, and microform catalogs would be time-consuming if the library's collection was large; however, OPACs could be readily reprogrammed so that recent materials are displayed first when a subject search is requested.

Some patrons rely on contents notes and annotations to help them make their choices (Palmer, 1972). Several authors (for example, Maltby and Duxbury, 1972; Simmons and Foster, 1982) found that these descriptions were considered of greater utility than much of the data normally included in a catalog entry. Unfortunately, too few notes and annotations are provided. This makes it difficult for patrons to determine, from the catalog entry, whether a book is relevant to their information needs and explains, in part, why one-third of the patrons who search in the catalog by subject simply note relevant call numbers before proceeding to the shelves to make their selections (Miura et al., 1980).

Abrera (1982) took a different viewpoint in studying how patrons chose needed materials. She examined 2,270 reference requests in a medium-sized public library and found that 95 percent asked for information by author, title, subject, or some combination of these. The other 5 percent of patron requests could have been met if access points had been provided by publication date, format (for example, videotape), and type of work (for example, textbook).

Two other studies investigated what data elements would meet most patron needs in subject searching (and, incidentally, in known-item searching as well). In the first, Palmer (1972) determined that a computer-based catalog that included an abbreviated citation of only five elements—author, title, call number, subject headings, and date of publication—would satisfy approximately 84 percent of patron requirements. This satisfaction rate could be raised to 90 percent if a contents note was added. Although patrons did not mind having information included on publisher and edition, few wanted or used data on the place of publication, illustrations, or pagination.

In the second study, Seal (1983) conducted an experiment to see how many errors would have resulted from use of a short-entry catalog. The short entries did not contain statements of responsibility, places of publication, publishers, series statements, or International Standard Book Numbers (ISBNs). They also omitted forenames from personal name headings. Some 215 searches were analyzed to determine whether failure occurred. Seal defined failure as "a user's being unable to locate an item which could have been located if the normal catalog was used or to distinguish between similar entries or to retrieve specific bibliographic details on a particular item" (p. 149). He found a failure rate of only 5 percent. If forenames had been retained, the failure rate would have been reduced to 3 percent. The few remaining failures could have been omitted if the entries had included ISBNs and publishers, two features often used by library staff.

OTHER ASPECTS OF CATALOG USE

Evaluators have looked at additional factors that influence the effectiveness of catalog searches. For example, some have discovered that the larger the card catalog, the less successful the user will be in his or her search (for example, American Library Association, 1958; Tagliacozzo et al., 1970). This finding led to speculations that dividing a card catalog into separate author/title and subject catalogs would facilitate searching by reducing the catalog's bulk and making it easier for patrons to understand how entries are filed in the catalog. Indeed, patrons prefer divided catalogs because the size of the search file is reduced (Aubry, 1972). This type of division has no relevance to the catalog in online form.

Other researchers have focused on less obvious errors made by catalog users, many of which have been discovered during focus group sessions with library patrons. For example, many patrons often believe that the catalog lists everything a library owns (Markey, 1983c; Matthews, Lawrence, and Ferguson, 1983). They do not understand that librarians sometimes

have logical reasons for not cataloging some items and for creating separate catalogs for other items. Separate catalogs, often with different levels of bibliographic control, may be established for different types of materials, such as government documents or audiovisual items; for special collections, such as a Far East collection; for different classification systems, particularly if one system is discontinued and a new one adopted; for different editions of cataloging rules, such as the adoption of AACR2; and for different periods of cataloging, for example, supplements to a COM [Computer Output Microform] catalog. (Senzig, 1984, p. 37)

Intner (1984), in a nationwide survey, documented that only 38 percent of public libraries had an integrated, omnimedia catalog. Bierbaum (1990a; 1990b) found that 50 percent of academic libraries and 60 percent of junior college libraries cataloged nonprint materials but did not list them in the regular catalog. This practice of not including materials can lead to patron error, as can delays in entering new acquisitions into the catalog. For example, a third of the patrons at the University of Oregon library made their selections exclusively from a frozen (and, therefore, retrospective) catalog, not realizing that microfiche supplements had to be used to gain access to current materials (Dwyer, 1981).

The problem is compounded by the fact that some patrons fail to understand that librarians never intended certain items to be included in the catalog (for example, periodical articles or ephemeral materials like those included in vertical files) (Moore, 1981). Further research is needed to explore how widespread patron misconceptions are about the coverage of catalogs in individual libraries. Where major misconceptions are found, steps should be taken to educate patrons or to solve the problem in some other way. The emergence of OPACs has led librarians to include an increasing variety of items in their catalogs, even periodical articles in some cases.

Another aspect of catalog use that needs further exploration is the types of actions taken when catalog failure is experienced. Seymour and Schofield (1973) studied this issue in four libraries and found that local conditions may affect these actions (Exhibit 7-9). For example, the exhibit shows that a very high percentage of the Institute of Education (London) group intended to try another

Action Planned After Failure	Proportions of readers intending different types of action in			
	Cambridge	Leicester	Institute of Education	Bradford
Total number of readers failing	110	90	105	69
	%	%	%	%
Recheck reference	5	–	–	7
Look on shelf	2	17	10	9
Ask library staff	11	18	35	13
Ask supervisor/colleague	12	4	5	2
Look in bibliography	6	2	5	1
Attempt to purchase	6	3	10	–
Try another library	18	14	39	25
Try interlibrary loan	2	12	3	9
Recommend to library	2	–	1	3
Try to find substitute	4	1	4	7
Other	4	2	17	4
Forget it	28	29	11	19

EXHIBIT 7-9   Actions planned by library users after encountering failure at the catalog. Reprinted from Seymour and Schofield (1973), courtesy of the American Library Association.

library, which may be explained by the close proximity of the main library of London University.

Other evaluators continue to focus on determining patron satisfaction with various formats of the catalog. Older studies concentrated on determining whether patrons were likely to prefer microfilm, microfiche, or book catalogs over the card catalog. Hodges and Bloch (1982) had patrons and staff search for items (by author, title, and subject) in microfiche and microfilm catalogs. Evaluators timed each search, checked answers to verify their accuracy, and surveyed patron satisfaction with and preference for each catalog format. Hodges and Bloch concluded that there were no significant differences in ease of use between the two catalogs.

Other studies have examined whether the online catalog is preferred over other formats. Frid (1987) and Pease and Gouke (1982) compared the speed and success of known-item searching in both the card and the online catalogs. Although patrons were faster and more successful in searching the card catalog, they preferred to use the online catalog when given a choice. In fact, patrons in all types of libraries have indicated that they prefer online catalogs to any other form of catalog (for example, Dowlin, 1980; Matthews, Lawrence, and

Ferguson, 1983; Siegel et al., 1984). The satisfaction rates are highest among people who are the heaviest users of the catalog (and of the library) and among those who have received initial training or assistance in use of the online system (Matthews and Lawrence, 1984).

The format of the card (or display) is also being studied. Fryser and Stirling (1984) asked 340 library patrons to rate different versions of a bibliographic record displayed on a terminal. One version presented the information in the format used on Library of Congress catalog cards (Exhibit 7-10). The other versions used either side headings or underheadings of each data element in the display. One of these screens is shown in Exhibit 7-11. Eighty-three percent of the patrons preferred the alternate displays over the Library of Congress card format, noting that they were easier to read and understand. Now that the use of online catalogs is becoming commonplace, the guidelines that Matthews (1987) and others have proposed for screen layout and design can be tested under controlled conditions.

In fact, a number of facets of online catalog design must be studied more thoroughly. For example, it needs to be determined whether or not patrons can effectively use command-driven, as opposed to menu-driven, search systems. One study indicates that some menu-driven systems, like the one at the Univer-

---

Doyle, Lauren B   1926

Information retrieval and processing / Lauren B Doyle. – – Los Angeles : Melville Pub. Co., 1975

xv, 410 p. : ill. ; 23 cm. – – (Information science series).

An up-to-date version of information storage and retrieval by J. Becker and R. M. Hayes.
"A Wiley-Becker & Hayes series book".
Includes bibliographies and indexes.
ISBN 0-471-22151-1

1. Information storage and retrieval systems. 2. Electronic data processing. 3. Information science. I. Becker, Joseph. Information storage and retrieval. II. Title.

Z699.D67	1975	029.7	75-1179
Library of Congress		75	MARC

EXHIBIT 7-10 Online screen display presenting catalog elements in a traditional Library of Congress format. Reprinted from Fryser and Stirling (1984), courtesy of John Wiley & Sons.

Author...............	Doyle, Lauren B
Book Title	Information Retrieval and Processing
Call Number	029.7 Z699.D67 75-1179

Notes .... An up-to-date version of information storage and retrieval by
J. Becker & R. M. Hayes.
"A Wiley-Becker & Hayes series book".
Includes bibliographies and indexes.
ISBN 0-471-22151-1

Phys. Features .... xv, 410 p. ; ill. : 23 cm. -- (Information science series).
Publisher & Pl .... Melville Pub. Co., Los Angeles

Sub. Tracings .... 1. Information storage and retrieval systems.
2. Electronic data processing. 3. Information science.
Tracings .... I. Becker, Joseph. Information storage and retrieval. II. Title.
Year 1975

EXHIBIT 7-11   Online screen display presenting catalog elements organized under side headings. Reprinted from Fryser and Stirling (1984), courtesy of John Wiley & Sons.

sity of California, have caused as many difficulties as the command systems at the same libraries (Matthews, Lawrence, and Ferguson, 1983). Another study suggests that some patrons need instruction to develop and create a good search strategy regardless of whether they are using menu-driven or command-driven systems (Trzebiatowski, 1984). A third study, conducted at the Bell Laboratories library, determined that patrons preferred the command mode of one system because it allowed keyword searches. Sixty-five percent of those using such keyword searches found what they were looking for, as opposed to 30 percent of those using the subject search mode of the menu-driven version of the same catalog (Geller and Lesk, 1983). In studies of this kind, however, results must be interpreted carefully. In the Bell study, for example, it was the keyword search feature, not the command feature per se, that made a difference to the users.

One encouraging sign is the attention that librarians are giving to determining what features patrons wish to have incorporated into online catalogs. For example, patrons want the ability to search the library's catalog from their home or office (for example, Besant, 1982; Dowlin, 1980; Larson and Graham, 1983). When this type of remote access has been provided, it has been heavily used; a study at the University of Calgary libraries showed, for instance, that initially high levels of use (16,000 transactions per month) more than quadrupled within a one-year period (deBruijn and Matheson, 1987). Another frequently requested feature is the status record, which tells whether a book is checked out, on reserve, or at some other location (Hammell and Goldberg, 1985; Weiming, 1988). Not surprisingly, this feature is desired most by patrons of libraries that have many branches or departments, because such a feature could save them a great deal of retrieval time and inconvenience. Other popular items among patrons include the ability to print out search results (Bosman, 1987), faster response time (Matthews, Lawrence, and Ferguson, 1983; Weiming, 1988), more terminals (Besant, 1982), and better error messages (Larson and Graham, 1983).

Because a major purpose of most libraries is to design their services so that they will receive maximum use, it is not surprising that a growing number of researchers are investigating whether changes in cataloging practices will affect the circulation of library materials. For example, Knutson (1986) and Rao (1982) both tried to determine if a significant relationship exists between the number of subject and other access points provided for a book and its annual circulation. Each determined the total number of access points for a randomly selected sample of titles in an academic library: the mean was 4.3 in Rao's study and 5.0 in Knutson's. Neither author found a significant correlation between the number of access points and recorded use of a title. It is interesting to speculate on reasons for this lack of significance:

One intriguing possibility is that an incremental increase in subject headings, such as from one or two up to three or four, is not significantly associated with circulation, but that a very large increase—up to perhaps ten or more—which would also allow access to subsets of information in monographs—may show an association in use figures. (Knutson, 1986, p. 468)

Aguilar's (1984) study also is intriguing. He randomly selected 198 books from the adult collection of a small public library and observed their circulation for 14 weeks. The books were then randomly divided into experimental and control groups. All related catalog entries (author, title, and subject) for books in the experimental group were removed from the card catalog. Catalog entries for the control group were left intact. Circulation then was remeasured for a second 14-week period. Although circulation of control group titles remained the same, the use of experimental titles dropped 17 percent. This decrease, however, was not statistically significant. Aguilar speculated that the small decline in use in small public libraries was because many patrons find materials by browsing rather than by selecting titles from the card catalog. This particular experiment should be replicated in larger libraries and in libraries of other types before any conclusions are drawn.

SUMMARY

This chapter provides an overview of studies that have measured or evaluated the use of the catalog in libraries. The major emphasis has been on the scope of these studies and the procedures used. The importance of such investigations has been well summarized by Gorman (1968), who claims that

the most vital aspect of cataloguing theory and practice that remains unexamined is the use made of the catalogue. Until the aim of catalogue construction has been clearly stated on the basis of objective and accurate surveys of catalogue use, all cataloguing theory will remain unscientific and open to doubt. (pp. 66–67)

Since Gorman wrote this, a number of valuable studies have been completed, but the subject is certainly far from exhausted.

The catalog is the major key to a library's collection. If designed and used effectively, it will increase the accessibility of the collection to library users. A patron's success in searching the catalog depends on many factors, which may vary, depending on the form of the catalog used (microform, card, book, or online). Some of these factors include

- The number of terminals or microform readers available for use
- The accuracy of the information brought to the catalog by the patron and the form in which it is brought (for example, written or memorized)
- The point of access chosen by the patron
- The amount of patron experience and training in using the particular form of catalog
- The number of entry points per item provided in the catalog
- The number of cross-references provided
- The order in which catalog entries are filed
- The extent of information included on a bibliographic record
- The size, complexity, and form of the catalog
- The quality of the labeling, guiding, and error messages given in the catalog
- The perseverance, diligence, and intelligence of the patron
- The availability and use of thesauri or other forms of controlled vocabulary used in the catalog

The various catalog studies reviewed provide some interesting and useful data on who uses the catalog in different types of libraries, for what purpose, how much, and with what degree of success. Most of the studies have used surveys, experiments, transaction-log analyses, or focus group interviews, although a few other techniques have also been tried. Some of the investigations have produced estimates of failure rates in catalog searching—both failures to find entries for items actually present (catalog failures) and failures to find entries for items not present (collection failures). Many cases of catalog failure have been documented, and analyses to determine causes of these failures have been undertaken.

REFERENCES

Aanonson, John. "A Comparison of Keyword Subject Searching on Six British University OPACs." *Online Review, 11*(5):303–313, October 1987.

Abrera, Josefa B. "Bibliographic Structure Possibility Set: A Quantitative Approach for Identifying Users' Bibliographic Information Needs." *Library Resources and Technical Services, 26*(1):21–36, January–March 1982.

Aguilar, William. "Influence of the Card Catalog on Circulation in a Small Public Library." *Library Resources and Technical Services, 28*(2):175–184, April–June 1984.

Alzofon, Sammy R., and Noelle Van Pulis. "Patterns of Searching and Success Rates in an Online Public Access Catalog." *College and Research Libraries, 45*(2):110–115, March 1984.

American Library Association. *Catalog Use Study.* Edited by Vaclav Mostecky. Chicago, Ill., ALA, 1958.

Armstrong, Margaret, and Betty Costa. "Computer Cat™ at Mountain View Elementary School." *Library Hi Tech, 1*(3):47–52, Winter 1983.

Aubry, John. "A Timing Study of the Manual Searching of Catalogs." *Library Quarterly, 42*(4):399–415, October 1972.

Aveney, Brian, and Mary Fischer Ghikas. "600 Users Meet the COM Catalog." *American Libraries, 10*(2):82–83, February 1979.

Baker, Betsy. "A New Direction for Online Catalog Instruction." *Information Technology and Libraries, 5*(1):35–41, March 1986.

Bates, Marcia J. "Factors Affecting Subject Catalog Search Success." *Journal of the American Society for Information Science, 28*(3):161–169, May 1977.

Berger, Mike, and Katharina Klemperer. "Developing an Effective Man/Machine Interface for a Large On-Line University Library Catalog." In: *The Information Community: An Alliance for Progress. Proceedings of the 44th ASIS Annual Meeting, 1981.* Volume 18. Edited by Lois F. Lunin, Madeline Henderson, and Harold Wooster. White Plains, N.Y., Knowledge Industry Publications, 1981, pp. 267–269.

Besant, Larry. "Users of Public Online Catalogs Want Sophisticated Subject Access." *American Libraries, 13*(3):160, March 1982.

Bierbaum, Esther G. "Beyond Print: Object Collections in Academic Libraries." *Collection Building, 10*(1/2):7–11, 1990a.

_____. "The Two-Year College LRC: Promise Deferred?" *College and Research Libraries, 51*(6):531–538, November 1990b.

Bishop, David F. "The CLR OPAC Study: Analysis of ARL User Responses." *Information Technology and Libraries, 2*(3):315–321, September 1983.

Borgman, Christine L. *End User Behavior on the Ohio State University Libraries' Online Catalog: A Computer Monitoring Study.* Dublin, Ohio, OCLC, 1983. (OCLC/OPR/RR-83/7)

Bosman, Fred. "Verslag Gebruikerson derzoek OPC bij de UB Groningen." (Report on the Survey of OPAC Users at Groningen University Library.) *PICA Mededelingen, 10*(5):2–6, December 1987.

Broadbent, Elaine. "A Study of the Use of the Subject Catalog, Marriott Library, University of Utah." *Cataloging and Classification Quarterly, 4*(3):75–83, Spring 1984.

Brooks, Benedict, and Frederick G. Kilgour. "Catalog Subject Searches in the Yale Medical Library." *College and Research Libraries,* 25(6):483–487, November 1964.

Bryant, Philip, and Angela Needham. "Review of the *U.K. Catalogue Use Survey* by Arthur Maltby." *Catalogue and Index,* (30):16, Summer 1973.

Byrne, Alex, and Mary Micco. "Improving OPAC Subject Access: The ADFA Experiment." *College and Research Libraries,* 49(5):432–441, September 1988.

Chan, Lois Mai. "Library of Congress Classification as an Online Retrieval Tool: Potentials and Limitations." *Information Technology and Libraries,* 5(3):181–192, September 1986.

Chwe, Steven Seokho. "A Study of Data Elements for the COM Catalog." *Journal of Library Automation,* 12(1):94–97, March 1979.

Cochrane, Pauline A., and Karen Markey. "Catalog Use Studies—Since the Introduction of Online Interactive Catalogs: Impact on Design for Subject Access." *Library and Information Science Research,* 5(4):337–363, Winter 1983.

Cooper, William S. "Expected Search Length: A Single Measure of Retrieval Effectiveness Based on the Weak Ordering Action of Retrieval Systems." *American Documentation,* 19(1):30–41, January 1968.

Corya, William M., and Gary C. Lelvis. "The Integration of Formats to Provide Catalog Access Services." In: *Information Round-up: A Continuing Education Session on Microforms and Data Processing in the Library and Information Science Center. Proceedings of the 4th ASIS Mid-Year Meeting, Portland, Oregon, May 15–17, 1975.* Edited by Frances G. Spigai et al. Washington, D.C., American Society for Information Science, 1975. (Unpaged)

deBruijn, Debbie, and Arden Matheson. "University of Calgary: Remote Access to On-Line Catalogues." *Canadian Library Journal,* 44(4):225–228, August 1987.

Dickinson, Elizabeth. "Of Catalogs, Computers and Communication." *Wilson Library Bulletin,* 50(6):463–470, February 1976.

Dickson, Jean. "An Analysis of User Errors in Searching an Online Catalog." *Cataloging and Classification Quarterly,* 4(3):19–38, Spring 1984.

Diodato, Virgil. "Tables of Contents and Book Indexes: How Well Do They Match Readers' Descriptions of Books?" *Library Resources and Technical Services,* 30(4):402–412, October–December 1986.

Donkersloot, H. B. "Zoeken op Titelwoorden: Een Onderzoek met de On-Line Publiekscatalogus." ("Searching by Title Word: A Study of the On-Line Public Catalogue.") *Open,* 17(12):542–546, December 1985.

Doszkocs, Tamas E. "CITE NLM: Natural Language Searching in an Online Catalog." *Information Technology and Libraries,* 2(4):364–380, December 1983.

Dowlin, Kenneth. "On-line Catalog User Acceptance Survey." *RQ,* 20(1):44–47, Fall 1980.

Drone, Jeanette M. "A Use Study of the Card Catalogs in the University of Illinois Music Library." *Library Resources and Technical Services,* 28(3):253–262, July–September 1984.

Dwyer, James R. "The Effect of Closed Catalogs on Public Access." *Library Resources and Technical Services,* 25(2):186–195, April–June 1981.

Ferguson, Douglas, et al. "The CLR Public Online Catalog Study: An Overview." *Information Technology and Libraries,* 1(2):84–97, June 1982.

Frarey, Carlyle J. "Studies of Use of the Subject Catalog: Summary and Evaluation."

In: *The Subject Analysis of Library Materials.* Edited by Maurice F. Tauber. New York, Columbia University, 1953, pp. 147–166.

Freiburger, Gary, and Marjorie Simon. "Patron Use of an Online Catalog." In: *Crossroads: Proceedings of the First National Conference of the Library and Information Technology Association, September 17–21, 1983, Baltimore, Maryland.* Edited by Michael Gorman. Chicago, Ill., American Library Association, 1984, pp. 106–111.

Frid, Hans Ove. "Perseverance as a Factor for Success at the Online Catalogue." In: *Online Information 87. Proceedings of the 11th International Online Information Meeting, London, 8–10, December 1987.* Medford, N.J., Learned Information, 1987, pp. 241–245.

Frost, Carolyn O. "Student and Faculty Subject Searching in a University Online Public Catalog: A Report to the Council on Library Resources." Washington, D.C., Council on Library Resources, Inc., August 1985. ERIC ED264872

——————. "Faculty Use of Subject Searching in Card and Online Catalogs." *Journal of Academic Librarianship, 13*(2):86–92, May 1987a.

——————. "Subject Searching in an Online Catalog." *Information Technology and Libraries, 6*(1):60–63, March 1987b.

Fryser, Benjamin S., and Keith H. Stirling. "The Effect of Spatial Arrangement, Upper-Lower Case Letter Combinations, and Reverse Video on Patron Response to CRT Displayed Catalog Records." *Journal of the American Society for Information Science, 35*(6):344–350, November 1984.

Geller, Valerie, and Michael Lesk. "An On-Line Library Catalog Offering Menu and Keyword User Interfaces." In: *National Online Meeting: Proceedings—1983, New York, April 12–April 14, 1983.* Compiled by Martha E. Williams and Thomas H. Hogan. Medford, N.J., Learned Information, 1983, pp. 159–165.

Golden, Gary A., et al. "Patron Approaches to Serials: A User Study." *College and Research Libraries, 43*(1):22–30, January 1982.

Gorman, Michael. *A Study of the Rules for Entry and Heading in the Anglo-American Cataloguing Rules, 1967.* London, Eng., Library Association, 1968.

Grathwol, Mary. "Bibliographic Elements in Citations and Catalog Entries: A Comparison." Master's Thesis. Chicago, Ill., University of Chicago, 1971.

Hafter, Ruth. "The Performance of Card Catalogs: A Review of Research." *Library Research, 1*(3):199–222, Fall 1979.

Hammell, Kathryn A., and Kay Goldberg. "The Evolution of an Online Union Catalog: Impact of User Feedback." *Information Technology and Libraries, 4*(2):162–168, June 1985.

Hancock, Micheline. "Subject Searching Behaviour at the Library Catalogue and at the Shelves: Implications for Online Interactive Catalogues." *Journal of Documentation, 43*(4):303–321, December 1987.

Hinkley, William A. "On Searching Catalogs and Indexes with Inexact Title Information." Master's Thesis. Chicago, Ill., University of Chicago, 1968.

Hodges, Theodora, and Uri Bloch. "Fiche or Film for COM Catalogs: Two Use Tests." *Library Quarterly, 52*(2):131–144, April 1982.

Holgate, Elizabeth, and Jane Lenton. "Planning for Automation: Catalogue Use Survey at Humberside College of Higher Education." *Program, 20*(1):77–81, January 1986.

Huestis, Jeffrey C. "Clustering LC Classification Numbers in an Online Catalog for Improved Browsability." *Information Technology and Libraries,* 7(4):381–393, December 1988.

Intner, Sheila S. "Access to Media: Attitudes of Public Librarians." *RQ, 23*(4):424–430, Summer 1984.

Jamieson, Alexis J.; Elizabeth Dolan; and Luc Declerck. "Keyword Searching vs. Authority Control in an Online Catalog." *Journal of Academic Librarianship, 12*(5):277–283, November 1986.

Kaske, Neal K. "A Comparative Study of Subject Searching in an OPAC Among Branch Libraries of a University Library System." *Information Technology and Libraries,* 7(4):359–372, December 1988.

Kaske, Neal K., and Nancy P. Sanders. "On-Line Subject Access: The Human Side of the Problem." *RQ, 20*(1):52–58, Fall 1980.

Kawakami, Kozo, and Yutaka Kobayashi. "Catalog Use Study with Intermittent Photography." *Library and Information Science,* (17):213–221, 1979.

Kern-Simirenko, Cheryl. "OPAC User Logs: Implications for Bibliographic Instruction." *Library Hi Tech, 1*(3):27–35, Winter 1983.

Kinsella, Janet, and Philip Bryant. "Online Public Access Catalog Research in the United Kingdom: An Overview." *Library Trends, 35*(4):619–629, Spring 1987.

Klugkist, A.; G. Jacobs; and A. Bossers. "Het PICA-Experiment met een On-Line Catalogus voor het Publiek: Resultaten van het Gebruikersonderzoek." ("The PICA On-Line Public Catalogue Experiment: Results of the User Survey.") *Open, 17*(12):536–541, December 1985.

Knutson, Gunnar. "Does the Catalog Record Make a Difference? Access Points and Book Use." *College and Research Libraries, 47*(5):460–469, September 1986.

Krikelas, James. "Catalog Use Studies and Their Implications." In: *Advances in Librarianship.* Volume 3. Edited by Melvin J. Voigt. New York, Seminar Press, 1972, pp. 195–220.

———. "Searching the Library Catalog: A Study of Users' Access." *Library Research, 2*(3):215–230, Fall 1980.

Larson, Ray R., and Vicki Graham. "Monitoring and Evaluating MELVYL." *Information Technology and Libraries, 2*(1):93–104, March 1983.

Lester, Marilyn A. "Coincidence of User Vocabulary and Library of Congress Subject Headings: Experiments to Improve Subject Access in Academic Library Online Catalogs." Doctoral Dissertation. Urbana, Ill., University of Illinois, 1988.

Lewis, David W. "Research on the Use of Online Catalogs and Its Implications for Library Practice." *Journal of Academic Librarianship, 13*(3):152–156, July 1987.

Library of Congress, Subject Cataloging Division. *Library of Congress Subject Headings.* 11th Edition. Washington, D.C., 1988.

Lipetz, Ben-Ami. *User Requirements in Identifying Desired Works in a Large Library.* New Haven, Conn., Yale University Library, 1970.

———. "Catalog Use in a Large Research Library." *Library Quarterly, 42*(1):129–139, January 1972.

Lipetz, Ben-Ami, and Peter J. Paulson. "A Study of the Impact of Introducing an Online Subject Catalog at the New York State Library." *Library Trends, 35*(4):597–617, Spring 1987.

Lipetz, Ben-Ami, and Peter Stangl. "User Clues in Initiating Searches in a Large Library Catalog." In: *Proceedings of the American Society for Information Science. Annual*

Meeting, Volume 5, Information Transfer, Columbus, Ohio, October 20–24, 1968. New York, Greenwood Publishing, 1968, pp. 137–139.

Maclaren, Grant E. "Evaluation of a COM Catalog in a Community College." *Community and Junior College Libraries,* 2(4):69–73, Summer 1984.

Malcolm, Roberta S. "The Student's Approach to the Card Catalog." Master's Thesis. Pittsburgh, Pa., Carnegie Institute of Technology, 1950.

Maltby, Arthur, and A. Duxbury. "Description and Annotation in Catalogues: Reader Requirements." *New Library World,* 73(862):260–262, 273, April 1972.

Mandel, Carol A. *Classification Schedules as Subject Enhancement in Online Catalogs.* Washington, D.C., Council on Library Resources, 1986. ERIC ED275326

Markey, Karen. *Research Report: An Analytical Review of Catalog Use Studies.* Columbus, Ohio, OCLC, 1980. ERIC ED186041

————. *Online Catalog Use: Results of Surveys and Focus Group Interviews in Several Libraries; Final Report to the Council on Library Resources,* Volume II. Dublin, Ohio, OCLC, 1983a. ERIC ED231403

————. *The Process of Subject Searching in the Library Catalog: Final Report on the Subject Access Research Project.* Dublin, Ohio, OCLC, 1983b. ERIC ED231390

————. "Thus Spake the OPAC User." *Information Technology and Libraries,* 2(4):381–387, December 1983c.

————. "Offline and Online User Assistance for Online Catalog Searchers." *Online,* 8(3):54–66, May 1984.

————. "Subject-Searching Experiences and Needs of On-Line Catalog Users: Implications for Library Classification." *Library Resources and Technical Services,* 29(1):34–51, January–March 1985.

————. "Class Number Searching in an Experimental Online Catalog." *International Classification,* 13(3):142–150, 1986.

————. "Searching and Browsing the Dewey Decimal Classification in an Online Catalog." *Cataloging and Classification Quarterly,* 7(3):37–68, Spring 1987.

————. "Integrating the Machine-Readable LCSH into Online Catalogs." *Information Technology and Libraries,* 7(3):299–312, September 1988.

Markey, Karen, and Anh N. Demeyer. *Dewey Decimal Classification Online Project: Evaluation of a Library Schedule and Index Integrated into the Subject Searching Capabilities of an Online Catalog.* Dublin, Ohio, OCLC, 1986. (OCLC Research Report 85-1) ERIC ED269021

Marshall, Joan. "Sexist Subject Headings: An Update." *Hennepin County Library Cataloging Bulletin,* (17):38–42, October 1, 1975.

Massicotte, Mia. "Improved Browsable Displays for Online Subject Access." *Information Technology and Libraries,* 7(4):373–380, December 1988.

Matthews, Joseph R. "Suggested Guidelines for Screen Layouts and Design of Online Catalogs." *Library Trends,* 35(4):555–570, Spring 1987.

Matthews, Joseph R., and Gary S. Lawrence. "Further Analysis of the CLR Online Catalog Project." *Information Technology and Libraries,* 3(4):354–376, December 1984.

Matthews, Joseph R.; Gary S. Lawrence; and Douglas K. Ferguson, eds. *Using Online Catalogs: A Nationwide Survey; A Report of a Study Sponsored by the Council on Library Resources.* New York, Neal-Schuman, 1983.

Mischo, William H. *A Subject Retrieval Function for the Online Union Catalog.* Dublin, Ohio, OCLC, 1981. (OCLC Technical Report 81-4) ERIC ED212263

Miura, Itsuo, et al. "Information-Seeking Behavior of Catalog Users in the Library of International Christian University." *Library and Information Science,* (18):29–57, 1980.

Moore, Carole Weiss. "User Reactions to Online Catalogs: An Exploratory Study." *College and Research Libraries,* 42(4):295–302, July 1981.

Nielsen, Brian. "What They Say They Do and What They Do: Assessing Online Catalog Use Instruction Through Transaction Monitoring." *Information Technology and Libraries,* 5(1):28–34, March 1986.

Nitecki, Joseph Z. "Significance of Date of Publication in the Subject Catalog: An Unfinished Experiment." *PLA Bulletin, 32*(3):53–54, 71, May 1977.

Norden, David J., and Gail Herndon Lawrence. "Public Terminal Use in an Online Catalog: Some Preliminary Results." *College and Research Libraries, 42*(4):308–316, July 1981.

Palmer, Richard P. *Computerizing the Card Catalog in the University Library: A Survey of User Requirements.* Littleton, Colo., Libraries Unlimited, 1972.

Pawley, Carolyn. "Online Access: User Reaction." *College and Research Libraries, 43*(6):473–477, November 1982.

Pease, Sue, and Mary Noel Gouke. "Patterns of Use in an Online Catalog and a Card Catalog." *College and Research Libraries, 43*(4):279–291, July 1982.

Pejtersen, Annelise Mark, and Jutta Austin. "Fiction Retrieval: Experimental Design and Evaluation of a Search System Based on Users' Value Criteria (Part 1)." *Journal of Documentation, 39*(4):230–246, December 1983.

Penniman, W. David, and W. D. Dominick. "Monitoring and Evaluation of On-Line Information System Usage." *Information Processing and Management, 16*(1):17–35, 1980.

Perrine, Richard H. "Catalog Use Study." *RQ, 6*(3):115–119, Spring 1967.

————. "Catalog Use Difficulties." *RQ, 7*(4):169–174, Summer 1968.

Pritchard, Sarah M. "SCORPIO: A Study of Public Users of the Library of Congress Information System." Washington, D.C., Library of Congress, 1981. ERIC ED198801

Rao, Pal V. "The Relationship Between Card Catalog Access Points and the Recorded Use of Education Books in a University Library." *College and Research Libraries, 43*(4):341–345, July 1982.

Sacco, Concetta N. "Book Catalog Use Study: Failure and Success." *RQ, 12*(3):259–266, Spring 1973.

Sage, Charles, et al. "A Queueing Study of Public Catalog Use." *College and Research Libraries, 42*(4):317–325, July 1981.

Seal, Alan. "Experiments with Full and Short Entry Catalogues: A Study of Library Needs." *Library Resources and Technical Services, 27*(2):144–155, April–June 1983.

Sears, Minnie Earl. *Sears List of Subject Headings.* 13th Edition. Edited by Carmen Rovira and Caroline Reyes. New York, Wilson, 1986.

Senzig, Donna. "Library Catalogs for Library Users." *RQ, 24*(1):37–42, Fall 1984.

Settel, Barbara, and Pauline A. Cochrane. "Augmenting Subject Descriptions for Books in Online Catalogs." *Database, 5*(4):29–37, December 1982.

Seymour, Carol A., and J. L. Schofield. "Measuring Reader Failure at the Catalogue." *Library Resources and Technical Services, 17*(1):6–24, Winter 1973.

Siegel, Elliot R., et al. "Research Strategy and Methods Used to Conduct a Comparative Evaluation of Two Prototype Online Catalog Systems." In: *National Online Meeting:*

Proceedings—1983, New York, April 12–14, 1983. Compiled by Martha E. Williams and Thomas H. Hogan. Medford, N.J., Learned Information, 1983, pp. 503–511.

_____. "A Comparative Evaluation of the Technical Performance and User Acceptance of Two Prototype Online Catalog Systems." *Information Technology and Libraries, 3*(1):35–46, March 1984.

Simmons, Peter, and Jocelyn Foster. "User Survey of a Microfiche Catalog." *Information Technology and Libraries, 1*(1):52–54, March 1982.

Spalding, C. Sumner. "The Use of Catalog Entries at the Library of Congress." *Journal of Cataloguing and Classification, 6*(4):95–100, Fall 1950.

Specht, Jerry. "Patron Use of an Online Circulation System in Known-Item Searching." *Journal of the American Society for Information Science, 31*(5):335–346, September 1980.

Spiller, David. "The Provision of Fiction for Public Libraries." *Journal of Librarianship, 12*(4):238–266, October 1980.

Steinberg, David, and Paul Metz. "User Response to and Knowledge About an Online Catalog." *College and Research Libraries, 45*(1):66–70, January 1984.

Swanson, Don R. "Requirements Study for Future Catalogs." *Library Quarterly, 42*(3): 302–315, July 1972.

Tagliacozzo, Renata. "Some Relations Between Queries and Search-Terms Generated by Catalog Users." *Journal of the American Society for Information Science, 23*(4):278–280, July/August 1972.

Tagliacozzo, Renata, and Manfred Kochen. "Information-Seeking Behavior of Catalog Users." *Information Storage and Retrieval, 6*(5):363–381, December 1970.

Tagliacozzo, Renata, et al. "Access and Recognition: From Users' Data to Catalogue Entries." *Journal of Documentation, 26*(3):230–249, September 1970.

Taylor, Arlene G. "Authority Files in Online Catalogs: An Investigation of Their Value." *Cataloging and Classification Quarterly, 4*(3):1–17, Spring 1984.

Taylor, Raymond G., Jr. "Determining the Minimum Number of Online Terminals Needed to Meet Various Library Service Policies." *Information Technology and Libraries, 6*(3):197–204, September 1987.

_____. "Measures of Expected Online Catalog Performance for Public Access Terminals." *Information Technology and Libraries, 7*(1):24–29, March 1988.

Tolle, John E. "Understanding Patrons' Use of Online Catalogs: Transaction Log Analysis of the Search Method." In: *Productivity in the Information Age. Proceedings of the 46th ASIS Annual Meeting, 1983, Washington, D.C., October 2–6, 1983*. Volume 20. Edited by Raymond F. Vondran et al. White Plains, N.Y., Knowledge Industry Publications, 1983, pp. 167–171.

Tolle, John E., et al. "Determining the Required Number of Online Catalog Terminals: A Research Study." *Information Technology and Libraries, 2*(3):261–265, September 1983.

Trzebiatowski, Elaine. "End User Study on BRS/After Dark." *RQ, 23*(4):446–450, Summer 1984.

University of Chicago. *Requirements Study for Future Catalogs. Progress Report No. 2.* Chicago, Ill., 1968.

Van Pulis, Noelle, and Lorene E. Ludy. "Subject Searching in an Online Catalog with Authority Control." *College and Research Libraries, 49*(6):523–533, November 1988.

Walker, Stephen. "OKAPI: Evaluating and Enhancing an Experimental Online Catalog." *Library Trends, 35*(4):631–645, Spring 1987.

_____. "Improving Subject Access Painlessly: Recent Work on the OKAPI Online Catalogue Projects." *Program, 22*(1):21–31, January 1988.

Walker, Stephen, and Richard M. Jones. *Improving Subject Retrieval in Online Catalogues. 1: Stemming, Automatic Spelling Correction, and Cross-Reference Tables.* London, Eng., The Polytechnic of Central London, 1987. (British Library Research Paper 24)

Wayland, Sharon. "User Study of an Online Library Catalog: Tarrant County Junior College District." *Community and Junior College Libraries, 1*(2):5–19, Winter 1982.

Weiming, Li. "User Reactions to OPACs: An Australian Case Study." *LASIE, 18*(4):92–101, January–February, 1988.

Weintraub, D. Kathryn. "The Essentials or Desiderata of the Bibliographic Record as Discovered by Research." *Library Resources and Technical Services, 23*(4):391–405, Fall 1979.

Wellisch, Hans. "Subject Retrieval in the Seventies: Methods, Problems, Prospects." In: *Subject Retrieval in the Seventies.* Edited by Hans Wellisch and Thomas D. Wilson. Westport, Conn., Greenwood Publishing, 1972, pp. 2–27.

Williamson, Nancy J. "The Library of Congress Classification: Problems and Prospects in Online Retrieval." *International Cataloguing, 15*(4):45–48, October–December 1986.

CHAPTER 8

EVALUATION OF REFERENCE SERVICES: QUESTION ANSWERING

The measurement of reference services has been discussed in the professional literature for many years. Rothstein (1964) categorized most of the articles as subjective attempts to describe what was happening. Since 1964, however, reseachers have conducted an increasing number of studies in an attempt to evaluate objectively the quality of reference work. A recent bibliography lists more than 60 studies, or overviews of studies, that discuss reference evaluation (Von Seggern, 1987). Such evaluation is being actively encouraged by library associations, which in some cases are even issuing detailed standards and policies regarding reference services, sample evaluation forms, and the like (for example, Association of Research Libraries, 1987.)

This expanded level of interest in reference service evaluation may be a result of more difficult financial times and the increased need to justify expenditures. Financial justification is crucial for reference services. Although reference departments are key components of every library, they are costly to maintain because of their largely professional staffs and the expensive sources needed to answer many questions. McClure (1984) argued that these costs may put reference departments under more critical scrutiny than other institutional departments, and that librarians should carefully assess the quality of reference services and make any needed changes before external pressure forces them to do so.

During the past 10 years or so, the profession has begun to realize the importance of evaluation. The Reference and Adult Services Division of the American Library Association (1979) has issued standards asking that libraries assign one or more staff with appropriate skills to act as evaluation specialists. Furthermore, these standards recommend that libraries undertake a systematic collection of reference statistics for use in evaluating the quality and quantity of reference services provided, as well as in policy decisions, reports, and budget preparation. Other uses may include reviewing staff performance, determining what type of initial or corrective training is needed, and evaluating staff work load. Today, when an ongoing system of reference evaluation is still the exception rather than the rule, reference statistics are collected and simple evaluations are performed in a growing number of libraries.

The expression "evaluation of reference service" means different things to different people, depending on each person's interpretation of what "reference service" really is. Most authors who discuss the scope of reference service distinguish between direct and indirect service. Direct service is "personal assistance provided [by library staff] to users in pursuit of information" (American Library Association, 1979). Much of this involves answering questions, many of a factual nature, by telephone, in person, or by mail. Conducting literature searches and instructing and guiding patrons in their use of library resources are also important direct services (Katz, 1987). Indirect service includes tasks such as preparing tools (for example, catalogs and bibliographies) to improve access to the collection, selecting and ordering materials, building data and resource files, training and supervising personnel, and handling interlibrary loans. In some specialized libraries, reference staff may even write abstracts and translate materials. This chapter examines only the evaluation of the primary activity of reference librarians: question answering.

Ingwersen and Kaae (1980) discussed the "ideal" reference transaction in some depth (Exhibit 8-1). The patron formulates a question and asks the librarian for assistance. Because the patron often fails to state the true information need, the librarian clarifies the question to determine exactly what information the patron wants and the amount, level, and difficulty of material that is needed. The librarian attempts to find the material, systematically choosing and searching specific tools that are likely to contain the answer. The search may require identifying the most appropriate subject terms, judging the relevance of the citations encountered, or evaluating the documents themselves. Finally, the librarian checks to see that the user is satisfied with the information received, and, if not, begins the process again.

WHAT DATA WILL BE GATHERED TO EVALUATE REFERENCE SERVICES?

It is important to distinguish between macroevaluation and microevaluation of reference services. Macroevaluation measures how well a system operates. It reveals that a particular system operates at a certain level but does not in itself indicate why the system operates at this level or what might be done to improve future performance. Microevaluation investigates how a system operates and why it operates at a particular level. Only microevaluation can lead to improved performance.

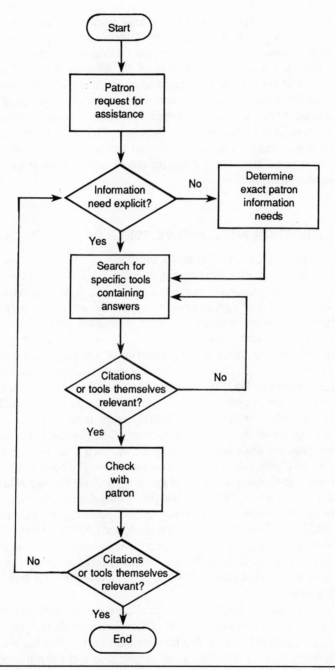

EXHIBIT 8-1   Steps in the reference interview process. Based on a discussion in Ingwerson and Kaae (1980).

Macroevaluation might determine the total number of questions received during a specified period, the proportion of these questions that the librarian attempted to answer, the proportion of the "attempted" questions for which answers were provided, the proportion of the answers that were complete and correct, and the average time taken to answer the questions. These types of data provide a good picture of how well a reference department answers user questions. Microevaluation, however, is needed to determine exactly why the department fails to answer some questions. This involves an analysis to determine why certain questions are handled but others are not, why answers are found for some questions but not for others, and why some questions are answered more quickly than others.

WILL A QUESTION ARISE AND BE ASKED OF THE LIBRARY?

Four events affect the probability that a question will arise and be submitted to the library: (1) the question must arise in an individual's mind, (2) the individual must recognize that the question needs to be answered, (3) the individual must be sufficiently motivated to seek an answer, and (4) the individual must approach the library to have the question answered (Lancaster, 1984). Librarians can influence only the fourth event.

Studies of the information-seeking behavior of various groups have consistently revealed that "consulting a librarian" is used relatively infrequently when information is needed. For instance, when Nelson (1973) surveyed faculty members at six California colleges, he discovered that only 61 percent knew the university library's reference service would answer factual questions. Sandock (1977) asked students the same question at an urban campus. Forty-two percent knew the reference librarians could help answer their questions; an additional 26 percent *were sure they could not.* Two more general studies were conducted to determine the everyday information needs of residents of California and New England and the sources they used to satisfy their information needs. Although libraries were mentioned as one source in both studies, they were not among the top choices (Chen, 1982; King Research, Inc., 1979). Overall, it appears that few people actually think of a library's reference department as a place where they can get questions answered. This is due, at least in part, to a general failure among libraries to adequately and continuously publicize their question-answering services.

Some of the studies addressing this issue have concentrated on publicity efforts to promote information and referral services, a specialized type of reference. Childers (1978b) stressed that libraries must engage in active and ongoing publicity campaigns to have successful information and referral services. Yet both Childers (1984) and Donohue (1976) found that information and referral services were less than effective (and in at least one case failed entirely) because promotion efforts decreased drastically once the programs were established and because few efforts were made to promote such services outside the library.

Other studies reinforce these findings, revealing that the primary users of reference services make up that small segment of the population that already uses libraries for other purposes, rather than the entire population. For example, Weech and Goldhor (1984) found that 58 percent of the users of reference services in public libraries were professionals, managers, or students. Sixty percent were 40 years old or younger; 78 percent had one or more years of college. In other words, the primary users of reference services were highly representative not of the general public, but rather of the current users of public libraries.

Even current library users might not ask a reference librarian for help when they have questions. This may reflect a lack of awareness about the availability of reference services, since most libraries spread such knowledge simply by referring users with questions to a reference librarian and since at least one study has shown that many users are not sure who to ask if they have a question. Westbrook (1984) found that only 53 percent of the freshmen and 38 percent of the visitors using an academic library knew where to go when they had questions. They lacked accurate information concerning the location, function, and identification of reference librarians. This pattern of intermittent, irregular promotion has caused the heaviest use of reference services to come from those who have used such services in the past. In fact, Weech and Goldhor (1984) found that 61 percent of those asking reference questions in five Illinois public libraries had done so previously. Another 20 percent asked questions because they had been made aware of the availability of reference services, although it was not clear when or how this occurred. Individuals referred 9 percent of the patrons to the reference departments, and other agencies referred an additional 5 percent.

But can the failure to ask reference questions be attributed solely to a lack of knowledge of the service by potential users? Not entirely. Swope and Katzer (1972) randomly selected 119 patrons of the Syracuse University library from three library areas: near the card catalog, in the reference room, and in the open stacks. They asked whether patrons (1) had questions and (2) would ask a librarian for assistance. Of the 41 percent of the patrons who did have questions, 65 percent said they would *not* ask a librarian for assistance. When the evaluators asked why, 75 percent of that group replied that they did not want to bother the busy librarian, that they felt the question was too simple, or that they were not satisfied with the image or past services of a librarian.

Other studies reinforce these ideas, particularly that users do not want to bother librarians. Half the users in several academic libraries avoided one or more librarians because at some time in the past the librarians had appeared too busy to help them, had given no help, or had given more help than needed (Durrance, 1986). In a different academic library, 39 percent of the people who

234 THE MEASUREMENT AND EVALUATION OF LIBRARY SERVICES

had questions did not ask for help because the librarians appeared too busy to assist them, 16 percent were unsure whether the librarians were willing to help them, and 2 percent felt the librarians actually were unwilling to help (Westbrook, 1984).

The apparent busyness of the librarians is understandable, since reference staff is not always adequate to cover potential use. Murfin (1983) confirmed this when she found that as the number of users in the library increases, the number of individuals who will ask reference questions decreases. This is because the number of reference staff hours does not usually increase in proportion to the number of users. Thus, increased competition for each available reference librarian leads to queues at the reference desk that discourage people from asking questions. Stayner (1980) also found a high correlation between the number of individual staff hours and various measures of public service effectiveness.

Many libraries are so short-staffed that, in the interests of economy, they require reference staff to fill up any "empty" time at the reference desk by performing other duties. This compounds the problem because it prevents reference staff from being alert to people who might need help. At least one study demonstrated the importance of being receptive to those who feel nervous or awkward about asking for help. Kazlauskas (1976) positioned himself where he could watch the nonverbal behavior of staff and patrons, then recorded the body movements of both. He found that some librarians, through the use of positive body movements, are more approachable than others. These librarians immediately acknowledge a patron's presence when the patron moves toward the reference desk—if not verbally then through establishing immediate eye contact or "flashing their eyebrows." Receptive librarians also smile at patrons and use evaluative gestures, such as nodding, to indicate that they are interested in and are absorbing patron requests. In cases where patrons could choose between asking for help from a receptive and a nonreceptive staff member, patrons always approached the former. When users had a choice between two similarly receptive staff members, they approached standing librarians rather than seated ones 10 out of 11 times, because they perceived a seated librarian as one who was busy and would rather not be interrupted.

Reference staff should also be willing to take an active role in approaching patrons who do not approach the desk but who might need help. This is rarely done; most librarians rely on patrons to initiate the reference query (Wilkinson, 1972). This is understandable in libraries that are so short-staffed that only one reference person is on duty at a time, but in more fully staffed libraries, efforts should be made to approach patrons who look as if they are having problems.

These studies show that the following questions must be asked when libraries begin to evaluate reference services:

- To what extent is the potential clientele aware that reference services are provided?

- Are the users of reference services already regular library patrons?
- How many reference users are first-time users?
- How many reference users belong to each of the library's potential target groups—for example, students, business people, or faculty?
- How did reference users find out about the service?
- Is the clientele not asking reference questions because of lack of knowledge about the service, or because of staff busyness, attitude problems, or past performance failures?

The first question should be asked not just of current library patrons, but of a random sample of all potential library users. The other questions can be addressed by surveying or interviewing a sample of all current users about their knowledge and use of reference services. The total effectiveness of the library as a source of reference information cannot be judged without considering these questions and the implications of the responses to them.

HOW MANY AND WHAT TYPE OF QUESTIONS DOES THE REFERENCE DEPARTMENT RECEIVE?

A second type of data collection that libraries can perform is a simple count of the number of reference questions received during a particular period and the number that the library attempted to answer. Most libraries collect the former figure. Gross counts of this kind have value in indicating a library's volume of business, and information on the pattern of query distribution throughout the day and the week is useful in developing efficient staff schedules. But in themselves, number counts provide no basis for evaluating the quality of reference service. They can, however, suggest areas for further research.

Two studies illustrate the potential of reference counts. Goldhor (1987) collected data on the number of reference questions asked in public libraries in the United States, Canada, and Great Britain between 1970 and 1985. His data show that as the size of the library increases, the percentage of reference questions asked in relation to total circulation count increases. For example, reference questions total 5 percent of circulation transactions in libraries serving fewer than 10,000 persons but 20 percent of circulation transactions in libraries serving more than 200,000 persons. Other studies (for example, Baker, 1986) indicate that information overload increases as the library's size increases. The pattern Goldhor observed suggests related points of fruitful research, such as verifying that patrons in larger libraries may be attempting to cope with information overload by asking for help more often and determining what steps public services staff could take to lessen this overload.

An older study by Harris (1966) is different in nature, but it too indicates that reference counts can alert librarians to factors that may influence the quality of service. Harris noted that some libraries receive many more reference questions than others and suggested that this might be because of the physical location of the reference department. After determining the number of questions routinely asked in a university library, Harris moved the reference desk to a location that was more visible and more physically accessible to patrons. The number of questions asked after the move increased significantly.

Currently, few libraries attempt to collect data on the number of questions the library attempts to answer. But this too is important. Libraries may reject many questions for legitimate policy reasons. Policy factors generally relate to who is eligible to use the library's service and whether the question is of a type acceptable to the library. For example, the librarian of a particular company may refuse to answer questions posed by nonemployees or questions that are not directly related to company business. Librarians may reject other questions because they think they will be unable to find the answer or will find it only after an arduous search.

A thorough evaluation should record all requests as they are made, tally questions that are rejected, and categorize reasons for rejection. An analysis of the latter could reveal the kinds of legitimate questions the library is poorly equipped to handle, perhaps because of weaknesses in the collection or because of inadequate tools for exploiting the collection. Or it could reveal a lack of training or experience among staff—for example, questions are rejected that actually could be answered, if not from the library's own resources, then from some easily accessible outside source.

Libraries that collect information about the numbers of questions asked and handled may also wish to categorize the types of inquiries they receive to help with collection development, staff training efforts, and staff scheduling. Many evaluators categorize a query by the reference source or the type of sources needed to answer it, the source from which the query came (a telephone, mail, or walk-in request), the amount of time needed to answer the query, or its subject matter. Katz (1987) noted four widely used categorizations:

1. Directional questions, which require only the location of a particular item, source, or service
2. Ready reference questions, which require a single, usually factual and uncomplicated answer from a standard reference work such as an encylopedia or almanac
3. Specific search questions, which require more information on a subject and are generally answered from one or more books, articles, bibliographies, or encyclopedias
4. Research questions, which require more information on often complicated questions and which may be answered from sources contained both within and outside the library

Many libraries modify this list, perhaps by grouping together all inquiries except directional ones.

Some authors have recommended or used different categorizations. Rothstein (1964) suggested a category for readers' advisory questions, which require that the librarian help choose a book. Hieber (1966) classed questions by the form and content of the response—for example, does the query require a fill-in-the-blank response? Spicer (1972) recorded bibliography questions separately, and Hood and Gittings (1975) separated questions about library policy, which they found formed almost one-third of the questions asked. Weech and Goldhor (1984) classed questions on location and selection of material separately from ready reference or search questions. Calabretta and Ross (1984) grouped questions by the action the librarian took while answering them: recommending sources, using sources, interpreting sources, or instructing patrons in what to use and how to use it. Ultimately, questions should be classed in the manner that will meet the objectives of the library, the reference department, or the evaluator.

Some libraries also ask staff to record the subject matter of the question and the source or types of sources used to answer the question. This information, and information about questions that could not be answered, can help the staff decide which subject areas need augmenting or weeding and which heavily used sources might be featured in staff development activities. Thus, Hebert's (1984) findings that certain types of information are requested more frequently in government documents libraries (legislative information, statistical information, and maps) could form the basis of a training program for new employees.

Evaluators should use caution when collecting and attempting to use traditional question counts as measures of reference activity. These lack reliability unless data collection procedures are tightly controlled. Two librarians could record similar transactions differently, on the basis of their perceptions of how much information was required. Kesselman and Watstein (1987) showed that this happens even when reference librarians think the categories are fairly well defined. Furthermore, busy librarians often fail to log the questions entirely, or fail to do this at the time the service is provided, relying on their memories to go back and fill in the needed information at a later time.

The problem of data reliability can be alleviated somewhat by giving reference librarians precise instructions about which questions fall into each recording category. Definitions of the categories should be contained on the data collection form whenever possible to prevent librarians from forgetting them over time. A partial solution to the busyness problem is to use recording forms designed so that much of the information can be noted merely by checking or circling an item (Exhibit 8-2). Department heads who regularly and judiciously emphasize the need for accuracy in recording such statistics may also help increase data reliability.

Evaluators can further improve reliability by sampling reference transactions, rather than collecting data on them every day, so long as the data are collected

DATE:	DAY: M Tu W Th F Sa Su	TIME:	ASKED	in person 1 by telephone 2 by mail 3	PATRON: Undergraduate 1 Graduate 2 Faculty 3

INFORMATION REQUESTED		Library staff	4
Address	1	Staff	5
Biog.	2	Other students	6
Book Review	3	Others	7
Check card cat.	4		
Critical sources:		ACTUAL TIME:	
poetry, fict., drama	5	Less than 5 min.	1
Explain ref. (in *Reader's*		5 to 15 min.	2
Guide to Periodical		15 to 30 min.	3
Literature, Book		30 to 60 min.	4
Review Digest,		1 to 2 hrs.	5
etc.)	6	2 or more hrs.	6
How to get a periodical	7		
Interpret card cat.	8		

SOURCES:					ANSWERED:	
Tel. dir.	1	DAS	11		Yes	1
City dir.	2	WW	12		Partially	2
College cat.	3	WWA	13		Hope so, patron	
Gale En. Asso.	4	Bio. Ind.	14		to return, if not	3
HEW Dir.	5	DNB	15		No	4
Am. Men Sc.	6	Ency.	16		Referred elsewhere	5
VF	7	Atlas	17			
Con. Auth.	8	Dict.	18			
Curr. Biog.	9					
DAB	10					

Patron's name and address

EXHIBIT 8-2   Reference question form used at the Walter Clinton Jackson Library, University of North Carolina at Greensboro. Reprinted from Hawley (1970), courtesy of the American Library Association.

on a representative sample of days. The best way to ensure representative data is through random sampling, with supervisors emphasizing the need for thoroughness and accuracy in recording the sampled transactions. For example, Kesselman and Watstein (1987) graphed weekly transaction totals for one year, then chose a systematic random sample to get a representative selection of high-, medium-, and low-use weeks during which data could be collected.

When properly conducted, reference counts can aid a library in reducing costs by determining more effective staffing patterns. Simple transaction counts may be supplemented by collecting information on the time and date of the reference transaction, its length, its mode (for example, telephone versus walk-in), and the level of activity at the reference desk during the transaction. They may also be augmented with turnstile count, which both Murfin (1983) and Slater (1981) found to be highly correlated with demand for reference services. Measuring the availability of staff to answer reference questions is also a possibility. Kantor (1980) suggested that observers, during representative time periods, record the number of patrons awaiting service, the number of reference personnel free to serve, the number of personnel engaged in providing service, and the number of personnel otherwise engaged. Spencer (1980) described a different approach to work sampling, based on the use of a randomly set alarm. When the alarm sounded, reference staff recorded the activities in which they were engaged. The sum of the staff observations, recorded each time the alarm rang during the selected working days, provided a good composite picture of the department's activities.

Libraries that record the number of questions received during a particular period, the average amount of time needed to answer a question, the length of the waiting queue, and other work load variables can decide whether fewer or more staff members are needed during particular periods. They also can consider other related matters. Suppose, for example, that an evaluator discovers that 60 percent of a library's reference transactions are directional. Various researchers (for example, Balay and Andrew, 1975; Young, 1970) showed that nonprofessionals can answer many simple directional and ready reference questions with only a small amount of training. Therefore, the head of reference might consider training a nonprofessional to answer these queries and to refer more difficult questions to professionals. In a large library, this could reduce significantly the cost of current reference service or at least permit professionals to spend their time working on projects in keeping with their training.

It is even possible to use simulation techniques to determine the most cost-effective model for staffing a reference desk. Shafa (1980) developed a computer program that examines information on when patrons arrive, the types of patrons, the types of questions users generally ask, the amount of time needed to answer the questions, and related factors. The possible numbers and skill levels of staff available to work at the reference desk, from student assistants to senior-level librarians, are other data used. Using these criteria, the computer develops various staffing models, predicting for each such factors as the costs of various levels of professional and nonprofessional staffing, the adequacy of the answers likely to be received, and the like. The library can then choose the model that is best suited to its particular operations.

DID PATRONS RECEIVE COMPLETE AND CORRECT ANSWERS?

Students at Drexel University said that the accuracy of the answer is the most important criterion they use to judge reference service (Halperin and Strazdon,

1980). It is to the profession's credit that some progress has been made in addressing this issue; researchers have conducted more than 30 studies on this topic since the late 1960s.

The simplest type of accuracy study asks the librarian to report whether he or she believes the question has been answered correctly. This evaluation of perceived "reference fill rate" has been promoted by the Public Library Association (Van House et al., 1987); however, it is not recommended. Granted, self-reported measures of fill rate are quickly and easily obtained and do readily detect questions for which no answers were found. Questions that are inaccurately or only partly answered, however, often go undetected by the librarian recording the information.

It is more valuable to have staff performance rated by an informed evaluator with less vested interest in the outcome. Evaluators can scrutinize performance obtrusively (with the reference librarian's knowledge) or unobtrusively. In most such studies, evaluators assemble a group of questions that a reference librarian in a particular library or group of libraries should be able to answer correctly. Evaluators choose various types of questions. Factual questions can be answered quickly from standard ready reference sources such as encyclopedias or almanacs. Evaluators use these questions most often in tests of accuracy, because such inquiries constitute the bulk of the queries received in an average library. Bibliographic questions require the use of standard sources to verify citations and possibly the locations of items. Research questions require that the librarian spend time helping patrons find in-depth information on specific subjects. And readers' advisory questions test the librarian's knowledge of current fiction and nonfiction sources to satisfy patron demands for good books. Evaluators also may ask questions about specific library services or policies (for example, whether the library charges a fee for filing an interlibrary loan request).

A relatively recent innovation is the inclusion of escalator questions, which measure whether the librarian probes for the patron's exact, underlying information need. Olson (1984) gave the following example of an escalator question:

Step 1: (Initial question): Where are your books on running?
Step 2: (Additional information): I'd like to find out who makes Vantage running shoes.
Step 3: (Ultimate level): I could use the address; I have a complaint to make to the manufacturer. (p. 327)

All the questions that are used to test accuracy should represent typical queries the staff might receive. The evaluator should draw questions either from a list of those received in the past by the library (or by a library similar to the one being studied) or compiled by experts who know the types of questions asked in a certain size or type of library. Because the results of the study will depend heavily on the choice of questions, evaluators should pretest the questions before they are used to ensure that they are unambiguous. The pretest can also reveal which questions are especially easy or difficult to answer. These can then be eliminated to ensure a better test of reference, especially if several libraries are being compared.

Before actually beginning the evaluation, the librarian needs to consider who will judge the correctness of the answers. Judging usually is done by a qualified and experienced evaluator or panel of evaluators. The use of a panel may help the library resolve any difficulties in categorizing a response. The librarian also needs to consider, in advance, the criteria that will be used to judge responses and the scale that will be used to rate them. Evaluators should consider the following criteria in tests of accuracy:

- Did the librarian conduct a reference interview to probe for the patron's underlying need?
- What strategies were used in the librarian's search?
- Was the complete and correct answer received?
- How long did the librarian take to respond?
- Did the librarian answer the question in a professional manner (for example, courteous, sympathetic)?
- Did the librarian provide the source of the answer?
- Did the librarian use more than one source, when appropriate?
- Did the librarian refer the question elsewhere if no answer could be provided?
- Was the patron referred to an agency that could provide the complete and correct answer?

Generally, a numerical scale is used to score the results. The criteria for scoring need to be as objective as possible to avoid introducing bias into the results. Wallace (1984) used a 10-point scale and subtracted points for various mistakes the librarian made. As Exhibit 8-3 shows, he subtracted 1 point if the librarian failed to give a source and increased the penalty with the seriousness of the mistake.

Many libraries prefer to use obtrusive tests to measure reference accuracy, in part because they are easy to conduct. In the simplest studies, each reference librarian is given a set of questions to answer, often within some specified time frame. The responses then are scored either to reveal the performance of the individual or the average performance of the library. This method has been used in a number of studies, including those by Powell (1978) and Weech and Goldhor (1982).

Researchers have proposed or tried more complicated techniques to measure accuracy. Jahoda (1977) collected a sample of reference questions from special libraries, then asked reference staff to tell what search strategy they would use to answer the questions. Bunge (1977) suggested having an informed expert observe the librarian's handling of questions posed by actual patrons,

Maximum possible points = 10

Correct and complete answer supplied within 48 hours of request	Subtract 0
Incomplete answer	Subtract 2
Partially correct answer (outdated, etc.)	Subtract 5
Totally incorrect answer	Subtract 10
No answer, but referred	Subtract 6
No answer, no referral	Subtract 8
Source of answer not volunteered	Subtract 1
Source of answer not supplied when requested	Subtract 2
Patron directed to source, answer in source	Subtract 2
Patron found answer independently after being referred to card catalog, vertical file, etc.	Subtract 4
Original answer not understandable to patron or not acceptable to patron without clarification	Subtract 2
For each 24 hours beyond the initial 48 hours	Subtract 0.5

Minimum score possible = 0

EXHIBIT 8-3 Index of quality scoring of reference service. Reprinted from Wallace (1984), courtesy of the Illinois State Library.

then conduct an in-depth interview with these patrons to determine their real information needs and the appropriateness of the answers. A variation of this method, used by Ingwersen (1982) and Ingwersen and Kaae (1980), had librarians verbalize and tape record their thoughts during reference interviews. These recordings were combined with systematic observation to get information on other details of the transactions, including the tools that were used and the nonverbal behavior of the librarians. Mucci (1976) used a third method in a large public library: videotaping librarians during reference transactions. These techniques all should gather more valid data than Jahoda's, because they measure the librarian's actual performance during the reference transaction rather than just the ability to identify sources or to tell how to structure searches.

One disadvantage of many of these methods is that the evaluator needs to spend a lot of time determining whether or not the librarian was supplying correct responses. An even greater concern with the obtrusive methods is that reference personnel may perform better when they know they are being evaluated than at other times.

Weech and Goldhor (1982) verified that a more accurate picture of performance can be obtained if reference services are evaluated without the librarian's knowledge. They rated 30 typical public library reference questions in terms of difficulty and divided them into two lists of equivalent difficulty. During the first part of the study, when staff were unaware that they were being tested, five patrons at each of five public libraries asked three different reference questions over a period of several weeks. When all unobtrusive evaluations were complete, reference librarians at the same libraries were given the second set of 15 reference questions and told that their performance would be judged. As was expected, library staff answered significantly more reference questions completely and correctly when they were aware they were being scrutinized (Exhibit 8-4). Crowley (1985) and Williams (1987) also found that unobtrusive evaluations result in lower accuracy figures.

Evaluators generally plan unobtrusive studies in the same way they plan obtrusive ones; however, observers posing as patrons ask the reference questions. Each surrogate patron, or *proxy*, must be carefully trained to present the question naturally and be ready to indicate why the answer is needed. If training and supervision of proxies are done carefully, proxies are indistinguishable from regular patrons and should receive "typical" answers to the questions they pose.

Surrogate patrons can ask reference questions in person, over the telephone, or through the mail. In-person requests are preferable, since many aspects of the

	Library					
	A	B	C	D	E	Total
Obtrusive evaluation*	80	87	67	93	100	85
Unobtrusive evaluation†	67	78	75	33	92	70

$\chi^2 = 4.45$, $p < .05$, $df = 1$.

*Obtrusive evaluation: $n = 15$ for all libraries.
†Unobtrusive evaluation: $n = 15$ for A, $n = 12$ for C and E, $n = 9$ for B and D.

EXHIBIT 8-4 Percentage of complete and correct answers given in obtrusive and unobtrusive evaluations in five Illinois public libraries. Reprinted, with additions, from Weech and Goldhor (1982), courtesy of the University of Chicago Press.

librarian's behavior that influence accuracy (for example, the search strategy) cannot be observed by proxies phoning or mailing in questions.

Unobtrusive evaluations are flexible enough to be used as part of a larger study. In the best example of this, Hernon and McClure (1987) unobtrusively measured staff performance on questions about statistical data disseminated by the Federal Government. Both reference and documents staff then attended either a workshop or a slide presentation designed to increase their awareness of and familiarity with the basic sources of such statistical information. Performance was then remeasured to determine if the staff's accuracy had significantly improved.

Unobtrusive tests of accuracy have their share of drawbacks. One of the biggest is that they may be more expensive to administer than obtrusive tests, since proxies need to be hired and trained. Tests conducted at more than one library location are also costly, because they require the use of long-distance phone calls or extensive travel funds. It is possible, however, to reduce some expenses. The Fairfax County (Virginia) Public Library joined with two neighboring libraries to reduce costs in a study of telephone reference services. Staff members from each system asked questions of librarians in the other systems, so no proxies were hired (Rodger and Goodwin, 1984). Weech and Goldhor (1982) used undergraduate student proxies, who could be paid less, and Hansel (1986) used volunteers.

Some researchers have also expressed concerns about the ethics of unobtrusive studies, suggesting that the results should be used to judge overall institutional quality but not individual staff performance (for example, McClure, 1984; Weech, 1974). Hansel (1986), however, argued that "it is only through individuals that improvement in service will come. Administrative commitment to excellence in library service is meaningless without the commitment of individual staff" (p. 74). This is reasonable, because an individual staff member's behavior and knowledge are the two factors most highly related to accuracy. Test results for individuals should at least be used to develop in-staff training programs or to set individual goals for improvement.

Evaluators who wish to measure their reference staff's performance unobtrusively should refer to Hernon and McClure (1987) for a more exhaustive review of the procedures involved, paying particular attention to the excellent overview of the ways in which the validity and reliability of such testing can be increased.

Although unobtrusive studies generally show that libraries answer completely and correctly little more than half of the questions received, librarians themselves tend to report better results. One example is a survey of questions received by the business departments of two large public libraries in the United Kingdom (Capital Planning Information, 1987). Staff at one of these libraries believed they had answered completely 79 percent of the questions received, and answered partially another 18 percent, leaving only 3 percent not answered satisfactorily. At the other library, the corresponding figures were 71 percent, 19 percent, and

9 percent. Between 80 percent and 90 percent of users, contacted by telephone, claimed to be completely satisfied with the service they received, but these figures were derived from small samples. High rates of success can be partly attributed to the fact that many of the questions (22 percent in one library, 31 percent in another) were of a simple name/address type, the source used being the British electoral registers.

User Ratings of Completeness and Accuracy

Most studies of reference accuracy have relied on judgments made by professional researchers or experienced practitioners, rather than by library patrons. Is this a good idea? Patrons may provide valuable information that can be obtained no other way—information that reflects their opinions about whether the answers they were given were satisfactory and whether they felt the ambiance of the transaction was favorable. Evaluating user satisfaction with the reference process is appropriate and is described in the last section of this chapter, "Was the Patron Satisfied with the Response?"

Results of past studies, however, have made a number of researchers question the user's ability to assess the accuracy of response received. Wallace's (1984) findings illustrate this most dramatically: 83 percent of the patrons he studied were fully satisfied with the answers they received, even though only 69 percent of them received complete, correct responses. Similar discrepancies between the patron's perception of accuracy and the actual accuracy rate have been noted by Bunge (1985), Goldhor (1979), Hansel (1986), and Weech and Goldhor (1984). In a study performed in 1989 at Illinois State University, students generally expressed satisfaction with the library staff even when the staff did essentially nothing for them (Elzy et al., in press). Several factors could cause patrons to report satisfaction even when they have not received the best service, such as unwillingness to criticize the performance of librarians they perceive to be friendly.

A recent breakthrough is the finding by Murfin and Gugelchuk (1987) that a major cause of the difference between evaluator and patron ratings of accuracy is the inadequacy of the forms that are used to survey patrons. These authors designed a form that asks more specific questions, uses a more precise measuring scale, and separates user ratings of satisfaction with the answer from user ratings of satisfaction with the librarian. The form proved to be highly reliable when tested under controlled conditions. Moreover, the authors reported that "Results of success on factual-type questions as reported by patrons in this study correspond to [those] obtained by testing reference librarians by unobtrusive observation on a preselected set of reference questions" (p. 329). If further studies show this particular form to be continually reliable in assessing the accuracy of responses provided, evaluators could substitute surveys of user satisfaction for the more expensive unobtrusive tests of question answering.

Source of Study	Year Study Was Published	Percentage of Questions Answered Completely and Correctly
Murfin and Bunge	1988	51 (paraprofessionals) 60 (professionals)
Benham	1987	53
Drone	1987	47
Williams	1987	64
Hansel	1986	75
Hernon and McClure	1986a	42
Hernon and McClure	1986b	62
Gers and Seward	1985	55
Myers	1985	56
Roy	1985a	71
Roy	1985b	62
Rodger and Goodwin	1984	56
Van House and Childers	1984	74
Wallace	1984	59
McClure and Hernon	1983	37
Myers	1983	50
Wallace	1983	80
Way	1983	65
Weech and Goldhor	1982	70
Jirjees	1981	56
Schmidt	1980a, 1980b	50
Childers	1978a	47
Powell	1978	59
Ramsden	1978	50
Halldorsson and Murfin	1977	32 (paraprofessionals)* 65 (professionals)*
Peat, Marwick, Mitchell and Company	1975	40
House	1974	40
King and Berry	1973	60
Childers	1971	55
Crowley	1971	54

*Calculated from raw data presented in original article.

EXHIBIT 8-5   Results of selected studies of reference accuracy.

Results of Tests of Accuracy

During the past two decades, evaluators have measured accuracy in a wide variety of obtrusive and unobtrusive studies (Exhibit 8-5 summarizes the results of selected studies). Some evaluators submitted questions by phone, some by personal visit, and some by a combination of the two. Studies varied by type and size of library and were conducted both by trained researchers and library practitioners. Each study used a different set of questions to test accuracy, and each scored the responses of reference librarians differently. Yet all the studies had something in common: they showed that library users face a surprisingly low probability of getting their questions answered accurately. Although some libraries do very poorly and others do much better, the average accuracy rate hovers at or slightly above 50 percent, causing Crowley (1985) to dub this phenomenon "half-right reference."

Both Ballard (1986) and Douglas (1988) have been highly critical of these types of accuracy tests. The fact that libraries consistently score around 50 percent on such tests, Douglas maintained, is at least partly because (1) very easy questions might be eliminated; (2) some questions are carried over from one test to another, creating a tendency for results to be similar across tests; and (3) sets of test questions typically contain a disproportionate number of queries that are unusually difficult or for which the answer has recently changed. Douglas and Ballard both were unwilling to accept that a score of, say, 55 percent truly reflects the success of libraries in answering reference questions. Douglas further criticized unobtrusive tests because they tend to focus primarily, if not exclusively, on questions with unequivocal factual answers—only one type of question handled by reference departments. He also maintained that the number of test questions is often too small to allow reliable diagnosis.

WHY ARE ACCURACY RATES SO LOW?

Since the early 1970s, microevaluation studies have tried to pinpoint the causes of reference failure. But confusion reigned because of a large body of seemingly disparate findings on the subject. Gers and Seward (1985) suggested that this problem, although complex, is resolvable. They found in their study of reference services in Maryland public libraries that three major factors influenced accuracy: (1) the librarian's behavior during the question-answering process, (2) the library's resources, and (3) the type of demand for service. The first strongly influenced performance; the last two influenced performance only slightly. The numerous studies that have explored reference performance indicate this same pattern: the librarian's behavior and knowledge are the primary predictors of accuracy, with resources and demand being secondary predictors. Two other factors, not considered by Gers and Seward, may also influence accuracy: library policies regarding question answering and characteristics of the question itself. All of these factors are discussed next.

Librarian Behavior and Knowledge

It is reasonable to suppose that the characteristics of the librarian are major factors affecting the quality of question answering. Theoretically, a large number of personal actions, skills, and attributes are involved in answering questions well, including the librarian's knowledge of the collection and of current events; the librarian's ability to make decisions; his or her perception of professional responsibilities and commitment to these responsibilities; the librarian's education and training; and his or her experience as a librarian and a reference librarian (Lancaster, 1984). Only recently has a large enough body of data been amassed to show some consistent patterns. The data reveal that, all other factors being equal, the librarian's behavior and knowledge are the strongest influences in determining whether a question will be answered completely and correctly.

The Librarian's Performance During the Reference Interview

Murfin (1970) reemphasized the need for a reference interview after discovering that a quarter of the questions asked were poor reflections of true patron needs. The ideal interview should determine the exact subject needed and pinpoint the patron's objective and motivation for asking the question, as well as any relevant personal characteristics that affect the information need. The librarian should also seek information about anticipated or acceptable answers—for example, is a book on the subject acceptable, or does the patron want only a short summary or a picture?

Librarians generally obtain information through a combination of open-ended and close-ended questions. The former encourage patrons to respond at length and generally are prefaced by the words "what," "when," "how," "who," "where," and "why." Although open-ended questions are thought to be preferable because of the larger amount of information that can be gleaned from them, Lynch (1978) found that librarians overwhelmingly tend to ask close-ended questions. These call for shorter responses to more specific inquiries. Ideally, the number and type of questions asked depend on the amount of information the user has about the topic and on how articulate the user is (White, 1981).

The ability of the librarian to pace the interview through the effective use of pauses also affects the content of the patron's response. Librarians who proceed on their own agenda, allowing patrons little or no time to respond, reduce the amount of information received. Conversely, librarians who pause for a very long time after the inquiries also have difficulty extracting information about the patron's true information need (Knapp, 1978; White, 1981).

Librarians who conduct a full and efficient reference interview to probe for the patron's underlying need give more complete and more accurate answers. Four aspects of the reference interview influence accuracy: (1) the degree to which the librarian negotiated the question, (2) how well the librarian understood the question and how much attention was given to it, (3) how comfortable the librarian was with the question, and (4) whether the librarian checked to see if the patron was satisfied with the final response (Gers and Seward, 1985).

The first and last aspects are particularly important to the process. If a librarian fails in the first instance, then asking "Have I really answered your question?" at the end of the transaction may reveal the failure. Murfin (1970) concluded this after asking reference users to examine critically the materials they were given and to state whether their needs were met. Only 60 percent of the users were satisfied. Routine follow-up should identify unsatisfied users for the purpose of helping them further. Unfortunately, few reference librarians ask follow-up questions (Gers and Seward, 1985).

At least two other studies affirmed that the major cause of inaccuracy was failure to conduct a good reference interview. The first study was an unobtrusive evaluation conducted at the Fairfax County (Virginia) Public Library. Evaluators asked five escalator questions at each of 14 branch libraries. The failure of system staff to negotiate these, either in part or in full, led to staff giving many incomplete answers (Rodger and Goodwin, 1984). The second study examined levels of accuracy in a college library that often used nonprofessionals to staff the reference desk (Halldorsson and Murfin, 1977). Professionals performed much better than nonprofessionals in situations involving escalator questions and faulty information questions—questions that were deliberately designed to be slightly misleading (Exhibits 8-6 and 8-7). This was because nonprofessionals spent less time trying to discover exactly what the patron wanted through a reference interview.

Type of Reference Interview	Total Number of Questions	Nonprofessionals		Professionals		Difference Between Nonprofessionals and Professionals
		Number Correct Solutions	Percent Correct Solutions	Number Correct Solutions	Percent Correct Solutions	
Success in personally obtaining correct information in reference interview (without referral or consultation)	25	5	20	13	52	32 pts.
Success with referral or consultation	25	7	28	15	67	39 pts.

EXHIBIT 8-6 Overall success of professionals and nonprofessionals in correcting faulty information in the reference interview. Reprinted in modified form from Halldorsson and Murfin (1977), courtesy of the American Library Association.

Type of Question	Example of Question	Total Number of Questions	Nonprofessionals		Professionals		Difference Between Nonprofessionals and Professionals
			Number of Questions Solved	Percent of Questions Solved	Number of Questions Solved	Percent of Questions Solved	
Indirect Questions	"Broad Subject" Example: "Where are your literature books?"	11	8	73	10	91	18 pts.
	"Wrong Type of Source" Example: "Where are your almanacs to history?"	10	5	50	9	90	40 pts.
Faulty Information Questions	Misspelling Example: Southy for Southey	12	3	25	9	75	50 pts.
	Example: Poem "Agnes Eve" by Shelley	13	2	16	5	38	22 pts.

EXHIBIT 8-7 Success of professionals and nonprofessionals in answering questions, by type of question. Reprinted in modified form from Halldorsson and Murfin (1977), courtesy of the American Library Association.

Durrance (1989) reported on an unobtrusive study of reference interviews in which an unspecified number of students in library and information science presented questions "of importance to them" at 142 public, academic, and special libraries. The objective was not to study the accuracy of responses (indeed, Durrance suggests that "accuracy may not be the most appropriate measure of success") but to evaluate the reference interview and the environment in which it occurs. Students either presented the questions to librarians themselves or "observed the interaction between a colleague and a librarian." The reference interview was evaluated through the use of a questionnaire that addressed the students' attitudes toward the librarian and his or her interpersonal behavior and interviewing skills. Durrance pointed out that the "environment" in which the reference interview takes place—usually some type of desk in a large, open area without a chair for the library user and without the user being certain that he or she is dealing with a professional—may itself be a significant barrier to effective communication. The data also suggest that interpersonal factors, such as friendliness and attentiveness of the librarian, are more important than the perceived accuracy of response in determining whether a library user will return to a particular librarian.

How often are reference interviews actually conducted? A number of studies have measured this. One of the earliest found that 65 percent of the reference staff in the business department of an academic library made no attempt to clarify the patron's question (King and Berry, 1973). Childers (1980) confirmed the low rate of interviewing in his unobtrusive study of 57 public library outlets in Suffolk County, New York. The study used escalator questions to examine whether librarians were determining exact user information needs. Sixty-seven percent of the reference librarians made no effort to probe for the precise need; only 20 percent were totally successful in identifying it. When measuring the quality of question answering in Illinois public libraries, Roy (1985b) documented that during each of the four years of the study, between 72 percent and 85 percent of the librarians failed to query proxies posing questions for any additional information. Other unobtrusive studies yielded similar results, although the percentages vary: Lynch (1978) found that 51 percent of staff asked no exploratory questions; Gers and Seward (1985), 49 percent; Goldhor (1979), 49 percent; and Weech and Goldhor (1984), 45 percent.

In a related study by Schmidt (1980a, 1980b), proxies asked 30 questions in three college libraries and recorded how the librarian responded to each. Eight reference librarians asked the proxies to explain specific terms contained in the question. But only 3 of the 30 asked for any background information, including the reason for the question. Three others asked how much information the proxies needed and in what detail.

These results show that many librarians fail to determine the real information need of their patrons and that this failure is a major cause of inaccurate responses. Although the findings are pessimistic, one recent study gives hope that correct behavior can be learned and, once learned, can improve accuracy rates. Stephan et al. (1988) showed that when reference librarians are fully and correctly trained to conduct effective reference interviews, their accuracy rates increase significantly. Initially, an unobtrusive study found that librarians in 60 Maryland public libraries gave accurate answers for only 55 percent of the posed questions. Consultants working for the Maryland State Library designed an experimental study to determine whether they could significantly increase this accuracy rate. One group of librarians attended an intensive three-day workshop that emphasized how to conduct a proper reference interview. The workshop required that librarians be made aware of how they were currently handling reference questions, receive intensive training in more appropriate behavior, be given ample opportunity to practice the new techniques, and receive feedback on their performance from individual coaches. The librarians thus trained accurately answered 77 percent of the questions in a posttest. In two libraries, staff completed the workshops, were extensively coached by peers on the job, and received support and praise from supervisors for any improvement. The accuracy rate in these libraries rose to 95 percent. These studies show conclusively that reference evaluators need to include, in their design, plans to measure the extent of, and the exact nature of, the reference interview; develop intensive and comprehensive corrective training programs; and remeasure performance once corrective action is taken.

Search Strategy

A related concern is the strategy a librarian follows to find the answer, once the true question is understood. House (1974) studied this topic by having library school students ask the same research question in 20 libraries and note in detail the strategies each librarian used to provide an answer. Students were instructed to ask for all available information on wildlife artist David Shepherd. A previous and intensive class search revealed that some information was available. *The British National Bibliography (BNB)* listed a volume of Shepherd's paintings, with 10 pages of introductory text, and several periodical articles were listed in either *British Humanities Index* or *Art Index*. No information was listed in other standard reference sources for this topic, such as *Who's Who in Art*.

When asked, 12 librarians could find no information on Shepherd. Six others produced some information, and only two found most or all of it. The 12 libraries in which no data were found owned at least two of the three sources that listed information.

What exactly were the librarian's search strategies?

In twelve cases out of twenty the [library card] catalogue was not consulted. Not once was *BNB* used. In seventeen cases out of twenty, periodical literature was entirely ignored. . . . "Method" in most cases, meant skimming through a random selection of reference works from the shelves and announcing that they contained no relevant information. (House, 1974, p. 223)

All the librarians who offered students the volume of Shepherd's paintings produced the title from memory, without using a bibliography or catalog. Most of these librarians stopped their searches at this point, thus failing to completely answer the question. House concluded that the librarians tended to rely too much on their personal knowledge of the collections and to limit their search areas, ignoring potentially useful sources of information.

House's findings regarding search strategy are not isolated ones. Bunge (1967) described the mental processes a librarian uses to locate information (Exhibit 8-8). These processes were later verified by Ingwersen (1982), Ingwersen and Kaae (1980), and Schmidt (1980a, 1980b). Each librarian mentally reviews a list of possible sources already known to him or her and focuses on one source that might contain the answer. The source is then located; other alternatives that might answer the question are not explored. The librarian repeats the process until an answer is found or he or she runs out of known sources.

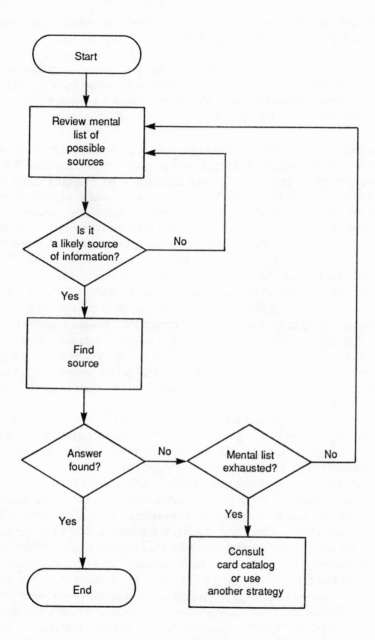

EXHIBIT 8-8 Reference librarian's mental search strategy. Based on a discussion in Bunge (1967).

Only then is the catalog consulted or other systematic search strategies used to find an answer (Bunge, 1967). Overall, this pattern can be characterized as

act[ing] before consideration of the problem in question. Activity is directed toward concrete titles on shelves, classes in classification schemes, or subject headings in indexes. . . . No real topic analysis takes place, as we initially supposed to occur, before the first search action. (Ingwersen, 1982, p. 183)

It is understandable why librarians, operating so often under time constraints, rely so heavily on quick action using known sources. But Myers (1980) showed that performance is poorest on queries that cannot be answered easily with the usual tools. In other words, librarians do not carefully exploit during a search the tools they have available to them, including the catalog. Other researchers discovered that librarians do not always find sources even when they are immediately available and that some librarians settle for searching only one source when more would provide a better response. Powell (1978) found that public librarians correctly answered only 78 percent of the questions for which their reference collection held appropriate sources. Schmidt (1980a, 1980b) discovered that half the questions asked in three college libraries were not answered completely or correctly even though sources were available in each library. Ramsden (1978) noted a number of times when reference librarians in Melbourne either overlooked an appropriate source or checked the right source unsuccessfully. And Myers (1980) found that staff did not consult, did not know how to use, or misinterpreted information contained in sources that offered the answers to patron questions.

Weech and Goldhor (1984) asked how many sources were searched to answer questions posed in five Illinois public libraries. Fifty-four percent of the librarians searched only one source, reinforcing Bunge's (1967) earlier discovery that most librarians tend to accept the first answer found. Twenty-three percent of the librarians in the Weech and Goldhor study searched two sources, 10 percent searched three, and 13 percent searched four or more. Some librarians consistently used multiple sources to answer a question, whereas others routinely used only one source. Weech and Goldhor's exploration stopped at this point, so it is not known whether librarians who used more sources provided more accurate answers. Future evaluators should certainly investigate this issue.

At least two other factors may influence searching success. A number of studies have shown that physical accessibility significantly influences *patron* selection of materials. To date, no studies have explored whether accessibility influences *librarian* selection of materials. Lancaster (1988), however, suggested that patrons are more likely to receive the correct answer to a question if a source containing the answer is in the ready reference section; the farther away from the librarian's desk an appropriate source is, the less likely it is that the librarian will be familiar with the source and use it. This hypothesis needs to be tested.

Lancaster also speculated that the search strategy is influenced by how well organized and indexed the reference sources are. For example, if a library uses a comprehensive subject index that is specifically compiled to provide better intellectual access to owned reference sources, the librarians should have a better chance of locating the answer. The findings of the one study that examined this (House, 1974) are inconclusive. Those libraries that compiled special indexes provided more accurate responses. But, it is not clear whether the indexes themselves contributed to the higher accuracy or whether the reference librarians in these libraries had, through the process of compiling the indexes, gained a more in-depth knowledge of the collection and its organization.

Several studies (Bunge, 1985; Childers, 1978a; Hood and Gittings, 1975) documented the importance of having the librarian help a patron search for information. Bunge found that patrons received correct answers only 47 percent of the time when they were merely directed toward the appropriate sources. This rate increased to 59 percent when librarians were busy but searched with patrons anyway and to 65 percent when the librarians were not busy and searched with patrons.

How often do librarians merely direct patrons toward sources? In a study by Hood and Gittings (1975), staff accompanied patrons 54 percent of the time when answering reference questions and 55 percent of the time when asked to find information on some broad subject. Childers (1978a) noted low rates of accompaniment when he had proxies record the number of occasions on which they were asked either to use an index or catalog or to browse on their own through shelves, books, chapters, or articles. Eighteen percent of the proxies were directed to go alone to the tools, whereas 26 percent were directed to browse alone. In all, one-third of the proxies were expected to find the responses to their reference questions with minimal guidance from librarians, a factor that may add significantly to reference failure. Clearly, evaluators measuring reference accuracy should focus on search strategies as one means of determining exactly why failure occurs.

Librarian Education, Experience, and Knowledge of the Collection

It would be expected that a librarian's education would affect the quality of question answering. To date, a number of researchers have examined this; however, their findings are mixed. Some authors (Myers, 1983; Powell, 1976; Schmidt, 1980a, 1980b) found that staff with a library degree answered factual questions more accurately. But others (Bunge, 1967, 1985; Ramsden, 1978; Weech and Goldhor, 1984) found little or no correlation between accuracy and a library degree. These conflicting findings seem to indicate that some factor other than education may have a stronger influence on reference performance.

Initially, the effects of reference experience on accuracy also appear mixed. Some authors (for example, Benham, 1981; Benham and Powell, 1987) documented that librarians with more years of reference experience are more accurate; others (for example, Weech and Goldhor, 1984) found no such relationship. When reference experience was measured not in years, but rather in terms of actual recent contact (the number of reference hours worked per week or the number of questions received per week), it did significantly affect accuracy (Benham and Powell, 1987; Myers, 1983; and Powell, 1976, 1978). This should come as no surprise. Accuracy should be closely associated with recent knowledge of and practice in searching current resources. Indeed, Halldorsson and Murfin (1977) found that knowledge of the current reference collection significantly influenced the accuracy rate. Bunge (1967) discovered a significant relationship between duties that allowed increased familiarity with the information contents of the library collection (for instance, selection of reference books) and reference efficiency. These findings suggest that it can be predicted, at least to some extent, which librarians will answer questions more accurately by testing their knowledge of a variety of reference sources. Thus, libraries may wish to conduct periodic tests of staff knowledge of specific sources shown to be useful in that setting. Pizer and Cain (1968) described a variation of this approach, in which staff members were asked to verify a sample of citations within a specified time frame and to answer reference questions from a set of documents known to be in the collection.

Personal subject knowledge also appears to affect accuracy. When Hernon and McClure (1987) unobtrusively measured the performance of general reference librarians and documents specialists on a series of questions about the U.S. government and its publications, the accuracy rate of documents librarians was more than twice that of general reference librarians. In a study at an academic library, both professionals and nonprofessionals performed better on "faulty" information questions when they were familiar with the subject matter in question (Halldorsson and Murfin, 1977). Neither group performed well when unfamiliar with the subject matter: professionals answered correctly 31 percent of the latter questions, whereas no questions were answered correctly by nonprofessionals. It is unclear, however, whether professionals did better because they were more familiar with sources, had a better search strategy, or conducted a more effective reference interview.

Bunge (1967) made one other important discovery. Increased knowledge of the collection refers not only to increased knowledge of specific sources, but also to increased knowledge of how the collection is organized. This includes familiarity with the subject classification system used, the formal languages used in the catalog and the indexes to the collection, and the relationships between the contents of various types of materials. Knowledge of collection organization, which is logically related to search strategy, is an area that needs further investigation.

Resources

Gers and Seward (1985) suggested that resources have only a slight influence on reference accuracy. Clearly, the resource that deserves the most attention is the reference collection itself. Theoretically, the larger the collection, the more sources it will contain to answer a particular question. Studies have generally confirmed that reference collection size will influence accuracy up to a point (for example, Myers, 1980, 1983). Powell (1978), in a study of 51 public libraries, found a strong relationship between reference collection size (measured by perceived adequacy of the collection and by actual number of volumes) and accuracy of response. The relationship, however, was not linear. The size of the reference collection "apparently reached a point of diminishing returns beyond which less was gained by continuing to expand the collections" (p. 9). For example, increasing a reference collection's size from 250 to 500 volumes should improve accuracy more than increasing its size from 2,500 to 2,750 volumes. Perceived currency of the reference collection was also found to be important to accuracy (Powell, 1976).

Complex relationships exist between the size of a reference collection and the ability of librarians to exploit it. On the one hand, the larger the collection, the greater the chance that it contains the answer to a particular question or, stated in another way, the more sources it is likely to include that could answer the question. On the other hand, the larger the collection, the more difficult it becomes for librarians to be thoroughly familiar with all its contents. Thus, a lack of knowledge of the collection or an illogical search strategy may counteract the effect of a large reference collection. This view is reinforced by the finding that librarians often fail to answer questions even when their library owns sources that contain the answers (Powell, 1978; Ramsden, 1978; Schmidt, 1980a, 1980b).

Many other studies have measured the effects of resources on accuracy. But again the findings have been mixed, suggesting that many types of resources are not closely associated with accuracy. Although Childers (1971) found a relationship between total expenditures and accuracy, other authors found none (Birbeck, 1986; Childers, 1978a; Crowley, 1971; Hernon and McClure, 1987). Nor was there a relationship between accuracy and expenditures on books (Birbeck). The size of the general collection was found to be related to accuracy by Childers (1971) and Myers (1983) but not by Birbeck and Hernon and McClure. Although Myers discovered a relationship between staff size and accuracy, Birbeck did not, nor did Hernon and McClure, who looked for differences between accuracy and five different measures of staffing in their unobtrusive study of answers given to government information questions in 26 academic and public libraries nationwide.

These findings suggest that libraries designing studies of reference accuracy would do well to pay attention primarily to the librarian's behavior and knowledge, giving secondary consideration to the size and currency of the reference collection.

Type of Demand for Service

A third category of factors that may affect accuracy is the type of demand for service, which includes both the way in which the question is asked and the amount of service required. Gers and Seward (1985) found that patrons are less likely to get complete answers when they ask their questions by telephone, in part because librarians are less likely to quote the source of an answer for a telephone inquiry.

Practicing librarians have also suggested that the librarian's degree of busyness will influence the accuracy of his or her response. Busyness is definitely and negatively related to whether a patron will even ask the question (Swope and Katzer, 1972). But evidence is divided about whether a busy librarian will give poorer answers. Gers and Seward found that busyness had little effect on performance; however, Bunge (1985) found that busy librarians provided the correct response less often than librarians who were not busy and that librarians who searched with patrons for the response (reflecting in part that they were not so busy) provided more accurate answers than those who did not. Further study is needed before final conclusions can be drawn.

Library Policies About Question Answering

Policy factors may influence the accuracy of the answer a patron receives. Many policy factors relate to how much time and expense the librarian can devote to answering questions. For example, can long-distance telephone calls be made or online reference sources be used to get the latest data? Theoretically, a librarian with unlimited time and money could find the complete, correct answer to most questions.

Unfortunately, these factors are the least researched, in part because most tests of accuracy that have been conducted to date contained simple, factual questions that can be answered quickly with sources contained in the library's collection. The rule of thumb in many libraries seems to be to answer a question if it can be done relatively quickly and with fairly little time or expense to the library. Bunge and Murfin (1987) examined data collected on more than 3,000 reference questions from 31 academic libraries and found that librarians spent very little time answering individual questions. Librarians took less than 2 minutes to answer 37 percent of the questions; 2–5 minutes to answer 43 percent; 5–15 minutes to answer 19 percent; and more than 15 minutes to answer only 3 percent of the questions.

If the question cannot be answered quickly, librarians often are instructed to refer it elsewhere or to tell the patron that they cannot provide the answer. Although the former practice is preferable, little referral actually occurs (for example, DeWath, 1981; Roy, 1985a). Hawley (1987) explored why this is so. He interviewed librarians in five public and five academic libraries and found that a number of different factors influenced whether a query would be referred. Some were related to the librarian's personality, such as empathy for the patron's problem and level of motivation. Some were related to the librarian's knowledge of outside sources. Factors related to the library itself (for example, the strength of its collection and the availability of referral tools) and to the user (for example, attitudes about referrals to libraries located far away) also affected the degree to which referral occurred.

Another factor that may influence accuracy is the library's policy of providing training for new reference librarians. Again, little research has been done, but one study in particular indicates that little training occurs and that new reference librarians are not satisfied with the training they receive. Stabler (1987) found that 55 percent of new reference librarians in the academic libraries she studied had not previously worked in a reference department. (Most of these librarians were recent library school graduates.) They generally received brief orientations in their respective libraries that included a tour of the library and the reference department, information about the university in general, and an introduction to other staff members. More than 40 percent, however, were not given procedures to follow when they were unable to find the answer to a question, information on their expected behavior as a reference librarian, guidelines for conducting an effective reference interview, a sample of typical reference questions asked in academic libraries, practice in answering sample reference questions, an indication of whether a telephone or a personal inquiry has higher priority, training in the use of particular reference tools, and instructions on how to work the telephone system.

Sixty percent of these newly employed librarians began working on the reference desk within their first week on the job, with little opportunity to observe experienced reference staff. These new staff members were overwhelmingly critical of the training programs, finding them poorly organized and ineffectual in communicating expectations about the quality of reference services that should be provided in a particular library. Evaluators who find very low accuracy rates may do well to examine the training program for new personnel, particularly in libraries with high staff turnover.

The Question Itself

Finally, accuracy must be considered in relation to the characteristics of the question itself. For example, is the answer to the question recorded somewhere? Some questions are so obscure or complex that no answer exists in a readily accessible form; therefore, the librarian cannot be blamed for failing to give a complete and accurate answer. And what about the question's subject? Is it within the scope of the library? Is the question "stable"? Or has its answer changed recently?

Few evaluators have explored how these factors affect the librarian's performance. This may be partly due to a tendency of evaluators to design or choose test questions that have an answer and that generally can be answered with known sources. Only the factor of stability has been addressed at all, and this was in an informal survey. Crowley (1985) found that librarians have a difficult time answering questions with unstable answers, such as "Who is the current _____ ?"

PATRON SATISFACTION WITH THE RESPONSE

Patrons have had difficulty in the past in evaluating whether the answers they receive to their questions are accurate. But they are able to reveal whether the answers they get meet their needs and whether they are satisfied with the way their queries were handled. The reference transaction assessment instrument developed by Murfin and Gugelchuk (1987) enables evaluators to investigate both these areas (Exhibit 8-9).

To judge satisfaction with an answer, a user should be given the information requested and the time to review it thoroughly. The evaluator should then ask the user specific questions to determine whether enough information was offered and whether it was, in the user's opinion, current, timely, relevant, neither too technical nor too general, or otherwise satisfactory. When Murfin (1970) did this, she discovered that 40 percent of the users were in some way dissatisfied with the information they were given.

One of the more recent and interesting studies on satisfaction was conducted by Murfin and Bunge (1988). Patron satisfaction with the answers they received was measured at 20 academic libraries of various sizes. Each of the libraries used professionals and paraprofessionals to answer reference questions. The researchers asked each patron to indicate whether the librarian had found just what the patron wanted; to indicate whether he or she was fully satisfied, partly satisfied, or not satisfied with the answer; and, if not fully satisfied, to check one of nine reasons for being dissatisfied. Evidence is mixed about whether the answers nonprofessionals provide are as accurate as the ones provided by professionals. But this study shows that patrons are significantly less satisfied with responses received from nonprofessionals. Sixty percent of the patrons seeking help from a professional reported that the exact information they needed was found and that they were fully satisfied. This figure dropped to 50 percent for patrons who sought help from a nonprofessional. Furthermore, professionals were significantly more successful than nonprofessionals in performing subject searches in the card catalog, in answering complex questions, and in answering questions posed by undergraduates.

Exhibit 8-10 pinpoints why patrons in Murfin and Bunge's (1988) study were not satisfied with the responses to their questions. Apparently, nonprofessionals

FILL IN DOT LIKE THIS ⎯⎯⎯⎯⎯⎯⎯⎯⎯⎯⎯→ ●

> The Reference Department is doing a survey of reference use and would appreciate it if you would mark the following brief checksheet. Thank you!
>
> (Deposit checksheet UNFOLDED in container on leaving this area or on leaving the library.)
> THANKS AGAIN FOR YOUR HELP!

USE NO. 2 PENCIL ONLY

STATUS

- O Freshman
- O Sophomore
- O Junior
- O Senior
- O Graduate student or teaching assistant
- O Continuing education or nondegree student
- O Alumni
- O Faculty
- O Staff
- O Not affiliated with Univ.

MAJOR OR TEACHING/ RESEARCH AREA

- O Arts or Humanities
- O Education
- O Law
- O Business/Management
- O Other Social Sci.
- O Medicine/Health
- O Agric./Biological Sci.
- O Math./Physical Sci.
- O Technology/Engineering
- O Interdisciplinary/Other
- O Major not declared

1. Did you locate what you asked about at the reference desk?
   - O Yes, just what I wanted
   - O Yes, with limitations
   - O Yes, not what I asked for, but oth. information or materials that will be helpful
   - O Yes, but not really what I wanted
   - O Only partly
   - O No

2. If yes, how did you find the information or materials?
   - O Librarian found or helped find
   - O Followed suggestions and found on my own
   - O Didn't follow suggestions but found on my own

3. Were you satisfied with the information or materials found or suggested?
   - O Yes
   - O Partly
   - O No

4. If partly or not satisfied, why? MARK ALL THAT APPLY.
   - O Found nothing
   - O Not enough
   - O Need more simple
   - O Too much
   - O Need more in-depth
   - O Not relevant enough
   - O Want different viewpoint
   - O Couldn't find information in source
   - O Not sure if information given me is correct

5. How important was it to you to find what you asked about?
   - O Very important
   - O Important
   - O Moderately important
   - O Somewhat important
   - O Not important

	Yes	Partly	No
6. Was the librarian busy (e.g., phone ringing, others waiting)?	O	O	O
7. Did the librarian understand what you wanted?	O	O	O
8. Did you get enough help and explanation?	O	O	O
9. Were the explanations clear?	O	O	O
10. Did the librarian appear knowledgeable about your question?	O	O	O
11. Was the service you received courteous and considerate?	O	O	O
12. Did the librarian give you enough time?	O	O	O
13. Did you learn something about reference sources or use of the library as a result of consulting the reference librarian?	O	O	O

14. Did you become acquainted with any reference sources you hadn't previously known about, as a result of consulting the reference librarian?
   - O Yes, one
   - O Yes, more than one
   - O No, none

■O■O■■O■■O■■O■■■■O○○○○   **15797**   FOR OFFICE USE ONLY

MAKE NO MARKS IN THIS AREA

⎯⎯⎯⎯⎯⎯⎯⎯⎯⎯⎯⎯⎯⎯⎯⎯⎯⎯⎯⎯⎯⎯⎯⎯⎯⎯⎯⎯⎯⎯⎯⎯⎯⎯⎯⎯⎯⎯

EXHIBIT 8-9 Reference transaction assessment instrument. Reprinted from Murfin and Gugelchuk (1987), courtesy of the American Library Association.

EXHIBIT 8-9   *(Continued)*

---

1. TYPE OF QUESTION Select <u>only</u> one category in A-D below that <u>best</u> fits type of answer wanted.

○ Librarian
○ Library Assistant
○ Other Assistant

A PARTICULAR TEXT(S) OR AUTHOR(S) WANTED
○ 1. Is particular book, serial, etc. in our collection?
○ 2. Smaller item in larger publication (<u>Particular</u> article, speech, quote, poem, law, etc.)
○ 3. Anything (or certain type of thing) by particular author

JOT DOWN QUESTION

B SHORT ANSWER WANTED (AND IS APPROPRIATE) (What, when, where, who, which, yes or no, etc.) (Answer of a few words. Includes verification and meaning of citations, bibliographical form, recommendations, etc., etc., etc.)

C GENERAL EXPL. OF CATALOG, LIBR., OR PRINTED REF. SOURCE WANTED (Rather than short answer)

D TYPE MATERIALS OR LONGER DESCRIPTIVE ANSWER WANTED (OR APPROPR.) (Answer usually in the form of printed materials)

1. SUBJECT (Mark one)
○ a. Single subject(s)
○ b. Relate 2 subj. or concepts

○ d. Focus on aspect, biog., hist., other.
○ e. Requests factual inf. in general (or source containing it) (names, addr., definitions, statistics, ratings, rankings, etc., etc.)

2. ASPECTS (MARK ALL THAT APPLY)
○ a. Something, anything, everything
○ b. Must be cert. time period, currentness, place, country, lang., etc.
○ c. Must be cert. type ref. source, publ., materials, or format (map, pict., etc., etc., etc., etc.)

○ f. Criticism, reviews, interpr., etc.
○ g. Analysis, trends, pro/con, cause/effect, how-to-do-it, how-it-works, & other
○ h. Requests that you compile list of references on a subject

---

2A RESULTS (MARK ONE)	2B RESPONSE (MARK ONE)	2C TIME (MARK ONE)
○ 1. Found	○ 1. Directed and suggested only	○ 1. 0-3 minutes (i.e. under 3 min.)
○ 2. Partly found	○ 2. Helped with or made search	○ 2. 3-5 minutes
○ 3. Not found	○ 3. Deferred	○ 3. 5-15 minutes
○ 4. Don't know	○ 4. Referred	○ 4. Over 15 minutes

---

3. SPECIAL FACTORS. DO NOT OMIT MARK ALL THAT APPLY

QUESTION AND PATRON	CONDITIONS
○ 1. Missing information or misinformation	○ 10. Difficult to think of source
○ 2. Concerned with foreign countr./lang.	○ 11. Difficult to find subj. headings
○ 3. Concerned with govt. docs.	○ 12. Books off shelf
○ 4. Inf. needed (or citat.) very recent	○ 13. Source difficult to consult
○ 5. Wants no. of things	○ 14A. Busy ○ 14B. Very busy
○ 6. Difficult citation	○ 15. Cataloging or tech. problem
○ 7. Patron in hurry	○ 16. Collection weak in that area or out-of-date
○ 8. Communic. diff. or confused question	○ 17. Need bks. in another area or location
○ 9A. Needs extra help ○ 9B. Returns freq.	

---

4. LIB. INSTRUCT. MARK ALL THAT APPLY
○ 1. Expl. sources, citations, search strat.
○ 2. Expl. cat., computer, holdings, locations

5. NUMBER OF SOURCES USED, REC., OR INTERP. ——   1 2 3 4 5+ ○○○○○

TYPE: MARK ALL THAT APPLY

○ 1. Indexes to period.
○ 2. Ref. books
○ 3. Cat. (card, online. etc.)
○ 4. OCLC, RLIN, etc
○ 5. Comp. database srch or CD-ROM

○ 6. Yr. own knowledge
○ 7. Inhouse prod. tools
○ 8. Phone bks., VF, Coll. cat.
○ 9. Circ. bks., period., newsp.
○ 10. Consult someone
○ 11. Refer

6. QUESTION DIFFICULTY (as perceived)	7. ASPECT (only if applicable)	8. SUBJECT	
		1st	2nd (if applic)
		○ 0	○ 0
○ Easy	○ Stat	○ 1 ○ 1	○ 1 ○ 1
	○ Biog	○ 2 ○ 2	○ 2 ○ 2
	○ Hist	○ 3 ○ 3	○ 3 ○ 3
		○ 4 ○ 4	○ 4 ○ 4
○ Medium		○ 5 ○ 5	○ 5 ○ 5
		○ 6 ○ 6	○ 6 ○ 6
○ Hard		○ 7 ○ 7	○ 7 ○ 7
		○ 8 ○ 8	○ 8 ○ 8
		○ 9 ○ 9	○ 9 ○ 9

Use separate guidesheet and select subj.
Mark boxes with no. of your subject.

	SUBJ. No. 2	SUBJ. No. 20
	○ 0	● 0
EXAMPLE	○ 1 ○ 1	○ 1 ○ 1
	● 2 ○ 2	● 2 ○ 2

▉○■○■○■○■○■■■○○○○   **15797**

MAKE NO MARKS IN THIS AREA

FOR OFFICE USE ONLY
⓪①②③④⑤⑥⑦⑧⑨
⓪①②③④⑤⑥⑦⑧⑨
⓪①②③④⑤⑥⑦⑧⑨

Printed in U.S.A   NCS Trans-Optic· M18-78714-321

	Percentage of Patrons Reporting	
Reason	Paraprofessionals	Professionals
Information not found	6.9	3.4
More in-depth information is needed to answer question	15.5	9.0
Different viewpoint is needed to answer question	3.8	1.9
Not enough help is given by librarian	12.7	6.8
Librarian's explanation is unclear	9.6	6.2
Librarian is not knowledgeable enough	15.2	9.4
Librarian did not devote enough time to answering question	7.6	4.7
Question is not understood well enough by librarian	8.6	4.4
Communication difficulty	13.4	7.8
Librarian only gave directions to the source; information found anyway	39.7	54.6

EXHIBIT 8-10 Reasons that patrons are not satisfied with reference librarians' responses to their questions. Adapted from Murfin and Bunge (1988), courtesy of the *Journal of Academic Librarianship*.

are committing more of the types of errors that have been described in this chapter. They are not as successful as professionals in conducting good reference interviews, they generally communicate poorly, and they use less-adequate search strategies. These deficits may be due to poor training in the reference process.

Judging satisfaction with the way user queries are handled involves examining the intangible atmosphere that the librarian has created through various verbal and nonverbal communication cues. This aspect has not been well researched; however, at least six studies show the possibilities of such examination. Lopez and Rubacher (1969) discovered a significant relationship between user satisfaction and the following personality and communication characteristics of academic librarians: empathy, respect, genuineness, concreteness, and specificity of expression. The first three characteristics suggest that users will be most satisfied when the librarian establishes, within the short time frame of the reference interaction, a friendly and caring atmosphere. Gothberg (1976) confirmed this during a controlled experiment in a public library. Reference librarians were trained to exhibit two different communication styles, using both verbal and nonverbal cues. Such actions as a friendly tone of voice, a listening attitude, and good eye contact characterized a caring style. The other style required the librarians to remain polite but to distance themselves from their patrons. As expected, library users were more satisfied when they dealt with the caring librarians. This was true even though patrons felt their queries were answered with equal competence by both types of librarians.

Crouch (1981) carried this research a step further by speculating that there was an ideal type of communicator who would verbally and nonverbally encourage patrons to communicate openly in reference interviews. He discovered that the personality trait most closely associated with communication ability was genuineness. He also found that the empathy and warmth of the librarian interact with those characteristics in the patron, thereby contributing to the ability of each to communicate with the other. Further evaluation of the effect of communication skills and other aspects of the librarian's behavior on user satisfaction is needed. The findings may be most beneficial if tied closely to research about the reference interview process.

Two studies were conducted to determine whether the librarian's level of warmth and inclusion (the degree to which the librarian instructed the patron in the use of reference tools) affected user and librarian views of competence. In the first study, Harris and Michell (1986) made 16 different videotapes in which a reference librarian answered a user's question about ridding houseplants of insects. In each videotape, the librarian successfully solved the problem. The scripts of each videotape were carefully varied, however; half featured a male librarian and half a female librarian. Within each set of eight videotapes, scripts also were varied to show the librarian exhibiting different levels of warmth and inclusion. The evaluators asked each of 160 male and 160 female public library users to view one of the five-minute tapes. The results show that the level of the librarian's warmth (whether the librarian smiled, spoke warmly, and looked at the patron during the interview) positively affected the patron's view of the librarian's competence. This finding confirms the results of studies in other disciplines that show that clients rate a professional's warmth as a major criterion for judging both trustworthiness and expertness (Lee, Uhlemann, and Haase, 1985). Harris and Michell (1986) also found that male and female patrons viewed inclusion differently: "The male observers seemed to interpret the teaching function (or more verbal behavior from the librarian) as an evidence of warmth on the part of the librarian" (p. 98). Again, this finding suggests that further exploration is needed of user reactions to and satisfaction with the reference librarians with whom they deal.

Michell and Harris (1987) reported on a spin-off of the study, which used a subset of the videotapes just described—four tapes showing a successful encounter between a female reference librarian and a female public library patron. Again, the level of warmth and inclusion exhibited by the librarian varied from tape to tape. Thirty-two male and 32 female librarians attending a professional meeting observed one tape each, then rated the reference worker's behavior on a 22-item scale. Even though the librarians were able to recognize the reference worker's competence in each videotape, they rated workers who displayed a high level of nonverbal warmth as significantly more professional than those who did not.

Finally, Durrance (1989) described an unobtrusive study in which students in library and information science presented questions that were important to them at 142 public, academic, and special libraries. Durrance's objective was to evaluate the reference interview. Each student either presented the question to the librarian or watched as a colleague did so. The reference interview was evaluated with a questionnaire that addressed student attitudes toward the librarian's interpersonal behavior and interviewing skills. The data suggested that interpersonal factors, such as the friendliness and attentiveness of the librarian, were more important than perceived accuracy of response in determining whether a library user would return to a particular librarian.

REFERENCES

American Library Association, Reference and Adult Services Division. "A Commitment to Information Services: Developmental Guidelines." *RQ, 18*(3):275–278, Spring 1979.

Association of Research Libraries, Office of Management Studies. *Performance Evaluation in Reference Services in ARL Libraries.* Washington, D.C., ARL, 1987. SPEC Kit 139

Baker, Sharon L. "Overload, Browsers, and Selections." *Library and Information Science Research, 8*(4):315–329, October–December 1986.

Balay, Robert, and Christine Andrew. "Use of the Reference Service in a Large Academic Library." *College and Research Libraries, 36*(1):9–26, January 1975.

Ballard, Thomas H. *The Failure of Resource Sharing in Public Libraries and Alternative Strategies for Service.* Chicago, Ill., American Library Association, 1986.

Benham, Frances. "A Prediction Study of Reference Accuracy Among Recently Graduated Working Reference Librarians (1975–1979)." Doctoral Dissertation. Tallahassee, Fla., Florida State University, 1981.

Benham, Frances, and Ronald R. Powell. *Success in Answering Reference Questions: Two Studies.* Metuchen, N.J., Scarecrow Press, 1987.

Birbeck, Vaughan P. "Unobtrusive Testing of Public Library Reference Service." *Refer, 4*(2):5–9, Autumn 1986.

Bunge, Charles A. *Professional Education and Reference Efficiency.* Springfield, Ill., Illinois State Library, 1967 (Research Series No. 11). ERIC ED019097

———. "Approaches to the Evaluation of Library Reference Services." In: *Evaluation and Scientific Management of Libraries and Information Centers.* Edited by F. W. Lancaster and Cyril W. Cleverdon. London, Eng., Noordhoff International Publishing, 1977, pp. 41–71.

———. "Factors Related to Reference Question Answering Success: The Development of a Data-Gathering Form." *RQ, 24*(4):482–486, Summer 1985.

Bunge, Charles A., and Marjorie E. Murfin. "Reference Questions: Data from the Field." *RQ, 27*(1):15–18, Fall 1987.

Calabretta, Nancy, and Rosalinda Ross. "Analysis of Reference Transactions Using Packaged Computer Programs." *Medical Reference Services Quarterly, 3*(3):23–47, Fall 1984.

Capital Planning Information. *Qualitative Assessment of Public Reference Services*. London, Eng., British Library, 1987.

Chen, Ching-Chih. "Information Seeking Patterns." In: *Information Seeking: Assessing and Anticipating User Needs*. Edited by Ching-Chih Chen and Peter Hernon. New York, Neal-Schuman, 1982, pp. 33–81.

Childers, Thomas. "Telephone Information Service in Public Libraries." In: *Information Service in Public Libraries: Two Studies*. By Terence Crowley and Thomas Childers. Metuchen, N.J., Scarecrow Press, 1971, pp. 73–204.

_____. *The Effectiveness of Information Service in Public Libraries—Suffolk County: Final Report*. Philadelphia, Pa., Drexel University, School of Library and Information Science, 1978a.

_____. "Evaluation and Prospects for the Future." In: *Public Library Information and Referral Service*. Edited by Clara S. Jones. Syracuse, N.Y., Gaylord Brothers, 1978b, pp. 154–165.

_____. "The Test of Reference." *Library Journal, 105*(8):924–928, April 15, 1980.

_____. *Information and Referral: Public Libraries*. Norwood, N.J., Ablex Publishing, 1984.

Crouch, Richard K. C. "Interpersonal Communication in the Reference Interview." Doctoral Dissertation. Toronto, Can., University of Toronto, 1981.

Crowley, Terence. "The Effectiveness of Information Service in Medium-Size Public Libraries." In: *Information Service in Public Libraries: Two Studies*. By Terence Crowley and Thomas Childers. Metuchen, N.J., Scarecrow Press, 1971, pp. 1–71.

_____. "Half-Right Reference: Is It True?" *RQ, 25*(1):59–68, Fall 1985.

DeWath, Nancy. *California Statewide Reference Referral Service: Analysis and Recommendations*. Rockville, Md., King Research, 1981. ERIC ED206311

Donohue, Joseph C. "The Public Information Center Project." In: *Information for the Community*. Edited by Manfred Kochen and Joseph C. Donohue. Chicago, Ill., American Library Association, 1976, pp. 79–93.

Douglas, Ian. "Reducing Failures in Reference Service." *RQ, 28*(1):94–101, Fall 1988.

Drone, Jeanette M. "An Index of Quality of Illinois Public Library Service, 1986." *Illinois Library Statistical Report*, (22):3–46, January 1987.

Durrance, Joan C. "The Influence of Reference Practices on the Client-Librarian Relationship." *College and Research Libraries, 47*(1):57–67, January 1986.

_____. "Reference Success: Does the 55 Percent Rule Tell the Whole Story?" *Library Journal, 114*(7):31–36, April 15, 1989.

Elzy, Cheryl, et al. "Evaluating Reference Service in a Large Academic Library." (Accepted for publication in *College and Research Libraries*, 1991.)

Gers, Ralph, and Lillie J. Seward. "Improving Reference Performance: Results of a Statewide Study." *Library Journal, 110*(18):32–35, November 1, 1985.

Goldhor, Herbert. "The Patrons' Side of Public Library Reference Questions." *Public Library Quarterly, 1*(1):35–49, Spring 1979.

_____. "An Analysis of Available Data on the Number of Public Library Reference Questions." *RQ, 27*(2):195–201, Winter 1987.

Gothberg, Helen. "Immediacy: A Study of Communication Effect on the Reference Process." *Journal of Academic Librarianship,* 2(3):126–129, July 1976.

Halldorsson, Egill A., and Marjorie E. Murfin. "The Performance of Professionals and Nonprofessionals in the Reference Interview." *College and Research Libraries,* 38(5):385–395, September 1977.

Halperin, Michael, and Maureen Strazdon. "Measuring Students' Preferences for Reference Service: A Conjoint Analysis." *Library Quarterly,* 50(2):208–224, April 1980.

Hansel, Patsy J. "Unobtrusive Evaluation for Improvement: The CCPL and IC Experience." *North Carolina Libraries,* 44(2):69–75, Summer 1986.

Harris, Ira W. "The Influence of Accessibility on Academic Library Use." Doctoral Dissertation. New Brunswick, N.J., Rutgers University, 1966.

Harris, Roma M., and B. Gillian Michell. "The Social Context of Reference Work: Assessing the Effects of Gender and Communication Skill on Observers' Judgments of Competence." *Library and Information Science Research,* 8(1):85–101, January–March 1986.

Hawley, George S. *The Referral Process in Libraries: A Characterization and an Exploration of Related Factors.* Metuchen, N.J., Scarecrow Press, 1987.

Hawley, Mary B. "Reference Statistics." *RQ,* 10(2):143–147, Winter 1970.

Hebert, Robert A. *The Measurement and Evaluation of Reference Service at the Public Documents and Maps Department of the Duke University Library.* Master's Thesis. Chapel Hill, N.C., University of North Carolina, 1984. ERIC ED252235

Hernon, Peter, and Charles R. McClure. "The Quality of Academic and Public Library Reference Service Provided for NTIS Products and Services: Unobtrusive Results." *Government Information Quarterly,* 3(2):117–132, May 1986a.

————. "Unobtrusive Reference Testing: The 55% Rule." *Library Journal,* 111(7): 37–41, April 15, 1986b.

————. *Unobtrusive Testing and Library Reference Services.* Norwood, N.J., Ablex Publishing, 1987.

Hieber, Caroline E. "Studies in the Man-System Interface of Libraries: An Analysis of Questions and Answers in Libraries." Master's Thesis. Bethlehem, Pa., Lehigh University, 1966.

Hood, Wyma J., and Monte J. Gittings. *Evaluation of Service at the General Reference Desk, University of Oregon Library.* Eugene, Oreg., University of Oregon, 1975. ERIC ED110038

House, David E. "Reference Efficiency or Reference Deficiency." *Library Association Record,* 76(11):222–223, November 1974.

Ingwersen, Peter. "Search Procedures in the Library—Analyzed from the Cognitive Point of View." *Journal of Documentation,* 38(3):165–191, September 1982.

Ingwersen, Peter, and Soren Kaae. *User-Librarian Negotiations and Information Search Procedures in Public Libraries: Analysis of Verbal Protocols.* (Final Research Report) Copenhagen, Denmark, Royal School of Librarianship, 1980. ERIC ED211051

Jahoda, Gerald. *The Process of Answering Reference Questions: A Test of a Descriptive Model.* Tallahassee, Fla., Florida State University, School of Library Science, 1977. ERIC ED136769

Jirjees, Jassim M. "The Accuracy of Selected Northeastern College Library Reference Information Telephone Services in Responding to Factual Inquiries." Doctoral Dissertation. New Brunswick, N.J., Rutgers University, 1981.

Kantor, Paul B. "Analyzing the Availability of Reference Services." In: *Library Effectiveness: A State of the Art.* Edited by Neal K. Kaske and William G. Jones. New York, Library Administration and Management Association, American Library Association, 1980, pp. 131–149.

Katz, William A. *Introduction to Reference Work.* 5th Edition. Volume 1: *Basic Information Sources.* New York, McGraw-Hill, 1987.

Kazlauskas, Edward. "An Exploratory Study: A Kinesic Analysis of Academic Library Public Service Points." *Journal of Academic Librarianship,* 2(3):130–134, July 1976.

Kesselman, Martin, and Sarah Barbara Watstein. "The Measurement of Reference and Information Services." *Journal of Academic Librarianship, 13*(1):24–30, March 1987.

King, Geraldine B., and Rachel Berry. *Evaluation of the University of Minnesota Libraries Reference Department Telephone Information Service: Pilot Study.* Minneapolis, Minn., University of Minnesota Library School, 1973. ERIC ED077517

King Research, Inc. "Information Needs of Californians." Report Commissioned by the California State Library for the California Governor's Conference on Libraries and Information Services, March 1979. Rockville, Md., 1979.

Knapp, Sara D. "The Reference Interview in the Computer-Based Setting." *RQ, 17*(4):320–324, Summer 1978.

Lancaster, F. W. "Factors Influencing the Effectiveness of Question-Answering Services in Libraries." *The Reference Librarian,* (11):95–108, Fall–Winter 1984.

—————. *If You Want to Evaluate Your Library* . . . Champaign, Ill., University of Illinois, Graduate School of Library and Information Science, 1988.

Lee, Dong Yul; Max R. Uhlemann; and Richard F. Haase. "Counselor Verbal and Nonverbal Responses and Perceived Expertness, Trustworthiness, and Attractiveness." *Journal of Counseling Psychology, 32*(2):181–187, April 1985.

Lopez, Manuel, and Richard Rubacher. "Interpersonal Psychology: Librarians and Patrons." *Catholic Library World, 40*(8):483–487, April 1969.

Lynch, Mary Jo. "Reference Interviews in Public Libraries." *Library Quarterly, 48*(2): 119–142, April 1978.

McClure, Charles R. "Output Measures, Unobtrusive Testing, and Assessing the Quality of Reference Services." *The Reference Librarian, 11*:215–233, Fall–Winter 1984.

McClure, Charles R., and Peter Hernon. *Improving the Quality of Reference Service for Government Publications.* Chicago, Ill., American Library Association, 1983.

Michell, B. Gillian, and Roma M. Harris. "Evaluating the Reference Interview: Some Factors Influencing Patrons and Professionals." *RQ, 27*(1):95–105, Fall 1987.

Mucci, Judith. "Videotape Self-Evaluation in Public Libraries: Experiments in Evaluating Public Service." *RQ, 16*(1):33–37, Fall 1976.

Murfin, Marjorie E. "A Study of the Reference Process in a University Library." Master's Thesis. Kent, Ohio, Kent State University, 1970.

—————. "National Reference Measurement: What Can It Tell Us About Staffing?" *College and Research Libraries, 44*(5):321–333, September 1983.

Murfin, Marjorie E., and Charles A. Bunge. "Paraprofessionals at the Reference Desk." *Journal of Academic Librarianship, 14*(1):10–14, March 1988.

Murfin, Marjorie E., and Gary M. Gugelchuk. "Development and Testing of a Reference Transaction Assessment Instrument." *College and Research Libraries, 48*(4):314–338, July 1987.

Myers, Marcia J. "The Accuracy of Telephone Reference Services in the Southeast: A

Case for Quantitative Standards." In: *Library Effectiveness: A State of the Art.* Edited by Neal K. Kaske and William G. Jones. New York, Library Administration and Management Association, American Library Association, 1980, pp. 219–233.

—————. "Telephone Reference/Information Services in Academic Libraries in the Southeast." In: *The Accuracy of Telephone Reference/Information Services in Academic Libraries.* Edited by Marcia J. Myers and Jassim M. Jirjees. Metuchen, N.J., Scarecrow Press, 1983, pp. vii–141.

—————. "Check Your Catalog Image." *The Reference Librarian,* (12):39–47, Spring–Summer 1985.

Nelson, Jerold. "Faculty Awareness and Attitudes Toward Academic Library Reference Services: A Measure of Communication." *College and Research Libraries, 34*(5):268–275, September 1973.

Olson, Linda M. "Reference Service Evaluation in Medium-Sized Academic Libraries: A Model." *Journal of Academic Librarianship, 9*(6):322–329, January 1984.

Peat, Marwick, Mitchell and Company. "California Public Library Systems: A Comprehensive Review with Guidelines for the Next Decade." Los Angeles, Calif., 1975. ERIC ED105906

Pizer, Irwin H., and Alexander M. Cain. "Objective Tests of Library Performance." *Special Libraries, 59*(9):704–711, November 1968.

Powell, Ronald R. "Investigation of the Relationship Between Reference Collection Size and Other Reference Service Factors and Success in Answering Reference Questions." Doctoral Dissertation. Urbana, Ill., University of Illinois, 1976.

—————. "An Investigation of the Relationships Between Quantifiable Reference Service Variables and Reference Performance in Public Libraries." *Library Quarterly, 48*(1):1–19, January 1978.

Ramsden, Michael J. *Performance Measurement of Some Melbourne Public Libraries.* Melbourne, Australia, Library Council of Victoria, 1978.

Rodger, Eleanor Jo, and Jane Goodwin. *Reference Accuracy at the Fairfax County Public Library.* Washington, D.C., Metropolitan Washington Library Council, 1984.

Rothstein, Samuel. "The Measurement and Evaluation of Reference Service." *Library Trends, 12*(3):456–472, January 1964.

Roy, Loriene. "An Index of Quality of Illinois Public Library Service, 1984." *Illinois Library Statistical Report,* (17):21–45, May 1985a.

—————. "An Index of Quality of Illinois Public Library Service, 1985." *Illinois Library Statistical Report,* (20):87–114, December 1985b.

Sandock, Mollie. "A Study of University Students' Awareness of Reference Services." *RQ, 16*(4):284–296, Summer 1977.

Schmidt, Janine. "Evaluation of Reference Service in College Libraries in New South Wales, Australia." In: *Library Effectiveness: A State of the Art.* Edited by Neal K. Kaske and William G. Jones. New York, Library Administration and Management Association, American Library Association, 1980a, pp. 265–294.

—————. "Reference Performance in College Libraries." *Australian Academic and Research Libraries, 11*(2):87–95, June 1980b.

Shafa, Zarrintaj M. "Staffing Reference Performance in University Libraries: A Cost-Effective Model for Administrative Decisions." Doctoral Dissertation. Denton, Texas, Texas Woman's University, 1980.

Slater, Margaret. *Ratio of Staff to Users: Implications for Library-Information Work and the Potential for Automation.* London, Eng., Aslib, 1981. (Aslib Occasional Publications No. 24)

Spencer, Carol C. "Random Time Sampling with Self-Observation for Library Cost Studies: Unit Costs of Reference Questions." *Bulletin of the Medical Library Association,* 68(1):53–57, January 1980.

Spicer, Caroline T. "Measuring Reference Service: A Look at the Cornell University Libraries Reference Question Recording System." *Bookmark, 31*(3):79–81, January–February 1972.

Stabler, Karen Y. "Introductory Training of Academic Reference Librarians: A Survey." *RQ, 26*(3):363–369, Spring 1987.

Stayner, Richard. "The Use of Empirical Standards in Assessing Public Library Effectiveness." In: *Library Effectiveness: A State of the Art.* Edited by Neal K. Kaske and William G. Jones. New York, Library Administration and Management Association, American Library Association, 1980, pp. 351–369.

Stephan, Sandy, et al. "Reference Breakthrough in Maryland." *Public Libraries, 27*(4):202–203, Winter 1988.

Swope, Mary Jane, and Jeffrey Katzer. "The Silent Majority: Why Don't They Ask Questions?" *RQ, 12*(2):161–166, Winter 1972.

Van House, Nancy A., and Thomas Childers. "Unobtrusive Evaluation of a Reference Referral Network: The California Experience." *Library and Information Science Research, 6*(3):305–319, July–September 1984.

Van House, Nancy A., et al. *Output Measures for Public Libraries: A Manual of Standardized Procedures.* 2nd Edition. Chicago, Ill., American Library Association, 1987.

Von Seggern, Marilyn. "Assessment of Reference Services." *RQ, 26*(4):487–496, Summer 1987.

Wallace, Danny P. "An Index of Quality of Illinois Public Library Service." *Illinois Library Statistical Report,* (10):1–46, September 1983.

———. "An Index of Quality of Illinois Public Library Service." *Illinois Library Statistical Report,* (14):61–84, August 1984.

Way, Kathy A. "Measurement and Evaluation of Telephone Reference/Information Service in Law School Depository Libraries in the Greater Los Angeles, California, Area." M.L.S. Specialization Paper. Los Angeles, Calif., University of California at Los Angeles, 1983.

Weech, Terry L. "Evaluation of Adult Reference Service." *Library Trends, 22*(3):315–335, January 1974.

Weech, Terry L., and Herbert Goldhor. "Obtrusive Versus Unobtrusive Evaluation of Reference Service in Five Illinois Public Libraries: A Pilot Study." *Library Quarterly, 52*(4):305–324, October 1982.

———. "Reference Clientele and the Reference Transaction in Five Illinois Public Libraries." *Library and Information Science Research, 6*(1):21–42, January 1984.

Westbrook, Lynn. "Catalog Failure and Reference Service: A Preliminary Study." *RQ, 24*(1):82–90, Fall 1984.

White, Marilyn Domas. "The Dimensions of the Reference Interview." *RQ, 20*(4): 373–381, Summer 1981.

Wilkinson, Billy R. *Reference Services for Undergraduate Students: Four Case Studies.* Metuchen, N.J., Scarecrow Press, 1972.

Williams, Roy. "An Unobtrusive Survey of Academic Library Reference Services." *Library and Information Research News, 10*(37–38):12–40, 1987.
Young, Arthur P. "Student Assistants: A Report and a Challenge." *RQ, 9*(4):295–297, Summer 1970.

CHAPTER 9

EVALUATION OF REFERENCE SERVICES: DATABASE SEARCHING

Librarians can use a number of criteria and methods to evaluate any type of literature-searching activity, manual or mechanized. ("Literature searching" is used here to mean any activity in which a search is conducted to find bibliographic material on a particular subject.) Twenty years ago, many special libraries were willing to undertake comprehensive literature searches for their users in order to generate bibliographies. Most public, school, and academic libraries, however, were not so willing, at least partly because of the high cost of staffing such services. This situation has changed, and continues to change, mainly because the availability of commercial databases (online or in CD-ROM format) has enabled even libraries with few staff members to conduct major searches quickly and inexpensively. Today many libraries have terminals connected via telephone to major online databases, and librarians routinely undertake complex and comprehensive bibliographic searches for their patrons. Some libraries also offer computer-based current awareness services, known generally as selective dissemination of information (SDI). The librarian in charge of an SDI service creates a profile of each patron's ongoing research and information needs; conducts, at regular intervals, literature searches designed to meet those needs; and sends the patron the results.

A number of authors have proposed models describing literature-searching activities (for example, Chen and Schweizer, 1981; Cochrane, 1981; Fenichel and Hogan, 1981; Somerville, 1977). One of the most comprehensive models was proposed by Meadow and Cochrane (1981). It suggests that a librarian take eight steps to meet a patron's information needs (although the librarian may not

---

NOTE: Throughout this chapter, "database" is used generically to refer to bibliographic resources in printed, online, or CD-ROM form.

necessarily proceed in the order set out or make clear-cut distinctions between actions taken in one step and those taken in another). These eight steps are:

1. Clarify and negotiate the information needs and the search objectives during a presearch interview.
2. Determine the type of output the patron wants (citations, abstracts, or the documents themselves).
3. Identify relevant sources in which the search can be conducted.
4. Choose the terms under which the search will be made.
5. Formulate the basic search logic and plan search strategy.
6. Carry out the search in the chosen retrieval system.
7. Evaluate preliminary search results. If these are unacceptable to the patron, determine why, then repeat any or all of the above steps to obtain better results.
8. Evaluate final search results. If these are unacceptable to the patron, determine why, then repeat any or all of the above steps to obtain better results.

Some of the steps involved in literature searching parallel those involved in answering reference questions (see Chapter 8). The patron asks the librarian for assistance with his or her information need. The librarian clarifies the inquiry to determine the exact information desired and attempts to find the material. Finally, the librarian checks to see that the patron is satisfied with the information given. If not, the process begins again.

Literature searching, however, may differ from question answering in at least two respects. The first may occur during the search itself. When answering reference questions, librarians search most often in a conventional manner, using card catalogs, printed indexes, and other manual tools.[1] Although librarians conduct some literature searches this way, they are more likely to perform a search in a database that is accessible in electronic form. Because of the relatively high cost of computer searching (a cost that either the library or the patron must pay directly to the information center making the database available), the librarian may take more time in constructing the initial search strategy and in getting feedback from the patron during the course of the search.[2]

---

[1] Even this situation is changing. Online databases are used increasingly to answer factual questions; see, for example, Anderson (1989).

[2] The cost of online searching is quite complex. The bill presented to a library by an online service center such as DIALOG will reflect several costs: the center's own costs for acquiring databases, manipulating them, and making them accessible; royalties to database producers; perhaps telecommunications costs; and some built-in profit. The largest single cost that is eventually passed on to consumers is that of building the databases. Online searches appear to be more expensive than manual searches because the cost of a librarian's time essentially is absorbed by the library, and, more important, the cost of acquiring and storing databases in printed form is rarely considered. If the real costs of manual searching were considered, a manual search would frequently cost more than an equivalent search in an online source (Elchesen, 1978; Lancaster, 1981). Anderson (1989) showed that database searching may even be cost-effective in many quick-reference applications.

The second difference may occur at the end of the searching process. At the end of a "quick reference" transaction, the librarian hands the patron an answer to a question or, in some cases, a document that is assumed to contain an answer. At the end of a literature search, the librarian gives the patron a list of document surrogates, that is, citations to or descriptions of items that should contain relevant information. The patron examines the list to see which items are most likely to meet his or her information needs. In most organizations, the patron then is responsible for obtaining these items from the collection of this or another library (generally via interlibrary loan). Although the responsibility of the librarian performing the search can be considered complete when a satisfactory bibliography is delivered to the patron, it is clear that the responsibility of the library is complete only when the patron has in hand the documents sought. This implies that the evaluation of literature searching is intertwined closely with the evaluation of the collection and the document-delivery capabilities of a particular library.

This chapter deals exclusively with the effectiveness, efficiency, and cost-effectiveness of literature searching done by librarians in libraries and information centers. Studies that consider the evaluation of literature searching from a technological or theoretical perspective that is of little use to the practicing librarian, as well as studies that address the evaluation of searches performed by library patrons themselves (for example, Trzebiatowski, 1984) are not dealt with.

WILL A QUESTION BE ASKED OF THE LIBRARY?

In a complete evaluation, one needs to determine whether potential patrons are aware that a library provides a literature-searching service, whether patrons who are aware of the service are using it, and why patrons who are aware of the service are not using it. Although recent research has focused on online searching activities, the findings have implications for manual search services as well.

The initial evaluation step is to ask whether a library's clientele knows about an existing search service. The evaluator should ask this question of a sample of all potential library patrons, rather than just current patrons, to get an accurate picture of awareness. If a high level of awareness is not present, corrective action should be taken.

Many library patrons know about literature-searching services but still do not use them (Curtis, 1977; Lawrence, Weil, and Graham, 1974). In this case, the evaluator needs to determine the reasons for nonuse. Many characteristics of the patron appear to be unrelated to use, including age, sex, level of education, job, area of research, past scholarly activity, and patron satisfaction with his or her own search efforts (Bayer and Jahoda, 1979; Curtis, 1977; Lawrence, Weil, and Graham, 1974). But use is related to patron perceptions of the time and effort it takes to use the literature-searching service. Nonusers perceive that the service requires more effort to use than it is worth; they believe that the costs outweigh the benefits. For example, many nonusers think online searching by a librarian takes more time than a manual search that they themselves would perform (Fosdick, 1977). In other words, many nonusers are unaware of the time savings and potentially higher success rates of a literature search conducted by a librarian. This situation must change before use will increase.

It is possible to change perceptions of the value of a searching service and thus to make a difference in subsequent use. As Bayer and Jahoda (1979) reported,

Substantially larger proportions of those who expressed a clear belief that [an] online service would improve their current information seeking methods, on the basis of what they had learned prior to the actual introduction of online search services in their work location, were likely to become users over the next year. Similarly, those who expressed generally positive comments to an open-ended question on the potential utility of an online search system to their work were substantially more likely than others to consequently become users of the system. (pp. 102–103)

This implies that evaluators need to determine which forms of education will most change nonuser perceptions. One simple way to do this is to determine how patrons who use the search service learned about it. This question should be routinely asked of people requesting searches. Several studies found that publicity materials such as press releases printed in the college bulletin were not particularly effective in increasing use; most potential users discarded these materials or just ignored them (Benenfeld et al., 1975; Fosdick, 1977; Warden, 1981). Direct promotion of search services by librarians was slightly more effective, but two other means of publicity were still better, perhaps because they were oriented toward the immediate, personal needs of the potential users. The first was informal, word-of-mouth advertising by peers or superiors who had already used the service. For example, satisfied colleagues were the highest promoters of online searching at General Electric (Warden, 1981); most college library patrons learned about online services from their professors or from other students (Hilchey and Hurych, 1985; Hoover, 1976). Direct demonstration of the service's value to patrons also is an effective promotion technique. Free or partly funded demonstrations such as those provided at the University of Delaware (Kobelski and Trumbore, 1978) and Nazareth College (Matzek and Smith, 1982) can substantially increase the number of patrons who try the service. And once patrons experience the benefits of search services, they are likely to use them again (Bayer and Jahoda, 1979, 1981; Lawrence, Weil, and Graham, 1974; Warden, 1981). In the University of Delaware study, 82 percent of the students who received half-cost online searches were very satisfied with search results; 70 percent said they would definitely have a search performed again; and 22 percent said they would do a further search contingent on the topic of the information they needed and the cost of the search.

It is not enough simply to determine the best ways to change patron perceptions of ease of use; actual barriers to use must be identified and removed. Fosdick (1977) reported that some engineers did not have online searches conducted because they needed the actual documents, not just references to them, and found it too difficult to obtain the documents themselves. Kobelski and Trumbore (1978) discovered that a major cause of student dissatisfaction with online searching was the inability of the library to supply everything on the list of citations retrieved. Bayer and Jahoda (1981) found that frequent users of online search services now relied more heavily on librarians than they had in their pre-online search days. This is because the online searches identified more items that were not directly accessible without the librarian's assistance. Once again, the responsibility of the library does not end with the printing out of citations; the library must be prepared to provide the documents from its own collection or from outside sources.

The failure to provide easy access to documents is not the only barrier to the use of literature-searching services. Other barriers include the cost of the service, the unavailability of the service during all the hours a library is open, and the inconvenient physical location of the service within a library (Benenfeld, Pensyl, and Marcus, 1975; Jahoda, Bayer, and Needham, 1978; Kerhuel, 1986). Decreasing such barriers should increase use, and, conversely, erecting barriers should decrease use. Indeed, several studies have shown that introducing or raising fees for online searching causes use to decline (Kobelski and Trumbore, 1978; Lehman and Wood, 1978; Maina, 1977; Summit and Firschein, 1977). And in all the studies, use declined among patrons who were well able to afford the service (for example, physicians), as well as among patrons who were thought to have a low ability to pay (such as undergraduate students in academic libraries).

HOW MANY LITERATURE SEARCHES ARE CONDUCTED, AND WHAT TYPES OF ANSWERS ARE SOUGHT?

Chapter 8 discussed the value of tabulating the number of reference requests that a library receives and the number the librarian attempts to answer. Counting the number of requests for literature searches enables an evaluator to see whether the popularity of this service is rising or falling. Recording the subject matter of all search requests, whether filled or not, can help evaluators determine whether a librarian rejected a request appropriately (say, because it did not fall within the library's scope) or inappropriately (perhaps, because no staff member was available to perform the search and the patron could not wait). Tabulating the times during which searches are requested can aid in developing staff schedules.

Evaluators might also wish to categorize literature searches according to the purpose of the search. Most searches are requested to aid with projects involving research, publication, or course work. Tso (1984) found that 77 percent of the online patrons at the University of Hong Kong were faculty members and that the rest were graduate students. Seventy-nine percent of the patrons used the information for research, and 12 percent used it for teaching purposes. Corporate libraries also have a high percentage of research uses. For example, 67 percent of the patrons in one corporate library used the results of their literature searches for research purposes, and an additional 13 percent used them for publication purposes. Another 21 percent used the information to aid in management or planning activities, and 5 percent used it to help with a contract or proposal (Warden, 1981). Evaluators can break down the major categories of literature searches even further, as Jahoda, Bayer, and Needham (1978) did when they studied differences between the information needs of scientists in industry and those in academia (Exhibit 9-1).

	Academic Scientists (Florida State University) %	Corporate Scientists (Monsanto) %	Level of Significance
Keeping current in own area (field)	53	41	0.002
Keeping current in related areas (fields)	17	10	0.02
Developing competence by relearning (brushing up)	9	8	NS
Developing competence by learning new specialty	20	19	NS
Supporting ongoing project (pertaining to):			
Theory	19	12	0.03
Facts	36	25	0.002
Procedure, apparatus, or methodology	25	53	0.001
Preparing reports for meeting or publication:			
Internal meeting	5	3	0.02
Internal report	1	5	0.004
Patent application	0	2	0.04
Paper for external dissemination	33	5	0.001
Grant proposal	6	0	0.001
Dissertation	20	1	0.001

NOTE: Totals are more than 100 percent because of multiple answers.

NS = not significant.

EXHIBIT 9-1   Anticipated use of search results by academic and industrial scientists (in percent of all searches). Reprinted from Jahoda, Bayer, and Needham (1978), courtesy of the American Library Association.

Even though the bulk of literature searches appear to be done for research and publication, the purposes for which searches are undertaken may vary, depending on the type of library or patron involved. Such variation may be greatest in those libraries in which the clientele is highly diverse (for example, in public and some special libraries). Specific information about why searches are requested is useful in other ways, too. If librarians know why patrons are using search services, they can target their audiences and tailor their advertising accordingly. Knowing the needs for a particular search also helps librarians understand more precisely what requesters really want.

Subject categorization of the questions also is important. Librarians can analyze this type of data to determine which databases to subscribe to. They also can record the types of subject searches that have been successful in various sources so that, in the future, staff members can conduct similar searches in the "best" sources. Roose (1985) reported on the statistical analysis of online searches carried out at the North Suburban Library System in Illinois. The number of requests that resulted in online searches, the subjects of the requests, the databases used to answer the requests, and the costs of each search all were tabulated.

WERE THE CITATIONS PROVIDED FROM THE LITERATURE SEARCH SATISFACTORY?

Researchers spend a great deal of time determining whether the answers provided to reference questions are complete and accurate. It is more difficult to measure the effectiveness of literature searching since the search usually is conducted to find general information on some topic, rather than to obtain an unequivocal answer to a specific question.

Satisfaction generally is measured by two different approaches. In the first, the evaluator examines the search product (the list of citations/abstracts retrieved); applies quantitative measures of the success of the search, the most common of which are recall, precision, and novelty; and reviews the steps used during the search to see where improvements could have been made. In the second approach, the evaluator asks the patron, as the person whom the information retrieval system is meant to serve, whether he or she was satisfied with the literature-searching services and, if not, why not. Most of this chapter is devoted to examining these two approaches.

THE EVALUATOR'S REVIEW OF THE SEARCH PRODUCT AND PROCESS

Library patrons find it difficult to assess whether the answers they receive to reference questions are correct. Patrons of literature-searching services have similar difficulties in judging objectively how successfully the searcher has met their information needs (Auster, 1983), although they can state whether they are satisfied with search results. Because searchers cannot judge objectively the quality of their own searches, tending to rate their own performances too favorably (Fenichel, 1980b), libraries should use impartial judges and objective measures to rate search results. Ideally, evaluators who have no vested interest in the outcome of the study should examine the patron's exact information needs and then scrutinize, either obtrusively or unobtrusively, the actual steps involved in the search process and the end product of the search, to determine whether the searcher has effectively met the patron's needs.

Obtrusive Versus Unobtrusive Evaluation of Literature Searching

The advantages and disadvantages of obtrusive and unobtrusive evaluation were described in detail in Chapter 8. In an unobtrusive study, the evaluator observes and records the searcher's behavior during the actual search process. A few evaluators supplement this by asking searchers to verbalize and record their thought processes during the search process for later examination (Fidel, 1984; *Individualized Instruction for Data Access*, 1978). Alternatively, searchers may be asked to comment further on their search strategies, using a written transcript of their thought processes as a guide. The evaluator may follow the review of the search process with an "exit interview" of the patron, a check to determine if his/her needs were met satisfactorily and, if not, why not. Obtrusive evaluations may be less accurate than unobtrusive ones, because searchers who know they are being evaluated probably are on their best behavior. McCue (1988) conducted one of the most comprehensive search studies using the unobtrusive method. She compared and analyzed the results of 42 online database searches conducted in 21 public libraries in 16 states.

A common approach to unobtrusive evaluation is to use a trained surrogate patron, who mentally notes each behavior of the librarian throughout the search process. Because the librarian is unaware of being observed, he or she performs the search in the normal fashion. It also is possible to use some other means to unobtrusively screen at least part of the search process. A number of libraries, such as the corporate research library at General Electric, have used special two-terminal setups for online searches (Warden, 1981). These can be located next to the searcher, so that a patron can review search results without having to peer over the librarian's shoulder, or away from the search site, so that patrons who are unable to physically come to the library can participate during the search through a conference call. With such a setup, it is possible for the evaluator to monitor the search strategy from the remote terminal, or to screen it obtrusively from a terminal located beside the searcher. Alternatively, it might be possible simply to generate a printout of a search dialogue, without the searcher's knowledge, so that the evaluator can analyze it later.

Regardless of whether the evaluation is obtrusive or unobtrusive, the evaluator needs to review two documents, a search request form and a printout of the dialogue between the searcher and the system. Many libraries require the completion of a search request form. This form should be filled out by the requester (Lancaster, 1968), although data can be added later by the librarian. Exhibit 9-2 shows a typical search request form. If such forms are designed appropriately, they can serve as permanent records of factors relating to each search, including the time when the search was begun and ended, the basic subject of the search, any constraints specified by the patron (for example, language of citations desired), the terms and logic to be used in the search, and the total cost of the search. The printout of the dialogue between the searcher and the system will help the evaluator understand certain aspects of the search. But even a conscientious and intensive review of these two documents will not give the evaluator insight into some aspects of the searcher's behavior, such as the process of question negotiation between the searcher and the patron.

REVIEWING THE SEARCH PRODUCT

The simplest way to begin an evaluation is to examine the final search product (the list of citations or abstracts retrieved) to verify that it meets the patron's requirements. Whenever possible, this should be done with the patron present, so that any questions the evaluator may have can be clarified.

It is easy to determine whether the search meets patron requirements for language, date, format of materials, the direct cost of the search, or the way in which the results are presented (for example, abstracts or simple citations). These are objective matters and are easily quantified. It also is easy to determine whether the information was provided within the time frame specified by the patron. When such patron requirements are not stated, it may be because the searcher forgot to ask about them. This type of error is easily corrected by developing better procedures for determining precisely what the patron wants— for example, preparing a list of questions that searchers can ask each patron requesting a literature search, either during an interview or on a request form completed by the user.

It is more difficult to determine whether the patron's real information needs are met. An evaluator usually tries to do this by examining three measures of the "relevance" of a particular search: precision, recall, and novelty. These measures are appropriate regardless of whether a search is manual or mechanized and whether the end product is a collection of actual documents or of document surrogates such as abstracts. Consider a person entering a library to find bibliographic materials on a particular subject. A finite number of items are

APPLICATION FOR A COMPUTERIZED BIBLIOGRAPHIC SEARCH
THE WICHITA STATE UNIVERSITY LIBRARY REFERENCE DEPARTMENT

NAME _____

(Include name of alternate contact person if applicable)

WSU Department;
Company or Agency _____

ADDRESS _____ DAYTIME _____
                                                        PHONES
CITY _____ ZIP _____   _____

___U-GRAD STUDENT   ___ FACULTY/STAFF   CAMPUS
                                        ACCT. NO.: _____
___ GRAD STUDENT   ___OTHER

I understand that computer searching in no way guarantees results. I agree to pay for this search. Failure to pay can result in legal action (e.g. transcript or registration holds, payroll deduction by university). Cost structure is on the back page.

                                        TODAY'S
                                        DATE: _____
_____
SIGNATURE

The maximum amount I want to spend is: $ _____

OFFICE USE ONLY

Date of
Search: _____

WSU Dept.: _____

STATUS: U   G   F   N   L

NAME OF
SEARCH: _____

NO. OF DATABASES
USED (NOT CROS OR DIAL): _____

HOW TO
BE PAID: A   C   N

Date bibliography
Prepared _____

Date Patron
Informed: _____

___ Mail   ___ Phone

VENDOR	DATABASE	SEARCH FEE PER DATABASE	CITATION CHARGES		TOTAL CITATION COST	TOTAL PER DATABASE
			1 — 30 NO. X ¢	31 + NO. X ¢		

TOTAL COST
OF SEARCH:

SEARCH TOPIC:
    Write a short statement describing your search. Include all important concepts and key words. Give any variant spelling or terminology if applicable.

List indexes already consulted and any known articles or authors of particular relevance to your topic.

SEARCHER'S USE

EXCLUSIONS: List any terms concepts, or aspects that should be excluded.

PUBLICATION TYPES:

journal articles	Y	N
books/monographs	Y	N
PhD dissertations	Y	N
conference papers	Y	N
A/V items	Y	N
gov doc/technical rpts	Y	N
ERIC docs	Y	N

___ English language only
___ All languages
___ Specific foreign language(s):
_____

___ Infant   ___ Animal
___ Child   ___ Human
___ Adolescent
___ Adult   ___ Male
___ Aged   ___ Female

YEARS: _____

AN INTERVIEW, by phone or in person, is required PRIOR TO SEARCH BEING RUN.

                                        Reference Dept.
                                        Phone Number: 689-3591

_____   _____
LIBRARIAN   SUBJECT SPECIALTY

EXHIBIT 9-2 Online search request form used at the Wichita State University library. Reprinted from Germann, Nowak, and Wilke (1987), courtesy of the American Library Association.

	RELEVANT	NOT RELEVANT	TOTAL
RETRIEVED	a HITS	b NOISE	a + b TOTAL RETRIEVED
NOT RETRIEVED	c MISSES	d CORRECTLY REJECTED	c + d TOTAL NOT RETRIEVED
TOTAL	a + c TOTAL RELEVANT	b + d TOTAL NOT RELEVANT	a + b + c + d TOTAL COLLECTION

EXHIBIT 9-3 Four specific outcomes of a literature search: two positive (relevant retrieved (a), and not relevant correctly rejected (d)), and two negative (relevant misses (c), and not relevant (noise) (b)).

capable of meeting this patron's information needs. If he or she was to look at every item in the collection, relatively few would be considered relevant. Relevance is a subjective quality; each patron has a different interpretation of what is and what is not "relevant."[3]

A typical subject search has four specific outcomes, two of which are positive (some relevant items will be retrieved and most irrelevant ones will not be retrieved) and two negative (some relevant items will be missed and some irrelevant ones will be retrieved) (Exhibit 9-3).

[3] Many factors actually influence relevance decisions, and the subject of relevance has generated a great deal of argument (for example, Cooper, 1971; Soergel, 1976; Swanson, 1986; Wilson, 1973, 1978).

Recall

Recall is the proportion of all relevant items in a particular collection or database that the search is able to retrieve. The recall ratio can be expressed by the formula a/(a + c) (Exhibit 9-3). If a database includes 15 items on a particular subject and the librarian finds 12 of these, the recall ratio of the search is 12/15, or 0.8.

All patrons require some recall (except in those rare situations when the search is conducted to confirm that nothing exists); otherwise, they would not have approached the system. But recall requirements vary among patrons. Many will be satisfied with a few relevant citations, but some will require high or even complete recall. The patron wanting to know if anyone else had patented an invention like his or hers would not be satisfied if the librarian missed the only two citations showing that this had occurred. Corporate scientists are less likely to want exhaustive searches than their academic counterparts (Jahoda, Bayer, and Needham, 1978). Rather, they tend to make more specific requests, seeking particular facts or information about specialized procedures or methodologies; they are more interested in obtaining the right information than in obtaining all the information (Exhibit 9-4).

One way to estimate the recall ratio of a search is by comparing actual search results against one or more searches conducted solely for the purpose of evaluation. Katzer (1973), Martin (1974), and Oldroyd and Citroen (1977) conducted studies of this type. The evaluator gives a written statement of the patron's search requirements to two or more additional members of the library staff, who then conduct a literature search on the same subject. The evaluator compares

	Academic Scientists (Florida State University) %	Corporate Scientists (Monsanto) %	Level of Significance
Exhaustive (everything available)	50	33	0.001
Specific facts, procedures	14	39	0.001
A few references (combined with browsing)*	22	14	NS
Current awareness	13	9	NS

*Two types of approaches on the information specialist's record, "a few references on topic" and "browsing," were combined for this analysis since it was difficult to differentiate between them in practice.

NS = not significant.

EXHIBIT 9-4 Type of approach to a literature search by academic and industrial scientists (percent of all searches). Adapted from Jahoda, Bayer, and Needham (1978), courtesy of the American Library Association.

the citations gathered during these parallel searches with those gathered during the original search. The evaluator then gives all the citations identified to the patron, who assesses their relevance. With this technique, the evaluator develops an estimated recall ratio for the original search as follows:

$$\text{Recall ratio of search A} = \frac{\text{Number of relevant items found by searcher A}}{\text{Total number of unique relevant items found by searchers A, B and C}}$$

The results of the second and third searches are not evaluated; they are used merely to estimate the performance of the first search.

Suppose that searcher A, a member of the staff of an industrial library, conducts a search in a particular database and locates 42 citations for a scientist who needs a comprehensive bibliography. The scientist judges 25 of these citations to be relevant. Two other staff members, B and C, conduct separate searches on the same topic. They find 18 items that were not retrieved by A. The scientist judges 12 of these items to be relevant. The recall ratio for the original search conducted by A is thus 25/(25 + 12), or 0.68.

This figure really represents an upper-bound estimate of the recall of A's search. The evaluator assumes that the sum of all the relevant references found by A, B, and C is the total relevant references that can be located in this particular database. This assumption may not be completely valid, because there may be some additional relevant items that were not found by any of the searchers. For most evaluation purposes, however, it is not necessary to determine absolute recall. An estimated recall ratio, established by the methods just described, is generally adequate.

Precision

Precision is the percentage of items retrieved and delivered (whether actual documents or references to them) that the patron judges to be relevant. Referring again to Exhibit 9-3, the precision ratio is expressed as $a/(a + b)$. To illustrate, suppose a scientist asks the company librarian to undertake a comprehensive literature search in *Chemical Abstracts (CA)* on a specific topic. A few days later, the librarian presents the scientist with the results: abstracts of 65 items appearing in *CA*. The scientist judges 41 of the items to be relevant to his/her information need and the remaining 24 to be irrelevant. The precision ratio is thus 41/65, or 0.63. Precision, then, is a valid measure of the performance of any type of delegated search—whether manual or mechanized—in which the information seeker submits a request to some system and awaits the results.

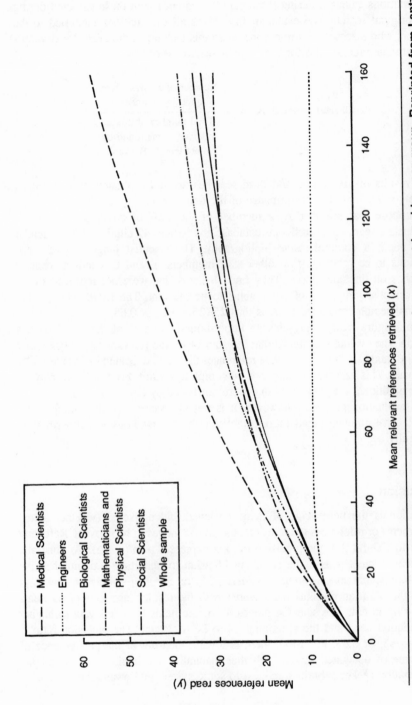

EXHIBIT 9-5 Mean references read, related to mean relevant references retrieved by user group. Reprinted from Lantz (1981), courtesy of the *Journal of Documentation*.

Precision is actually an indirect measure of patron time and effort; that is, the higher the precision ratio, the less time and effort the patron will need to expend in separating relevant items from irrelevant ones. In a search with low precision, considerable patron time and effort might be required to identify the relevant items in a list. This is especially true if the list contains only bibliographic citations rather than abstracts, since the patron usually must retrieve copies of the documents before deciding which are relevant.

As the principle of least effort predicts, most patrons prefer precise retrieval. Lantz (1981) examined the results of a patron questionnaire completed by almost 1,600 users of an online search service at the University of London. Immediately after the initial search, patrons were asked to indicate how many of the retrieved abstracts were relevant to their needs. One month later, patrons were asked to indicate how many of the abstracts they had read. Lantz speculated that, as the number of relevant abstracts increased, the actual number read by a patron would increase up to some saturation point. The patron would cease reading at that point, even though more relevant abstracts were available to meet his or her information needs, because he or she would eventually decide that gaining additional knowledge on the subject was not worth the effort it would take to read more abstracts. Although the saturation level varied among patrons and among disciplines, this general pattern held true (Exhibit 9-5). On the average, no more than 34 abstracts were read, no matter how many relevant abstracts were produced.[4] This finding suggests that arranging abstracts in order of probable relevance would significantly reduce a patron's effort and improve satisfaction with search results.

At least two studies (Lloyd, 1988; Morris, Holtum, and Curry, 1982) suggested that as a patron gains familiarity with the capabilities of online searching, the precision of the searches the librarian conducts for the patron may increase. In other words, patrons who understand the strengths and weaknesses of online searches and of various search strategies may be able to communicate more effectively with the librarian. In fact, many repeat users of search services even present the searcher with a list of subject descriptors, synonyms, and possible strategies for search logic. These suggestions may be very valuable to the librarian if the requester is truly familiar with the online search process and with the terminology used in a particular database. On the other hand, if the requester has an imperfect knowledge of these things, the suggestions could actually mislead rather than help (Lancaster, 1968).

Novelty

Novelty is an extension of precision, since it represents the percentage of relevant

---

[4] This will not surprise librarians who have read any of the research on how information overload affects patrons in libraries (for example, Baker, 1986; Rudd and Rudd, 1986).

items retrieved during a search that are *new* to the requester (that is, brought to his or her attention for the first time). If a patron has never conducted a search on a topic, the novelty may be quite high, even 100 percent. If the patron is knowledgeable about the search topic, novelty might be low, even if the search was technically excellent (high recall and high precision).

The evaluator determines the novelty ratio by asking how many relevant citations are new to the patron. Two different formulas can be used. In one, the number of new and relevant references retrieved is divided by the total number of references retrieved. Alternatively, the number of new and relevant references retrieved is divided by the total number of relevant references retrieved. Consider the hypothetical search referred to earlier for which precision was 41/65 (0.63). If 20 of the 41 relevant items were new to the requester, the novelty ratio could be calculated as 20/65 (0.31) or as 20/41 (0.49).

RESULTS OF EVALUATOR REVIEWS OF THE SEARCH PRODUCT AND PROCESS

The evaluator can compare the precision, recall, and novelty ratios to statements made by the patron about the type of search wanted, especially its completeness, and can also ask the patron to indicate satisfaction with the results obtained. Requesters can be dissatisfied with the results of a search for any of several reasons, including the following:

- The search fails to retrieve enough items on the subject. In other words, the recall is low in relation to the user's expectations. In two major studies of many different searches, the average recall ratio achieved was remarkably low—in the neighborhood of 20 percent (Saracevic and Kantor, 1988; Wanger, McDonald, and Berger, 1980).

- The search retrieves too much on the subject when only a few relevant items are wanted. According to Lantz (1981), the number of citations considered by most patrons to be too many is fairly low.

- The search retrieves too much that is irrelevant or only marginally relevant. In other words, high precision is desired but not attained. The patron is forced to exert extra effort to screen relevant materials from irrelevant ones, violating Ranganathan's rule about saving the patron's time. According to Schroder (1983), unacceptable levels of precision occur quite often. Saracevic and Kantor (1988) showed an average precision of around 55 percent after examining a large number of online searches.

- The search retrieves many items that are relevant but few that are new to the requester. Novelty is low. This may make the patron question whether the search was worth conducting.

Evaluators should always try to determine why certain searches appear to have gone awry. The actual precision, recall, and novelty ratios for a search are less important than that failures have been identified—some items that should have been retrieved were not and some that were retrieved should not have been. The important diagnostic purpose of the evaluation is served only by analyzing why the failures occurred. If the evaluator can identify the reasons behind the failures, corrective action can be taken to avoid similar failures in the future. Searcher strengths can be reinforced, and weaknesses can be communicated, along with suggestions for improvement.

The research on causes of failures in literature searching parallels that on the causes of failures in answering reference questions. Many factors that might be predicted to cause search failure actually have little or no impact on success rates. For instance, the type of training the librarian received and the amount of experience the librarian has with literature searching in general or with the use of a particular database seem to have little effect on search quality (Fenichel, 1979, 1981; Oldroyd and Citroen, 1977; Wanger, McDonald, and Berger, 1980). Nonetheless, the human element has a tremendous effect on the outcome of a search. Studies have documented large individual differences in search performance, even when the searchers are experienced and are using the same database. In fact, differences in performance among individual searchers vary by as much as a factor of 10 (Bourne, Robinson, and Todd, 1974; Fenichel, 1979; Katzer, 1973; Martin, 1974; Oldroyd and Citroen, 1977). Such wide variations in performance are rather depressing, all the more so because different searchers tend to retrieve different sets of documents and because each searcher tends to retrieve some relevant items that were not found by the other searchers.

A search may not be fully successful because of factors within the library's control—for example, the searcher may have failed to determine a requester's true information needs or to develop a good search strategy. If the evaluator has access to the search request forms and printouts and has observed (or trained others to observe) the interview and the search process in its entirety, he or she may be able to pinpoint specific failures on the searcher's part and suggest corrective tactics. Of course, some search failures are due to factors beyond the library's control, such as errors in the database. Database failures may be caused by inadequate cross-references (in a printed index), lack of specificity in the vocabulary (for example, of a thesaurus), inconsistent or inadequate assignment of subject terms, and spelling and typographical errors (see Bourne, 1969a, 1969b; Davison and Matthews, 1969; de Jong-Hofman and Siebers, 1984; Funk and Reid, 1983). From the user's point of view, other database failures may be caused by lack of adequate coverage or delays in getting items into the database.

This chapter does not deal with diagnostic studies designed to improve the effectiveness of a database, but only with studies designed to determine why a searcher does not locate certain relevant items that should be readily accessible within a particular database or why a searcher retrieves an unacceptably high number of irrelevant items.[5] There are several questions that an evaluator should address in reviewing the quality of a literature search.

Did the Searcher Successfully Determine the Patron's Real Information Needs During the Presearch Interview?

A reference librarian who thoroughly questions patrons about their true information needs generally provides more accurate answers. The quality of the dialogue between a patron and the librarian is just as important for literature searches. It may be even more important when an online search is involved, because mistakes are more visible and have a greater impact on the cost of the search (Somerville, 1982).

Evaluators initially should try to determine whether the searcher actually conducted an interview, since the quality of search results (measured objectively and from the patron's point of view) increases if the searcher and the patron have an identical understanding of the topic and purpose of the search. This mutual state of understanding is easier to achieve if the searcher talks with the patron in person or on the telephone. The former is preferable, since the patron's presence throughout the search process increases the librarian's chances of successfully meeting the patron's demand, increases patron satisfaction with search results, and yields the highest ratio of benefits to costs per citation retrieved (Jensen, Asbury, and King, 1980; Morris, Holtum, and Curry, 1982; Warden, 1981).

If no interview was conducted, the evaluator should determine whether this was the librarian's fault or due to some factor beyond the librarian's control. For example, the locations of the search site and the requester may determine how many requesters can be present during the initial interview (Jahoda, Bayer, and Needham, 1978). Or, in libraries where the responsible librarian is on duty only during limited hours, the user may write out a request and leave it for later handling. Neither of these situations is the librarian's fault; however, the librarian may contribute to a poor search if he or she fails to call a patron who left a written request when there are ambiguities in the information requirements.

If an interview was conducted, the evaluator tries to determine whether it was superficial or in-depth by examining the length of time that was devoted to the interview and determining whether the librarian asked a standard series of questions. There is no absolute length of time needed to conduct effective presearch interviews, but evaluators rating search performance should know that interviews conducted before searches of broad, interdisciplinary topics may take longer than ones conducted before searches of narrow topics. Searchers

---

[5] Lancaster (1977) and White and Griffith (1987) examined procedures that can be used by publishers and others who want to improve a database. Interested readers are referred to these sources.

faced with a broad topic must spend a great deal of time trying to determine exactly what the patron is looking for if the search is to be successful. This explains why Somerville (1977) found that interviews conducted before searches of online databases in broad disciplines (those within the social sciences and the humanities) lasted an average of 40 minutes, whereas those held before a search in physical science databases usually lasted less than 10 minutes. The searchers in the latter situation did not have to work as hard to define the real questions because the terminology in the physical sciences is more precise and the searches tend to be in more specific fields (Jahoda, Bayer, and Needham, 1978). The evaluator or surrogate patron can note the length of the interview as part of the data recorded on the actual search. To aid with staffing schedules, some libraries also keep logs that show how long the search interview lasts.

The evaluator then determines whether the searcher has asked, and received clear answers for, a series of questions to clarify the patron's information requirements. In an unobtrusive observation, the evaluator sets, and thus knows, the search requirements for each trained surrogate. The surrogate simply notes whether the searcher has asked each question and successfully identified the requirements. If the evaluator is obtrusively observing an actual interview, he or she initially records whether the questions have been asked and later interviews the patron to determine whether the librarian correctly identified the patron's information needs. Following is a discussion of each question the librarian should address in a presearch interview.

What are the patron's exact information needs? It is well known that library users often do not state clearly their information needs. A patron's need frequently is clarified if it is written, in the patron's own words, on the formal search request form. Indeed, completing such a form has been shown to improve patron satisfaction with search results (Daniels, 1978; Fitzgerald, 1981; Lancaster, 1968). Nevertheless, additional probing by the librarian usually is necessary to increase the chances of a successful search. Whenever possible, the librarian should probe with open-ended questions, which elicit better statements of the information needs and tend to increase patron satisfaction with search results (Auster and Lawton, 1984). The evaluator's job is to see that this probing has occurred and to compare the librarian's impression of the question with the patron's intent, to see if they match.

What is the objective of the search? Knowing why a search is being conducted may help the librarian understand the requester's real information needs (Lancaster, 1968). For example, "heat transfer across the skin in humans" is put into a more meaningful context if the requester is led to explain that he or she is doing research on the thermal comfort of astronauts in spacecraft.

What are the patron's requirements in terms of recall, precision, and novelty? The type of literature search that should be performed depends largely on the answer to this question. The choice of database, search terms, and search strategies are all affected by whether the patron wants a comprehensive search, a few good citations, or new citations to add to an already large collection of materials gathered on the subject.

Searches conducted with the patron present tend to yield better results, whatever the evaluation criteria used (Fosdick, 1977; Lawrence, Weil, and Graham, 1974; Morris, Holtum, and Curry, 1982; Warden, 1981). This is because the interaction involves all major factors in the process: the librarian, the patron, and the database. The librarian may retrieve a few citations from an online database and have the patron confirm that they are relevant. If they are not, the librarian and the patron, working together, refine the search strategy.

If the patron cannot be physically present at the search site, the librarian might suggest that the patron view the search from a remote location with a terminal connected by telephone lines. This has been done, for example, at the Eastern Oregon State College library. Searchers at the main site obtained feedback during the course of the search from patrons at 20 other library sites and made the necessary modifications to their searching strategies (Anderson, 1987).

Has the patron already conducted his or her own literature search? If so, where did he or she look? Jahoda, Bayer, and Needham (1978) discovered that many patrons requesting online searches in academic and industrial settings had already searched their personal collections, discussed possible sources with colleagues, or examined printed indexes. The librarian who obtains specific information on prior manual or online search strategies may discover clues that reveal which sources might be searched next, which sources should be avoided, and which searching terms might be useful.

Does the user already have some references to items known to be relevant? Full bibliographic citations to items that the requester already knows to be relevant to the information need can be valuable to the librarian in at least three ways (Lancaster, 1968). First, the librarian can compare the titles of these publications with the planned request statement to determine if the latter is either too broad or too narrow. Second, the librarian may choose to begin a search by retrieving the known items, by author search, from the database and checking to see what terminology occurs in the abstracts or how the items have been indexed. Third, once the search is completed, the librarian may use the relevant references as a check on the completeness of the search; if they appear in the database and are known to be relevant, they should have been retrieved.

Has the patron made any other preparations for the literature search, such as writing down synonyms for key terms or thinking about the logic that might be needed during the course of the search? More patrons of searching services do this than might be expected or will do it during the interview if asked. Auster and Lawton (1984) found that most patrons in academic libraries supplied synonyms for use in searching. Jahoda, Bayer, and Needham (1978) discovered that 57 percent of the patrons in an industrial environment supplied synonyms when requesting online searches and 17 percent supplied searching logic; in an academic environment, 43 percent supplied synonyms and 22 percent, logic.

Are there any search constraints? A number of patrons will mention constraints if asked. For instance, they may wish to limit the search to materials published within a particular time period, in a certain language, or of a certain type. Determining these and other constraints before the search begins may increase patron satisfaction with the results.

When is the information needed? This depends, at least partly, on the nature of the patron's request, but may nevertheless influence a patron's satisfaction with the response. Although many patrons will say they need the information immediately, others may be willing to wait a few days to obtain it.

In what format does the patron want to receive the response? The form of output could be the actual documents or microfiche copies, abstracts, full bibliographic citations, titles, or the like. Form of output is not a quantifiable performance measure, but it certainly affects patron satisfaction and will influence the patron's judgment of the relevance of retrieved items. For example, it will be easier for the patron to decide which items are relevant if he or she is given abstracts rather than only bibliographic references. The more complete the information supplied, the easier it will be for the patron to judge the item's relevance and the lower the precision ratio that he or she may tolerate. Providing information in a certain format may also help overcome other difficulties. For example, if the patron needs the information immediately, he or she may be more satisfied with a copy of the abstract that is provided today than with the actual document, available on interlibrary loan but with a 10-day delay.

The nature of the database searched and the library's policy will influence whether the librarian can provide search results in the form preferred by a particular user. Searchers have no direct control over the contents of a database, so they must accept the limitations imposed in terms of providing abstracts, citations, or the full text. But library policy is also an issue. In most public, school, and academic libraries, patrons are expected to obtain the documents themselves, after the librarian presents them with the citations or abstracts. This policy can be changed, but only if the library has enough staff to retrieve the actual documents. In any case, the library staff handling document delivery probably will not be the same as the staff performing bibliographic searches.

How much can the patron afford to pay? The answer to this question may determine whether a manual or online search is conducted, which database is searched, how comprehensive the search is, and in what form the final product may appear. It also might influence the level of patron satisfaction with the search; a patron who expects to pay $25 for a search may be very dissatisfied when presented with a bill for $125, even if the search has retrieved many relevant documents.

Is the patron aware of both the benefits and the limitations of the literature-searching service? Somerville (1977, 1982) suggested that it is particularly important for the searcher to ask this question of new or infrequent patrons of online search services, since the patron must often bear the direct cost of the search. Inexperienced patrons should be given short explanations of the process, procedures, and search strategies typically used during such a search.

Did the Librarian Search the Appropriate Databases?

At some point in the search process, the librarian selects one or more sources in which to perform the search. One task of the evaluator is to review the patron's requirements to determine whether the librarian chose the most appropriate sources for searching. A number of experts have specified factors that searchers should consider in database selection (for example, Brand, 1979; Ewbank, 1982; Hunter, 1981). These include, for instance, the currency of the materials desired; the cost of searching the source; the language, date, or geographic area covered; the subject coverage; and the nature of the topic (is it a very specific topic likely to be found only in one highly specialized database or is it an interdisciplinary topic that might occur in several?).

One problem the evaluator will face is that databases sometimes lack the kind of detailed, comprehensive descriptions that are needed to judge whether the source chosen for the search is a good one. For example, the description may fail to indicate coverage of certain topics or to reveal the depth of indexing (Shaw, 1986). Evaluators may be able to overcome this problem in several ways. They could scan the terms appearing in the database to determine their relevance. They could check the large number of published guides to various indexes and databases, although these too vary in the quality of their descriptions (Borgman, Case, and Ingebretsen, 1985). Or they could check the indexes to databases (for example, DIALINDEX) maintained by the vendors.

The coverage that a database provides on a specific subject is important to some patrons.[6] Suppose that a scientist wishes to find all possible references to the use of lasers in eye surgery. An obvious source would be the MEDLINE database of the National Library of Medicine. Even if a search in this source achieves 100 percent recall (unlikely), the patron who needs a really comprehensive search will want to know the exact coverage of the database—that is, what proportion of all the literature on eye surgery using lasers is contained in the database? Searching a particular database may result in a very high recall, but the database itself may be low in overall coverage of the literature. Although absolute coverage is not important to the typical patron (who simply wants a

---

[6] Coverage is actually an extension of recall.

few relevant citations on some topic), it is of great concern to the person who needs a comprehensive search.

Coverage, like recall, precision, and novelty, can be expressed as a proportion or percentage. If an investigator was evaluating the results of a search conducted in *Chemical Abstracts,* he or she could estimate recall using the procedures discussed earlier in this chapter; let's say it is 75 percent. This individual could also estimate (for example, by comparing with other databases) that the coverage of *CA* in the subject area of the search is 40 percent. The overall estimate of the comprehensiveness of the search, therefore, would be 0.75 × 0.40, or 0.3.

Evaluators can estimate the coverage of one database by performing comparative searches in others. The following three studies, all conducted in the same year with different online databases, exemplify this kind of evaluation.

Brody and Lambert (1984) tried to determine which databases were most appropriate for literature searches in anthropology. They conducted searches on three very specific topics in the fields of linguistics, cultural anthropology, and physical anthropology. Only two databases gave a number of highly relevant citations for all areas; some databases that were expected to yield good citations did not; and a few databases that were not in the "core" of the social sciences provided better results than many of those that were.

Gruner and Heron (1984) wanted to see which DIALOG databases had the best coverage of federal securities regulations. They prescreened all of DIALOG's databases and found 34 that were likely to contain relevant citations. After conducting six searches in each database, they ranked the databases by the number of relevant citations yielded. They ultimately identified eight databases with high potential for securities regulation research.

Another study used forensic medicine as the subject. Snow and Ifshin (1984) searched 10 different topics in five databases. They calculated recall, precision, and novelty for each topic. Novelty in particular is of great help when an evaluator is comparing the coverage of one database with another to determine which might be more useful in answering specific types of questions, especially those on narrow subject areas like telecommunications patents. Snow and Ifshin also constructed a measure of utility for each database. The concept of utility reflects the reality that most patrons want abstracts rather than mere citations and want materials written in their native language. These authors measured utility by determining the percentage of English-language documents cited, the percentage of abstracts that were available for the relevant citations retrieved, and the percentage of English-language abstracts that were available for the non-English source documents cited.

Evaluators also can estimate coverage by finding specialized bibliographies in subject areas within the stated scope of a database, then determining the percentage of the items in the bibliography that appear in the database. Several classic studies of this type were conducted by Bourne (1969a, 1969b), Davison and Matthews (1969), and Martyn and Slater (1964). If no current, specialized bibliographies are available, evaluators can use review articles. For an accurate estimate of coverage, several review articles, comprehensive in scope and diverse in subject matter, should be used.

Suppose that evaluators wanted to determine how comprehensive *Index Medicus (IM)* is in its coverage of nutrition disorders. They could begin by locating several comprehensive review articles covering specific aspects of nutrition disorders in the *Bibliography of Medical Reviews*. Suppose they located four such review articles and that these articles collectively cited 160 unique papers in various sources. They could then use these citations to assess the extent to which *IM* covered the literature of this subject field. This would be done by checking each citation against the author index of *IM* to determine which items were and which were not included until the percentage of the 160 citations that this index covers was determined. The same technique could be used to compare the coverage of two or more related indexes, such as *Current Index to Journals in Education* and *Education Index*.

Another aspect of coverage is the proportion of articles judged relevant (in a group of literature searches) that the library can supply from its own resources. If this proportion is small, it may indicate inadequacies in the library's holdings of the primary literature on a particular subject.

Evaluators should be aware of the following four common patterns when investigating whether or not a librarian has chosen the best databases for a particular search:

1. There is frequently no single source that will give a very high percentage of all citations available to answer a patron's question, nor is there a high overlap between most sources (Bawden and Brock, 1982; de Jong-Hofman and Siebers, 1984; Foreman and Baldwin, 1976; Gruner and Heron, 1984; Hawkins, 1978; McCain, White, and Griffith, 1987; Van Camp and Foreman, 1977). Evaluators should check to see if multiple databases were searched for patrons who wanted comprehensive results.

2. Searches in databases covering areas tangential to the subject may not be very cost-effective because they are unlikely to retrieve many items that have not been found elsewhere. Evaluators should verify that these sources are searched only when patrons want truly comprehensive searches performed.

3. The impressions of searchers about which sources will be most helpful are often wrong (Brody and Lambert, 1984). This reinforces the fact that evaluators should not assume that a search is satisfactory just because the search strategy used within a database was good. If the initial selection of the source was poor, poor results will follow.

4. Some searchers tend to search sources that are highly subject-specific. This can be appropriate when the patron is sophisticated and needs research findings, but general interest or multidisciplinary indexes should be used to

answer general inquiries on a subject (Shaw, 1986). Evaluators should compare the subject specificity of the index with the patron's search requirements.

The evaluator may also review whether the librarian has chosen the mode of searching that best meets the patron's needs: a manual search of a printed source or a search of an electronic source through an online service center or in CD-ROM form. The choice of search mode may hinge on a number of factors, the most common being cost and the perceived effectiveness of the search mode. Some patrons may not want to pay the direct costs of online searching, so the librarian will need to conduct a manual search or direct the user to a CD-ROM source, if an appropriate one is available. Other libraries let staff decide which search mode will be the most cost-effective, given staffing constraints. For example, a library might search online to satisfy a patron's request for a comprehensive list of citations on the impact of acid rain on conifer forests in Finland and manually to satisfy a request for three references on the broad topic of acid rain.

Generally, for comprehensive requests, evaluators have found that searching for materials online is faster, less costly (measured in total cost to the library, including staff time), and more effective (in terms of achieving acceptable recall, precision, and novelty levels) than searching for materials in a printed index (Bivans, 1974; Buckley, 1975; Elchesen, 1978; Gardner and Siebert, 1981; Michaels, 1975; Naber, 1985; Truelson, 1984). Nevertheless, even a "comprehensive" search in a database, printed or online, may be incomplete because of limitations in the indexing of the database or other factors. This was shown by de Jong-Hofman and Siebers (1984) when they compared the effectiveness of an online search with that of a completely manual search conducted by librarians without reference to printed indexes. They conducted a comprehensive search for references published in 1980 on a very specific topic: the modeling of the role of sediments as an internal nutrient source in shallow lakes. They performed online searches in four databases that emphasized the field of water quality management and manually searched professional journals and items listed by current awareness services. Eventually, 121 relevent references were identified. Although both means of searching failed to find all the articles, the direct manual search of primary sources uncovered more references than the online searches. This was attributed to indexing, titling, and abstracting errors in the databases, rather than the failure of the databases to include the references or because of an error in search strategy. Although this type of manual search, without reference to any indexes at all, is useful for certain evaluation purposes, it is impractical in most real information service environments.

Did the Librarian Select the Appropriate Search Terms?

The librarian's choice of search terms for locating materials within a database also influences the results of the search. The librarian must translate the patron's information needs into the language of the source. Generally, if a librarian is searching a printed index, the translation occurs at the time of the search. If the librarian is searching online, the translation may occur before the search; that is, to save money, the librarian may decide before going online which terms will be used, at least for the initial search.

The librarian's ability to translate the patron's needs into the language of the database depends on a number of factors, including

- The patron's ability to express his or her needs.
- The degree to which the vocabulary of the database matches the search requirements. Of particular importance is whether the vocabulary is sufficiently specific to match the patron's precise requirements.
- The assistance and guidance provided by the database, particularly in terms of its organization, structure, and extent of cross-referencing.
- The librarian's ability to overcome any shortcomings in the first three factors.

In theory, the librarian has already overcome the patron's inability to express his/her needs during the presearch interview. Therefore, in this stage of the search, the librarian attempts to overcome problems with indexing quality and with inadequacies in the vocabulary used to index the database. Most indexing, for both print and electronic sources, is not as exhaustive as possible (too few terms are assigned to each item indexed) or as consistent (literature on a topic may be scattered over several subject headings with few or no references linking them). Carroll (1969) discovered that abstracts of papers relating to virology were found in at least 20 sections of *Biological Abstracts,* other than those dealing directly with virology. Oppenheim (1975) found that less than half of the chemical patents actually included in *Chemical Abstracts* could be retrieved with the appropriate terms in the subject and formula indexes. The librarian's search strategy should strive to surmount problems that are associated with the vocabulary, organization, and structure of a database.

The mistakes made at this stage of the search generally relate to the amount of effort the librarian puts into solving the problem of which terms to search under. Common librarian errors include ignoring the thesaurus used by a database, choosing the wrong search terms because of unfamiliarity with a subject, selecting only a few search terms when more are needed for a particular search, or overlooking obvious synonyms (Fenichel, 1979, 1981; Oldroyd and Citroen, 1977). Many searchers also fail to ask patrons to check the terms that are chosen, although patrons (particularly those with special subject expertise) often are able to indicate which terms are relevant, tangential, or irrelevant and which of the relevant terms are most important. Salton and Waldstein (1978), among others, showed how this type of patron verification results in more precise searches.

A recent study has shown that mistakes could be caused by the librarian's failure to understand complex words or to relate these words to other words. Saracevic and Kantor (1988) used a standard test to measure the ability of librarians to associate some words with others of a similar nature. Those librarians who scored high on the Remotes Associates Test retrieved significantly more relevant documents than their lower scoring counterparts. The evaluator's job is to verify that librarians are choosing the correct search terms to begin with (especially important when patrons want high precision) and choosing appropriate synonyms to expand the search (especially important when patrons want high recall or novelty). For this purpose, the evaluator must have some tangible evidence of the terms actually used. During online searches, the search strategy may be printed on paper as the search is conducted so that both patron and searcher can tell what terms are being used. In an obtrusive manual search, the staff member (or evaluator) can record on a special form which subject headings are consulted and in what sequence.

To determine the quality of term selection, the evaluator may need to perform additional searches in the database to determine if the original searcher chose terms that closely corresponded to the concepts sought by the patron and, if high recall or novelty is desired, whether the searcher looked under all possible terms. One should not be surprised to find little agreement among searchers in the selection of search terms; Saracevic and Kantor (1988) found an average overlap of only 27 percent among terms used by different searchers working on the same problem. It is examples of irrelevant items retrieved (determined by feedback from the requester) and of relevant items not retrieved (which may be located through further searching or may be items known in advance by the requester) that will be most valuable in determining whether the terms used by a searcher were the most appropriate for a particular topic and for the type of search specified by the requester.

Was the Librarian's Search Logic Appropriate?

A search strategy consists of more than a group of terms. The terms must be combined in appropriate logical relationships, and other search features, like truncation and word proximity, might be used. The evaluator should focus on whether the searcher used an appropriate strategy, given the patron's request, and, if not, why not.

Fidel (1984) suggested that experienced librarians use one of two basic approaches to conduct the literature search: operational or conceptual. Operationalist searchers design search strategies to maximize precision; they usually begin by selecting and combining only the most relevant terms for a search. Conceptualist searchers design search strategies to maximize recall (and often, in the process, novelty); they begin by selecting a large number of search terms for several concepts before making any logical combinations to reduce the size of the citation set retrieved. These two camps are similar to those that Oldroyd and Citroen (1977) identified in a study of 20 experienced searchers at the European Space Agency network. Various, more specific approaches to online searching, as identified by Hawkins (1983) and by Markey and Atherton (1978), can be grouped under the operational or conceptual approach.

The evaluator is more concerned with whether the approach used by the searcher is appropriate to meet the needs of the user than with the approach itself. Indeed, several possible approaches could each yield similar results. When Fidel (1984) observed five experienced searchers, she found that they tended to consistently search in one mode, regardless of the nature of the request. Since Fidel studied only five searchers, no generalizations can be made from her findings to the entire searcher population. Nonetheless, one should be alert to the fact that librarians may habitually use the same search approach for each request, rather than the one that is best suited to the patron's needs in terms of precision, recall, and novelty.

A number of studies have explored factors that might affect the success of the type of search chosen. The librarian's level of search experience—overall or with a particular database—affects search success less than one might suppose (Fenichel, 1980a), although lack of familiarity with the vocabulary used within a database can have a profound impact on search results (Howard, 1982; Lancaster, 1972; Sewell and Bevan, 1976). Saracevic and Kantor (1988) indicated that searchers who are comfortable in dealing with abstractions may get better results than those who have difficulty thinking in abstract terms.

Most errors in search strategy, however, may be caused simply by the librarian's lack of search effort (Fenichel, 1979; Lancaster, 1968). Searchers who put more effort into an online search—that is, used more commands, searched more descriptors, browsed more citation sets, and modified search strategies more frequently—achieved the highest recall in searches studied by Fenichel (1980a). There is also evidence that experienced searchers often put more effort into solving difficult search problems (Fenichel, 1980a; Harris, 1986; Howard, 1982).

Most librarians working with online databases conduct very simple subject searches, ignoring more advanced techniques; use the most basic techniques for selecting and combining terms; and use only a small portion of the commands that are available for searching (Bourne, Robinson, and Todd, 1974; Fenichel, 1979; Oberhauser, 1986; Penniman, 1975; White, 1986). Many do not adapt search strategy to account for differences in file structure and do not fully exploit the interactive capabilities of the systems used (Fenichel, 1979; Martin, 1974; Oldroyd and Citroen, 1977; Pollitt, 1977; Vigil, 1988).

The concept of effort also applies when examining specific aspects of the search strategy, including whether the librarian should use a controlled vocabulary or a free-text search, search one or more parts of the document surrogate (for example, the title, the abstract, or both), or use a more complicated search approach designed to achieve high recall at an acceptable level of precision.

The pros and cons of searching by using either a controlled vocabulary or free-text (natural) language have been debated for years. There is conflicting evidence on whether one mode of search is preferable to the other when particular requirements exist for recall or precision. The comparison is complicated by the fact that other variables have a profound effect on the results of a search—most important, the length of the record searched. The fact that a database of abstracts gives higher recall than a database with shallow indexing reflects length of record, not the property of free text per se (Lancaster, 1991). What is certain is that free-text and controlled vocabulary searches both retrieve some relevant documents that are not found by the other (Bates, 1987; Dubois, 1987; Hersey et al., 1970, 1971). Thus, a combination of the two seems logical for the patron who needs high recall or novelty. The evaluator's task is to verify that the type of search used (free text, controlled vocabulary, or a combination of the two) is appropriate to meet the patron's recall, precision, and novelty requirements.

When a free-text search is used, the evaluator needs to examine which part of the document surrogate the searcher used to retrieve the citations, since this can greatly influence results. Researchers agree that searching any one part of the document record will not achieve complete recall (Katzer et al., 1982; McGill, 1979; Olive et al., 1973). Hodges (1983) found that fewer than 50 percent of relevant items were retrieved with a title keyword search. Cleverdon (1984) verified that recall is significantly higher when searching abstracts as compared with titles, but neither search method retrieves all relevant citations. Researchers generally have found that full text achieves significantly better results than any other single element of the document (Durkin et al., 1980; Hood, 1987; Stein et al., 1982; Terrant et al., 1983). But even full-text searches do not usually achieve total recall. This was illustrated by Tenopir (1984, 1985) when she conducted several searches on various business-related topics in the online version of the *Harvard Business Review*. Searches were performed on abstracts, index terms, full text, and abstracts combined with index terms. Not unexpectedly, the full text gave very high recall (73.9 percent) but very low precision (18 percent). Searches on abstracts alone were very poor on recall (19.3 percent) but achieved better precision (35.6 percent). The searches on index terms achieved 34 percent precision and a recall of only 28 percent. The combination of abstracts plus index terms gave 44.9 percent recall and 37 percent precision. Even the best searches in terms of recall (on full text) missed some 26 percent of the relevant items.

Tenopir's results agree with those of Saracevic and Kantor (1988): each search approach tends to retrieve some relevant items not found by the others.

Precision can also vary considerably, depending on which parts of the record are searched. Cleverdon (1984) showed that precision is significantly higher when searching titles than when searching abstracts. Full-text searching tends to give the lowest precision (Hood, 1987; Tenopir, 1985).

Many studies have shown that searches which rank output, so that items appearing first in a printout are most likely to be relevant, will tend to optimize results from the user's point of view (for example, Cleverdon, 1984). There are many possible ways of ranking output, a simple one being the "quorum function search" described by Cleverdon and illustrated in Exhibit 9-6. Documents at the top of the ranking achieved in a quorum search are more likely to be relevant to the patron's needs (Exhibit 9-7). This type of search is very valuable when high precision is desired. Moreover, a ranked output alleviates some of the information overload that Lantz (1981) identified and reduces the patron's level of effort.

Boolean:

A *or* B *or* C *or* (D *and* E) *or* (F *and* (G *or* H))
and
J *or* K *or* (L *and* M)
and
N *or* (P *and* R) *or* (S *and* T)

Quorum:

1. A *and* B *and* C *and* D *and* E *and* F *and* G *and* H *and* J .... *and* T
2. Search (1) less any single term
3. Search (1) less any two terms
4. Search (1) less any three terms
5. Search (1) less any four terms
   .
   .
   .
15. Any three terms from Search (1)
16. Any two terms from Search (1)
17. A *or* B *or* C *or* D *or* E *or* F *or* G *or* H *or* J *or* K *or* L .... *or* T

EXHIBIT 9-6   Example of Boolean and quorum function searches for the same set of terms. Reprinted from Cleverdon (1984), courtesy of Elsevier Science Publishers and Cyril Cleverdon.

	Total retrieved	Total relevant	Recall ratio (%)	Precision ratio (%)
Boolean	344	175	30	51
Quorum function				
Level 9	6	6	1	100
Level 8	12	12	2	100
Level 7	26	26	5	100
Level 6	59	57	10	97
Level 5	143	116	21	81
Level 4	314	314	39	68
Level 3	606	409	74	67
Level 2	1,588	546	99	34

EXHIBIT 9-7 Accumulated figures for 14 searches comparing Boolean and quorum function search methods. Reprinted from Cleverdon (1984), courtesy of Elsevier Science Publishers and Cyril Cleverdon.

Did the Librarian Follow Up on the Results of a Search?

When the patron is present at a search, the librarian and patron review the search results as the search proceeds, modifying the direction of the search accordingly. When the patron cannot be present, the librarian would be well-advised to follow up with the patron to determine how valuable the search results have been. This can be achieved through the use of an evaluation form such as that shown in Exhibit 9-8 or through a post search interview, performed perhaps by telephone.

How Long Did the Search Take?

The time taken to perform a search must also be considered in a complete evaluation because it exerts a significant influence on the cost of the search and, thus, its cost-effectiveness. A number of factors (aside from system response time) influence online search time and cost. These include the cost-consciousness of the librarian, the librarian's familiarity with the database, the effort expended by the librarian on the search, and the presence of the patron during the search.

A librarian's cost-consciousness is affected by the institutional setting in which he or she works. Librarians employed by institutions that pass fees on to patrons make a particular effort to ensure that the patron gets a high-quality product. They participate in more continuing education opportunities to upgrade their skills, and they spend more time developing a search strategy with the patron prior to conducting the search (Bourne, Robinson, and Todd, 1974; Cooper and DeWath, 1977; Nielsen, 1983). This last action directly increases searching efficiency while online, even as it reduces direct connect time

---

Search Evaluation

The printout attached presents the results of the search recently undertaken for you on the subject of _____ .

To help us monitor and improve our services would you please study the search results and answer the following questions:

1. Would you judge this search to be:

   Of great value _____   Of value _____
   Of little value _____   Of no value _____

2. Give a brief statement to explain the reason for your value judgment.

3. The search retrieved a total of _____ items. Please indicate how many were useful in contributing to the satisfaction of your information need according to scale presented below. (NOTE: In judging the importance of an item do *not* take into consideration whether or not you were previously familiar with it. Indicate how many items you were previously familiar with in the final column.)

	Number of items	Number previously familiar to you
A. These items are very important to me. The value of the search would have been greatly reduced had these been missed.	_____	_____
B. These are pertinent to my interests but of lesser importance. Nevertheless, it is good that they were retrieved.	_____	_____
C. These are pertinent but of very marginal value. The search would have been just as valuable without them.	_____	_____
D. These are not at all pertinent to my interests.	_____	_____

4. For the items judged D above please give some explanation as to why they were not pertinent:

5. If you are aware of any pertinent items that were not retrieved in this search, but probably should have been, please give bibliographic details below:

EXHIBIT 9-8   Draft of a search evaluation questionnaire. Reprinted from Lancaster (1988) by permission of the author.

significantly (Cannell and Mowat, 1982). Thus, charging fees may paradoxically result in searches that are more cost-effective.

Searcher familiarity with the database also affects costs. As might be expected, novices (people with little literature-searching experience in general or with little experience searching a particular source) take longer to conduct a search (Fenichel, 1980b; Howard, 1982). Although the search results of novices may be similar in terms of precision, recall, and novelty to those of more experienced searchers, the cost per search may be considerably higher.

Librarians who put more effort into the search have longer connect times than any other group except the novice users (Fenichel, 1979, 1981). But since the recall achieved by these librarians may well be higher, their searches may be more cost-effective when measured by the cost per relevant item retrieved.

Finally, the amount of time spent online, measured in minutes, is significantly higher when the patron is present, since the interaction with the searcher to refine the strategy takes time; therefore, the actual cost per search is increased. Because patron presence usually produces better results, however, as well as higher patron satisfaction, the searches are more cost-effective overall (Morris, Holtum, and Curry, 1982).

SUBJECTIVE EVALUATION OF PATRON SATISFACTION

Most patrons are satisfied with the results of a search even if the search was less than optimal. This tends to be true regardless of the cost of the search or the type of library in which it was conducted. Studies finding very high satisfaction rates (more than 70 percent of the patrons were highly satisfied) include those by Benenfeld, Pensyl, and Marcus (1975); Kobelski and Trumbore (1978); Ruhl and Yeates (1976); and Summit and Firschein (1975). Some authors have suggested that patrons cannot judge objectively the results of a literature search (for example, Auster, 1983). But patrons can state their level of satisfaction with the results of a particular search, with the interaction they had with the librarian, and with service policies and the library in general (Hitchingham, 1977; Tessier, 1981; Tessier, Crouch, and Atherton, 1977).

Patron Satisfaction with Search Results

The form recommended by the American Library Association's Machine-Assisted Reference Section (Blood, 1983) to evaluate patron satisfaction is shown in Exhibit 9-9. Note that this form addresses precision and novelty but not recall. The form could be improved in other ways as well. For example, the requester could be asked why some retrieved citations are not relevant, since this information may help the evaluator understand how the search might have been improved. Many patrons want high precision; Hilchey and Hurych (1985), for

In order to evaluate and improve computerized literature search services, we would appreciate your taking a few moments to complete and return this questionnaire.

Search number _____

Since only a limited sample of users is asked to evaluate the results of their computerized literature searches, the validity of the sample results depends on subsequent follow-up of nonrespondents. The search number was entered by a member of the library staff in order to identify users who return their questionnaires and to eliminate them from a subsequent telephone follow-up of nonrespondents. If you prefer to complete and return this questionnaire without indicating your name in order to remain anonymous, the search number will *not* be used to identify your response. Whether or not you choose to remain anonymous, your response will be kept strictly confidential.

Name: _____

Address: _____

Telephone number(s): _____

Status: (Categories vary by type of library—local option phrasing)

    e.g. *Academic Library:*   Faculty _____ Graduate student _____

                                         Undergraduate _____ Staff _____

                                         Other (specify) _____

    e.g. *Special Library:*   Administrator _____ Salesman _____

                                           Laboratory technician _____

                                         Other (specify) _____

1. What was your main purpose in requesting this search? In other words, at the time you submitted your search request, what had you planned to do with the results?

   (Local option—provide list of possible responses, e.g. term paper, Ph.D. dissertation, faculty research, grant proposal, etc.)

2. Was the purpose of this search to determine that no previous work had been done on this topic?

   Yes _____ No _____

EXHIBIT 9-9   Search evaluation questionnaire to assess patron satisfaction, recommended by the American Library Association's Machine-Assisted Reference Section Committee on Measurement and Evaluation of Service. Reprinted from Blood (1983), courtesy of the American Library Association.

EXHIBIT 9-9 *(Continued)*

3. Does this search provide enough *relevant* citations for the purpose for which you submitted the search request?
   Yes _____
   No, but didn't expect to see anything _____
   No (please comment) _____
4. Among the total citations provided by this search, what percentage appears *relevant* to the specific question or topic for which you submitted a search request?
   0% _____
   1 to 25% _____
   26 to 50% _____
   51 to 75% _____
   76 to 100% _____
5. Among the total citations provided by this search, what percentage appears *relevant* to your overall information need, rather than simply relevant to the specific question submitted as a search topic or question?
   0% _____
   1 to 25% _____
   26 to 50% _____
   51 to 75% _____
   76 to 100% _____
6. Among the *relevant* citations provided by this search, what percentage is new to you, or, in other words, was unknown to you at the time you examined the search results?
   0% of the *relevant* citations are new to me _____
   1 to 25% of the *relevant* citations are new to me _____
   26 to 50% of the *relevant* citations are new to me _____
   51 to 75% of the *relevant* citations are new to me _____
   76 to 100% of the *relevant* citations are new to me _____
7. Do you feel that the citations that are both *relevant* and previously *unknown* to you are worth the cost that you paid for the search?
   Yes _____ No _____
   If "No," please comment:
   (Optional question—may be omitted if library does not charge)
8. Was the time lapse between submitting your search request and receiving your search results reasonable?
   Yes _____ No _____
   If "No," please comment:
9. Were the results of the search of value to you?
   Yes _____ No _____
   If "No," please comment:
10. The major reason for the Search Evaluation Questionnaire is to obtain your comments and suggestions for improving the computerized literature searching service. If you have suggestions as to how *any aspect* of the search service can be improved, please comment *in detail:*

example, found a strong positive relationship between the relevance of citations retrieved and the patron's statement of search value (see Exhibit 9-10).

Librarians working with patrons who have prior experience with search services tend to achieve higher precision. This may be because experienced patrons are able to communicate their needs more clearly to the librarian and to offer suggestions for term choice and search strategy. This enhanced communication may help explain why patron satisfaction with the precision of search results is highest for the most experienced group of patrons (Morris, Holtum, and Curry, 1982).

Although the librarian can perhaps increase precision, recall, or novelty by conducting a better search, there is one factor beyond his or her control: the degree of importance that the requester places on the search results. Patrons placing high importance on the information sought tend to have lower satisfaction scores (Auster and Lawton, 1984). An evaluator should not ignore this important factor, because dissatisfaction can be caused not only by some error on the part of the librarian but also by the unrealistic expectations of the patron.

Patron satisfaction rates also are related to response time, the time elapsing between submission of a request by the patron and delivery of a satisfactory response. Many patrons prefer quick retrieval to solve immediate information needs; therefore, their satisfaction with the service can be influenced by response time.

Relevance	Major Value	Considerable Value	Minor Value	No Value	Row Total
All Relevant	5	4	0	0	9 (5.9%)
Most Relevant	48	23	1	0	72 (47.1%)
Half Relevant	12	32	5	0	49 (32.0%)
Most Irrelevant	1	5	15	1	22 (14.4%)
All Irrelevant	0	0	0	1	1 (0.7%)
Column Total	66 (43.1%)	64 (41.8%)	21 (13.7%)	2 (1.3%)	153 (100.1%)

NOTE: Percentages do not add to 100.0 because of rounding.

χ-square = 167.33810; df = 12; $p < .01$; contingency coefficient = 0.72276.

EXHIBIT 9-10 Cross-tabulation of relevance of references by patron's statement of search value. Reprinted from Hilchey and Hurych (1985), courtesy of the American Library Association.

	Frequency	Valid Percent	Cumulative Percent
Yes	111	73.5	73.5
Partly	31	20.5	94.0
No	9	6.0	100.0
Total	151	100.0	

EXHIBIT 9-11 Did search results justify the expense? Reprinted from Hilchey and Hurych (1985), courtesy of the American Library Association.

A third and major factor related to satisfaction is the ratio of the user's cost of a search to the perceived benefits of the search. Cost has two components: the effort the patron must make to use the service and any direct charges the patron must bear. For the service to be used (and reused), the patron must consider that the cost expended is exceeded by the benefit received.

Three types of effort affect patron satisfaction. The first is the effort needed to interrogate the system. Most patrons have some initial perceptions of the ease or difficulty of accessing the literature-searching service. These may be related to the distance the patron must travel to use the service, the physical location of the service inside the library, the availability of staff to help the patron with the request, or the total amount of time needed to negotiate the inquiry with the librarian. A second type of effort is that needed to use the form of output provided to meet the patron's request. Does the form of output make it easy for the patron to separate the relevant items from those that are not relevant (which is directly influenced by the precision ratio)? Patron satisfaction can be improved by decreasing the effort needed at this stage. For example, the librarian could provide abstracts rather than citations or (in some systems) could print out the final output in ranked order. The third type of effort is that involved in retrieving the documents brought to the user's attention by the search. Most libraries are confusing to nonlibrarians, and the typical patron may be overwhelmed with the mechanics of retrieving specific items.

It may be that many members of the general public perceive that the effort needed to use literature-searching services is greater than the benefits that will result. Once patrons use the service, however, they may change their minds, realizing that it generally "costs" them less to have librarians conduct the searches than to conduct the searches themselves. Most (60–80 percent) of those who actually use literature-searching services rate the benefits higher than the costs (Benenfeld et al., 1975; Collette and Price, 1977; Fosdick, 1977). Exhibit 9-11 illustrates this for a study that Hilchey and Hurych (1985) conducted in an academic library. The primary benefit received seems to be time saved. For example, Kobelski and Trumbore (1978) discovered that 87 percent of those

Number of Citations Retrieved	Frequency	No Response or Unquantifiable (%)	0 Hours Saved (%)	1–10 Hours Saved (%)	More than 10 Hours Saved (%)
1–20	117	6.0	9.4	55.6	29.1
21–40	49	10.2	10.2	44.9	34.7
41–60	32	0.0	6.3	56.3	37.5
61–80	14	0.0	0.0	42.9	57.1
81–100	13	0.0	0.0	30.8	69.2
101+	29	10.3	0.0	34.5	55.2

EXHIBIT 9-12   User perceptions of the amount of time saved by number of citations retrieved. Reprinted from Markee (1981). Reproduced from *Online Review*, Volume 5, Number 6, courtesy of Learned Information, Inc.

who used an online search service claimed to have saved at least 10 hours of their time.

Patron perceptions of the extent of time savings are likely to be influenced by the number of relevant citations retrieved. As Exhibit 9-12 shows, the more citations patrons receive, the more time they believe they have saved by using the search service (Markee, 1981).

There is little point in comparing the cost-benefit ratios of searching in different libraries. Figures vary widely from facility to facility, because some libraries pass along all service costs to patrons, others pass on direct costs only (for example, those for online connect time), and a few do not charge at all.

Some investigators claim that the cost-benefit ratio is greater within a particular library for those patrons who stay during the search than it is for those who deposit their search request and leave before the search is conducted. For example, clients who participated in an interactive search in an industrial environment estimated their search results would yield a benefit of more than $34 for every dollar invested in the search, whereas clients who did not stay for the search predicted that results would yield a benefit of $18 for every dollar invested (Jensen, Asbury, and King, 1980). Any "benefit" data that can be collected from a library user are, of course, only considered estimates of how much time or money might have been saved. Although this does not negate the value of such analyses, it does mean that data should be interpreted very cautiously.

Patron Satisfaction with the Quality of the Interaction

Evaluators need to consider patron satisfaction with the quality of the personal interaction with library staff. Research on this aspect is scarce, but studies do show that the nature of the interaction affects patron satisfaction. For example, Genova (1981) found that nonverbal communication (for example, postural shifts, facial cues such as laughter, eye contact, and hand and head movements) affected patron satisfaction (but not search results).

Another interesting study was based on the communications theory that people are always concerned with three characteristics of interpersonal interactions: liking, responsiveness, and power. Tessier, Crouch, and Atherton (1977) related this theory to patron satisfaction with their interaction with the librarian who is performing the literature search. "Liking" is linked to the patron's perceptions of the librarian's availability, willingness to provide service, and supportiveness (of the patron as a person and of the patron's needs for information). "Responsiveness" refers to the patron's need for the librarian to acknowledge the patron's presence and attend to his or her needs. "Power" relates to the patron's satisfaction with who is controlling the interaction. Some patrons want the librarian to control the transaction, some patrons would rather control it themselves, and others wish to work on an equal basis with the librarian. Thus, patron satisfaction with power depends on how well the librarian picks up patron clues as to who should control the situation and plays the desired role.

Patron Satisfaction with the Library and Its Policies

A third aspect of patron satisfaction relates to overall satisfaction with the library and its policies. The librarian should take great care in interpreting the results of these general studies of satisfaction with the library, because so many variables affect library use (D'Elia and Walsh, 1985). It is possible, however, to ask patrons whether their attitudes toward the library have changed as a result of using the search services. At least two studies show that they may. Carmon and Park (1973) found that patron attitudes about the library improved after they were introduced to online searching. Patrons found this type of searching to be a highly personalized service that greatly reduced the effort they needed to get their work done. In a second study, patrons said they would use the library more often as a result of their positive experiences with online search services (Hilchey and Hurych, 1985).

EVALUATION OF SUBJECT SEARCHES IN THE LIBRARY CATALOG

The evaluation criteria and procedures described in this chapter are applicable to any subject searches, including those conducted in the library catalog by library staff. In this case, the precise topic of a search would be recorded, along with the subject headings consulted, the items selected to meet search needs, and the time spent on the search. The end product would be evaluated by asking patrons about their perceptions of relevant titles and their overall satisfaction with the search and by having exhaustive parallel searches conducted to estimate how much relevant material the original search might have missed.

This type of evaluation identifies searches that have produced poor results so that a diagnostic analysis can be undertaken to determine why the failures occurred. For instance, there may be defects in the catalog's design or comprehensiveness that could be improved by more access points per title, more specific subject headings, or more extensive use of cross-references. Chapter 7 examines in detail the ways in which catalog use can be evaluated.

EVALUATION OF SDI SERVICES

The evaluation criteria mentioned in this chapter also apply to the SDI services offered by a particular library. Novelty is a particularly appropriate measure because it shows how well a service increases a patron's awareness of new literature in some field.

An early SDI evaluation was conducted by Scheffler and March (1971), who interviewed 63 patrons of SDI services offered by the Aerospace Materials Information Center. Patrons indicated that too many abstracts were being received and that too few were relevant. The evaluators refined patron profiles on the basis of more precise statements obtained during patron interviews. Precision improved from 38 percent to 52 percent, showing how useful patron feedback can be in increasing both patron satisfaction and the quality of search results.

Because SDI services can be expensive, evaluators may want to determine the benefits that patrons receive in order to justify the cost of the service. When evaluators examined SISMAKOM, a free computerized SDI service in operation at five Malaysian universities, they determined that 78 percent of the patrons were better informed since they started using SISMAKOM, that patrons saved an average of three hours per week by using SISMAKOM, that 90 percent of the patrons wanted to continue using the service, and that 40 percent valued it so much that they were willing to begin paying for it (Universiti Sains Malaysia Library, 1983). Estabrook (1986) found that $2 was saved by the SDI service at a large engineering firm for every dollar expended. Houlson and Jax (1987) identified a number of benefits to staff and faculty users of the SDI program at the University of Wisconsin–Stout, including heightened current awareness, a filling-in of existing gaps in specialized subject areas, time savings averaging 6–15 hours per week, a positive impact on teaching and research, and greater access to comprehensive sources of information.

CONCLUSION

In any database search, some relevant items may be missed because the librarian failed to determine the patron's exact information needs, looked under the wrong terms, or used inadequate search strategies. Other relevant items may be missed because of poor indexing. It is the cumulative nature of these effects that makes it so difficult to conduct a search that will achieve a high recall at a tolerable level of precision.

As with the other aspects of evaluation discussed in this book, an evaluation of the literature-searching service offered by a library should be performed with the goal of improving the service. This improvement will come primarily from additional training of staff. Corrective training might involve general instruction in search strategy, interviewing methods, or database selection, or it might be tailored to particular problem areas like subjects or databases that seem to present the most difficulties. Libraries should also review the number of staff performing search services, because inadequate staffing is likely to affect both the quantity and the quality of searches conducted.

REFERENCES

Anderson, Charles R. "Online Ready Reference in the Public Library." In: *Questions and Answers: Strategies for Using the Electronic Reference Collection. Proceedings of the 24th Annual Clinic on Library Applications of Data Processing*. Edited by Linda C. Smith. Urbana, Ill., University of Illinois, Graduate School of Library and Information Science, 1989, pp. 71–84.

Anderson, Verl A. "Simultaneous Remote Searching: An Aid to the End User." In: *National Online Meeting. Proceedings 1987. New York, 5–7 May 1987*. Edited by Martha E. Williams and Thomas H. Hogan. Medford, N.J., Learned Information, 1987, pp. 5–8.

Auster, Ethel. "User Satisfaction with the Online Negotiation Interview: Contemporary Concern in Traditional Perspective." *RQ, 23*(1):47–59, Fall 1983.

Auster, Ethel, and Stephen B. Lawton. "Search Interview Techniques and Information Gain as Antecedents of User Satisfaction with Online Bibliographic Retrieval." *Journal of the American Society for Information Science, 35*(2):90–103, March 1984.

Baker, Sharon L. "Overload, Browsers, and Selections." *Library and Information Science Research, 8*(4):315–329, October–December 1986.

Bates, Marcia J. "Optimal Use of Controlled Vocabularies in Online Searching." In: *Online '87, Proceedings of the Conference, Anaheim, California, 20–22 October 1987. Part 1*. Weston, Conn., Online, Inc., 1987, pp. 14–19.

Bawden, David, and Alison M. Brock. "Chemical Toxicology Searching." *Journal of Information Science, 5*(1):3–18, October 1982.

Bayer, Alan E., and Gerald Jahoda. "Background Characteristics of Industrial and Academic Users and Nonusers of Online Bibliographic Search Services." *Online Review, 3*(1):95–105, March 1979.

_____. "Effects of Online Bibliographic Searching on Scientists' Information Style." *Online Review*, 5(4):323–333, August 1981.

Benenfeld, Alan R., et al. *NASIC at MIT: Final Report, 1 March 1974 through 28 February 1975.* Cambridge, Mass., Massachusetts Institute of Technology, Electronic Systems Laboratory, 1975. Report ESL-FR-587. ERIC ED107226

Benenfeld, Alan R.; Mary E. Pensyl; and Richard S. Marcus. "User Receptivity to Fee-for-Service Computer-Based Reference in a University Community." In: *Proceedings of the American Society for Information Science, October 26–30, 1975. Boston, Mass.* Vol. 12. Edited by Charles W. Husbands and Ruth L. Tigre. Washington, D.C., American Society for Information Science, 1975, pp. 151–152.

Bivans, Margaret M. "A Comparison of Manual and Machine Literature Searches." *Special Libraries*, 65(5–6):216–222, May–June 1974.

Blood, Richard W. "Evaluation of Online Searches." *RQ*, 22(3):266–277, Spring 1983.

Borgman, Christine L.; Donald O. Case; and Dorothy Ingebretsen. "University Faculty Use of Computerized Databases: An Assessment of Needs and Resources." *Online Review*, 9(4):307–332, August 1985.

Bourne, Charles P. *Characteristics of Coverage by the Bibliography of Agriculture of the Literature Relating to Agricultural Research and Development.* Palo Alto, Calif., Information General Corp., 1969a. NTIS Report PB185425

_____. *Overlapping Coverage of Bibliography of Agriculture by 15 Other Secondary Services.* Palo Alto, Calif., Information General Corp., 1969b. NTIS Report PB185069

Bourne, Charles P.; Jo Robinson; and Judy Todd. *Analysis of ERIC On-Line File Searching Procedures and Guidelines for Searching.* Berkeley, Calif., University of California, Institute of Library Research, 1974. ERIC ED101757

Brand, Alice A. "Searching Multiple Indexes and Databases in the Behavioral Sciences: Which and How Many?" *Behavioral and Social Sciences Librarian*, 1(2):105–112, Winter 1979.

Brody, Fern, and Maureen Lambert. "Alternative Databases for Anthropology Searching." *Database*, 7(1):28–33, February 1984.

Buckley, Jay S. "Planning for Effective Use of On-Line Systems." *Journal of Chemical Information and Computer Science*, 15(3):161–164, August 1975.

Cannell, Sheila E., and Ian R. M. Mowat. "Charges for On-Line Searches in University Libraries: A Report on a Survey." *Journal of Librarianship*, 14(3):176–203, July 1982.

Carmon, James L., and Margaret K. Park. "User Assessment of Computer-Based Bibliographic Retrieval Services." *Journal of Chemical Documentation*, 13(1):24–27, February 1973.

Carroll, Kathleen H. "An Analytical Survey of Virology Literature Reported in Two Announcement Journals." *American Documentation*, 20(3):234–237, July 1969.

Chen, Ching-Chih, and Susanna Schweizer. *Online Bibliographic Searching: A Learning Manual.* New York, Neal-Schuman, 1981, p. 2.

Cleverdon, Cyril. "Optimizing Convenient Online Access to Bibliographic Databases." *Information Services and Use*, 4(1–2):37–47, April 1984.

Cochrane, Pauline A. *Tasks Performed by Online Searchers in Presearch Interviews: A Report of the Presearch Interview Project.* Syracuse, N.Y., Syracuse University, School of Information Studies, April 1981. ERIC ED205189

Collette, A. D., and J. A. Price. "A Cost/Benefit Evaluation of Online Interactive

Bibliographic Searching in a Research and Engineering Organization." In: *The Value of Information: Collection of Papers Presented at the 6th American Society for Information Science Mid-Year Meeting, May 19–21, 1977.* Washington D.C., American Society for Information Science, 1977, pp. 24–34.

Cooper, Michael D., and Nancy A. DeWath. "The Effect of User Fees on the Cost of On-Line Searching in Libraries." *Journal of Library Automation, 10*(4):304–319, December 1977.

Cooper, William S. "A Definition of Relevance for Information Retrieval." *Information Storage and Retrieval, 7*(1):19–37, June 1971.

Curtis, Dade T. "Online Retrieval as an Information Source for Bench Bioscientists." *Online Review, 1*(4):279–288, December 1977.

Daniels, Linda. "A Matter of Form." *Online, 2*(4):31–39, October 1978.

Davison, P. S., and D. A. R. Matthews. "Assessment of Information Services." *Aslib Proceedings, 21*(7):280–284, July 1969.

de Jong-Hofman, M. W., and H. H. Siebers. "Experiences with Online Literature Searching in a Water-Related Subject Field: Aqualine, Biosis, CA Search and PASCAL, Compared Using the ESA/Information Retrieval System." *Online Review, 8*(1):59–73, February 1984.

D'Elia, George, and Sandra Walsh. "Patrons' Uses and Evaluations of Library Services: A Comparison Across Five Public Libraries." *Library and Information Science Research, 7*(1):3–30, January–March 1985.

Dubois, C. P. R. "Free Text vs. Controlled Vocabulary: A Reassessment." *Online Review, 11*(4):243–253, August 1987.

Durkin, Kay, et al. "An Experiment to Study the Online Use of a Full-Text Primary Journal Database." In: *Proceedings of the 4th International Online Information Meeting, 9–11 December, 1980, London, England.* Oxford, Eng., Learned Information, Ltd., 1980, pp. 53–56.

Elchesen, Dennis R. "Cost-Effectiveness Comparison of Manual and On-Line Retrospective Bibliographic Searching." *Journal of the American Society for Information Science, 29*(2):56–66, March 1978.

Estabrook, Leigh Stewart. "Valuing a Document Delivery System." *RQ, 26*(1):58–62, Fall 1986.

Ewbank, W. Bruce. "Comparison Guide to Selection of Databases and Database Services." *Drexel Library Quarterly, 18*(3–4):189–204, Summer–Fall 1982.

Fenichel, Carol Hansen. "Online Information Retrieval: Identification of Measures that Discriminate Among Users with Different Levels and Types of Experience." Doctoral Dissertation. Philadelphia, Pa., Drexel University, 1979.

─────────. "An Examination of the Relationship Between Searching Behavior and Searcher Background." *Online Review, 4*(4):341–347, December 1980a.

─────────. "Intermediary Searchers' Satisfaction with the Results of Their Searches." In: *Proceedings of the American Society for Information Science Conference, Anaheim, California, October 5–10, 1980.* Vol. 17. *Communicating Information.* New York, Knowledge Industry Publications, 1980b, pp. 58–60.

─────────. "Online Searching: Measures that Discriminate Among Users with Different Types of Experience." *Journal of the American Society for Information Science, 32*(1):23–32, January 1981.

Fenichel, Carol Hansen, and Thomas H. Hogan. *Online Searching: A Primer.* Medford,

N.J., Learned Information, 1981, pp. 67–76.

Fidel, Raya. "Online Searching Styles: A Case-Study-Based Model of Searching Behavior." *Journal of the American Society for Information Science, 35*(4):211–221, July 1984.

Fitzgerald, Evelyn L. C. "The Value of the Search Request Form in the Negotiation Process Between Requester and Librarian." Doctoral Dissertation. Urbana, Ill., University of Illinois, 1981.

Foreman, Gertrude, and Carol Baldwin. "Use of Multiple Data Bases in Bibliographic Services." *Bulletin of the Medical Library Association, 64*(1):55–57, January 1976.

Fosdick, Howard. "An SDC-Based On-Line Search Service: A Patron Evaluation Survey and Implications." *Special Libraries, 68*(9):305–312, September 1977.

Funk, Mark E., and C. A. Reid. "Indexing Consistency in MEDLINE." *Bulletin of the Medical Library Association, 71*(2):176–183, April 1983.

Gardner, Trudy A., and Judy A. Siebert. "Consumer Health Information Needs and Access Through Existing Indexes." *RQ, 20*(4):366–372, Summer 1981.

Genova, Bissy. *Nonverbal Behaviors in Presearch Interviews: A Report of the Presearch Interview Project.* Syracuse, N.Y., Syracuse University, School of Information Studies, April 1981. ERIC ED205188

Germann, Malcolm P.; Elizabeth Nowak; and Janet Stoeger Wilke. "Form Design Simplifies Online Search Services Procedures." *Information Technology and Libraries, 6*(4):313–316, December 1987.

Gruner, Richard, and Carol E. Heron. "New Resources for Computer-Aided Legal Research: An Assessment of the Usefulness of the DIALOG System in Securities Regulation Studies." *Database, 7*(4):13–29, December 1984.

Harris, Margaret A. "Sequence Analysis of Moves in Online Searching." *Canadian Journal of Information Science, 11*(2):35–56, 1986.

Hawkins, Donald T. "Multiple Database Searching: Techniques and Pitfalls." *Online, 2*(2):9–15, April 1978.

_____. "Online Information Retrieval Bibliography: Sixth Update." *Online Review, 7*(2):127–187, April 1983.

Hersey, David F., et al. "Comparison of On-Line Retrieval Using Free Text Words and Scientist Indexing." In: *The Information Conscious Society: Proceedings of the American Society for Information Science 33rd Annual Meeting: 11–15 October 1970, Philadelphia, Pa.* Washington, D.C., American Society for Information Science, 1970, pp. 265–268.

_____. "Free Text Word Retrieval and Scientist Indexing: Performance Profiles and Costs." *Journal of Documentation, 27*(3):167–183, September 1971.

Hilchey, Susan E., and Jitka M. Hurych. "User Satisfaction or User Acceptance? Statistical Evaluation of an Online Reference Service." *RQ, 24*(4):452–459, Summer 1985.

Hitchingham, Eileen E. "Selecting Measures Applicable to Evaluation of On-Line Literature Searching." *Drexel Library Quarterly, 13*(3):52–67, July 1977.

Hodges, Pauline R. "Keyword in Title Indexes: Effectivenes of Retrieval in Computer Searches." *Special Libraries, 74*(1):56–60, January 1983.

Hood, William. "Full-Text Searching in Bibliographic Databases." *LASIE, 18*(2):42–48, September–October 1987.

Hoover, Ryan E. "Patron Appraisal of Computer-Aided On-Line Bibliographic Retrieval Services." *Journal of Library Automation,* 9(4):335–350, December 1976.

Houlson, Van C., and John J. Jax. "An Automatic Current Awareness Service: The Stout Experience." Menomonie, Wis., University of Wisconsin–Stout, 1987. ERIC ED283523

Howard, Helen. "Measures that Discriminate Among Online Searchers with Different Training and Experience." *Online Review,* 6(4):315–327, August 1982.

Hunter, J. A. "Quantifiable Characteristics of Bibliographic Databases." *Information Services and Use,* 1(1):31–43, March 1981.

Individualized Instruction for Data Access. Philadelphia, Pa., Drexel University, School of Library and Information Science, and Franklin Institute Research Laboratories, 1978.

Jahoda, Gerald; Alan Bayer; and William L. Needham. "A Comparison of On-line Bibliographic Searches in One Academic and One Industrial Organization." *RQ,* 18(1):42–49, Fall 1978.

Jensen, Rebecca J.; Herbert O. Asbury; and Radford G. King. "Costs and Benefits to Industry of Online Literature Searches." *Special Libraries,* 71(7):291–299, July 1980.

Katzer, Jeffrey. "The Cost-Performance of an On-Line, Free-Text Bibliographic Retrieval System." *Information Storage and Retrieval,* 9(6):321–329, June 1973.

Katzer, Jeffrey, et al. *A Study of the Impact of Representations in Information Retrieval Systems.* Syracuse, N.Y., Syracuse University, 1982.

Kerhuel, Marie-Christine. "Un Ticket Valable sur Toutes les Lignes." (A Ticket Valid on All Lines.) *Bulletin des Bibliotheques de France,* 31(6):580–585, 1986.

Kobelski, Pamela, and Jean Trumbore. "Student Use of Online Bibliographic Services." *Journal of Academic Librarianship,* 4(1):14–18, March 1978.

Lancaster, F. W. *Evaluation of the MEDLARS Demand Search Service.* Bethesda, Md., National Library of Medicine, 1968.

—————. "Evaluation of On-Line Searching in MEDLARS (AIM-TWX) by Biomedical Practitioners." Urbana, Ill., University of Illinois, Graduate School of Library Science, 1972.

—————. *The Measurement and Evaluation of Library Services.* Arlington, Va., Information Resources Press, 1977.

—————. "Some Considerations Relating to the Cost-Effectiveness of Online Services in Libraries." *Aslib Proceedings,* 33(1):10–14, January 1981.

—————. *If You Want to Evaluate Your Library . . .* Champaign, Ill., University of Illinois, Graduate School of Library and Information Science, 1988.

—————. *Indexing and Abstracting in Theory and Practice.* Champaign, Ill., University of Illinois, Graduate School of Library and Information Science, 1991.

Lantz, Brian E. "The Relationship Between Documents Read and Relevant References Retrieved as Effectiveness Measures for Information Retrieval Systems." *Journal of Documentation,* 37(3):134–145, September 1981.

Lawrence, Barbara; Ben H. Weil; and Margaret H. Graham. "Making On-Line Search Available in an Industrial Research Environment." *Journal of the American Society for Information Science,* 25(6):364–369, November–December 1974.

Lehman, Lois J., and M. Sandra Wood. "Effect of Fees on an Information Service for Physicians." *Bulletin of the Medical Library Association,* 66(1):58–61, January 1978.

Lloyd, D. A. "Scientists and Information: How They Get It." *Bibliotheca Medica Canadiana,* 9(4):198–202, 1988.

Maina, William E. "Undergraduate Use of Online Bibliographic Retrieval Services: Experiences at the University of California, San Diego." *Online,* 1(2):45–50, April 1977.

Markee, Katherine M. "Economies of Online Retrieval." *Online Review,* 5(6):439–444, December 1981.

Markey, Karen, and Pauline Atherton. "ONTAP: Online Training and Practice Manual for ERIC Data Base Searchers." Syracuse, N.Y., Syracuse University, 1978. ERIC ED160109

Martin, W. A. "A Comparative Study of Terminal User Techniques in Four European Countries on a Large Common On-Line Interactive Information Retrieval System." In: *First European Congress on Documentation Systems and Networks, Luxembourg, 16th, 17th, and 18th May 1973.* Luxembourg, Commission of the European Communities, 1974, pp. 107–164.

Martyn, John, and Margaret Slater. "Tests on Abstracts Journals." *Journal of Documentation,* 20(4):212–235, December 1964.

Matzek, Dick, and Scott Smith. "Online Searching in the Small College Library—The Economics and the Results." *Online,* 6(2):21–29, March 1982.

McCain, Katherine W.; Howard D. White; and Belver C. Griffith. "Comparing Retrieval Performance in Online Data Bases." *Information Processing and Management,* 23(6):539–553, 1987.

McCue, Janice Helen. *Online Searching in Public Libraries: A Comparative Study of Performance.* Metuchen, N.J., Scarecrow Press, 1988.

McGill, Michael J. *An Evaluation of Factors Affecting Document Ranking by Information Retrieval Systems.* Syracuse, N.Y., Syracuse University, 1979. NTIS Report PB80-119506

Meadow, Charles T., and Pauline Atherton Cochrane. *Basics of Online Searching.* New York, Wiley, 1981.

Michaels, C. J. "Searching CA Condensates On-Line vs. the CA Keyword Indexes." *Journal of Chemical Information and Computer Science,* 15(3):172–173, August 1975.

Morris, Ruth Traister; Edwin A. Holtum; and David S. Curry. "Being There: The Effect of the User's Presence on MEDLINE Search Results." *Bulletin of the Medical Library Association,* 70(3):298–304, July 1982.

Naber, G. "Online versus Manual Literature Retrieval: A Test Case Shows Interesting Results in Retrieval Effectiveness and Search Strategy." *Database,* 8(1):20–24, February 1985.

Nielsen, Thomas Brian. "The Impact of a User Fee on Librarian Responsiveness: An Examination of Online Bibliographic Searching and Reference Practice." Doctoral Dissertation. Chapel Hill, N.C., University of North Carolina, 1983.

Oberhauser, Otto. "Klassifikation in Online-Informationssystemen." (Classification in Online Information Systems.) *International Classification,* 13(2):79–87, 1986.

Oldroyd, Betty K., and Charles L. Citroen. "Study of Strategies Used in On-Line Searching." *Online Review,* 1(4):295–310, December 1977.

Olive, G., et al. "Studies to Compare Retrieval Using Titles with that Using Index Terms." *Journal of Documentation,* 29(2):169–191, June 1973.

Oppenheim, C. "The Performance of the *Chemical Abstracts* Subject and Formula Indexes in Retrieving Compounds Disclosed in Chemical Patents." *Information Scientist, 9*(3):107–111, September 1975. Errata, *10*(1):31–32, March 1976.

Penniman, William David. "Rhythms of Dialogue in Human-Computer Conversation." Doctoral Dissertation. Columbus, Ohio, Ohio State University, 1975.

Pollitt, Arthur Steven. "CANCERLINE Evaluation Project: Final Report." Leeds, Eng., University of Leeds School of Medicine, Medical Library, 1977.

Roose, Tina. "A Month of Searches." *Library Journal, 110*(4):66–67, March 1, 1985.

Rudd, Joel, and Mary Jo Rudd. "Coping with Information Load: User Strategies and Implications for Librarians." *College and Research Libraries, 47*(4):315–322, July 1986.

Ruhl, Mary Jane, and Elizabeth J. Yeates. "Introducing and Implementing Online Bibliographic Retrieval Services in a Scientific Research and Development Organisation." *Journal of Chemical Information and Computer Science, 16*(3):147–150, August 1976.

Salton, G., and R. K. Waldstein. "Term Relevance Weights in On-Line Information Retrieval." *Information Processing and Management, 14*(1):29–35, 1978.

Saracevic, Tefko, and Paul Kantor. "A Study of Information Seeking and Retrieving: III. Searchers, Searches, and Overlap." *Journal of the American Society for Information Science, 39*(3):197–216, May 1988.

Scheffler, F. L., and J. F. March. "Evaluation of the Selective Dissemination of Information (SDI) Program for the Aerospace Materials Information Center." Dayton, Ohio, University of Dayton Research Institute, March 1971. Report No. AFML-TR-71-11. ERIC ED050775

Schroder, J. J. "Study of Strategies Used in Online Searching: 3. Query Refining." *Online Review, 7*(3):229–236, June 1983.

Sewell, Winifred, and Alice Bevan. "Nonmediated Use of MEDLINE and TOXLINE by Pathologists and Pharmacists." *Bulletin of the Medical Library Association, 64*(4):382–391, October 1976.

Shaw, Debora. "Nine Sources of Problems for Novice Online Searchers." *Online Review, 10*(5):295–303, October 1986.

Snow, Bonnie, and Steven L. Ifshin. "Online Database Coverage of Forensic Medicine." *Online, 8*(2):37–43, March 1984.

Soergel, Dagobert. "Is User Satisfaction a Hobgoblin?" *Journal of the American Society for Information Science, 27*(4):256–259, July–August 1976.

Somerville, Arleen N. "The Place of the Reference Interview in Computer Searching: The Academic Setting." *Online, 1*(4):14–23, October 1977.

_____. "The Pre-Search Reference Interview—A Step by Step Guide." *Database, 5*(1):32–38, February 1982.

Stein, D., et al. "Full Text Online Patent Searching: Results of a USPTO Experiment." In: *Online '82 Conference, Proceedings, 1–3 November 1982, Atlanta, Georgia.* Weston, Conn., Online, Inc., 1982, pp. 289–294.

Summit, Roger K., and Oscar Firschein. "Fee for Online Retrieval Service in a Public Library Setting." In: *Information Revolution: The 38th ASIS Annual Meeting.* Vol. 12. Edited by Charles W. Husbands and Ruth L. Tighe. Washington, D.C., American Society for Information Science, 1975, p. 155.

—————. "Public Library Use of Online Bibliographic Retrieval Services: Experience in Four Public Libraries in Northern California." *Online, 1*(4):58–62, October 1977.

Swanson, Don R. "Subjective Versus Objective Relevance in Bibliographic Retrieval Systems." *Library Quarterly, 56*(4):389–398, October 1986.

Tenopir, Carol. "Retrieval Performance in a Full Text Journal Article Database." Doctoral Dissertation. Urbana, Ill., University of Illinois, 1984.

—————. "Full Text Database Retrieval Performance." *Online Review, 9*(2):149–164, April 1985.

Terrant, Seldon W., et al. "ACS Primary Journal Online Database." In: *Proceedings of the Fourth National Online Meeting: 12–14 April 1983, New York.* Edited by Martha E. Williams and Thomas H. Hogan. Medford, N.J., Learned Information, 1983, p. 551.

Tessier, Judith A. "Satisfaction Measures in Presearch Interviews." Syracuse, N.Y., Syracuse University, School of Information Studies, 1981. ERIC ED205186

Tessier, Judith; Wayne W. Crouch; and Pauline Atherton. "New Measures of User Satisfaction with Computer-Based Literature Searches." *Special Libraries, 68*(11): 383–389, November 1977.

Truelson, Judith A. "Applying Benefit-Cost Analysis to Online Ready Reference: The Los Angeles Public Library Experience." In: *National Online Meeting Proceedings, New York, April 10–12, 1984.* Medford, N.J., Learned Information, 1984, pp. 395–403.

Trzebiatowski, Elaine. "End User Study on BRS/After Dark." *RQ, 23*(4):446–450, Summer 1984.

Tso, P. S. "On-Line Information Services in the University of Hong Kong Libraries: Three Years Experience." *International Library Review, 16*(2):175–182, April 1984.

Universiti Sains Malaysia Library. "The Evaluation of SISMAKOM (Computerized SDI Project)." Paris, United Nations Educational, Scientific, and Cultural Organization, 1983. Report No. PGI-83/WS/16. ERIC ED241060

Van Camp, Ann J., and Gertrude Foreman. "BIOSIS Previews and MEDLARS—A Biomedical Team." *Online, 1*(1):24–31, 40–42, January 1977.

Vigil, Peter J. *Online Retrieval Analysis and Strategy.* New York, Wiley, 1988.

Wanger, Judith; Dennis McDonald; and Mary C. Berger. *Evaluation of the Online Search Process: A Final Report.* Santa Monica, Calif., Cuadra Associates, 1980. NTIS Report PB 81-132565

Warden, Carolyn L. "User Evaluation of a Corporate Library Online Search Service." *Special Libraries, 72*(2):113–117, April 1981.

White, Howard D. "Cocited Author Retrieval." *Information Technology and Libraries, 5*(2):93–99, June 1986.

White, Howard D., and Belver C. Griffith. "Quality of Indexing in Online Data Bases." *Information Processing and Management, 23*(3):211–224, 1987.

Wilson, Patrick. "Situational Relevance." *Information Storage and Retrieval, 9*(8):457–471, August 1973.

—————. "Some Fundamental Concepts of Information Retrieval." *Drexel Library Quarterly, 14*(2):10–24, April 1978.

CHAPTER 10

THE RELEVANCE OF STANDARDS TO THE EVALUATION OF LIBRARY SERVICES

Lynch (1982) writes that "Standards for libraries generally are used for purposes of evaluation. Thus, the task of designing a set of standards becomes the task of designing an instrument of evaluation" (p. 46). This strongly suggests that standards have an important role to play in the evaluation of library services. In this chapter, the discussion will focus on how standards are developed and used in an attempt to determine whether or not this is true.

Standards are essential to the successful conduct of many activities, especially manufacturing, maintenance, and engineering operations. But they have potential value in virtually all fields, and library science is no exception. Library standards differ markedly from industrial and engineering standards. The latter are generally precise and enforceable; a product is manufactured to satisfy the requirement of some standard (in terms of composition or mechanical or physical properties, for example). When applied to libraries, however, *standards* refers to a set of guidelines or recommended practices, developed by a group of experts, that serve as a model for good library service. The work of these experts generally is sponsored and promoted by professional associations at the state, regional, national or international level. But few of these associations attempt to actually enforce the standards.

Library standards can be categorized into two broad types:

1. *Technical standards* are uniform practices that libraries have adopted to accomplish certain work well. They include cataloging codes, rules for thesaurus construction, and standards for the representation of bibliographic data in machine-readable form. *Library Trends* (Rush, 1982) reviewed many of these standards, and Paul (1984) provided a simple overview of the process for creating technical standards.

2. *Performance standards* are more general statements that are related to the quality or quantity of services offered. They usually are written for libraries of a particular type. One notable example is *Information Power: Guidelines for School Library Media Programs* (American Association of School Librarians, 1988).

Technical standards have little real relevance to evaluation; a library either follows them or it does not. Therefore, this chapter focuses on performance standards.

Performance standards were envisioned as a way to help speed library development by providing librarians with suggested levels of services and collections (statements of what ought to be) against which to measure their own libraries. Librarians then could focus their efforts on areas that were found to be inadequate, using the standards to support requests for increased funding from the library's governing body (Bloss, 1980; Knightly, 1979; McClure, 1980). For example, a school librarian receiving $4.20 per capita for materials could show the school principal that the state standards specified an expenditure of $6.00 per capita.

Librarians have also used standards as a kind of preset agenda to aid in setting goals and planning for improvements. Thus, if the state's public library standards call for library facilities to be located within 10 miles of every county resident, the library director may set a long-term goal of adding a small branch in an isolated corner of the county. Standards also may assist with the establishment of new services or the spread of new ideas. For example, the document *Minimum Standards for Public Library Systems, 1966* (American Library Association, 1967) was instrumental in promoting the concept that larger library units could provide better service.

Standards may be written to address many aspects of library service or to focus on a specific aspect. A recent set of public library standards for the state of Iowa addressed the library's finances, administration, public relations, materials, accessibility, physical facilities, reference services, and outreach programs (State Library of Iowa, 1985). In contrast, the Public Library Association issued "Guidelines for Establishing Community Information and Referral Services in Public Libraries" (Public Library Association, 1986). The Association of College and Research Libraries (ACRL) has adopted a number of specialized standards, including those for bibliographic instruction; for ethical conduct of rare book, manuscript, and special collections librarians; and for the handling of thefts (Association of College and Research Libraries, 1977, 1987, 1988). Other standards are predicated on the fact that the services of a library are only as good as the staff that provides them. Thus, personnel standards cover the minimum qualifications required for various types of positions, hours of employment, vacations, and promotions. One set of national personnel guidelines is *Library Education and Personnel Utilization* (American Library Association, 1976).

ISSUES IN COMPILING STANDARDS

Library standards have been the source of considerable controversy ever since the first standard (for school libraries) was issued early in this century (Certain, 1917). Five major questions have dominated the discussion of the form that standards should take. Each is addressed in turn.

Should Standards Be Qualitative or Quantitative?

Most standards documents today are both qualitative and quantitative. Qualitative standards are general statements of principle about what constitutes good library service. For example, the 1979 guidelines for university libraries in the United States contain the following requirement: "A university library's collections shall be of sufficient size and scope to support the university's total instructional needs and to facilitate the university's research programs" (Association of College and Research Libraries, 1979a, p. 102).

Such standards appropriately reinforce general principles that libraries should follow and may be useful when the libraries to which the standards apply are so diverse that they can agree on nothing but these principles. For example, the "Standards for University Libraries" issued by the International Federation of Library Associations (1987) were designed to meet the needs of universities of all sizes, with differing goals, in both developed and third world countries. Generally, however, qualitative standards contain too many subjective criteria (for example, "sufficient size") to be of any real use in evaluation. Vague statements have little practical value in helping librarians determine at what level their library is performing. Two examples illustrate this point. Originally, the 1972 edition of "Guidelines for Two-Year College Learning Resources Programs" included only qualitative standards. Seven years later, however, the Association of College and Research Libraries (1979b) issued supplementary quantitative standards to meet recurring requests for quantitative figures to help in planning and evaluating programs. These proved so popular that the 1982 revision of the guidelines included both qualitative and quantitative standards (Association of College and Research Libraries, 1982a, 1982b).

The impracticality of issuing a standards document that contains only qualitative measures was also illustrated by Lynch (1982), who surveyed university library directors in the United States about their use of "Standards for University Libraries" (Association of College and Research Libraries, 1979a). Of 184 questionnaires submitted, only 88 (48 percent) were completed, not a very strong endorsement of interest in qualitative standards. Although 82 percent of the respondents were familiar with the standards, 54 percent of all respondents indicated that they made no use of them whatsoever, and the majority claimed that they found them to be of little practical use.

FORMULA A

1. Basic collection	85,000 vols.
2. Allowance per FTE faculty member	100 vols.
3. Allowance per FTE student	15 vols.
4. Allowance per undergraduate major or minor field*	350 vols.
5. Allowance per master's field, when no higher degree is offered in the field*	6,000 vols.
6. Allowance per master's field, when a higher degree is offered in the field*	3,000 vols.
7. Allowance per 6th year specialist degree field*	6,000 vols.
8. Allowance per doctoral field*	25,000 vols.

A "volume" is defined as a physical unit of a work which has been printed or otherwise reproduced, typewritten, or handwritten, contained in one binding or portfolio, hardbound or paperbound, which has been catalogued, classified, or otherwise prepared for use. Microform holdings should be converted to volume-equivalents, whether by actual count or by an averaging formula which considers each reel of microfilm, or ten pieces of any other microform, as one volume-equivalent.

*For example of List of Fields, see Gerald S. Malitz, *A Classification of Instructional Programs*. Washington, D.C.: National Center for Education Statistics, 1981.

EXHIBIT 10-1   Formula A for determining the adequacy of college library collections. Reprinted from Association of College and Research Libraries (1986), courtesy of the American Library Association.

In contrast, the last few editions of "Standards for College Libraries" have contained both qualitative and quantitative standards (Association of College and Research Libraries, 1986). The former give guiding principles for good library service, and the latter set out precise definitions of what good library service is. For example, one of the quantitative standards suggests a certain size of core collection, with a specific (minimum) number of volumes to be added for each full-time-equivalent faculty member, student, and field of study (Exhibit 10-1). Studies have found that such quantitative standards are viewed much more positively by library directors, who can use them to evaluate their own services and resources and to argue for increased funding to improve areas where inadequacies exist. Hardesty and Bentley (1981) found that more than 94 percent of the directors were aware of the college library standards, more than 83 percent thought they were useful or moderately useful, and only 13 percent had not used them to improve their libraries.

Not all aspects of library service are easily quantifiable (for example, having a friendly staff); however, many aspects are, including

1. *The size of the collection.* Size can be related to the size of the population served in a very direct way (for example, in the case of a public library) or in a more complex way that takes into account diversity in the groups that make up the population (for example, in an academic setting, doctoral students, although relatively few, require much greater and wider resources than undergraduates).

2. *The size and composition of the staff.* This can also be related to the population served.

3. *The budget of the library* related to some larger budget (for example, of the school, university, company, or city) or to the population served.

4. *The space occupied by the library* and, a special aspect of space, seating capacity. Overall space and seating capacity can both be related to the population served.

Should Standards Be Based on the Best Thinking of the Profession or on the Best Empirical Research?

In the past, it was common for a standards committee to meet, confer, and set certain standards on the basis of their collective expertise and with no reference to current research showing what libraries were currently doing. One major problem these committees faced was reaching agreement on the numbers to go into any kind of quantifiable standard. For example, Vaughan (1982), referring to work performed in the United Kingdom by the Public Libraries Research Group (PLRG), mentioned that one proposed standard was to ensure that books and material wanted by children were immediately available in *n* percent of cases. Unfortunately, PLRG was never able to agree on the value that should be assigned to *n*.

When standards committees do reach agreement, it usually is after a number of compromises have been made. Therefore, the resulting standards are mixed in quality. Many of the suggestions reveal the depth of experience and knowledge of committee members about what good library service should be. But others are not as well received. Critics feel that some standards are formed by arbitrary value judgments, whereas others are based on assumptions, reflect the personal prejudices or vested interests of individual committee members, or are set unrealistically high relative to current practice. For example, the National Commission on Libraries and Information Science recommended that two-year colleges should have a minimum collection of 40,000 volumes, augmented by additional items for each full-time faculty member and student and for each field of study; almost all two-year institutions were deficient when measured against this standard (Wallace, 1982). Standards with these types of flaws may (justifiably) be ignored.

A growing number of standards committees have addressed these concerns during the last two decades. Most are beginning to realize that the most realistic and authoritative standards are written after an examination of statistical and research data documenting current library practices. The Downs Committee, charged with the task of proposing standards for university libraries, identified 50 leading institutions in North America and collected from them data on finances, resources, personnel, space, and circulation (Lynch, 1982). Other standards committees—for instance, those that developed public library standards in Illinois and in North Carolina—have examined average resource and performance levels before setting quantitative standards (Illinois Library Association, 1989; North Carolina Library Association and North Carolina Public Library Directors Association, 1988).

Should Standards Be Set at Minimum or Optimal Levels of Adequacy?

In the past, many of the standards promoted by professional library associations were minimum requirements; they suggested levels of adequacy rather than excellence. They were designed to stimulate and improve future library development, particularly the development of substandard libraries ("laggards") that could use the recommendations to show funding sources how much they needed to improve. Such minimum standards still are supported by librarians in smaller, less-efficient organizations (Lynch, 1982).

Unfortunately, quantitative standards or formulas of this type can be misinterpreted. Although they are intended to prescribe minimum requirements, some funding bodies have used minimum standards against wealthier libraries, reducing levels of financial support and impeding growth and expansion on the grounds that these libraries already exceeded the standards. Some years ago, for example, the State University of New York libraries had to argue strongly against having the size of their collections restricted to the minimum levels set out in a set of academic library standards (State University of New York, 1970). "Leader" libraries actually could suffer financially if their performance was compared with levels specified by minimum standards (Bloss, 1980).

One solution to the "laggards versus leaders" dilemma is to include both minimum and diagnostic standards. Diagnostic (or benchmark) standards specify normative practices beyond the minimal level toward which libraries may strive. They are based on models of conditions present in libraries that are thought to be in some sense "good." They generally are used to allow comparison with other institutions for self-evaluation. Because they represent existing conditions, these standards are valid and beneficial only when constantly updated and revised.

Many of the more recent standards documents appropriately include both minimum and diagnostic elements. For example, the Illinois public library standards (Illinois Library Association, 1989) include quantitative standards for libraries that are striving to meet a "C" (minimum) level, an "A" (excellence) level, or a "B" (in-between) level of performance. "Guidelines for Two-Year College Learning Resources Programs" (Association of College and Research

Libraries, 1982a, 1982b) lists standards for five levels of adequacy, ranging from minimum to outstanding.

Should Standards Measure Input or Output?

Because of a general (and mostly unsubstantiated) belief that increased resources result in better service, many older standards focused on resources (inputs) instead of services. But critics have correctly noted that input standards are institution oriented rather than user oriented and therefore do not necessarily deal with the library's effectiveness or the quality of its services (Hamburg et al., 1974; Bloss, 1980). An input standard might recommend, for example, that a public library serving 5,000 patrons should receive at least $50,000 in operating funds. It is possible, however, for two similar public libraries, serving the same number of patrons and receiving the same funding, to provide very different levels of service. Recently, standards have begun to address the quantity and quality of direct patron service (output). An output standard might recommend, for instance, that 75 percent of the reference questions received be answered completely and accurately. The trend toward the use of output measures is a positive one, because it is only these standards that consider library effectiveness.

How Can Standards Be Written to Allow for the Diversity of Individual Libraries?

There is great diversity among the communities and institutions that libraries serve and, therefore, among the goals and requirements of different libraries. This individuality makes it possible to adapt library services to meet local needs but poses a very real problem in the formulation of state and national standards. For evaluation purposes, standards should be precise, quantifiable, and measurable. But there is the danger that precise, quantifiable standards would equalize all institutions and generalize libraries without taking into account differences attributable to local conditions. Standards that might help one library may stultify another.

Consider, for example, the paradoxical nature of special library standards: the word *special* implies uniqueness, and the word *standard* implies generality. Because special libraries, as a group, are so heterogeneous, any attempt to define common elements inevitably leads to meaningless generalities. Special libraries have widely differing objectives and use a variety of means to achieve them. No single set of standards could apply equally to all special libraries, which explains why no comprehensive standards have been issued since "Objectives and Standards for Special Libraries," a set of general guiding principles, was published by the Special Libraries Association (1964). Some individual sets of standards, however, have been issued for various types of special library services, such as *Standards for Libraries at Institutions for the Mentally*

Retarded (Association of Specialized and Cooperative Library Agencies, 1981) and *Revised Standards and Guidelines of Service for the Library of Congress Network of Libraries for the Blind and Physically Handicapped* (Association of Specialized and Cooperative Library Agencies, 1984).

Academic libraries have dealt with the problem of creating standards to meet local conditions in several ways. For example, they have realized that different types of academic libraries have different purposes and have adopted different sets of standards, reflecting the needs of two-year colleges and four-year colleges and universities (Association of College and Research Libraries, 1979a, 1982a, 1982b, 1986). The standards committee for the most diverse of these three groups, university libraries, eventually wrote qualitative standards, reasoning that local needs could be met only if each library had great leeway in defining good library service.

Public and school libraries have adopted a somewhat different approach. In 1974, two authors argued that the Public Library Association (PLA) should depart from its normal approach to standards and develop instead a process that would allow libraries to "(1) understand the particular community they are serving; (2) choose objectives in the light of that understanding; and (3) measure the degree to which these objectives are being met" (Blasingham and Lynch, 1974, p. 6). Currently, PLA does not issue national standards for public libraries. Instead, it encourages libraries to use two tools to develop their own performance measures. The first, a manual entitled *Planning and Role Setting for Public Libraries* (McClure et al., 1987), guides librarians through the process of analyzing the needs of their communities, choosing the "roles" on which they want to concentrate (for example, a popular materials center), and setting goals and objectives to effectively provide these services. The second, *Output Measures for Public Libraries* (Van House et al., 1987), describes procedures for collecting data that indicate the quantity or quality of service provided (for example, title fill rate, document delivery rate, and in-library materials use). The new standards for school library media centers (American Association of School Librarians, 1988) follow a similar approach, emphasizing a planning philosophy based on the needs of individual libraries and including quantitative recommendations only when they are supported by professional research and consensus.

Although many individual librarians applaud the new direction of standards for public and school libraries, not all of them feel comfortable with dropping prescriptive standards entirely. They still want published quantitative figures to help them argue for additional resources when their services are less than optimum. Some efforts are now ongoing to collect quantitative data that can indicate service norms. For example, Zweizig reported the data collected by a self-selected sample of public libraries nationally (1985a) and a sample of children's departments in Wisconsin (1985b). The usual scope of such collection efforts is small; however, PLA is working to establish a national cooperative system of public library data collection by persuading state libraries to coordinate their annual collection of public library statistics and to use uniform definitions in their collection efforts. PLA then plans to create a national database from which librarians can obtain comparative data with which to evaluate their libraries. In the meantime, at least 40 states still retain prescriptive standards to provide public librarians with quantitative figures that they can use to argue for increased resources (Weech, 1988).

OTHER PROBLEMS WITH CURRENT STANDARDS

Committees writing standards and evaluators using standards need to recognize several other potential problems. First, the definitions used in some standards are not as clear as needed. For standards to be used effectively, they must convey the same meaning and purpose, whether they are read by librarians, administrators, committee members, or others.

Second, some standards have been written for libraries of an indiscriminate (medium) size, failing to reflect the needs of large and small libraries. This problem is easily corrected by setting various standards by size of population served. For example, Weech (1988) indicated that most of the state standards for public libraries have set lower minimum standards for small libraries, reflecting the realities of support levels in these institutions.

Third, although some standards (for example, those relating to dollar figures) may quickly become obsolete, they tend to be used as norms for many years. This may impose rigidity on the profession by freezing practices at present levels. Therefore, standards should be revised frequently to reflect changing needs. Some organizations have speeded up their revision calendars; ACRL's 1959 edition of "Standards for College Libraries" was not updated for 16 years, but the 1975 edition was updated 11 years later. Alternatively, standards could be written with built-in correction devices. For example, if a dollar figure is used within the standards documents, a statement could be added that the figure needs to be adjusted annually for inflation.

Fourth, there is often no enforcement of standards. Rohlf (1982) compared hospitals and libraries. If a hospital fails to meet standards, it is closed; no such fate faces the library. This may be a reflection of the low value accorded to libraries by society or that libraries operate in a noncompetitive environment.

Because standards must be used to be effective, it is not surprising that standards-making bodies now are encouraging research to determine how many libraries fail to meet certain minimum standards and how many libraries ignore the standards altogether. For example, White (1986) determined that libraries in the 19 state universities in California met the minimum requirements listed in "Standards for College Libraries" in the areas of total collection size and volumes added; however, one-third failed to meet the standards for adequate personnel. The Illinois State Library has recently begun listing, in its annual analysis of public library statistics, the number of libraries that fail to meet selected minimum standards. This excellent practice pinpoints areas of inadequacy and allows corrective action to be taken. For example, after realizing that most public libraries did not meet the stock turnover rate standards, the state library sponsored experimental research to see how these rates could be increased. It then distributed study findings, at no charge, to all public libraries in the state (Roy, 1987). Several states, including Illinois, have adopted policies of reducing or denying state aid if a library fails to meet certain minimum standards. Library leaders in other states, not wishing to remove state aid from those libraries that may benefit the most from it, are trying other ways to encourage compliance with standards. For example, public libraries in Iowa that meet the state standards are "accredited" and benefit from whatever local publicity the accreditation generates.

National library associations, which have no formal authority over individual libraries, use various strategies to educate librarians about, and persuade them to adopt, national standards. PLA has issued a manual that teaches library leaders how to train others in the use of the role-setting and output measures manual (O'Donnell, 1988), and the American Association of School Librarians has promoted its standards through a national teleconference. One idea that has great potential is the linking of national standards to state standards. Baker (1987) studied the use of PLA's planning process and output measures in the state of North Carolina. She found that only one-quarter of the library directors were using the recommended five-year planning cycle and that less than half were measuring service levels with specific output measures. The lack of use was believed to be due to several different factors, most notably the lack of promotion of the measures within the state and the lack of staff time and expertise to collect those measures that required the use of a separate survey and a reasonable amount of time for data collection and analysis. Baker suggested that the state library, the North Carolina Library Association, and the North Carolina Public Library Directors Association work together to promote the use of the national standards by

- Adopting proposed state standards that recommend the use of the planning process and output measures
- Developing continuing education programs to promote the standards
- Adopting a formula tying performance on certain standards to state aid
- Revising the annual statistical report completed by public libraries to include measures of output
- Providing consulting assistance to libraries that need additional help in collecting data

Such recommendations, if followed, have the potential to encourage greatly the use of national standards within a particular state.

HAVE STANDARDS CAUSED SERVICES TO IMPROVE?

With such criticism and controversy, it is legitimate to question whether or not standards have benefited the library profession. To date, a number of authors have stated that they have (for example, Downs and Heussman, 1970), but little evidence is offered to support this point of view. A typical statement to this effect was made by Lynch (1982): "In 1959 only a few libraries in the 1,500 or so colleges in the United States could meet the minimums set forth in the standards. By 1970 these libraries had improved substantially in the very ways the standards proposed" (p. 33). Unfortunately, there is no clear causal link between the writing of standards and the improvement of libraries.

Existing standards may or may not have benefited the library profession to any significant extent. What is clear is that some types of standards are of limited value in the types of evaluation described in this book. The qualitative standards are too nebulous to be converted into objective evaluation criteria, whereas many quantitative standards deal with resources, which are linked only indirectly to the goodness of service in libraries. Only standards of output are related to the true studies of effectiveness that this book addresses. The future of standards as an evaluation tool, therefore, depends on the integration of output measures into standards documents.

It has been suggested that other associations would do well to adopt PLA's approach to standards; however, this approach has both strengths and weaknesses. On the one hand, the standards that libraries develop for themselves when using PLA's approach do not need to be limited to minimum levels of service. Moreover, the standards are flexible enough to consider the needs of different libraries (rural versus urban, large versus small, quality oriented versus demand oriented). The standards focus on the services given as well as the resources held and are quantifiable, thus facilitating evaluation. On the other hand, the PLA process is more concerned with the establishment of goals and objectives than with true evaluation of existing services. Moreover, the output measures recommended for use by PLA have several flaws. First, the data collection procedures have not been validated and may give inconsistent results. Second, the output measures included are only macroevaluation measures, telling what levels of service a library is attaining, but not why certain levels are attained; this makes it difficult to determine how to correct service flaws. Third, output measures are of limited use unless standards or norms are developed to indicate acceptable levels of performance for certain services in libraries of a certain size or in libraries concentrating on a particular role. For example, is an immediate title fill rate of

40 percent acceptable for a library that has chosen the role of popular materials center, or should it be 60 percent or 80 percent?

If PLA's envisioned national center for data collection comes to fruition, it could provide the norms of service on which true standards could be based. It is only when the flaws just reviewed are corrected that the standards will be useful in the types of evaluation discussed in this book.

SUMMARY AND CONCLUSIONS

Library performance standards tend to be guidelines rather than truly enforceable standards. The most useful standards are based on research about current practices at existing institutions; contain quantitative elements to supplement qualitative statements of principles of good library service; emphasize services (outputs) as well as resources (inputs); and are flexible enough to meet the needs of libraries of different types, with different purposes, and of different sizes and levels of resources. Library standards as they now exist are useful in providing evidence for budget requests. But they are often too general and imprecise to be used in the detailed evaluation of library services. Although the profession has improved standards immeasurably during the last 20 years, it must concentrate on developing standards that an institution can use to evaluate its own performance in relation to the needs of its user population; that is, standards or guidelines are needed for conducting the type of evaluative studies (effectiveness studies) discussed in this book. The approach adopted by PLA moves in this direction but does not go far enough. To improve overall quality, the profession must develop standards that reflect acceptable levels of output for various services—no easy task.

REFERENCES

American Association of School Librarians. *Information Power: Guidelines for School Library Media Programs.* Chicago, Ill., American Library Association, 1988.

American Library Association. *Minimum Standards for Public Library Systems, 1966.* Chicago, Ill., ALA, 1967.

_____. *Library Education and Personnel Utilization.* Chicago, Ill., ALA, 1976.

Association of College and Research Libraries. "Guidelines for Bibliographic Instruction in Academic Libraries." *College and Research Libraries News,* 38(4):92, April 1977.

_____. "Standards for University Libraries." *College and Research Libraries News,* 40(4):101–110, April 1979a.

_____. *Statement on Quantitative Standards for Two-Year Learning Resources Programs.* Chicago, Ill., ACRL, 1979b.

_____. "Guidelines for Two-Year College Learning Resources Programs (Revised), Part I." *College and Research Libraries News,* 43(1):5–10, January 1982a.

_____. "Guidelines for Two-Year College Learning Resources Programs (Revised), Part II." *College and Research Libraries News, 43*(2):45–49, February 1982b.

_____. "Standards for College Libraries, 1986." *College and Research Libraries News, 47*(3):189–200, March 1986.

_____. "Standards for Ethical Conduct for Rare Book, Manuscript, and Special Collections Librarians." *College and Research Libraries News, 48*(3):134–135, March 1987.

_____. "Guidelines Regarding Thefts in Libraries." *College and Research Libraries News, 49*(3):159–162, March 1988.

Association of Specialized and Cooperative Library Agencies. *Standards for Libraries at Institutions for the Mentally Retarded.* Chicago, Ill., ASCLA, 1981.

_____. *Revised Standards and Guidelines of Service for the Library of Congress Network of Libraries for the Blind and Physically Handicapped.* Chicago, Ill., American Library Association, 1984.

Baker, Sharon L. "Exploring the Use of *Output Measures for Public Libraries* in North Carolina Public Libraries." Iowa City, Ia., University of Iowa, School of Library and Information Science, 1987. ERIC ED288538

Blasingame, Ralph, Jr., and Mary Jo Lynch. "Design for Diversity: Alternatives to Standards for Public Libraries." *PLA Newsletter, 13*:4–22, June 1974.

Bloss, Meredith. "Research; and Standards for Library Service." *Library Research, 2*(4):285–308, Winter 1980.

Certain, C. C. "Standard Library Organization and Equipment for Secondary Schools of Different Sizes." *Educational Administration and Supervision, 3*:317–338, 1917.

Downs, Robert B., and John W. Heussman. "Standards for University Libraries." *College and Research Libraries, 31*(1):28–35, January 1970.

Hamburg, Morris, et al. *Library Planning and Decision-Making Systems.* Cambridge, Mass., MIT Press, 1974.

Hardesty, Larry, and Stella Bentley. "The Use and Effectiveness of the 1975 Standards for College Libraries: A Survey of College Library Directors." Unpublished paper presented at the Second National Conference of the Association of College and Research Libraries, October 2–3, 1981, Minneapolis, Minn.

Illinois Library Association. *Avenues to Excellence. II: Standards for Public Libraries in Illinois.* Springfield, Ill., ILA, 1989.

International Federation of Library Associations. "Standards for University Libraries." *IFLA Journal, 13*(2):120–125, May 1987.

Knightly, John J. "Overcoming the Criterion Problem in the Evaluation of Library Performance." *Special Libraries, 70*(4):173–178, April 1979.

Lynch, Beverly P. "University Library Standards." *Library Trends, 31*(1):33–47, Summer 1982.

McClure, Charles R. "From Public Library Standards to Development of Statewide Levels of Adequacy." *Library Research, 2*(1):47–62, Spring 1980.

McClure, Charles R., et al. *Planning and Role Setting for Public Libraries: A Manual of Options and Procedures.* Chicago, Ill., American Library Association, 1987.

North Carolina Library Association, Public Libraries Section, and North Carolina Public Library Directors Association. *Standards for North Carolina Public Libraries.* Raleigh, N.C., North Carolina Department of Cultural Resources, Division of State Library, 1988.

O'Donnell, Peggy. *Public Library Development Program, Manual for Trainers*. Chicago, Ill., American Library Association, 1988.

Paul, Sandra K. "Library Standards: An Introduction to Organizations and the Standards Process." *Library Hi Tech*, 2(3):87–90, 1984.

Public Library Association. "Guidelines for Establishing Community Information and Referral Services in Public Libraries." *Public Libraries*, 25(1):11–15, Spring 1986.

Rohlf, Robert H. "Standards for Public Libraries." *Library Trends*, 31(1):63–76, Summer 1982.

Roy, Loriene. "An Investigation of the Use of Weeding and Displays as Methods to Increase the Stock Turnover Rate in Small Public Libraries." *Illinois Library Statistical Report*, (24):28–69, August 1987.

Rush, James E., ed. "Technical Standards for Library and Information Science." *Library Trends*, 31(2):189–358, Fall 1982.

Special Libraries Association. "Objectives and Standards for Special Libraries." *Special Libraries*, 55(10):672–680, December 1964.

State Library of Iowa. *In Service to Iowa: Public Library Measures of Quality*. Des Moines, Ia., State Library of Iowa, 1985.

State University of New York, Associates for Library Services and Chancellor's Advisory Committee on Libraries. *Proposals for the Growth of Library Collections of the State University of New York: A Formula for Liminal Adequacy, with Recommendations for Growth Beyond*. Albany, N.Y., State University of New York, 1970.

Van House, Nancy A., et al. *Output Measures for Public Libraries: A Manual of Standardized Procedures*. 2nd Edition. Chicago, Ill., American Library Association, 1987.

Vaughan, Anthony. "Standards for British Libraries." *Library Trends*, 31(1):155–171, Summer 1982.

Wallace, James O. "Two-Year College Learning Resources Standards." *Library Trends*, 31(1):21–31, Summer 1982.

Weech, Terry L. "Small Public Libraries and Public Library Standards." *Public Libraries*, 27(2):72–74, Summer 1988.

White, Phillip M. "College Library Formulas Applied." *College and Research Libraries News*, 47(3):202–206, March 1986.

Zweizig, Douglas L. "Any Number Can Play: The First National Report of Output Measures Data." *Public Libraries*, 24(2):50–53, Summer 1985a.

————. *Output Measures for Children's Services in Wisconsin Public Libraries: A Pilot Project, 1984–1985*. Madison, Wis., University of Wisconsin, 1985b.

CHAPTER 11

THE RANGE AND SCOPE
OF LIBRARY SERVICES

One way of judging a library is by the range and scope of services it provides. It is difficult, however, to determine the precise services of a particular library without following some form of standardized inventory procedure. Use of such a procedure also allows comparison of the services provided by different libraries.

EARLY INVENTORIES OF SERVICES

Orr et al. (1968) were among the first to standardize a method for comparing the range of services offered by libraries. Although their work is now more than 20 years old, it remains the most comprehensive study of its kind. Moreover, it has influenced many later studies. Conducted for the Institute for the Advancement of Medical Communication (IAMC), the study was designed to determine the type and extent of services offered nationwide by medical libraries in academic institutions. The investigators held highly structured interviews with the director of each library surveyed and used a detailed checklist of the various services offered to users and the library's stated policies with regard to these services. A detailed interview guide was used to explicate the checklist, and each interviewer asked the questions exactly as they appeared in the guide. The questions were presented in a yes/no branching form, similar to a flowchart used in systems analysis. On the basis of the library director's answers to the questions, the interviewer checked the appropriate boxes on the accompanying checklist. The interview guide also contained notations about additional information that the interviewer was to seek from the library director, including matters that might

---

NOTE: For the reader's convenience, all exhibits in this chapter appear at the end of the chapter, following the references.

affect the user's time, effort, or expense. Examples from the interview guide, relating to various document services, are shown in Exhibits 11-1 through 11-8. The complete survey instrument consisted of 54 sections and took approximately two hours to complete.

An advantage of the inventory approach is that it allows the range and scope of the services offered by various libraries to be compared in a completely standardized way and is quite sensitive to differences among libraries.

As part of the effort to make answers obtained in the interviews comparable, investigators in the IAMC study weighted the categorical data obtained in the inventory to develop a quantitative score that would reflect the range and scope of the services provided by various libraries. They asked three separate groups to assign point values to express the importance they placed on both the large categories of services offered (for example, document delivery services, citation services, question-answering services) and on various service alternatives within each category. Eight undergraduates studying administrative processes, 4 library school students, and 15 hospital librarians each weighted the services using a 1,000-point scale. The weight assigned to a particular service policy was viewed as the "score" that a library would earn if it claimed this policy. An "ideal" library would have earned all 1,000 points. Exhibit 11-9 shows, at the broad category level, how these three groups weighted the services covered by the inventory. The potential usefulness of this method for comparing the services of a number of libraries is shown in Exhibit 11-10. Six academic medical libraries were compared, using a weighting scheme established by averaging the point allocations of two practicing medical librarians. Clearly, the resulting index of library performance is highly sensitive to the weighting method adopted, and Exhibit 11-10 should be regarded merely as demonstrating the application of the technique, using the "optimal" point allocation shown in the first column and applying it to the six libraries.

Although the IAMC inventory technique was developed for use by trained interviewers who wanted to compare the services offered in various biomedical libraries, it has been applied to other types of libraries and has been found suitable for use by librarians in "interviewing themselves." The checklist used was based on a broad categorization of user services, shown in Exhibit 11-11 and is easily adapted to the needs of other types of libraries. The checklist could also be self-administered and is, therefore, usable in a library self-survey.

Moreover, the IAMC inventory had a value beyond pure description and comparison of libraries. Data collection was designed to "give a comprehensive but detailed picture of what the library does and does not offer to, or do for, its users, including any significant differences in policy for different user groups" (Orr et al., 1968, p. 388). The resulting picture stimulated analysis and reappraisal of policies by the libraries surveyed. Participating librarians refocused their attention on the services and related policies of the organization and identified weaknesses and inconsistencies that required correction.

The IAMC investigators also described the development of another inventory, which covered the services offered by a library to other libraries—an "inventory of interlibrary services." It covered interlibrary loan, cataloging and binding for other libraries, exchange services, maintenance of union lists, and the provision of training and management services. Such an inventory may be useful in evaluating the services offered to member libraries by system headquarters.

Olson (1970), a former member of the IAMC study team, went on to develop a comprehensive survey of service policies in Indiana libraries. The object of his survey was to "describe and evaluate the prevailing pattern of service policies in Indiana libraries, including academic, public, school, and special libraries and information centers" (p. ix). He developed an expanded, modified interview guide of the type used in the IAMC study. It was designed for use in a mail survey and was self-administered by Indiana librarians participating in the survey. A sample page from the questionnaire is shown in Exhibit 11-12. The questionnaire was mailed to all academic libraries (excluding departmental libraries), to all special and public libraries, and to a sample of school libraries in the state. The data collected were weighted on the basis of "value preferences of groups of Indiana librarians from all types of libraries surveyed," using the method reported earlier by Orr et al. (1968), namely, the allocation of 1,000 points among the various service options. Three weightings were developed: one by a group of public librarians, another by a group of academic librarians, and the third by a group of school librarians. Exhibit 11-13 shows how the 1,000 points were allocated to the broad service categories by the three groups. A point allocation made by one special librarian is included for comparison purposes. Note that the academic and school librarians placed more emphasis on access to materials and less emphasis on question-answering services than did the public librarians. Exhibit 11-14 shows how closely the policies of each type of library match the service policies of an "ideal" library (1,000-point score) of the same type.

Olson's survey instrument proved to be highly discriminating because it revealed a wide range of performance levels among libraries of a particular type. For example, some small public libraries scored as low as 90/1,000, whereas some scored 630/1,000. In some instances, small public libraries achieved higher scores than their larger counterparts. Olson's survey includes much data on the detailed policies of Indiana libraries with regard to circulation of materials in the collection, provision of bibliographic citations, question-answering services, user instruction and educational programs, user relations, "wherewithal" (hours available, space available, and other factors affecting the use of the library's resources), and other special services. The data are worth studying. They provide a good example of how the standard inventory technique can be applied to a large group of libraries and show the ability of this technique to discriminate among libraries and to rank them by overall service scores.

One limitation of the inventory approach as developed by IAMC and used by

Olson is that it reflects only the librarian's weighting and perception of library services. This could be corrected easily if the weighting was established by a group of library users and if the users' perceptions of library policies were recorded.

USER PERCEPTIONS OF SERVICES

A more user-oriented approach to the evaluation of library services was used by Loertscher (1973) in evaluating the services provided by school media centers. Teachers from nine participating schools were presented with a list of 64 services that a media center might provide. Each teacher was asked to indicate how often the media center provided each service, using the following scale:

> 3 = regularly, as the need arises
> 2 = occasionally
> 1 = rarely or never
> X = do not know or does not apply

This technique permitted the ranking of services in order of the degree to which they were provided at the institutions surveyed (or, at least, the degree to which they were provided according to the perceptions of the users). A service that all users recorded as regularly provided would receive the perfect score of 3. The higher the score achieved by a particular service, the more agreement there would be among respondents that this service was regularly provided by the media centers they used. Loertscher also had users rate—again on a 3-point scale—the quality of the services provided. He further studied the services of the media center from the staff viewpoint, asking each staff member to judge the importance of each service and to indicate how frequently each service was provided. Loertscher compared the users' perceptions of the quality of services provided with the perceptions of the suppliers of the services. Some sample data obtained from both media staff and teachers are presented in Exhibit 11-15. All of these tabulations are based on a maximum possible score of 3.

Chwe (1978) advocated a somewhat similar approach. He developed a questionnaire (Exhibit 11-16) that took into account user needs for comfort, information (defined broadly to include recreational needs), convenience, and cooperation (defined as the cooperative attitudes of the library staff). Each user rated the "present condition" and "perceived importance" of each service on a 7-point scale. The difference between present condition and perceived importance was an indicator of a service deficiency. The worst possible situation, of course, would be one in which a service is given a 7 for importance but only a 1 for existing condition. An instrument of this type could be used over a considerable period of time to monitor changes in user attitudes or the effects of modifications to services or service policies.

Other researchers have also built on the framework of earlier studies. Fleming (1981) performed a comparative study similar to Loertscher's, using questionnaires and interviews to compare perceptions of actual and desired services offered by senior high school media centers in North Carolina. He discovered that the three groups surveyed—principals, teachers, and media staff—agreed more than they disagreed on the degree of importance of the current and desired services.

Working in an industrial library, McElroy (1982) used the IAMC classification of library services (document services, citation services, question-answering services, work-space services, instruction and consultation services, and adjunct services) as a framework within which to describe and discuss the services with library users. Users were asked to rank the services in order of importance. This ranking was compared with the library staff's view of the relative importance of the services and with actual demand as reflected in various statistics of library use.

Over the years, the types of service inventories described here have been incorporated into a systematic process for program planning. The most comprehensive effort, developed by Liesener (1976) for use in school media centers, asks the librarian to follow a logical sequence of steps:

1. *Compile the inventory of services.* The inventory should include services that are currently provided and services that are not provided but are thought to be desirable. Liesener included in his book a sample inventory that may be used as is or modified by the librarian.

2. *Separately survey students and teachers to determine their perceptions of what services are provided and the relative importance to users of these services.* This will alert the librarian to current services that would benefit from promotional efforts, identify important services that should be added, and indicate services that could be dropped.

3. *Determine the resources required to provide the various services considered important.* The costs of the services are calculated from this.

4. *Determine the range and level of services possible within resources now available to the media center.* This requires ranking the most important services and considering the range of options available within any one service. For example, a school library could provide unlimited online searching services for both teachers and students, unlimited searching for teachers and limited searching for students, or limited searching for both teachers and students.

5. *Inform administrators, teachers, and students which services can and cannot be provided with existing resources.* This alerts everyone to specific needs that cannot be met with existing funds and can stimulate users to request increased resources to allow provision of important services.

6. *Insofar as possible, reallocate the available resources to reflect user preferences in terms of the range and level of services.* Concentrate funding on important services and drop or deemphasize less important ones.

7. *Repeat steps 1–6 periodically.* This will ensure that the services provided continue to be responsive to user needs.

Liesener's book is especially valuable for its appendixes, which include a variety of data-gathering instruments that could be modified for use by libraries of all types.

Other recently developed planning processes could also be adapted for use with service inventories. *Planning and Role Setting for Public Libraries* (McClure et al., 1987) encourages librarians to identify the various roles their libraries undertake to support user needs in a particular community (formal education support center, community information center, recreational reading center, and so on). Each role is addressed from four perspectives: what is involved (a detailed description of the role), potential benefits to the community, resources needed, and evaluation criteria. A simple worksheet allows the weighting of roles with a 100-point scale (Exhibit 11-17). Because the worksheet assumes an understanding of the range of services that may be included within each role, it usually is completed only by the planning committee, the library board, or library staff. The descriptions of the various roles, however, could be used (or in some cases expanded) to develop a more detailed inventory of services and service components of the type described earlier in this chapter and a survey instrument to determine user priorities. Numerical scores could be assigned to the various roles (and their component services) to reflect the present allocation of resources, and comparable scores could be assigned to reflect user priorities. The librarian could compare the two sets of scores to identify discrepancies between the present situation and the priorities established by the user community.

Although service priorities can be established through the type of point allocation systems mentioned, investigators also can ask users to allocate an actual budget (the real library budget or a hypothetical one) to reflect their service priorities. This technique has been used by Raffel and Shishko (1969). The method they chose was unusual in the library environment, although it had been used in other situations (for example, in studying preferences for transportation systems). It involved a type of management "game" in which the players (in this case users of the libraries of the Massachusetts Institute of Technology) were given hypothetical library budgets and asked to allocate them over a range of possible library services. Each participant was given a list of 20 service alternatives, together with an indication of the cost of implementation and a summary of "benefit considerations" for each. Benefit considerations were both positive and negative; they indicated the losses that might be associated with a particular action as well as the possible gains. The list of alternatives, with accompanying instructions, is reproduced in Exhibit 11-18. The library user was given three budgets:

1. A supplemental budget of $200,000 (that is, an increase of $200,000 over the library budget in effect at the time of the study)
2. A supplemental budget of $100,000
3. No new funds (that is, the user was required to work with the present budget and reallocate it as he or she wished—a new service or an improvement to an existing one could be implemented only if needed funds were available owing to the curtailment of some other operation)

The survey was mailed to 700 students and faculty members; 283, or approximately 40 percent, responded. The major ranking of alternatives (reflecting the preferences of the entire group of respondents) is shown in Exhibit 11-19, and the percentage of respondents choosing particular alternatives at each budget level is given in Exhibit 11-20. Note that the rankings differ little among the three budget levels. The entire group of respondents placed great emphasis on the importance of improving availability and reducing the cost of materials for use outside the library. Most respondents would reallocate resources to reduce the cost of photocopying. If current levels of funding were maintained, virtually no one would cut acquisitions, but only some 20 percent would favor radical increases in that area; respondents did favor substantial increases in acquisitions, however, if funding was significantly increased. The idea of centralizing the reserve collections was generally popular, but the proposed inexpensive storage systems were less popular.

A number of special orientations were evident when library users were categorized by type. For example, undergraduates tended to reallocate funds from research activities to improve reserve collections. Graduate students were more oriented toward outside use of library materials (especially lower photocopying rates) and wanted improved access to collections of other libraries. Faculty expressed preferences for departmental libraries and were less opposed to methods for inexpensive storage. Those respondents who claimed heavy use of the library generally were research oriented; those who indicated light use preferred to use materials outside the library.

Raffel and Shishko (1969) described the benefits of this type of survey:

First, it gives an indication of the systems all members of the M.I.T. community would like to have. Second, the number of people supporting or vociferously opposing certain systems may be determined. The decrease in the popularity of a positive cost system as the budget level decreases may be a measure of the intensity of feeling, if any, for that system. Thus those items vigorously supported by a minority may be located. Few librarians feel comfortable basing their decisions only on the vocalized fears of a few concerned faculty members. Third, the inclusion of costs as a decision criterion eliminates the necessity of speculating (by the respondent or the decision maker) as to whether individuals would continue to support a given system if "they knew what it cost." Fourth, the survey can provide librarians with information to permit them to encourage the use of the library and to support library programs which they feel are educationally superior. (p. 57)

Norton and Gautschi (1985) also used a budget reallocation method as part of a user study in a special library.

CONCLUSION

Use of the inventory technique as a means of evaluating library service is not new. Smith (1954), for example, used a checklist of adult services to assess the scope of adult education activities offered by public libraries. The checklist was used to determine which of 37 services a particular public library provided; the reasons why certain services were not provided; and the types of services offered to various categories of users, including adult education agencies and community groups of various types. The means by which libraries provide these services also were investigated. The studies of Orr et al. (1968) and Olson (1970) occurred more than 20 years ago, but their methods are still useful today as a model for similar studies, although their survey instruments need to be expanded and updated to take into account online access, CD-ROM, and other services that have recently emerged.

Studies of this type often lead eventually to the derivation of a numerical value on some scale, for example, a library may score 750 out of 1,000 possible points. Some evaluators have tried to arrive at a meaningful "single figure of merit" for library services. For example, a working group of the (Canadian) Council of Federal Libraries (1979) proposed the following scoring method:

	Points or Weight
Information delivery	100
Document delivery	100
Timely document delivery	85
Current awareness	70
Collections	40
Catalogs	25
TOTAL	420

If procedures were developed for evaluating each of these library services, it would be possible to derive some composite score.

This type of index of effectiveness has strong appeal: if it was possible to achieve consensus on point allocation and testing procedures, a scoring method could be developed to compare different libraries. Unfortunately, it is almost impossible to achieve such consensus among librarians. And even if consensus was obtained, the single figure of merit obscures important data. For example, a library might do extremely well on document delivery but very poorly on question answering. The single score does not indicate such important differences. White (1977) gave a useful review of various approaches to arriving at a single figure of merit for libraries, including the advantages and disadvantages of each.

O'Connor (1982) took the single index approach one step further by developing "standard scores" for public libraries where a library's position on a particular scale is a function of the positions of all other libraries. Note, however, that O'Connor's scores are based only on data that are readily collected, such as total expenditures or total circulation, and not on data that truly reflect success (for example, shelf availability rates).

In concluding this chapter, it is important to note that D'Elia and Walsh (1985) questioned the value of data collected from library users in judging the performance of libraries. Questionnaires were distributed to users in the main library and four branches of a public library system, and more than 2,000 were completed. The data collected covered personal characteristics of the users, uses of the library, evaluations of specific services and collections, overall evaluation of the library, and general satisfaction with the library. No statistically significant correlations could be found between measures of patron use of the library and measures of patron evaluation. D'Elia and Walsh suggested that there may be some minimum (but unspecified and perhaps unspecifiable) level of acceptable service, that service improvements in a library operating at or above this minimum level may not be perceived by patrons and may not increase their use of the library, and that decreases in the quality of service may not be perceived by patrons or adversely affect their use of the library until service drops below the minimum acceptable level.

REFERENCES

Chwe, Steven S. "A Model Instrument for User-Rating of Library Service." *California Librarian*, 39(2):46–55, April 1978.

Council of Federal Libraries. *Performance Measurement in Federal Libraries: A Handbook*. Ottawa, Can., National Library of Canada, 1979.

D'Elia, George, and Sandra Walsh. "Patrons' Uses and Evaluations of Library Services: A Comparison Across Five Public Libraries." *Library and Information Science Research*, 7(1):3–30, January–March 1985.

Fleming, Joseph E. "Assessment of Media Center Services: An Investigation into the Preferences and Perceptions of Media Staff Members, Principals, and Teachers of Senior High Schools in North Carolina." Doctoral Dissertation. Pittsburgh, Pa., University of Pittsburgh, 1981.

Liesener, James W. *A Systematic Process for Planning Media Programs*. Chicago, Ill., American Library Association, 1976.

Loertscher, David V. "Media Center Services to Teachers in Indiana Senior High Schools, 1972–1973." Doctoral Dissertation. Bloomington, Ind., Indiana University, 1973.

McClure, Charles R., et al. *Planning and Role Setting for Public Libraries: A Manual of Options and Procedures.* Chicago, Ill., American Library Association, 1987.

McElroy, A. Rennie. "Library-Information Service Evaluation: A Case-History from Pharmaceutical R and D." *Aslib Proceedings, 34*(5):249–265, May 1982.

Norton, Robert, and David Gautschi. "User-Survey of an International Library—Resource Allocation: Preferred Allocations of the Library Budget." *Aslib Proceedings, 37*(9): 371–380, September 1985.

O'Connor, Daniel O. "Evaluating Public Libraries Using Standard Scores: The Library Quotient." *Library Research, 4*(1):51–70, Spring 1982.

Olson, Edwin E. *Survey of User Service Policies in Indiana Libraries and Information Centers.* Bloomington, Ind., Indiana State Library, 1970. Indiana Library Studies No. 10

Orr, Richard H., et al. "Development of Methodologic Tools for Planning and Managing Library Services. III. Standardized Inventories of Library Services." *Bulletin of the Medical Library Association, 56*(4):380–403, October 1968.

Raffel, Jeffrey A., and Robert Shishko. *Systematic Analysis of University Libraries.* Cambridge, Mass., MIT Press, 1969.

Smith, Helen L. *Adult Education Activities in Public Libraries.* Chicago, Ill., American Library Association, 1954.

White, G. Travis. "Quantitative Measures of Library Effectiveness." *Journal of Academic Librarianship, 3*(3):128–136, July 1977.

SECTION (1)
DOCUMENT SERVICES

Means of Obtaining Documents When User Is at Library

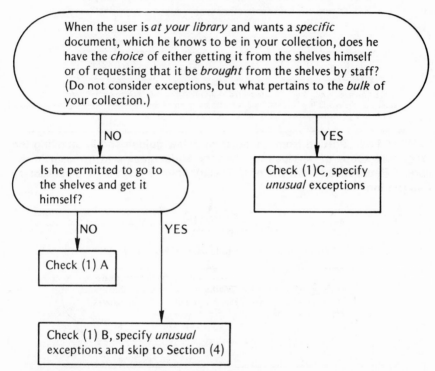

When the user is *at your library* and wants a *specific* document, which he knows to be in your collection, does he have the *choice* of either getting it from the shelves himself or of requesting that it be *brought* from the shelves by staff? (Do not consider exceptions, but what pertains to the *bulk* of your collection.)

NO

YES

Is he permitted to go to the shelves and get it himself?

Check (1)C, specify *unusual* exceptions

NO

YES

Check (1) A

Check (1) B, specify *unusual* exceptions and skip to Section (4)

NOTE: Check (1) A *only* if *most* of the stacks are closed to the given category of user. Checking (1) B for a given user category indicates that the *only* way a user in that category can obtain *most* of documents in the collection is by going to the shelves himself. Even where a self-service *only* policy is followed, exceptions are commonly made for documents in special locations (e.g., locked shelves) or in storage. It is not necessary to note such exceptions *when they are common to most libraries.*

EXHIBIT 11-1   Portion from the IAMC interview guide used in studying the range and scope of services for obtaining documents when the user is in the library. Reproduced from Orr et al. (1968), courtesy of the Medical Library Association.

SECTION (2)
DOCUMENT SERVICES

Requests for Staff Delivery of Documents When User Is at Library

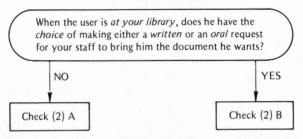

NOTE: A check in (2) A will be interpreted as meaning that *only* written requests are accepted- the possibility that *only* oral requests are accepted was considered unlikely. If this should be the case, check (2) A and *specify* this unusual policy.

EXHIBIT 11-2   Portion from the IAMC interview guide used in studying the range and scope of services for delivery of documents to the user in the library. Reproduced from Orr et al. (1968), courtesy of the Medical Library Association.

SECTION (3)
DOCUMENT SERVICES

Delivery of Documents to Locations Within Library

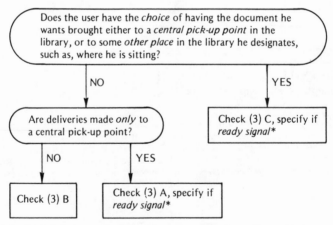

*Ready signal: A display system that enables the user to see from a distance his document is ready for him to pick-up.

NOTE: Checking (3) B means that deliveries within the library are made *only* to a seat location or a carrel, etc., as contrasted to a central pick-up point.

EXHIBIT 11-3   Portion from the IAMC interview guide used in studying the range and scope of services for delivery of documents within the library. Reproduced from Orr et al. (1968), courtesy of the Medical Library Association.

SECTION (4)
DOCUMENT SERVICES

Requests for Documents When User Is Away From Library

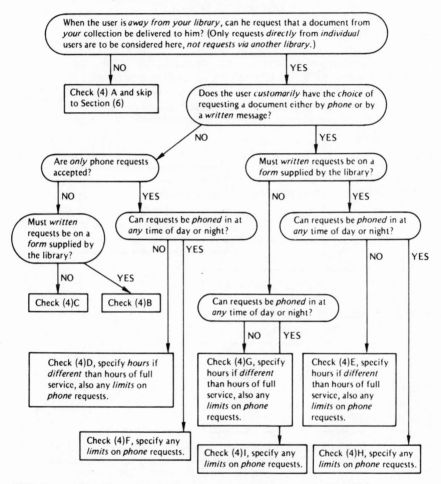

NOTE: Checking (4) B or (4) C means that the library does not *customarily* accept *phone* requests directly from its users. Checking (4) D or (4) F means that it does not *customarily* accept *written* requests.

EXHIBIT 11-4 Portion from the IAMC interview guide used in studying the range and scope of services for requesting documents when away from the library. Reproduced from Orr et al. (1968), courtesy of the Medical Library Association.

SECTION (5)
DOCUMENT SERVICES

Delivery of Documents to Locations Outside Library

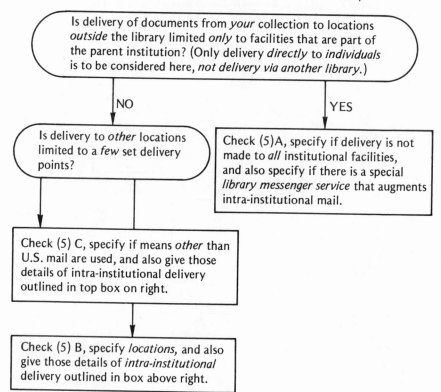

NOTE: Checking (5) C means that documents are delivered to *any* address the user designates. The possibility that a library delivers documents *only* to *extra-institutional* locations has been ignored. If this is the case, check (5) B or (5) C, as appropriate, and specify this unusual policy.

EXHIBIT 11-5 Portion from the IAMC interview guide used in studying the range and scope of services for delivery of documents outside the library. Reproduced from Orr et al. (1968), courtesy of the Medical Library Association.

SECTION (6)
DOCUMENT SERVICES

Reservation and Notification

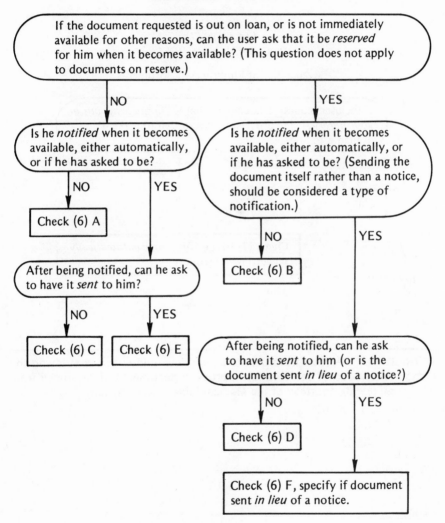

EXHIBIT 11-6 Portion from the IAMC interview guide used in studying the range and scope of services for reservations and notification. Reproduced from Orr et al. (1968), courtesy of the Medical Library Association.

SECTION (7)
DOCUMENT SERVICES

Availability of "In Process" Documents

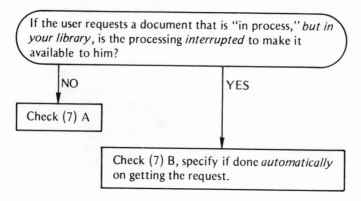

EXHIBIT 11-7   Portion from the IAMC interview guide used in studying the range and scope of services for in-process documents. Reproduced from Orr et al. (1968), courtesy of the Medical Library Association.

SECTION (8)
DOCUMENT SERVICES

Circulation of Serials

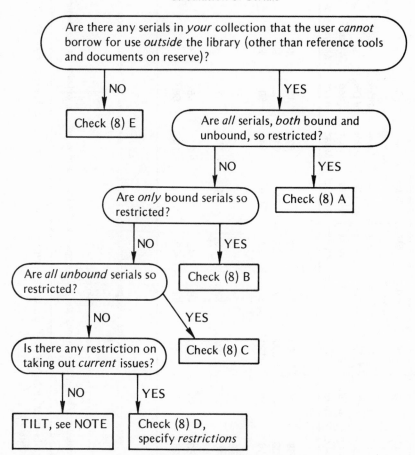

Are there any serials in *your* collection that the user *cannot* borrow for use *outside* the library (other than reference tools and documents on reserve)?

NO → Check (8) E

YES → Are *all* serials, *both* bound and unbound, so restricted?

    NO → Are *only* bound serials so restricted?

    YES → Check (8) A

        NO → Are *all unbound* serials so restricted?

        YES → Check (8) B

            NO → Is there any restriction on taking out *current* issues?

            YES → Check (8) C

                NO → TILT, see NOTE

                YES → Check (8) D, specify *restrictions*

NOTE: Here, as elsewhere, when a question tree leads to TILT, it means that some dichotomy has either broken down or has been misunderstood. Often this can be remedied by starting down the tree again and clearing up yes-no choices either by more explanation or by specifying the exceptions that caused the difficulty. For example, in this tree, TILT might be reached if the only serials not circulated were specific titles or specific volumes. In this case the difficulty could be handled by checking (8) E, and specifying the exceptions.

EXHIBIT 11-8 Portion from the IAMC interview guide used in studying the range and scope of services for circulation of serials. Reproduced from Orr et al. (1968), courtesy of the Medical Library Association.

Services	8 Undergraduate Students			4 Library Students			15 Hospital Librarians			All Groups*		
	(1) Mean Number Points Allotted	(2) Average Deviation from Mean	(3) Index of Disagreement	(4) Mean Number Points Allotted	(5) Average Deviation from Mean	(6) Index of Disagreement	(7) Mean Number Points Allotted	(8) Average Deviation from Mean	(9) Index of Disagreement	(10) Overall Mean	(11) Average Deviation from Mean	(12) Index of Disagreement
Document Services	420	38	9	390	40	10	450	82	18	420	20	5
Citation Services	230	22	10	230	62	27	280	61	22	250	23	9
Answer Services	88	16	18	120	39	32	110	64	58	110	11	10
Instruction and Consultation Services	61	18	30	65	29	45	61	25	41	62	2	3
Work-Space Services	130	63	48	110	46	42	47	21	45	95	33	35
Adjunct Services	68	26	38	85	34	40	48	28	58	67	13	19

Columns (1), (4), (7), and (10) may not total exactly 1,000 points because of rounding errors. All values are rounded to 2 significant figures or nearest whole number.

Index of Disagreement = [Average Deviation from Mean ÷ Mean No. Points Allotted] × 100.

*Here the mean for each group is treated as a single "observation," and the average deviation from the mean reflects variation among the three groups.

EXHIBIT 11-9   Results of trials of weighting method with various groups. Reproduced from Orr et al. (1968), courtesy of the Medical Library Association.

Services	"Optimal" Library* Points Allotted	Library A Points Earned	Library A Relative Score	Library B Points Earned	Library B Relative Score	Library C Points Earned	Library C Relative Score	Library D Points Earned	Library D Relative Score	Library E Points Earned	Library E Relative Score	Library F Points Earned	Library F Relative Score
Document Services	524	212	40%	382	73%	296	56%	394	75%	394	75%	192	37%
Citation Services	285	243	85%	119	42%	243	85%	184	65%	142	50%	236	83%
Answer Services	82	75	91%	75	91%	68	83%	75	91%	59	72%	59	72%
Other Services†	109	50	46%	29	27%	62	57%	68	62%	23	21%	46	42%
All Services	1,000	580	58%	605	60%	669	67%	721	72%	618	62%	533	53%

Relative Score = [Points Earned ÷ Points Allotted for "Optimal" Library] × 100.

*The values in this column were obtained by averaging the number of points allotted by two of the authors (V.P. and I.P.).

†Here "Other Services" includes "Work-Space Services," "Instruction and Consultation Services," and "Adjunct Services."

EXHIBIT 11-10 Demonstration scoring of inventory data for six academic medical libraries relative to "optimal" library. Reproduced from Orr et al. (1968), courtesy of the Medical Library Association.

LIBRARY SERVICES CLASSIFIED BY USER-FUNCTION SERVED

I. DOCUMENT SERVICES—providing documents* for which user has correct bibliographic descriptions (citations)
   A. *Making documents available for temporary use*
      1. On one-time basis
      2. On continuing basis (e.g., routine specified journal titles)
   B. *Supplying user with personal copies of documents*
      1. Originals (ordering for user)
      2. Facsimile copies
II. CITATION SERVICES—providing citations to documents
   A. *On one-time basis*
      1. Providing correct citations when user has incomplete or inaccurate bibliographic descriptions ("verification")
      2. Providing citations to documents relevant to user-specified subjects
         (a) Sample bibliographies (e.g., "several recent papers")
         (b) Exhaustive bibliographies
         (c) Critical bibliographies (selected for "merit")
   B. *On continuing basis*
      1. General alerting services (e.g., current journal shelves, monthly acquisitions list)
      2. Specific alerting services
         (a) Relevant to user-specified subjects or tailored to interests of user groups
         (b) Tailored to user's individual interests
III. ANSWER SERVICES—providing *specific* information to answer user's questions
   A. *Simple facts* (e.g., address, spelling of name)
   B. *Simple summaries* (e.g., biographical sketch prepared from multiple sources)
   C. *Complex facts* (e.g., compilation of conflicting data)
   D. *State-of-the-art summaries or critical reviews*
IV. WORK-SPACE SERVICES—providing space equipped for user to "work"[†] within library
   A. *Work involving library materials*
   B. *Other work*
V. INSTRUCTION AND CONSULTATION SERVICES
   A. *Formal and informal instruction in library-related subjects*
   B. *Helping with user's personal information system*
   C. *Exhibits*
VI. ADJUNCT SERVICES
   A. *Translations*
   B. *Editing*
   C. *Non-print media and equipment* (e.g., films, sound recordings)
   D. *Special services* (e.g., preparation of illustrations)

---

*The term "document" as used here. . . refers to a discrete bibliographic unit of recorded information, regardless of its type or form; it can be a journal article, book, reprint, technical report, etc., or a facsimile copy of any of these types of documents.

†"Work" is defined very broadly to include any user activity the library accommodates as a matter of policy; e.g., it may provide rooms for group discussions.

EXHIBIT 11-11   Categorization of library user services. Reproduced from Orr et al. (1968), courtesy of the Medical Library Association.

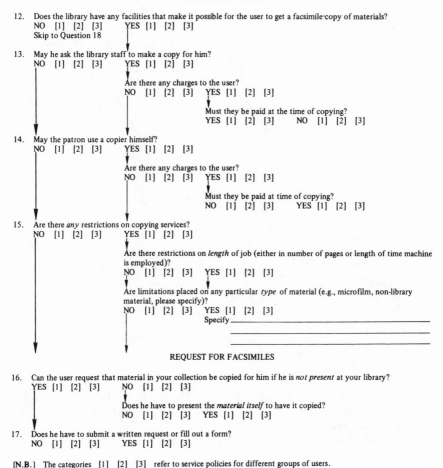

FACSIMILE COPYING

12. Does the library have any facilities that make it possible for the user to get a facsimile-copy of materials?
    NO [1] [2] [3]   YES [1] [2] [3]
    Skip to Question 18

13. May he ask the library staff to make a copy for him?
    NO [1] [2] [3]   YES [1] [2] [3]

                            Are there any charges to the user?
                            NO [1] [2] [3]   YES [1] [2] [3]

                                                  Must they be paid at the time of copying?
                                                  YES [1] [2] [3]   NO [1] [2] [3]

14. May the patron use a copier himself?
    NO [1] [2] [3]   YES [1] [2] [3]

                            Are there any charges to the user?
                            NO [1] [2] [3]   YES [1] [2] [3]

                                                  Must they be paid at time of copying?
                                                  NO [1] [2] [3]   YES [1] [2] [3]

15. Are there *any* restrictions on copying services?
    NO [1] [2] [3]   YES [1] [2] [3]

                            Are there restrictions on *length* of job (either in number of pages or length of time machine
                            is employed)?
                            NO [1] [2] [3]   YES [1] [2] [3]

                            Are limitations placed on any particular *type* of material (e.g., microfilm, non-library
                            material, please specify)?
                            NO [1] [2] [3]   YES [1] [2] [3]
                                                  Specify _____
                                                  _____
                                                  _____

REQUEST FOR FACSIMILES

16. Can the user request that material in your collection be copied for him if he is *not present* at your library?
    YES [1] [2] [3]   NO [1] [2] [3]

                            Does he have to present the *material itself* to have it copied?
                            NO [1] [2] [3]   YES [1] [2] [3]

17. Does he have to submit a written request or fill out a form?
    NO [1] [2] [3]   YES [1] [2] [3]

[N.B.] The categories [1] [2] [3] refer to service policies for different groups of users.

EXHIBIT 11-12 Sample page from questionnaire used in survey of Indiana libraries. Reproduced from Olson (1970), courtesy of Indiana State Library.

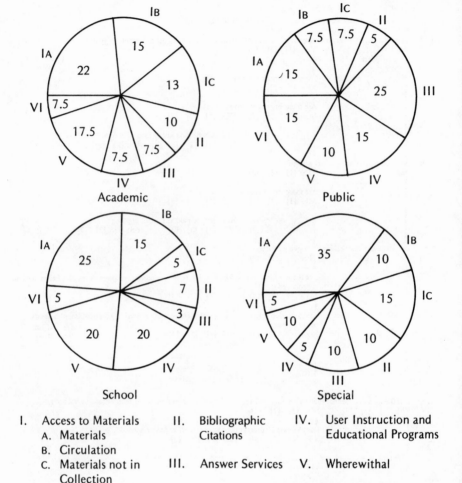

I.   Access to Materials   II.   Bibliographic   IV.   User Instruction and
     A. Materials   Citations   Educational Programs
     B. Circulation
     C. Materials not in   III.   Answer Services   V.   Wherewithal
        Collection
                                                           VI.   User Relations

EXHIBIT 11-13   Distribution of 1,000 points among major service policy categories for academic, public, school, and special libraries. Reproduced from Olson (1970), courtesy of Indiana State Library.

	Maximum Score (Points) for "Ideal" Library	Median % of Maximum Score	Mean % of Maximum Score	Confidence Interval of Mean (%)	Range of Individual Library Scores	
					Minimum % of Maximum Score	Maximum % of Maximum Score
SCHOOL LIBRARIES						
Elementary, Total	1,000	38	39	*	12	85
By Enrollment						
251–500	1,000	36	36	± 4	12	57
501–700	1,000	47	48	± 7	20	79
Over 700	1,000	33	38	± 6	12	67
Middle	1,000	52	50	± 4	18	83
High	1,000	47	49	± 2	13	85
PUBLIC LIBRARIES						
Central, Total	1,000	40	39	*	9	78
By Population						
Under 4,000	1,000	32	31	± 2	9	63
4,000–9,999	1,000	41	40	± 3	13	60
10,000–29,999	1,000	44	42	± 3	23	58
Over 30,000	1,000	57	58	± 4	34	78
Branches	1,000	42	42	± 3	9	73
ACADEMIC LIBRARIES	1,000	51	51	± 2	30	68

*Not computed.

EXHIBIT 11-14 Match of scores of Indiana libraries with optimal service policies of an ideal library: total scores for all service policies. Reproduced from Olson (1970), courtesy of Indiana State Library.

Service number and description	(1) Importance of services as perceived by media staffs in 40 schools		(2) Frequency of services given (received)						(3) Satisfaction rating of the teachers in 9 schools	
			(a) By the media staffs in 40 schools		(b) By the media staffs in 9 schools		(c) By the teachers in 9 schools			
	Mean	Rank	Mean	Rank	Mean	Rank	Mean	Rank	Mean	Rank
14. Makes media center facilities readily accessible to groups or individual students upon teacher request	2.92	7	2.88	5	2.88	6	2.61	3	2.47	5
15. Plans with teachers to correct students' problems in finding and utilizing resource materials through classroom or individualized instruction	2.61	25	2.30	24	2.16	31	1.88	28	2.07	31
MAKING TEACHERS AWARE OF SERVICES AND MATERIALS										
16. Informs teachers about new equipment acquired by the media center	2.92	5	2.82	8	2.80	9	2.45	7	2.46	8
17. Informs teachers about new materials acquired by the media center	2.98	1	2.88	3	2.88	5	2.55	5	2.57	1
18. Informs and reminds teachers about services offered by the media center	2.82	10	2.64	10	2.58	13	2.21	16	2.33	13
19. Orients new teachers to media center services	2.92	6	2.58	14	2.50	14	1.95	24	2.33	15
20. Provides information about services and materials available to teachers from other libraries and media centers in the area	2.36	52	2.12	34	1.96	46	1.72	41	1.93	49

NOTE: This is an example of the data collected by Loertscher. Each mean score is on a 3-point scale. Each column presents mean score for a particular service and the rank of this service when the services are ordered on the basis of mean score.

EXHIBIT 11-15 Sample of data from a survey of services offered by media centers in Indiana high schools: mean responses and rankings by all media staffs and teachers. Reproduced from Loertscher (1973), courtesy of the author.

QUESTIONNAIRE FOR USER-RATING OF LIBRARY SERVICES

As part of our constant effort to improve library services for you, we are asking your help by expressing your opinion as to various aspects of service of this library by completion of the following questionnaire. Please be assured you will not be identified. We appreciate your cooperation.*

Sex: Male (   )   Female (   )

Age: Under 20   (   )   20–29   (   )   30–39 (   )   40–49 (   )
        50–59   (   )   60 or over (   )

Education:
        Under 7th grade (   )   7th–9th grade   (   )   10th–12th grade   (   )
        Some college   (   )   Junior college   (   )   Baccaulaureate degree (   )
        Master's degree (   )   Doctoral degree (   )

Vocation: (   )

Instructions: There are two questions for each of the library service aspects listed below. Question "A" is to evaluate the present level of service of the aspect being asked. Please circle appropriate number in the rating scale, 1 to 7: 1 being the lowest score and 7 the highest. Question "B" is to request your value judgment of the same aspect of library service. That is, how important is the aspect to you. Please circle an appropriate number in the rating scale, 1 to 7: 1 being the least important, and 7 the most important.

I. COMFORT NEEDS.

  1. Correct temperature in the library.
     A. Present condition.   (Minimum) 1 2 3 4 5 6 7 (Maximum)
     B. How important?   (Minimum) 1 2 3 4 5 6 7 (Maximum)
  2. Variety of seating.
     A. Present condition.   (Min) 1 2 3 4 5 6 7 (Max)
     B. How important?   (Min) 1 2 3 4 5 6 7 (Max)
  3. Variety of reading desks.
     A. Present condition.   (Min) 1 2 3 4 5 6 7 (Max)
     B. How important?   (Min) 1 2 3 4 5 6 7 (Max)
  4. Right amount of light for reading.
     A. Present condition.   (Min) 1 2 3 4 5 6 7 (Max)
     B. How important?   (Min) 1 2 3 4 5 6 7 (Max)
  5. Control of noise in the library.
     A. Present condition.   (Min) 1 2 3 4 5 6 7 (Max)
     B. How important?   (Min) 1 2 3 4 5 6 7 (Max)
  6. Adequate carpeting.
     A. Present condition.   (Min) 1 2 3 4 5 6 7 (Max)
     B. How important?   (Min) 1 2 3 4 5 6 7 (Max)
  7. Keeping the library clean and neat.
     A. Present condition.   (Min) 1 2 3 4 5 6 7 (Max)
     B. How important?   (Min) 1 2 3 4 5 6 7 (Max)
  8. Keeping separate smoking and non-smoking reading rooms.
     A. Present condition.   (Min) 1 2 3 4 5 6 7 (Max)
     B. How important?   (Min) 1 2 3 4 5 6 7 (Max)

*Please check one.

EXHIBIT 11-16 Questionnaire rating user needs for comfort, information, convenience, and cooperation. Reprinted from Chwe (1978), courtesy of the California Library Association.

EXHIBIT 11-16 *(Continued)*

II. INFORMATION NEEDS.

1. Availability of local newspapers.
   A. Present condition.   (Min) 1 2 3 4 5 6 7 (Max)
   B. How important?   (Min) 1 2 3 4 5 6 7 (Max)
2. Availability of major out-of-town newspapers.
   A. Present condition.   (Min) 1 2 3 4 5 6 7 (Max)
   B. How important?   (Min) 1 2 3 4 5 6 7 (Max)
3. Availability of journals and magazines meeting your interests.
   A. Present condition.   (Min) 1 2 3 4 5 6 7 (Max)
   B. How important?   (Min) 1 2 3 4 5 6 7 (Max)
4. Availability of current best seller books.
   A. Present condition.   (Min) 1 2 3 4 5 6 7 (Max)
   B. How important?   (Min) 1 2 3 4 5 6 7 (Max)
5. Availability of general books of your interest.
   A. Present condition.   (Min) 1 2 3 4 5 6 7 (Max)
   B. How important?   (Min) 1 2 3 4 5 6 7 (Max)
6. Strong reference collection.
   A. Present condition.   (Min) 1 2 3 4 5 6 7 (Max)
   B. How important?   (Min) 1 2 3 4 5 6 7 (Max)
7. Availability of recreational audio-visual materials.
   A. Present condition.   (Min) 1 2 3 4 5 6 7 (Max)
   B. How important?   (Min) 1 2 3 4 5 6 7 (Max)
8. Good inter-library loan arrangement for materials unavailable in this library.
   A. Present condition.   (Min) 1 2 3 4 5 6 7 (Max)
   B. How important?   (Min) 1 2 3 4 5 6 7 (Max)
9. Union list of holdings of nearby libraries.
   A. Present condition.   (Min) 1 2 3 4 5 6 7 (Max)
   B. How important?   (Min) 1 2 3 4 5 6 7 (Max)
10. Library catalog well arranged and easy to use.
    A. Present condition.   (Min) 1 2 3 4 5 6 7 (Max)
    B. How important?   (Min) 1 2 3 4 5 6 7 (Max)
11. Availability of on-line computer information retrieval system.
    A. Present condition.   (Min) 1 2 3 4 5 6 7 (Max)
    B. How important?   (Min) 1 2 3 4 5 6 7 (Max)
12. Knowledgeable librarians available for help when needed.
    A. Present condition.   (Min) 1 2 3 4 5 6 7 (Max)
    B. How important?   (Min) 1 2 3 4 5 6 7 (Max)
13. Subject specialists to help with particular problems.
    A. Present condition.   (Min) 1 2 3 4 5 6 7 (Max)
    B. How important?   (Min) 1 2 3 4 5 6 7 (Max)
14. Quality answers provided by reference librarians.
    A. Present condition.   (Min) 1 2 3 4 5 6 7 (Max)
    B. How important?   (Min) 1 2 3 4 5 6 7 (Max)
15. Availability of actual books on the shelf listed in the library catalog.
    A. Present condition.   (Min) 1 2 3 4 5 6 7 (Max)
    B. How important?   (Min) 1 2 3 4 5 6 7 (Max)
16. Multiple copies of library materials.
    A. Present condition.   (Min) 1 2 3 4 5 6 7 (Max)
    B. How important?   (Min) 1 2 3 4 5 6 7 (Max)

EXHIBIT 11-16   *(Continued)*

III.   CONVENIENCE NEEDS.

1. Library staff stations located for help throughout the library.
   A. Present condition.   (Min) 1 2 3 4 5 6 7 (Max)
   B. How important?   (Min) 1 2 3 4 5 6 7 (Max)
2. Library catalog on each floor (if multi-floor).
   A. Present condition.   (Min) 1 2 3 4 5 6 7 (Max)
   B. How important?   (Min) 1 2 3 4 5 6 7 (Max)
3. Availability of conference or group study rooms for users.
   A. Present condition.   (Min) 1 2 3 4 5 6 7 (Max)
   B. How important?   (Min) 1 2 3 4 5 6 7 (Max)
4. Pay typewriters.
   A. Present condition.   (Min) 1 2 3 4 5 6 7 (Max)
   B. How important?   (Min) 1 2 3 4 5 6 7 (Max)
5. Free typewriters.
   A. Present condition.   (Min) 1 2 3 4 5 6 7 (Max)
   B. How important?   (Min) 1 2 3 4 5 6 7 (Max)
6. Vending machines.
   A. Present condition.   (Min) 1 2 3 4 5 6 7 (Max)
   B. How important?   (Min) 1 2 3 4 5 6 7 (Max)
7. Availability of pay-copy machines on each floor (if multi-floor).
   A. Present condition.   (Min) 1 2 3 4 5 6 7 (Max)
   B. How important?   (Min) 1 2 3 4 5 6 7 (Max)
8. Free copy machines.
   A. Present condition.   (Min) 1 2 3 4 5 6 7 (Max)
   B. How important?   (Min) 1 2 3 4 5 6 7 (Max)
9. Proper arrangement of book shelves for finding books easily.
   A. Present condition.   (Min) 1 2 3 4 5 6 7 (Max)
   B. How important?   (Min) 1 2 3 4 5 6 7 (Max)
10. Proper signs for directional guidance where needed.
    A. Present condition.   (Min) 1 2 3 4 5 6 7 (Max)
    B. How important?   (Min) 1 2 3 4 5 6 7 (Max)
11. Loan period long enough.
    A. Present condition.   (Min) 1 2 3 4 5 6 7 (Max)
    B. How important?   (Min) 1 2 3 4 5 6 7 (Max)
12. Reasonable fine for over-due materials.
    A. Present condition.   (Min) 1 2 3 4 5 6 7 (Max)
    B. How important?   (Min) 1 2 3 4 5 6 7 (Max)
13. Answering reference questions by telephone.
    A. Present condition.   (Min) 1 2 3 4 5 6 7 (Max)
    B. How important?   (Min) 1 2 3 4 5 6 7 (Max)
14. Renewal of loan-period by telephone.
    A. Present condition.   (Min) 1 2 3 4 5 6 7 (Max)
    B. How important?   (Min) 1 2 3 4 5 6 7 (Max)
15. Coin-change machines located near machines requiring change.
    A. Present condition.   (Min) 1 2 3 4 5 6 7 (Max)
    B. How important?   (Min) 1 2 3 4 5 6 7 (Max)
16. Library open sufficient hours during the week.
    A. Present condition.   (Min) 1 2 3 4 5 6 7 (Max)
    B. How important?   (Min) 1 2 3 4 5 6 7 (Max)

EXHIBIT 11-16   *(Continued)*

17. Library open sufficient hours during the weekend.
    A. Present condition.   (Min) 1 2 3 4 5 6 7 (Max)
    B. How important?   (Min) 1 2 3 4 5 6 7 (Max)
18. Books shelved correctly.
    A. Present condition.   (Min) 1 2 3 4 5 6 7 (Max)
    B. How important?   (Min) 1 2 3 4 5 6 7 (Max)
19. Simplified system for charging library materials.
    A. Present condition.   (Min) 1 2 3 4 5 6 7 (Max)
    B. How important?   (Min) 1 2 3 4 5 6 7 (Max)
20. Availability of audio-visual equipment for library users.
    A. Present condition.   (Min) 1 2 3 4 5 6 7 (Max)
    B. How important?   (Min) 1 2 3 4 5 6 7 (Max)
21. Prompt shelving of library materials returned from circulation.
    A. Present condition.   (Min) 1 2 3 4 5 6 7 (Max)
    B. How important?   (Min) 1 2 3 4 5 6 7 (Max)

IV. COOPERATION NEEDS.

1. Librarian's attitude to help when needed.
   A. Present condition.   (Min) 1 2 3 4 5 6 7 (Max)
   B. How important?   (Min) 1 2 3 4 5 6 7 (Max)
2. Librarian's kindness.
   A. Present condition.   (Min) 1 2 3 4 5 6 7 (Max)
   B. How important?   (Min) 1 2 3 4 5 6 7 (Max)
3. Librarian's taking enough time to understand and help with your problem.
   A. Present condition.   (Min) 1 2 3 4 5 6 7 (Max)
   B. How important?   (Min) 1 2 3 4 5 6 7 (Max)
4. Librarian's attitude in making sure you have found what you want.
   A. Present condition.   (Min) 1 2 3 4 5 6 7 (Max)
   B. How important?   (Min) 1 2 3 4 5 6 7 (Max)
5. Librarian's not being indifferent or fussy when you return for more help, that is,
   librarian's willingness to give additional help.
   A. Present condition.   (Min) 1 2 3 4 5 6 7 (Max)
   B. How important?   (Min) 1 2 3 4 5 6 7 (Max)
6. Proper treatment received from librarians.
   A. Present condition.   (Min) 1 2 3 4 5 6 7 (Max)
   B. How important?   (Min) 1 2 3 4 5 6 7 (Max)
7. Helpful suggestions provided by librarians.
   A. Present condition.   (Min) 1 2 3 4 5 6 7 (Max)
   B. How important?   (Min) 1 2 3 4 5 6 7 (Max)
8. Librarian's willingness to accept or respond to your complaints or suggestions.
   A. Present condition.   (Min) 1 2 3 4 5 6 7 (Max)
   B. How important?   (Min) 1 2 3 4 5 6 7 (Max)
9. Promptness of librarian's action on your requests or suggestions.
   A. Present condition.   (Min) 1 2 3 4 5 6 7 (Max)
   B. How important?   (Min) 1 2 3 4 5 6 7 (Max)

WORKFORM E   Selecting Library Roles Worksheet

(Group)

In the columns below, please allocate 100 points. You need not divide points equally, and some roles may receive no points. Note that 20 of the 100 points have already been assigned to cover basic library activities and roles not selected for emphasis. In the first column, distribute the 80 remaining points based on how you see *current* library activities being directed. In the second column, distribute the 80 points the way you feel library activities *should* be directed.

Role	Current Activities	Desired Commitment
Community Activities Center		
Community Information Center		
Formal Education Support Center		
Independent Learning Center		
Popular Materials Library		
Preschoolers' Door to Learning		
Reference Library		
Research Center		
Miscellaneous Activities and Roles Not Selected for Emphasis	20	20
Total	100	100

EXHIBIT 11-17   Worksheet used to help select the roles that public libraries should play. Reprinted from McClure et al. (1987), courtesy of the American Library Association.

TABLE 89   Service Alternatives and Associated Benefit Considerations[71]

Alternative	Benefit Considerations	Annual Additional Cost to Present Library Budget
1. 50% of the library's holdings of books which account for about 25% of total library circulations for the year, would be removed to an on-campus storage facility. There, these books would be stored as they are presently arranged (i.e., according to conventional Library of Congress classification) but access to the stacks would be restricted. Librarians would retrieve requested books on demand.	1. Browsing possible only under special circumstances, such as for theses, special projects, etc. Users would also encounter an average delay of 1/2 hour to retrieve stored books.	1. $−10,000
2. Again, 50% of the library's holdings of books which account for about 25% of total library circulations for the year, would be removed to an on-campus storage facility. There, these books would be stored *compactly* (i.e., shelved chronologically and by size). Access to the stacks would be closed, and librarians would retrieve requested books on demand. (Note: 1 and 2 cannot *both* be selected.)	2. Browsing impossible since books are not stored by subject classification. Users would also encounter an average delay of 1/2 hour to retrieve stored books.	2. $−25,000
3. *Expand* seating (all types) in libraries by *10%*. (Note: From systems 3 through 6, only one may be selected.)	3. Users would be able to find "choice" seating accommodations more easily.	3. $+25,000
4. *Expand* seating (all types) in libraries by *20%*.	4. Users would be able to find "choice" seating accommodations more easily.	4. $+50,000
5. *Cut* seating (all types) in libraries by *10%*.	5. Users would find it more difficult to obtain a seat in the library.	5. $−25,000
6. *Cut* seating (all types) in libraries by *20%*.	6. Users would find it more difficult to obtain a seat in the library.	6. $−50,000
7. The decentralized reserve collections would be replaced by two main reserve-study centers (one already in the Student Center, and another similar facility located near the Sloan-Hermann complex). Overnight circulation would be permitted from this latter facility. Areas now in the libraries devoted to study-reserve would be converted into stacks.	7. Replacing the decentralized reserve systems with two main study-reserve centers would lessen the current convenience of the more localized reserve collections, but would allow students to do all their work at one location.	7. $−75,000
8. The library would lower the charge for Xeroxing to local commercial rates, provide an operator, and encourage users to reproduce library material.	8. Users could duplicate important material at low cost and would be able to use the material outside the library.	8. $+10,000

9. Ten supplemental *departmental* libraries located near class-rooms would be built to house 10 years of the 20 most used journals and a collection of 3,000 books, including some required and recommended reading. These libraries would also have about 15 seats, but would provide no services beyond minimal cataloging. These might be contiguous to graduate lounges and study areas.

10. Instead of providing a reserve article per 10 students, the libraries would make enough complete Xerox copies of all articles 60 pages or less for *each* student in the relevant course and would distribute these articles.

11. *Increase* annual acquisitions by *10%*. (Note: From systems 11 through 14, only one may be selected.)

12. *Increase* annual acquisitions by *20%*.

13. *Decrease* annual acquisitions by *10%*.
14. *Decrease* annual acquisitions by *20%*.
15. The amount of time spent by professional catalogers on each book would be limited to a shorter period. The proof-reading and checking of catalog cards would also be curtailed.

16. The library would cut its reference staff by *10%*.

17. The library would add to its reference staff by *10%*.

18. The library would implement a direct telephone line to, say, Wellesley, staffed by additional professional librarians on station at Wellesley. In addition, interlibrary loan would be improved by increasing internal operating efficiency and direct messenger pickup.

19. The library would operate a long-range messenger service to the Library of Congress in Washington.

20. The library would purchase paperbacks of about 1/2 of books on reserve. This would treble the book:student ratio from 1:10 to 3:10. Circulation periods for these books would be lengthened to two days.

9. Such departmental libraries would provide more conveniently located working collections, and increase the availability of required and recommended reading.

10. Students could have a complete file of required articles for future use, and could read and study them at any time, in or out of the library.

11. Libraries could buy more new books as well as older books to "round out" the M.I.T. collection.

12. Libraries could buy more new books as well as older books to "round out" the M.I.T. collection.

13. Libraries could buy fewer books.
14. Libraries could buy fewer books.
15. The number of subject references for a given book would be limited. There would also be minor errors and other shortcomings in the catalog.

16. Bibliographic services and information aids would suffer.

17. Bibliographic services and information aids would be improved.

18. Users would be able to find out about books at another university library and would be able to obtain books within hours.

19. Users would be able to obtain books from the Library of Congress if they could not be obtained from a nearby collection.

20. Users would find required reading more readily available and would be able to take out these books for longer periods.

9. $+160,000
10. $+80,000
11. $+80,000
12. $+160,000
13. $-80,000
14. $-160,000
15. $-75,000
16. $-25,000
17. $+25,000
18. $+30,000
19. $+10,000
20. $+50,000

EXHIBIT 11-18 Service alternatives and associated benefit considerations. Reproduced from Raffel and Shishko (1969), courtesy of MIT Press.

	Budget Levels		
	$200,000	*$100,000*	*$0*
Positive Cost Systems			
Increase acquisitions	1*	2	2
Lower Xerox rates	2	1	1
LC messenger	3	3	3
Expand seating	4	4	4
Add reserve copies	5	5	4
Add reference	6	7	6
Increase access	7	6	7
Departmental libraries	8	9	9
All-Xerox reserve	9	8	8
Negative Cost Systems			
Centralize reserve	1*	1	1
Inexpensive storage	2	2	2
Cut reference	3	3	4
Cut seating	4	4	3
Decrease acquisitions	5	5	5

*Rank of system where rank of 1 means the system was chosen the most at that budget level.

EXHIBIT 11-19   Ranking of service alternatives by budget level. Reproduced from Raffel and Shishko (1969), courtesy of MIT Press.

System*	Budget Levels		
	$200,000	*$100,000*	*$0*
[Increase acquisitions, 10% or 20%]	[78%]	[61%]	[41%]
Lower Xerox rates	74	65	54
LC messenger service	55	44	32
[Expand seating, 10% or 20%]	[48]	[32]	[16]
Add reserve copies	43	28	18
Increase acquisitions, 20%	43	8	4
Centralize reserve	41	48	62
Increase acquisitions, 10%	35	53	37
Add reference librarians	33	19	13
Expand seating, 10%	31	23	12
Increase access to other libraries	30	23	12
Departmental libraries	28	16	6
All-Xerox reserve	27	17	8
[Conventional or compact storage]	[24]	[24]	[34]
Expand seating, 20%	17	9	4
Conventional storage	16	16	21
[Cut seating, 10% or 20%]	[11]	[14]	[24]
Cut reference staff	10	16	20
Limit cataloging	8	12	17
Compact storage	8	8	13
Cut seating, 10%	8	10	12
Cut seating, 20%	3	4	12
Decrease acquisitions, 10%	0	0	3
Decrease acquisitions, 20%	0	0	0

*Related pairs of alternatives are combined within brackets.

EXHIBIT 11-20 **Percentage of respondents choosing alternative services at three budget levels. Reproduced from Raffel and Shishko (1969), courtesy of MIT Press.**

CHAPTER 12

USER STUDIES IN LIBRARIES

The first edition of this book included a chapter on library surveys. This term is somewhat imprecise. Most of the studies described throughout the book are, in one form or another, surveys performed within the library. A study of the range and scope of services offered by a library, as discussed in Chapter 11, is certainly a type of survey. The term "library survey," however, is most often applied to a study that surveys the population served by a library to determine how the library is used and with what degree of success. It is a type of "use" or "user" study.

Hundreds of studies of the uses and users of information sources have been conducted. These studies vary widely in scope and include

- Studies of the information needs or information-seeking behavior of broad communities (for example, physicists or research and development personnel within the Department of Defense)
- Studies of the information needs or information-seeking behavior of individuals in a single institution (for example, a research center)
- Studies of the use made of particular information services, information centers, or libraries
- Studies of the use made of a particular service, tool, or product (for example, use of a catalog in a library or the "readership" of a particular journal)

The vast literature of "user studies" defies effective summarization. The authors who have attempted as much generally have concentrated on describing studies within a specific type of library or focusing on some specific topic or service (for example, Powell, 1988; Roberts and Wilson, 1988). This chapter intends only to outline several possible approaches to the conduct of user studies in libraries, to draw attention to various pitfalls that may occur, to alert the librarian to recent sources that discuss these pitfalls in more depth, and to assess the value of user studies to the librarian.

Library patrons can be studied using direct or indirect survey methods. Direct methods involve getting information directly from the user and include questionnaire or interview studies, diary keeping, and observational techniques. Indirect methods imply looking at some results of user behavior and trying to deduce something about the user. Some sources of indirect data on user behavior include records of circulation, in-house use, and interlibrary loan requests. Indirect methods are discussed elsewhere in this book (especially in Chapters 4, 5, and 6) and thus are not dealt with in this chapter.

QUESTIONNAIRES

One of the simplest ways to find out what someone is doing or thinking is to ask, and the most frequently used methods of asking are a written, self-administered questionnaire and a personal interview. Some kinds of information, such as opinions, personal preferences, intentions, or recent experiences, are difficult, if not impossible, to obtain any other way.

The questionnaire is used in preference to the interview when any of the following conditions exist: a large number of people have to be approached; the potential respondents are geographically dispersed; the quantity of information to be collected is small; the information to be collected is simple or contains factual data; little probing is needed to obtain the information; and frank, thoughtful answers are required (for example, a psychologist asking a question about sexual preferences and activities would probably administer a questionnaire rather than conduct an interview).

The evaluator who wishes to survey people by using a questionnaire

- Selects the sample to be questioned
- Designs the questionnaire
- Pretests the questionnaire and makes any necessary revisions
- Distributes the questionnaire and follows up on any unreturned questionnaires, as necessary
- Analyzes the results
- Interprets the results and writes up the findings

Because the first four of these steps are essentially the same in any questionnaire study, they are discussed briefly here. For information on the last two steps, the reader is referred to the works on research design mentioned in the last section of this chapter, "The Value of User Studies in Libraries."

In many cases, the group to be studied is selected automatically—for example, by being defined as the student body of a particular university or as all persons using the library on a particular day. The problem of sample selection is avoided if one is able to contact the whole population of interest. If, for example, the librarian in a small consulting company wanted to determine the extent to which the 55 employees were aware of library services, he or she could easily survey all of them.

Only in cases where the sample to be studied is not self-selecting or is too large to be surveyed in entirety does drawing a sample become an issue. The problem then is one of ensuring that those individuals questioned fully represent the population to be served. In other words, any bias in the results because of the way the sample was selected must be avoided. Selecting a representative sample requires an understanding of various sampling methods that will reduce bias (for example, random sampling or stratified sampling). For instance, in an academic environment, the evaluator might attempt to obtain proportional representation of each discipline present in the population to be surveyed. It is not the intent of this chapter to discuss sample selection, since most statistics textbooks and many texts on library research contain relevant chapters. Three recent works that are especially clear on sampling techniques are Kalton's *Introduction to Survey Sampling* (1983), Powell's *Basic Research Methods for Librarians* (1985), and Simpson's *Basic Statistics for Librarians* (1988).

Once the sample is selected, the evaluator must attempt to design a good questionnaire—a difficult undertaking. The ideal questionnaire is brief, easy to complete, unambiguous, and free of bias.

The length of the questionnaire is important because it affects response rate. The longer the questionnaire, the lower the response rate is likely to be. The total response rate is important because the higher the percentage of responses received, the more likely it is that the answers will be representative of the population surveyed.

The proper way to design a concise questionnaire is to list the specific pieces of information needed, then to frame questions that will collect the relevant data and no more. The temptation to ask questions beyond the survey's purpose should be resisted. For example, many questionnaires request personal particulars, such as name, age, or level of education. This type of information is appropriate and useful only if it affects the characteristics under investigation. If a survey on the extent of library use is being conducted, information on age and educational level might be appropriate, because age and education may both affect the extent of use; however, it is unlikely that the respondent's name would be useful. Some evaluators request that patrons sign their names so that sample members who did not reply can be identified and sent follow-up questionnaires. Even this practice is not recommended, however, since a master address list and serially numbered questionnaires would accomplish the same purpose and cut down on the amount of information the respondents must supply. Moreover, patrons are more likely to respond (and may respond more honestly) if they think their individual responses are anonymous.

Brevity and anonymity are not the only factors that affect response rate. The questionnaire should also be easy to answer. If it is not, a frustrated respondent may simply discard it. The layout of the questionnaire should be attractive and encourage the respondent to feel that answering the questionnaire will be easy. For example, if the evaluator is seeking information on four different facets of library service, the questionnaire might be subdivided into four sections that are set off by appropriate headings. Within each section, the questions should proceed from general to specific. Any questions that may be perceived as threatening for the respondent should be at the end, rather than the beginning, of a section. Another way to increase the attractiveness of the questionnaire is to have it printed rather than photocopied.

Evaluators also need to be sure that clear instructions are given for each question. A good example is, "Please check, in the space provided to the right of each question, the *one* alternative that best describes how well you feel your reference question was answered." If a particular question is appropriate to only part of the population being studied, the questionnaire should direct other respondents to another section of the questionnaire: "If your answer to question 4 is 'no,' please go to question 7."

Question format needs to be considered because it affects ease of completion as well as ease of analysis by the evaluator. The simplest questions for users to complete and for evaluators to tabulate are dichotomous or multiple-choice questions. Evaluators should use close-ended questions whenever the possible responses are known, limited in number, and clear-cut.

In a dichotomous question, the respondent chooses between two alternatives (for example, yes/no or agree/disagree). The dichotomous scale gives the respondent little flexibility in replying. Therefore, it is suitable only for those questions where the answer is clear-cut for most respondents. Frequently, such questions can be used to lead into other questions; that is, the yes/no or agree/disagree question can be used as a screening device. Consider the following:

The library is open from 12 noon until 5 p.m. on Sunday. Are these hours satisfactory to meet your needs?   Yes _____   No _____

If the answer is no, the respondent is asked more questions about the hours he or she would prefer to see the library open on Sunday. If the respondent answers yes, he or she is directed to a different section of the questionnaire. The dichotomous scale should not be used if many respondents want to qualify their answers; in this situation, a more flexible response scale should be chosen.

Multiple-choice questions fall between the extremes of the open-ended question and the dichotomous question. These are particularly suitable for determining attitudes or opinions because they allow for gradations in attitudes. Multiple-choice questions involve the use of checklists from which respondents select answers. Three types of checklists are (1) the list from which the respondent chooses the single best or most appropriate response, (2) the list from which the respondent chooses all responses that apply to his or her particular situation, and (3) the list that the respondent is asked to put in order of preference to produce a ranking of responses. Consider the following example:

Select the one statement that best indicates the novelty of the items retrieved in this search.

Most were new to me   _____
At least half were new to me   _____
Less than half were new to me _____
All were previously known to me _____

This type of multiple-choice question lists all responses to a particular question, then asks the respondent to check or circle the single answer that reflects his or her response. Such questions must be carefully designed to ensure that all reasonable alternatives are listed. For example, one student in a research methods class designed a question that asked public library patrons how they selected their books. Unfortunately, the student failed to include several obvious choices, including browsing. Often, evaluators list the alternatives in this type of question, then pretest the question on some members of the population to be studied to ensure that important alternatives have not been missed. Evaluators also should include, whenever possible, an "other" category among the alternatives so that responses that were not foreseen or that occur infrequently can be included.

Many multiple-choice questions use some type of attitude scale, such as the Likert scale. Here respondents indicate their degree of agreement with a positive or negative statement. The scale usually extends from "strongly agree" to "strongly disagree" and consists of four categories: "strongly agree" (SA), "agree" (A), "disagree" (D), and "strongly disagree" (SD). It might also include a fifth category, "undecided" (U), that appears at the center of the scale. The "undecided" category frequently is omitted, which forces the respondent to choose among the four positive and negative response categories. A Likert-type scale also can be used with "like/dislike" or "accept/reject" response ranges.

Many evaluators apply the Likert scale to a complete set of statements about a service. Ideally, approximately half these statements should be favorable and half unfavorable. The scoring of negative statements is the reverse of the scoring of positive statements. If a 4-point scale is assumed, the positive and negative statements can be scored according to the following scheme:

	SA	A	D	SD
Positive statement	4	3	2	1
Negative statement	1	2	3	4

With this scoring method, the most positive attitude is represented by the highest score. Thus, when the scores for all responses are averaged, the scores that are closest to 4 are the ones that represent the most positive attitudes.

Another popular, although more complex, scale is the Thurstone scale. The evaluator constructs a series of statements about various aspects of a particular service. Some of these statements should be favorable to the service, some unfavorable, and some neutral. The Thurstone scale needs to be calibrated before it can be applied in an actual survey. Calibration is achieved by pretesting the set of statements with a group of individuals similar to those who will participate in the actual evaluation. Each "judge" ranks the statements into, say, 10 levels, according to the degree to which the statement is considered positive or negative. For each statement, the distribution of the scaled values assigned by the judges is plotted, and the median of each distribution is located. The more ambiguous statements (indicated by major discrepancies among the judges as to where the statement appears on the favorable/unfavorable scale) are eliminated. From the remaining statements, a set of perhaps 20 statements is selected that contains statements ranging over the entire 10-point scale. The scale value for each statement is the mean of the judges' rankings. The statements are arranged randomly within the questionnaire, and respondents simply check off the statements with which they agree. A respondent's score is the sum of the scale values for the statements he or she has checked; the higher the score, the more positive the response.

The Thurstone scale is useful in determining the attitudes of individual respondents. It also is valuable in ascertaining whether attitudes have changed because of some additional experience. For example, this scale could be used to measure the attitude of library users before and after exposure to a new online catalog or some other new service.

Another type of scale is the semantic differential, which uses bipolar adjectives (weak/strong, good/bad, important/unimportant). The respondent is asked to rate a particular activity by marking a point on a scale between the two extremes represented by the bipolar adjectives:

Good – – – – – – Bad

A scale on which a respondent marks a point on a continuum frequently is referred to as a graphic scale. A group of graphic scales is created to measure an attitude toward a particular event or activity. The semantic differential is readily converted to a numerical score reflecting the degree of positiveness in the respondent's attitude, as in the following examples:

Weak   7 6 5 4 3 2 1   Strong
Incomplete 7 6 5 4 3 2 1   Complete

Users' attitudes toward a particular information service can be evaluated by a semantic differential incorporating a series of graphic scales.

In all the scales discussed so far, the respondent checks the most appropriate response or marks a particular point on a scale of values. As an alternative, questions can be included for which respondents must select all the statements with which they agree.

At this point, attention should be given to a particular class of questions that are more difficult for respondents to complete. These questions involve ranking a number of choices in order of preference or perceived merit. There are two basic possibilities. One is to ask for a true ranking of alternatives by some criterion; the other requires the respondent to group the alternatives into classes, such as good, bad, and indifferent, or very important, less important, and unimportant.

True ranking is very difficult. When a person is faced with a dozen kinds of information services and is asked to rank them in order of usefulness, only the values assigned at the ends of the scale can be considered meaningful. People tend to be clear about what they consider useful or useless, but the middle ground contains a much less clearly defined range of values. Ranking of this kind gives the spurious appearance of quantification, because the items being ranked seldom can be considered strictly as elements from a homogeneous continuum. Often, it is more preferable to ask respondents to assign values to each item on the list than to ask them to rank all services in order of usefulness.

Also, because of the difficulty most people experience in rating on an extended value scale, the value options should be restricted to no more than five; if possible, this should include a "no opinion" column to cover alternatives for which the respondent has no experience on which to base a judgment. Thus, in seeking ratings of various ways to acquire information, a librarian can ask respondents to characterize the usefulness of the methods as high, moderate, or low. Sometimes five grades—excellent, good, satisfactory, unsatisfactory, and bad—are used, but a natural unwillingness to label anyone or anything as "bad" results in most of the ratings being clustered at the more favorable end of the scale. This problem is less pronounced with a scale having only three values. Inevitably, some respondents will attempt to subdivide grades, assigning school-like marks such as B++—anything but an A.

Open-ended questions are used less frequently in questionnaires because they require more time for respondents to complete and for evaluators to tabulate and analyze. They must be used, however, when alternative answers for some question are not known (as in an exploratory study) or when the range of answers is wide, like for the question "Which journals do you scan regularly?" Before answers to open-ended questions can be analyzed, the researcher must tabulate each response and then group similar responses. This is a time-consuming process and often requires subjective decisions on the part of the researcher. This is not to suggest that open-ended questions should be avoided; there are occasions when they are unavoidable. Frequently, it is desirable to provide space on a questionnaire for the respondents to comment on the survey subject. Even when the opportunity is not given, respondents often add comments. These comments are valuable because they can add substance to a quantitative study and can provide insight into a respondent's attitudes about or relationship with the survey subject, insight not easily gained from close-ended questions.

Once the format of the question has been decided, the evaluator must concentrate on accurately phrasing the questions. This is one of the most difficult parts of questionnaire design. If any conceivable ambiguity exists in a question, someone will find it. Take the following question as an example: "Do you read many books?" This sounds like a reasonable question, but consider what is really meant. Does "read" mean read all the way through, read only those parts that are of interest, scan quickly to get an idea of content, or borrow from the library? How many is "many"? Words like "often" and "many" can be used only if they are followed by "how often?" or "how many"? But it would have been better to ask for exact numbers, or to give a range of values, in the first place. Also, the time frame for the number of books read needs qualification—for instance, "this week," "in a year," or "in your lifetime." If not qualified, the answers may indicate how respondents feel, not how they behave; to some people, a dozen books a year seems like many. And, finally, what is meant by "book"? The librarian may not include magazines, comic books, reports, theses, symposia, or conference proceedings in the definition, but the respondent might. "Do you read many books?" is a bad question because the terms are not defined.

Such questions can be reworked to eliminate ambiguities. For example, rather than asking patrons whether the reference librarian who just helped them was good, the evaluator might question specific behaviors of the librarian (for example, Did the librarian find an answer for the question? Did the librarian listen to the patron's needs? Was the librarian's attitude courteous?).

Ambiguity may also arise from bad phrasing. One form of question commonly used in exploring attitudes presents a number of statements and asks whether the respondent agrees with each of them. This device can be very useful but can also be dangerous if not handled properly. Consider the following: "Do you agree or disagree with the following statement: 'Too much trash is published.'?" To disagree could imply that the respondent thinks not enough trash is published, which may not be what the questioner intended. The statement should have been written, "Much of what is published is trash." "Much" is not a good choice of words, but it works here because the questioner is seeking an attitude, not a quantification, which is why "too" has been dropped.

The questionnaire designer should always be as definite and explicit as possible. For example, questions such as "Do you prefer abstracts or references with keywords?" should be avoided because users' preferences for one or the other may vary depending on the context—prefer them for what? A better practice is to word the question so that it applies to a particular incident. For example, if the evaluator wants to discover the format in which all persons using an online search service during the second week of March want to receive their searches, he or she could ask each person who used the service during that time, "For the online search you just requested, would you prefer to receive (1) a list of relevant references with indexing keywords or (2) a list of references with brief abstracts?"

Evaluators must strive to keep bias out of question design. Several possible sources of bias exist. For example, most people prefer the familiar to the unfamiliar. If given a choice between familiar and unfamiliar alternatives, most respondents choose the former. A question that asks whether users prefer a particular tool in printed form or on a CD-ROM might result in an overwhelming preference for the former if few of the respondents have experience with CD-ROM. Bias in this case could be controlled by filtering out patrons who have little experience with CD-ROM. For example, the evaluator could ask two separate questions. The first could determine whether the patron had used the tool in both printed and CD-ROM form. Only those respondents who had used both forms of the tool would be directed to the second question, "Which do you prefer and why?"

Leading the respondent is another form of bias that the evaluator should strive to avoid. Leading questions of the direct kind—"Do you not think that . . . ?"— are easy to avoid, but subtler forms of influence can intrude if emotionally laden words like "censorship" are used. A subtle form of leading the respondent may result from question order. For example, one research study tested the effects of question order when asking respondents whether a married woman should be allowed to obtain an abortion if she does not want any more children. Responses were considerably different when this question was asked alone than when it followed a question about allowing an abortion if there was a strong chance that the child would have a serious birth defect (*Institute for Social Research Newsletter*, 1982).

Another form of bias occurs when respondents give answers based on what they think is expected rather than on what they truly believe. For example, studies that ask library users how satisfied they are with the library generally indicate that users are satisfied or very satisfied. To avoid generating this kind of meaningless (for purposes of improvement) response, ask instead for instances of dissatisfaction or failure. Respondents also tend to play down their own "bad" behavior. Thus, students may be reluctant to admit that they rarely consult the catalog and use no printed indexes; this behavior can be discovered only by asking questions that will gradually reveal the truth without asking for it directly.

Pretesting the questionnaire is necessary if survey results are to be valid. Before a questionnaire is printed, the evaluator should obtain informal comments on the design of specific questions and the overall questionnaire from colleagues and selected individuals from the group of people to be surveyed. The pretest's main purpose is to alert the investigator to ambiguous or biased questions. For example, one library school student at the University of Iowa wanted to determine how many patrons read fiction that was shelved in the adult fiction section, as opposed to fiction shelved in sections for children and teenagers. Unfortunately, her question, "Have you read any adult books lately?" was misinterpreted by a number of patrons to mean "Have you read any risque books lately?" Pretests also are useful in showing researchers whether there is sufficient variation in response for a particular question to be worth asking and in ensuring that all major alternatives are identified in multiple-choice questions.

Distribution of the questionnaire is important because the representativeness of the sample often is determined by the percentage of people who respond. How the questionnaire is actually distributed depends on who is being surveyed. For example, if the population to be surveyed is library users only, the questionnaire can be handed out to each person who enters the library during randomly selected days or weeks. But if a library wants to survey a sample of all community residents, then the survey should be distributed through the mail.

Because the overall response rate for mail surveys is especially low (the addressee feels little pressure to respond so it is easy to discard the survey), the evaluator should take particular care in designing the cover letter. The letter should be written on the library's official stationery, since the respondent is more likely to heed a request from a representative of a known institution than a request from some unknown and unaffiliated individual. The evaluator should indicate in the letter, in general terms, the purpose of the study and the value of the results to the user. The latter statement could be as simple as "We will use the results to tailor our services to better meet the needs of individuals and the community and to help contain operating costs." The importance of receiving a reply should be stressed and, whenever possible, anonymity should be guaranteed. Finally, to make it as easy as possible to respond, the evaluator should include a self-addressed, stamped envelope in which the questionnaire can be returned. After allowing a reasonable period for return of the questionnaires, the investigator should send a follow-up letter and a second questionnaire to those who have not replied, since the goal is to achieve as high a response rate as possible.

Distribution of the questionnaire within the library is appropriate when only users are to be surveyed. Higher response rates will be achieved if a staff member or volunteer approaches each patron to be surveyed, briefly explains the purpose of the survey, gives each patron who agrees to cooperate a pen or pencil, and personally collects the completed questionnaires. Leaving the questionnaires out on tables or at the circulation desk for patrons to fill out and return is not recommended because most patrons will ignore them.

The questionnaire is cheaper than the interview and may be the only technique that can reach a large and widely dispersed audience, a factor to be considered in studies of library systems. The major problem with the questionnaire is that it must be self-explanatory, and every possible attempt must be made to avoid ambiguity. Even with great care, however, one cannot be sure that all respondents have interpreted a particular question in the way the investigator intended.[1] Questionnaires are most applicable to surveys in which facts or opinions can be recorded on a simple scale. They are less satisfactory for discursive opinion gathering, for which many open-ended questions are needed. The interview, particularly if recorded, is likely to be more satisfactory in this application.

INTERVIEWS

The kinds of information that can be obtained in interviews (and from other methodologies) range from the purely factual to what can be described as insight. Because interviews are expensive to conduct (involving costs for the interviewer's time and, possibly, the transcription of answers, travel costs, or long-distance telephone fees), the evaluator who wants essentially factual responses is more likely to use the questionnaire, which is well suited to collecting these types of data and costs much less to administer. The interview is preferred for situations in which insight is desired; the quantity of information to be obtained is so large that it would inhibit the response rate if a questionnaire was used; or the questions need considerable explanation, are difficult to answer, or require spontaneous answers.

The characteristics of the interviewer are important to the success of this method. The interview lets the respondents interact with the researcher and seek clarification when necessary. In many situations, particularly when the subject is complex or technical, it is essential that the interviewer be perceived as competent in the field. Moreover, the professional who understands the area of inquiry is more likely to ask better follow-up questions and, thus, to obtain more insight into the problem at hand.

Although it is possible to have a completely unstructured interview, which generally resembles an informal talk with a library user, the data obtained will be more reliable if the evaluator develops a structured questionnaire (known as an interview schedule) for the interviewer to use when speaking to respondents. This schedule is designed in the same way as the questionnaire but has greater built-in flexibility, allowing the interviewer to ask follow-up questions to clarify the respondent's answers (thus reducing the ambiguity that can be such a problem with the questionnaire) or to expand on certain answers (to obtain more insight into patron feelings and behaviors).

The sample selection, survey design, and pretesting stages are almost identical to those used in designing a questionnaire. One small difference is that the interviewer can design a long questionnaire and still expect a reasonable response

---

[1] Much literature exists on the difficulties associated with gathering data reliably through questionnaires. These problems have been highlighted for libraries by Bookstein (1985) and Kidston (1985). Bennion (1982) dealt specifically with the problem of bias in questionnaire design.

rate for both telephone and in-person interviews. This is because people are often uneasy about refusing to participate in a study when asked by a professional and polite interviewer, even though they find it easy to discard questionnaires.

A few other differences exist between questionnaires and interviews. For example, responses in a structured interview may differ slightly from those that would appear on a questionnaire because, in the former, the respondent does not have an overview of the whole schedule and so cannot foresee later questions. Therefore, interview responses show greater spontaneity than do questionnaire answers. Interview answers may be more complete or revealing than questionnaire answers, since many respondents may be more willing to "talk" in person than on paper (although the opposite may be true for sensitive topics, as noted in the previous section on questionnaires). There may be slightly more confusion during an interview if a respondent is asked to remember a long list of alternative answers to a close-ended question. To help alleviate this confusion, the evaluator may wish to present the alternatives to the respondent in written form, say, on index cards.

There are two bigger problems that are particularly important for the investigator to avoid. The first is possible bias that may be introduced by the interviewer, especially if the interviewer is inexperienced or has a vested interest in the results of the study. A good interviewer should have an agreeable personality, but not be so agreeable or attractive that the respondent's answers are colored by the desire to impress. The interviewer should be interested in the topic of the survey, but not so interested as to be emotionally involved; a clever interviewer may appear to argue to explore a reaction (this practice is not advocated) but should never persuade. The need for a neutral interviewer cannot be emphasized too strongly. Opinions of library service gathered from users within a library by interviewers posing as staff may differ from those gathered from respondents leaving the library by interviewers appearing to be from an agency not related to the library. Although the telephone interviewer's tone of voice can influence a respondent's answers, the danger is less than in a face-to-face situation, where tone of voice, facial expression, and even the interviewer's physical appearance can affect certain responses.

Second, the interviewer should avoid bias in asking questions and recording answers. The interviewer should not deviate from the exact wording of the questions (unless it becomes clear that the patron has misinterpreted or misunderstood the question), since they have already been pretested and shown to be effective. Bias in the way the interviewer interprets and records the answer is especially difficult to avoid. It is not much of a problem when the responses are factual, unambiguous, and short, so that they can be recorded exactly as given. But when answers are long or have to be interpreted or fitted into a classification scheme, interviewer bias can determine the answer recorded, often subconsciously. To avoid this, the interviewer should record the answers in the respondent's own words whenever possible. Writing the answers verbatim can be difficult, not only because long answers take time to record but also because the procedure may inhibit the respondent. Therefore, tape recording is now generally acceptable, so long as the consent of the person being interviewed has been obtained. Of course, the answers then must be transcribed.

A special type of interview is the focus group interview, which is specifically directed toward gaining insights. Individual interviews are fundamentally confrontations, but the essence of a group interview is interaction among the participants. Generally, 8–10 persons are chosen to represent the diversity of people sharing a common interest in the topic to be explored. Because little quantifiable information that will be subjected to statistical analysis is likely to emerge from a focus group interview, the group does not have to be fully representative. More than one point of view should be present, however, because otherwise little profitable interaction will take place. For example, a group interview dealing with a projected policy change in an academic library should include representation from students of various levels, as well as from staff and faculty.

The object of the focus group interview is to explore attitudes, opinions, and motives, which will more likely be revealed in the emotionally provocative interaction of group members than in a solo interview. The interviewer is the moderator of the process and guides the interview on the basis of predetermined questions to which the library desires answers. The interviewer, however, does not lead the discussion; his/her function is not to persuade but to provoke discussion, which may entail role playing to the extent of feigning ignorance to seek explanation, or of expressing attitudes to secure reaction. The group interview differs from brainstorming, which it superficially resembles, because it is conducted with a group of interested persons ("stakeholders") rather than with experts and because of the intensive analysis to which the discussions (which should be recorded) may be subjected.

In some types of surveys it may be possible to combine the advantages of both the questionnaire and the interview. The investigator can personally distribute and collect questionnaires, allowing him or her to clarify or interpret some of the difficult questions and perhaps even supplement them with additional open-ended questions in a face-to-face encounter. Or the questionnaire can be mailed with a cover letter asking recipients to examine the questions, consider their responses, and gather any data needed to complete the study. Recipients are told *not* to mail back the questionnaire; instead, the questionnaire is completed by the investigator during a subsequent telephone interview. Recipients may also be sent return postcards to indicate a telephone number and days and times at which they can be reached. This technique has several advantages. The respondent, by returning the postcard, indicates agreement to participate. The respondent is not surprised by a call at an inconvenient time. Interview scheduling is more efficient because the investigator has a better chance of reaching respondents on the first call. The telephone interview can help clarify possible ambiguous questions; further information can be elicited from the respondent by asking "probing" questions during the telephone interview. Also, more information can usually be obtained, because many people who are reluctant to write at length are willing to express their views at length in conversation.

DIARIES

Diary studies constitute one method of obtaining detailed information on the behavior (for example, in seeking information) of a sample of library users. As with any other survey methodology, the maximum information will be returned by those people who are most interested in the topic being investigated. The information sought from diarists should be defined carefully and structured at the outset so that it can be recorded by checking a preprinted form. The length of time for which diaries are kept should be the minimum necessary to collect reliable data. A relatively long period is necessary to observe changes resulting from innovation (perhaps requiring fewer observations from the diarist might compensate for the extra length of the study). Estimating the average time needed to perform a routine activity, such as scanning the latest issue of a book list, requires few observations, however, and so the recording period can be short.

In diary studies, there often is uncertainty about the completeness and accuracy of the responses obtained. Keeping a diary is a chore, and diarists may subconsciously reduce the effort by eliminating or forgetting to enter less-significant occurrences. Another way in which diarists often try to lessen the load is to complete diaries at the end of the day or week; this practice tends to promote underrecording of less-memorable or less-significant items. So far as is practical, the solution is to require that information be recorded as soon as it is generated, perhaps by using some form of "event card." For example, academic researchers can be asked to fill out a simple card for the first x document needs they encounter in a particular time period (Line, 1973).

The effect of conditioning poses one of the greatest problems in conducting diary studies. References have been made to the "sympathy" effect in answering questions, where a subject's reported behavior differs from reality because the subject sympathizes with the researcher. Or subjects may report their own behavior as better than it is. Furthermore, there is the well-known situation in which observing someone's behavior can alter the behavior, sometimes permanently, even when the observer is the subject himself. Keeping a diary can change the diarist's behavior pattern so that, even if accurately recorded, the behavior differs from the behavior pattern that might prevail were a diary not being kept. In other words, the diary may serve as a constant reminder that the diarist should more often be doing something "virtuous," like reading a journal. A diarist may conduct a literature search that he or she might not otherwise have done so that it can be recorded. Or diarists may advance the progress of a project for the same reason. Little can be done to allow for this effect. Any direct method of user study influences the users to some extent. Even a brief questionnaire about literature-searching habits reminds users that there is literature to be searched and that searching it is considered desirable.

A special form of diary involves the use of random alarm devices. A random alarm is a small mechanical or electronic device that emits a noise some predetermined number of times a day at random, or at least unpredictable, intervals. Random alarms are used in studies that examine the total behavior patterns of a group of persons. The devices are small enough to be carried by the study subjects; each time the alarm rings, subjects are required to note whatever they are doing. For an older, but still relevant, discussion of the problems and uses of this technique, see Halbert and Ackoff (1959). Although use of random alarms may underrepresent the low-probability event (unless the study continues for a long time and includes a large enough sample), the method probably gives the most accurate quantification of work-oriented activities. Examples of the use of random alarms in the library field can be found in Divilbiss and Self (1978) and Spencer (1971, 1974).

CRITICAL INCIDENT TECHNIQUE

The theory behind the critical incident technique is that people have less difficulty accurately recalling what they do on one occasion than what they do in general. People usually remember most clearly the latest incident of a particular type; this event usually becomes the critical incident. For example, suppose one wants to learn something about the reading habits of a group of students. The investigator could ask the students some general questions about what types of books they read, why they do so, and where they obtain the books. Or the researcher could ask each student to name the book he or she is reading now or the one completed most recently and then ask more specific questions on why the book was chosen, where it was obtained, and so on. Information gathered this way is probably more precise than information gathered about reading behavior in general, and the sum of the critical incidents contributed by all students probably presents a clearer picture of their reading habits and preferences than the sum of the answers to more general questions.

An obvious danger in applying this technique, however, must be guarded against. One must avoid asking critical incident questions when the response is likely to be atypical of the respondent's behavior at other times. For example, if an evaluator wants to determine how often students use an academic library as a study hall, he or she should not base the findings on a critical incident study conducted during exam week, when the library is used for studying much more frequently than normal.

Critical incident studies do not need to be used alone but can be incorporated into interviews or mail questionnaires. The investigator might begin a survey, for example, with some questions on library use, then ask the respondent to focus on a single critical incident.

The critical incident technique seems particularly suited to studies of the information-gathering behavior of a community—for example, the engineers in an industrial organization. Suppose one wanted to learn about the information needs of these individuals, which sources they used to satisfy their needs, and their degree of success in getting the needed information. An appropriate series of questions might resemble those shown in Exhibit 12-1.

Once respondents focus on some single critical incident, they can be asked precise questions about the event. Some precise responses can be expected. For example, knowing that the first source a respondent consulted was *The Electrical Engineers' Handbook* or *Engineering Index* is more valuable than learning that the individual uses handbooks or indexes. Note that in Exhibit 12-1, the respondent is asked to list documentary or personal sources in the sequence that they were consulted. The consultation outcome also is recorded. If the first source was unproductive, the same questions are applied to the second source, the third, and so on, until the answer is located or the search is abandoned. For a successful search, the respondent can be asked about the specific use of the information, the amount of time spent obtaining the information, and the value of the information in solving problems or making decisions. Exhibit 12-2 shows a possible approach to identifying sources and indicating where they were found.

Selecting the latest event as the critical incident is usually desirable, since the respondent should be able to remember this clearly. Sometimes, however, an evaluator may want the respondent to concentrate on another event, one that had a strong effect on his or her behavior. In that case, the opening question might be phrased, "Can you remember some occasion on which you urgently needed a particular item of information to make a decision or solve a problem?" Choosing events that the respondents consider significant is likely to yield results different from those obtained when only the latest events are requested. In the context of a complete survey, latest events are essentially random occurrences. Some are important, but others are trivial. A large number of latest events, each contributed by a different individual, should form a coherent picture of the typical information needs and information-seeking behavior of the population studied. Concentrating on only the most important events does not yield a typical picture. For certain kinds of studies, however, focusing on the most important events may be appropriate.

One useful example of the application of the critical incident technique in a library setting can be found in Kremer (1980). She incorporated two separate critical incidents in her survey of information flow among engineers in a design company. One incident relates to the latest purposive information-seeking act and the other relates to the most recent discovery of a useful item of information not deliberately sought.

1. When was the last time you needed some specific item of information to help solve a problem or make a decision in your work for the company?

Today ☐	Yesterday ☐
In the past week ☐	More than a week ago ☐

2. What was the information that you needed? Please be as complete as possible in your description of this information.

3. Was the first source you consulted to find the information

    (a) A book or other document? ☐   Go to question 4
    (b) Another person? ☐   Go to question 5

If you have not yet attempted to find the needed information, proceed to question 10.

4. Please identify, as completely as possible, the book or other document that you first consulted.

Where did you find this document?

    In your personal collection ☐
    In a department or office collection ☐
    In the company library ☐
    In some other place ☐   Please specify:

What did this source provide?

    (a) A complete answer to your question ☐
    (b) A partial answer ☐
    (c) No answer at all ☐

If you checked (b) or (c), did you seek the information from a second source?

    Yes ☐   Go to question 6
    No ☐   Go to question 10

5. Please give the name and organizational affiliation of the person you first asked for this information. If you have forgotten the person's name, please give the organizational affiliation and title or position of the person you asked. For example,

    Brenda Smith, the company librarian
    One of the librarians in the company library
    John Brooks in the Design Engineering Department
    Mr. Johnson of the Farmers' Bank
    One of the officers of the Farmers' Bank

What did this person provide?

    (a) A complete answer to your question ☐
    (b) A partial answer ☐
    (c) No answer at all ☐

If you checked (b) or (c), did you consult a second source?

    Yes ☐   Go to question 6
    No ☐   Go to question 10

EXHIBIT 12-1 Partial interview schedule using the critical incident technique to determine the information sources used by engineers working in an industrial organization.

Please identify the sources used to seek the information in the sequence in which they were used. If the source was personal, such as a colleague, a vendor, or a client, please name the person and his organization. If a printed source, please give title and/or author and indicate where it was obtained.

SOURCES (Printed or Personal)	PLACE SOURCE OBTAINED (Printed Sources Only)		
First source used: ——————— ———————————————— ———————————————— ————————————————	Library of your organization In your office Other library or other source Please specify: ————————	(((	)))
Second source used: —————— ———————————————— ———————————————— ————————————————	Library of your organization In your office Other library or other source Please specify: ————————	(((	)))
Third source used: ——————— ———————————————— ———————————————— ————————————————	Library of your organization In your office Other library or other source Please specify: ————————	(((	)))
Fourth source used: —————— ———————————————— ———————————————— ————————————————	Library of your organization In your office Other library or other source Please specify: ————————	(((	)))
Fifth source used: ——————— ———————————————— ———————————————— ————————————————	Library of your organization In your office Other library or other source Please specify: ————————	(((	)))

EXHIBIT 12-2 Interview schedule using the critical incident technique to determine the sequence in which information sources are used.

CONCLUSION: THE VALUE OF USER
STUDIES IN LIBRARIES

A number of authors have suggested that user studies are not as valuable to the individual library or the profession as they might be. Generally, the criticisms are that the studies use vague or varying methods of measurement, are subjective, collect information that is too general (or that does not require library users to be critical enough) to be useful in correcting problems, or have methodological defects (for example, Brittain, 1982; White, 1985). Surveys with these problems may produce no firm recommendations or recommendations that inspire little confidence.

These difficulties, however, can be overcome if particular attention is paid to research design. Samples must be scientifically derived, and all proposed approaches to the gathering of data must be critically examined to determine their validity and reliability. Appropriate statistical procedures must be applied in the analysis and interpretation of the survey results.

Many of the studies described elsewhere in this book can be regarded as special-purpose library surveys. Most of these attempt to gather quantitative data in an objective manner using acceptable research techniques. Subjective surveys—those that seek the opinions of library users—also have value. After all, it is important to know how people feel about the services being provided.

A well-conducted survey of users can produce data of potential value in the evaluation of library services. At the very least it can give a useful indication of how satisfied users are with the services provided and can identify areas of dissatisfaction that may require closer examination through more sophisticated microevaluation techniques. Such data can be used in a variety of ways. For example, Anderson and Miller (1983) reported on an opinion survey conducted at the University of Cincinnati libraries before the adoption of an automation program. The survey proved its value because it revealed "notable discrepancies between long-standing assumptions about user behavior . . . and the actual user perceptions." The automation program then was designed to meet actual user needs. Whitlatch (1983) and Hannabus (1987) also pointed to the value of user surveys in establishing service priorities and planning future services. And Powell (1988), in a comprehensive review, stressed the importance to librarians of user studies and user-oriented performance measures of the type discussed elsewhere in this book.

The library profession will continue to debate the value of studies that attempt to collect data and opinions from library users. There is no doubt that the design and implementation of reliable user studies is a difficult task, and it is likely that many studies of little or no utility have been performed in libraries. Nevertheless, the intrinsic value of opinion surveys, especially those conducted through some form of questionnaire or interview, should not be underestimated; after all, opinion surveys are at the heart of much social science research and also play an important role in the marketing activities of many corporations. The fact that surveys of users and potential users form an essential component of the American Library Association's Planning Process for Public Libraries (McClure et al., 1987) suggests that user studies will continue to be valuable to librarians for some time to come.

This chapter has not attempted to provide a complete overview of the problems of user studies in libraries. Indeed, there are full-length texts that discuss this issue. Readers who wish a more complete treatment should refer to the numerous general and library research texts that are available, as well as to more specialized works discussing various aspects of user surveys or research design (for example, Berdie, Anderson, and Niebuhr, 1986; Burns, 1978; Busha and Harter, 1980; Powell, 1985, 1988; Schuman and Presser, 1981; Swisher and McClure, 1984).

REFERENCES

Anderson, Paul M., and Ellen G. Miller. "Participative Planning for Library Automation: The Role of the User Opinion Survey." *College and Research Libraries, 44*(4):245–254, July 1983.

Bennion, Bruce C. "Some Hazards and Nonhazards of Mailed Questionnaire Surveys." *Public Library Quarterly, 3*(4):57–68, Winter 1982.

Berdie, Doug R.; John F. Anderson; and Marsha A. Niebuhr. *Questionnaires: Design and Use.* 2nd Edition. Metuchen, N.J., Scarecrow Press, 1986.

Bookstein, Abraham. "Questionnaire Research in a Library Setting." *Journal of Academic Librarianship, 11*(1):24–28, March 1985.

Brittain, J. Michael. "Pitfalls of User Research and Some Neglected Areas." *Social Science Information Studies, 2*(3):139–148, July 1982.

Burns, Robert W., Jr. "Library Use as a Performance Measure: Its Background and Rationale." *Journal of Academic Librarianship, 4*(1):4–11, March 1978.

Busha, Charles H., and Stephen P. Harter. *Research Methods in Librarianship: Techniques and Interpretation.* New York, Academic Press, 1980.

Divilbiss, James L., and Phyllis C. Self. "Work Analysis by Random Sampling." *Bulletin of the Medical Library Association, 66*(1):19–23, January 1978.

Halbert, Michael H., and Russell L. Ackoff. "An Operations Research Study of the Dissemination of Scientific Information." *Proceedings of the International Conference on Scientific Information.* Washington, D.C., National Academy of Sciences, 1959, pp. 97–130.

Hannabus, Stuart. "The Importance of User Studies." *Library Review, 36*:122–127, Summer 1987.

Institute for Social Research Newsletter. "Questions and Answers," 10(1/2), Spring–Summer 1982.

Kalton, Graham. *Introduction to Survey Sampling.* Beverly Hills, Calif., Sage Publications, 1983.

Kidston, James S. "The Validity of Questionnaire Responses." *Library Quarterly,* 55(2):133–150, April 1985.

Kremer, Jeannette. "Information Flow Among Engineers in a Design Company." Doctoral Dissertation. Urbana, Ill., University of Illinois, Graduate School of Library Science, 1980.

Line, Maurice B. "The Ability of a University Library to Provide Books Wanted by Researchers." *Journal of Librarianship,* 5(1):37–51, January 1973.

McClure, Charles R., et al. *Planning and Role Setting for Public Libraries: A Manual of Options and Procedures.* Chicago, Ill., American Library Association, 1987.

Powell, Ronald R. *Basic Research Methods for Librarians.* Norwood, N.J., Ablex Publishing, 1985.

_____. *The Relationship of Library User Studies to Performance Measures: A Review of the Literature.* Urbana, Ill., University of Illinois, Graduate School of Library and Information Science, 1988. (Occasional Papers No. 181)

Roberts, N., and T. D. Wilson. "The Development of User Studies at Sheffield University, 1963–1988." *Journal of Librarianship,* 20(4):270–290, October 1988.

Schuman, Howard, and Stanley Presser. *Questions and Answers in Attitude Surveys: Experiments on Question Form, Wording, and Context.* New York, Academic Press, 1981.

Simpson, I. S. *Basic Statistics for Librarians.* 3rd Edition. London, Eng., Library Association, 1988.

Spencer, Carol C. "Random Time Sampling with Self-Observation for Library Cost Studies: Unit Costs of Interlibrary Loans and Photocopies at a Regional Medical Library." *Journal of the American Society for Information Science,* 22(3):153–160, May–June, 1971.

_____. "How to Allocate Personnel Costs of Reference." In: *Proceedings of the Symposium on Measurement of Reference.* Edited by Katherine Emerson. Chicago, Ill., American Library Association, 1974, pp. 35–41.

Swisher, Robert, and Charles R. McClure. *Research for Decision Making.* Chicago, Ill., American Library Association, 1984.

White, Herbert S. "The Use and Misuse of Library User Studies." *Library Journal,* 110(20):70–71, December 1985.

Whitlatch, Jo Bell. "Library Use Patterns Among Full- and Part-Time Faculty and Students." *College and Research Libraries,* 44(2):141–152, March 1983.

CHAPTER 13

CONCLUSION

This book has reviewed various possible approaches to measuring and evaluating some of the major facets of library service. Orr (1973) referred to the process as "measuring the goodness of library services." He recognized two aspects of measurement, which are reflected in the following questions: "How good is the service?" and "How much good does it do?"

Chapter 1 referred to the first of these aspects as the measurement of effectiveness and to the second as the measurement of benefits. The effectiveness of library services (as well as their cost-effectiveness) can be measured and evaluated, but in many situations the benefits of library services cannot be measured in any objective way. The emphasis of this book, therefore, has been on the measurement of effectiveness and, to a lesser extent, the cost-effectiveness of library services.

The approach taken has been mainly fragmentary, in the sense that each of the several major facets of library operations or library services has been viewed independently. This is the only reasonable approach, because the evaluation of materials availability differs considerably from the evaluation of question answering, which differs from the evaluation of the catalog, and so on. Each of these facets can and should be evaluated separately; the evaluation of one does not depend on the evaluation of another. If a complete evaluation of a library was undertaken, each facet of service would be studied independently and all the results would be synthesized to present a composite picture of library effectiveness.

Creation of such a composite has been tried sporadically throughout the years with mixed success. Generally, composites rely on the use of a single index of library effectiveness, an equation usually designed to count the total volume of library use, total days of use, or total hours of use. To date, these indexes have been inherently flawed. Some represent only selected library services, usually those that are easy to measure. Others distinguish successes from failures in some parts of the equation (for example, measurement of the quality of question answering) but represent only the successes in other instances (for example, books checked out). And many indexes concentrate almost entirely on quantity while ignoring quality of use. Instead of relying on this type of equation to determine overall effectiveness, librarians should focus on evaluating separately as many of their current services as feasible.

For an evaluation program to work, it must be an integral part of the library's regular planning cycle. Evaluation efforts that are conducted only sporadically, or in isolation from the planning process, may solve an immediate problem without appreciably affecting long-term change.

During the past 20 years, many libraries have begun evaluation efforts. But few have committed themselves to the kind of ongoing, comprehensive evaluation program intertwined with regular operating procedures that is truly needed to make libraries more effective and more cost-effective. Although the situation is changing, especially in large libraries (see, Association of Research Libraries, 1987), comprehensive evaluation programs are needed in all libraries so as to deal with the problems the profession is now facing. In these days of tight funding, increased demands for accountability, and rapid technological change, evaluation efforts may make a difference in the survival of individual libraries and of the profession as now known.

This book has emphasized the need for going beyond macroevaluation— the simple description of what is happening with some library service—and embracing the microevaluation of library service. Microevaluation is a diagnostic tool. As applied to library services, it implies the use of evaluative and analytical procedures to determine how well a particular library performs in a given situation and to identify major sources of weakness, failure, and inefficiency. Of course, these deficits vary significantly from library to library. An institution that performs one type of service well may perform another service poorly. Evaluation must therefore occur at the level of the local institution. Nevertheless, it is possible to identify some major factors that are likely to influence the success or failure of the most important services that libraries offer. An attempt was made in this book to present these factors. Only by applying appropriate measurement and evaluation techniques can a library determine the circumstances under which it performs well or less well and identify the causes of its failures with sufficient precision to allow corrective actions to improve the overall level of performance and to raise the level of user satisfaction with the services provided.

REFERENCES

Association of Research Libraries, Office of Management Studies. *Planning for Management Statistics in ARL Libraries.* Washington, D.C., ARL, 1987. SPEC Kit 134

Orr, R. H. "Measuring the Goodness of Library Services: A General Framework for Considering Quantitative Measures." *Journal of Documentation,* 29(3):315–332, September 1973.

INDEX